UNITED STATES
EXTERNAL ADJUSTMENT
AND THE WORLD ECONOMY

United States

GP 89 01202

WILLIAM R. CLINE

External Adjustment and the World Economy

INSTITUTE FOR INTERNATIONAL ECONOMICS
Washington, DC 1989

William R. Cline is a Senior Fellow at the Institute for International Economics. He was formerly a Senior Fellow at The Brookings Institution; Deputy Director for Development and Trade Research at the US Treasury Department; Ford Foundation Visiting Professor at the Instituto de Planejamento Econômico e Social Aplicado (IPEA) in Brazil; and Assistant Professor at Princeton University.

INSTITUTE FOR INTERNATIONAL
ECONOMICS
11 Dupont Circle, NW
Washington, DC 20036
(202) 328-9000 Telex: 261271 IIE UR
Fax: (202) 328-5432

C. Fred Bergsten, *Director*

The Institute for International Economics was created by, and receives substantial support from, the German Marshall Fund of the United States.

Printed in the United States of America
93 92 91 90 89   5 4 3 2 1

Library of Congress Cataloging-in-Publication Data

Cline, William R.
   United States external adjustment and the world economy / William R. Cline.
      p.   cm.
   Includes index.
   1. Exports—United States—Econometric models.   2. Exports—United States—Forecasting.   3. Balance of trade—United States—Econometric models.   4. Balance of trade—United States—Forecasting.   5. United States—Commercial policy.   I. Title.
HF3003.C53   1989
382'.6'0973—dc19   89-2038

ISBN 0-88132-048-X

Contents

Preface *C. Fred Bergsten*   **xiii**

Acknowledgments   **xv**

1 **Overview**   1
   Origins and Importance of the External Imbalance   2
   Medium-Term Prospects for the US External Deficits   4
   Distortions in International Payments   13
   The Impact of Policy Measures   20
   An International Adjustment Program   28
   Real Adjustment in the United States and Abroad   40
   Policy Implications   45

2 **Origins of the Problem**   51
   The Economic Legacy of the 1980s   51
   Fiscal Deficits   53
   External Imbalance   57
   Dangers of the US External Imbalance   63
   The Rise and Fall of the Dollar   66
   Inadequacy of US External Adjustment to Date   70
   The Need for Symmetrical Adjustment Abroad   73
   Conclusion   75

3 **Medium-Term Prospects for the US External Accounts**   79
   The Helkie–Hooper Model   79
   Modifications   85
   Medium-Term Projections   88
   Factor Services   97
   Alternative Projections   100
   Impact of Exchange Rate Depreciation   102
   Impact of Differential Growth   115
   Policy Parameters   122

Sensitivity 126

The Bubble of 1988 128

Conclusion 129

4 **A Multicountry Model of International Trade** **131**

A Model of External Adjustment with Growth 132

Data 138

Estimation 146

Empirical Results 148

Statistical Annex 169

5 **The Impact of US External Adjustment on Trade and Current Accounts of Other Countries** **179**

Projection Variables 180

Current Account Model 183

Base Case Projections 186

Policy Scenarios 202

A Feasible Adjustment Package 213

Alternative Adjustment Packages 231

Policy Implications 233

Statistical Annex 241

6 **Real Effects of US External Adjustment and Macropolicy Implications** **259**

Real Trade Changes and Output 259

Trade Balance Drag on US Growth in the 1980s 262

US Trade Stimulus to Foreign Growth, 1980–86 266

The Scope of Real Adjustment: United States 269

Real Impact of US External Adjustment on Foreign Countries 273

Early Evidence of Real Adjustment 281

Policy Implications 284

7 **US External Adjustment and the Developing Countries** **295**

The Debt Crisis and US Trade 295

Impact of Improved Credit Access 300

Conclusion 311

APPENDICES   **313**

A   Recalibration of the EAG Model for Projection Purposes   315

B   The Cross-Price Elasticity   321

C   Trade Prices During the Dollar's Decline   327

D   Trends in US and International Oil Trade   337

E   Current Accounts for Major Countries: Trends and Adjustments   343

F   Real Versus Nominal External Adjustment   355

INDEX   **363**

BOXES

2.1   US external adjustment and global aggregate demand   76

3.1   The impact of exchange rate changes on imports
and exports: the gap factor   112

3.2   Variability in trade balance projections   127

5.1   Adverse trends in the United Kingdom   192

5.2   The impact of alternative elasticity assumptions   234

TABLES

1.1   Trends in trade and current account balances, 1987–92   14

1.2   Trends in US bilateral trade balances, 1987–92   15

2.1   United States: Resource and current account balance, 1979–87   60

3.1   Assumptions for medium-term projections   90

3.2   US balance of payments, actual and projected
(HHC, base case), 1980–92   94

3.3   Alternative projections of the US current account balance   101

3.4   Impact of real dollar depreciation on US external accounts,
1988–92   106

3.5   Impact of growth on US external accounts, 1988–92   118

3.6   Policy parameters for US external accounts, 1992   123

4.1   Trade matrix, 1987   142

4.2   Comparison of *Direction of Trade Statistics* (DOTS)
to US balance of payments (BOP) data   144

4.3   Country-specific trade elasticities and trade-weighted
averages   155

4A.1   Export growth rates, 1973–87   170

4A.2	Matrix of income elasticities	172
4A.3	Matrix of price elasticities	174
4A.4	Matrix of cross-price elasticities	176
4A.5	EAG trade equations: adjusted R^2	178
5.1	Base case assumptions for projections	187
5.2	Baseline trends in trade, 1987–92	190
5.3	Current account projections, base case, 1987–92	194
5.4	US trade projections, base case, 1987–92	198
5.5	Policy parameters for the United States	209
5.6	Individual country unilateral policy parameters, results for 1992	211
5.7	A Feasible Adjustment Package	216
5.8	Current account projections under the Feasible Adjustment Package	220
5.9	Distribution of adjustment under the Feasible Adjustment Package	221
5.10	Exchange rate changes implied by the Feasible Adjustment Package	228
5A.1	Matrix of adjusted cross-price elasticities	242
5A.2	Estimated current account balances, 1987	244
5A.3	Parameters for the current account model	245
5A.4	Baseline trade projections, 1992	246
5A.5	Scenario 1: 1992 trade with a 10 percent dollar depreciation against strong countries	248
5A.6	Scenario 2: 1992 trade with 1 percent higher growth in strong countries, 1989–92	250
5A.7	Scenario 3: 1992 trade with 1 percent lower US growth, 1989–92	252
5A.8	Trade projections under the Feasible Adjustment Package, 1992	254
5A.9	US balance of payments, projected (HHC, Feasible Adjustment Package), 1988–92	256
5A.10	Trade balances under alternative policy scenarios and elasticities, 1992	257
6.1	Real impact of trade on US production, 1980–88	264
6.2	Changes in real trade balances with the United States relative to trade and GNP, 1980–86	266

6.3   Changes in real trade in the projection models   272
6.4   Changes in real nonoil trade, 1987–92   275
6.5   Changes in real nonoil trade balances, 1987–92, relative to
      1987 production   277
6.6   Changes in real trade flows, base case, 1987–92   280
6.7   Changes in real trade flows, Feasible Adjustment Package,
      1987–92   282
7.1   Trends in US nonoil trade with troubled debtor countries
      and other areas, 1981–87   296
7.2   Trade impact of $20 billion in increased credit to debtor
      nations, constant shares analysis   304
7.3   Alternative scenarios for debtor country finance   307
7.4   Changes in trade from baseline under DEBT1 scenario, 1992   308
7.5   Changes in 1992 current account balances from baseline
      under alternative financing scenarios   310
D.1   US oil imports, actual and projected, 1985–95   341
E.1   Global statistical discrepancy, 1979–86   351
E.2   Current account balance: reported and adjusted, 1979–86   352
F.1   Ratio of trade balance volume change to trade balance value
      change   360

FIGURES

2.1   US private consumption, private saving, and government
      dissaving, 1979–87   55
2.2   US fiscal deficits and debt, 1979–87   58
2.3   US trade and current account balances, 1980–87   59
2.4   Government purchases of goods and services, 1979–87   61
2.5   Real dollar exchange rates, 1979–89   62
2.6   US monthly trade, seasonally adjusted, 1986–88   71
2.7   Keynesian income equilibrium before and after US external
      adjustment   75
3.1   The gap factor   112
4.1   Predicted and actual exports and imports, 1975–87   158
4.2   US bilateral trade with major countries, 1975–87   165
5.1   US exports: alternative projections, 1987–92   199
5.2   US imports: alternative projections, 1987–92   199
5.3   US trade balance: alternative projections, 1987–92   200

5.4   US current account balance: alternative projections, 1987–92   201

6.1   US manufacturing and total GNP, 1960–86   260

6.2   US manufacturing and total employment, 1960–86   261

6.3   Growth in real domestic demand and GNP, major industrial countries, 1980–88   285

7.1   Current account deficits of debtor countries, 1980–88   301

7.2   Net interest payments of debtor countries, 1980–88   302

C.1   Actual and expected export prices in six countries, 1970–85   328

C.2   Consumer and wholesale prices in six countries, 1970–85   332

D.1   Trade and reserves of oil-exporting countries, 1971–87   338

D.2   Real trade of oil-exporting countries, 1971–87   338

D.3   US oil imports and prices, 1971–87   339

E.1   Current account trends in 18 countries and regions   344

E.2   Statistical discrepancy on current account, 1979–86   348

UNITED STATES
EXTERNAL ADJUSTMENT
AND THE WORLD ECONOMY

Preface

This book presents a comprehensive analysis by William R. Cline of the outlook for the international imbalances of the United States and the world's other leading countries through 1992. It concludes that the progress of 1986–88 in reducing these imbalances is likely to end soon and in fact go into reverse, on the basis of present policies and exchange rates, and that substantial additional policy measures are therefore needed promptly both in the United States and in a number of other countries.

As with several earlier Institute studies, we are releasing our findings from this project in two different formats in an effort to meet the needs of different groups of readers. Chapter 1 of this book, which presents Dr. Cline's main analytical conclusions and policy recommendations, was released separately in March 1989 as *American Trade Adjustment: The Global Impact.*

The Institute has published several previous studies on the international imbalances of the major countries and their effects on the world economy. The first was *Deficits and the Dollar: The World Economy At Risk,* by Stephen Marris, originally released in December 1985 and updated in September 1987. Most recently, my own *America in the World Economy: A Strategy for the 1990s,* published in November 1988, draws heavily on the analyses presented here. Also related was a joint effort by 33 economists from 13 countries, released in December 1987, entitled *Resolving the Global Economic Crisis: After Wall Street.* In all these publications, the Institute has attempted to assess the "big picture" of where the world economy is headed and what policy changes may be needed to promote its successful evolution in the future.

The Institute for International Economics is a private nonprofit institution for the study and discussion of international economic policy. Its purpose is to analyze important issues in that area, and to develop and communicate practical new approaches for dealing with them. The Institute is completely nonpartisan.

The Institute was created by a generous commitment of funds from the German Marshall Fund of the United States in 1981 and now receives about 20 percent of its support from that source. In addition, major institutional grants are being received from the Ford Foundation, the William and Flora Hewlett Foundation, and the Alfred P. Sloan Foundation. A number of other foundations and private corporations are contributing to the increasing diversification of the Institute's resources. The American Express Foundation helped to finance the present study.

The Board of Directors bears overall responsibility for the Institute and gives general guidance and approval to its research program, including identification of topics that are likely to become important to international economic policymakers over the medium run (generally one to three years), and which thus should be addressed by the Institute. The Director, working closely with the staff and outside Advisory Committee, is responsible for the development of particular projects and makes the final decision to publish an individual study.

The Institute hopes that its studies and other activities will contribute to building a strong foundation for international economic policy around the world. We invite readers of these publications to let us know how they think we can best accomplish this objective.

C. FRED BERGSTEN
Director
March 1989

Acknowledgments

The author thanks Paul Armington, C. Fred Bergsten, Bela Balassa, Richard N. Cooper, Anne K. McGuirk, Richard Portes, John Williamson, and Masaru Yoshitomi for insightful comments. He gratefully acknowledges the cooperation of William Helkie and Peter Hooper of the US Federal Reserve Board in the use of their forecasting model. He expresses his great appreciation for the excellent work of research assistants Jonathan Conning, who prepared the data and programming for the multicountry model, and Alex Pfaff and John Hopkins. Andrea Pinkney and Anthony Stancil provided word processing assistance.

Overview

Since the mid-1980s the United States has run huge external deficits, which reached as high as $154 billion on the current account (merchandise trade and services, including capital income) in 1987. Prudence requires that this annual imbalance be cut by at least $100 billion over the next few years. Although the current account deficit did decline to $135 billion in 1988,[1] under present policies it is likely to remain well above $100 billion in 1989 despite further modest reduction, and the deficit is then likely to widen again in 1990 and beyond (as analyzed in this study). Elimination of the US fiscal deficit and some further real decline of the dollar are likely to be required to achieve a sustainable external balance.

The solution of the US external deficit problem, however, could cause new economic difficulties for other countries, many of which relied heavily on exports to the United States to fuel their economic growth earlier in the 1980s. Patterns of major imbalances among other nations persist, as large surpluses remain in Japan and Germany, as well as Taiwan and Korea, while external positions of Third World debtor countries remain weak. In addition, there are rising deficits in the United Kingdom and some other intermediate industrial countries. These emerging weaknesses could intensify once the United States does begin to deal forcefully with its own deficits. In particular, the weaker foreign economies could bear a disproportionately large share of the counterpart of falling US external deficits, in the absence of special measures to concentrate the impact on the high-surplus countries.

This study examines what measures will be needed to achieve the required correction in the US external accounts, and goes on to analyze the nature of

---

1. The trade deficit on a balance of payments basis stood at $126.5 billion. US Department of Commerce, *Summary of US International Transactions: Fourth Quarter and Year 1988* (Washington: US Department of Commerce, BEA 89-09, 14 March 1989), hereafter referred to as *Commerce 1988 Current Account*.

international adjustment necessary to ensure that correction of the US external deficit can occur smoothly, without provoking new imbalances abroad and risking international recession.

Origins and Importance of the External Imbalance

As discussed in Chapter 2, the large US external deficit is the legacy of economic policies adopted in the early 1980s. The central feature of these policies was an unusual combination of fiscal stimulus with monetary restraint. Tax revenues failed to rise as rapidly as many supply-side advocates had hoped after the 1981 tax cut, and the total fiscal deficit (federal, state, and local) rose from 1 percent of GNP in 1981 to an average of 3.4 percent of GNP in 1982–86.[2] This stimulus pulled the economy out of the severe 1982 recession, and permitted the creation of 17 million jobs during the course of the decade. Meanwhile monetary restraint, aided by the good fortune of falling oil prices, made possible a reduction of US inflation from its peak of nearly 14 percent in 1980 to about 4 percent by 1988.

Unfortunately, these gains came only at the expense of the so-called "twin deficits": the internal fiscal deficit and the external deficit on trade and services. The rising fiscal deficit caused a widening gap between the domestic use and availability of resources. Private saving did not rise to offset the decline in public sector saving—on the contrary, gross private saving fell from approximately 18 percent of GNP in 1979–81 to 16 percent in 1985–87, largely because of falling personal savings rates. Instead, foreign resources had to be called upon to fill the resource gap. Nor was the resulting inflow of foreign capital (and the goods and services it financed) dedicated to a boom in US investment, which might have justified borrowing abroad. The ratio of gross private investment to GNP actually declined from 17 percent in 1979–81 to less than 16 percent in 1985–87. The nation had simply gone on a spree of private and government consumption, financed by foreigners.

The resource gap caused high real interest rates, as the government vied with the private sector to borrow in the credit market. High interest rates attracted capital from abroad, and this capital inflow bid up the real price of the dollar by some 40 percent or more. The overvalued dollar acted like a tax of this amount on exports, and a subsidy of the same size to imports. As a result (and because of a higher rate of growth in the United States than abroad, as well as curtailed US exports to the debtor nations following

---

2. References for these and other data not otherwise cited in this overview are given in the subsequent chapters.

the debt crisis), in the first half of the 1980s the value of US exports stagnated while imports rose by nearly 50 percent despite lower oil prices.

The large US external deficit poses three major risks. The first is that failure of the deficit to show progress toward further reduction could at some point provoke a collapse in foreign confidence in the dollar and in the US economy, causing a sharp decline in the dollar well beyond the moderate further reduction from current levels needed to correct the external deficit. Under these circumstances, US monetary authorities would be likely to permit (or even encourage) a large rise in interest rates to stem the excessive fall of the dollar and its threat to revive inflation. A surge in interest rates by perhaps some 5 percentage points would be likely to lead to domestic recession. There would thus be a "hard landing" for both the dollar and the US economy.[3] There have already been storm warnings that the hard-landing scenario could occur, as two episodes of rising US interest rates in 1987 (when foreign private finance began to dry up and central banks had to finance most of the US external deficit) provoked first a bond market collapse and then the stock market crash of October.

The second risk of a large external deficit is that, if it continues over the longer term, the United States will be forced to maintain high real interest rates indefinitely to attract ongoing financing from abroad. High interest rates would discourage investment and thus limit longer-term economic growth. The burden imposed on the next generation would be twofold: not only would Americans have to service a large net external debt (already projected at close to $1 trillion by 1992), but in addition the American economy would have a smaller production base from which to make these payments.[4]

The third risk is an outbreak of protectionism. Congress was already moving toward higher protection in 1985 before the Plaza Agreement among governments to bring the dollar down from its excessively strong levels. If the US trade and current account deficits fail to decline after 1989 and begin to widen again, as projected in this study, there is considerable risk that

---

3. For the first and definitive statement of this risk, see Stephen Marris, *Deficits and the Dollar: The World Economy at Risk.* POLICY ANALYSES IN INTERNATIONAL ECONOMICS 14 (Washington: Institute for International Economics, December 1985). Note that the crucial dynamic of the hard landing is one of "bandwagon" expectations that cause a falling dollar to plunge far below its longer-term equilibrium level. The rise of the dollar in 1988 (after its three-year decline) somewhat reduces this risk by serving notice to speculators that simple extrapolation of past trends can be costly. However, from another standpoint the risk of the hard landing rises while net external debt is rising faster than exports or GNP.

4. If the external deficit were being used to finance unusually high domestic investment, this concern would not be relevant. However, as noted, the foreign financing has been used for consumption rather than investment.

politicians will conclude that macroeconomic policies such as exchange rate changes have had their chance and failed, and that the time has come to impose direct import restrictions. New protectionist measures and the foreign retaliation they would be likely to incite could only push the world economy toward recession.[5]

Medium-Term Prospects for the US External Deficits

Because of the risks of persistent high external deficits, it is crucial to diagnose whether the US trade and current account balances are well on their way toward correction, or whether instead more energetic policy measures are required to achieve adjustment. This study applies two econometric models to project the medium-term path of the US external accounts.

Recent Trends

In 1987 the exchange markets began to despair that the US trade deficit would ever decline. Although the dollar had begun its descent by the second quarter of 1985, the nominal trade deficit for 1987 was larger than ever before at $160 billion versus $122 billion in 1985 and $145 billion in 1986 (see table 3.2 in Chapter 3).[6] Actually the continued widening of the trade deficit should have come as no great surprise, in view of past lags of up to two years in the exchange rate–trade relationship.[7] It takes time for firms

---

5. For an overview of these risks and comprehensive policy proposals for correcting the US external deficit, see C. Fred Bergsten, *America in the World Economy: A Strategy for the 1990s* (Washington: Institute for International Economics, 1988).

6. In real terms the merchandise trade deficit did decline in 1987, from $168.6 billion to $158.9 billion at 1982 prices. However, the rise in dollar import prices meant that the nominal value widened. Note that the trade balance data used here refer to the balance of payments concept, which treats imports on an f.a.s. (free alongside ship) basis and excludes sales by military agencies. Press reports more commonly refer to the trade balance with imports on a c.i.f. (cost including insurance and freight) basis. That deficit stood at $170.3 billion in 1987 and $137.3 billion in 1988. US Department of Commerce, *US Merchandise Trade: December 1988,* FT 900 (Washington: US Department of Commerce).

7. Whether this time there was a "hysteresis" that fundamentally reduced or unusually delayed the trade response to the exchange rate remains a matter of debate. One popular argument has been that foreign firms accepted reduced profit margins rather than raise their dollar prices. However, tests comparing actual dollar export prices to what would have been expected on the basis of foreign wholesale prices divided by dollar exchange rates show an extremely close tracking for the cases of Germany,

to recognize the exchange rate change as permanent and to change their prices accordingly; then, for purchasers to change their buying decisions; and thereafter, for deliveries to arrive following new orders. Only after such lags do the increased volumes of exports and decreased volumes of imports begin to more than offset the initial adverse effect of higher nominal import prices after depreciation (the J-curve phenomenon).

By 1988, enough time had elapsed for trade to respond, and by the first quarter of that year the nominal value of US exports stood fully 32 percent higher than in the same period of 1987 (balance of payments basis), in contrast to their lackluster rise of only 2.3 percent from 1986 to 1987 as a whole. Favorable trade data brought exchange market euphoria, while the Group of Seven (G-7) moved forcefully to support the dollar at the beginning of the year, and the dollar began to rise again.

By late 1988 there were signs that the export boom was beginning to slow down, and progress in reducing the trade deficit appeared even more in jeopardy. Seasonally adjusted exports for the fourth quarter compared with those of the second showed that the annual growth rate had decelerated to 11 percent; and while the average quarterly trade deficit had fallen from $40 billion in 1987 to approximately $30 billion by the second quarter of 1988, it remained stuck at that plateau through the end of the year.[8] Under these circumstances, the dollar began to weaken again in the fourth quarter of 1988, and its renewed strength in early 1989 came not from favorable trade data but in response to rising US interest rates.

Despite the deceleration of improvement, the full-year results for 1988 were encouraging. On a balance of payments basis, US exports rose by 28.2 percent, imports rose by only 8.9 percent, the trade deficit declined by $33.8 billion (to $126 billion), and the current account deficit declined by $19 billion (to $135 billion).[9]

Modeling Trade and Current Accounts

The abrupt shift from further deterioration of the US trade balance in 1987 to brisk improvement in early 1988, followed by a seeming halt to the gains

---

France, and Italy, with little room for supposed breaks in the exchange rate–export price relationship. Tests for Japan and the United Kingdom show somewhat more evidence of lagging export price adjustment after 1985.

8. *Commerce 1988 Current Account.* The fourth quarter outcome (− $32 billion) was actually slightly worse than that of the third (− $29 billion).

9. *Ibid.*

by the second half, highlights the risks of simple straight-line projections of current trends as a basis for policy formation. For meaningful analysis of the external sector outlook, especially over a horizon of up to five years, it is necessary to apply an econometric model.

This study uses two such models. The first is an adaptation of the quarterly current account model developed at the Federal Reserve Board by Helkie and Hooper.[10] The second is an original multicountry model that provides a second opinion on the prospects for US external accounts, as well as a basis for analyzing the impact of US external adjustment on major foreign countries and regions.[11]

The HHC Model—The adapted Helkie–Hooper model (HHC) predicts aggregate US nonoil imports, oil imports, nonagricultural exports, and agricultural exports.[12] Export prices are determined by the US wholesale price index with export weights, and by a variable for foreign prices (based on foreign consumer prices divided by exchange rates against the dollar). US export prices rise by about 1 percent when the US export-weighted wholesale price rises by 1 percent, and by 0.2 percent when foreign prices rise by 1 percent. There is thus some feedback from exchange rate changes to US export prices: as the dollar depreciates, part of the benefit to US firms takes the form of higher dollar prices, instead of being completely "passed through" to foreign buyers in the form of lower foreign currency prices.

Export volume (nonagricultural) in the HHC model depends on foreign income (with an elasticity, or responsiveness, of 2.2, so that a 1 percent rise in GNP abroad causes a 2.2 percent increase in US exports); on the size of the US capital stock relative to the foreign stock (as a measure of trend capacity); and on the price of US exports relative to foreign consumer prices divided by foreign exchange rates, with price lags stretching over two years. Dollar export value equals the quantity of exports multiplied by the price.

Prices of nonoil imports depend on foreign consumer prices, on foreign exchange rates against the dollar (with lags over seven quarters), and on an index of commodity prices. The elasticity of import prices with respect to foreign prices is almost unity, as is the elasticity with respect to the exchange

---

10. William L. Helkie and Peter Hooper, "An Empirical Analysis of the External Deficit, 1980–86," in Ralph C. Bryant, Gerald Holtham, and Peter Hooper, eds., *External Deficits and the Dollar: The Pit and the Pendulum* (Washington: Brookings Institution, 1988), 10–56.

11. The full exposition of the first model appears in Chapter 3, and that of the second, multicountry model in Chapter 4.

12. The reader not interested in the analytical structure of the models may wish to skip this section and the next.

rate, so that the pass-through of foreign price and exchange rate movements over time is nearly total. The volume of nonoil imports depends on capacity utilization in foreign industrial countries, on US income (with a total two-year elasticity of approximately 2), on relative capital stock, and on the ratio of import prices to the US GDP deflator (with lags over seven quarters). The price elasticity is minus 1.15. Since it is close to unity, this elasticity means that nominal import values remain relatively unchanged in response to exchange rate changes, because quantity changes are approximately offset by dollar price changes in the opposite direction.

The HHC model also encompasses services, transfers, and the current account. Capital services play an important role. They are separated into earnings on direct investment, private portfolio holdings, and government obligations. Rates of return depend on interest rates, and the exchange rate has an important valuation effect on direct investment: depreciation of the dollar contributes to higher earnings on assets held abroad by American firms by virtue of a markup in their dollar value. In general, the capital services segment of the model shows a comparative advantage for the United States in international financial intermediation, as rates of return on US assets abroad tend to exceed those on US liabilities to foreigners. The model also cumulates the current account so that net foreign liabilities build over time as the US remains in deficit, in turn causing the capital services account to deteriorate.

For purposes of this study, two adaptations have been made in the original Helkie–Hooper model. The first is to streamline the model from 431 equations to 130, to facilitate simulation. Numerous equations concerning oil imports and agricultural exports are replaced by simplified projections for these sectors. Agricultural exports are projected to grow by 3 percent annually in volume and by 4 percent in nominal dollar prices. World oil prices are projected on the basis of the "low price" scenario estimated by the National Petroleum Council (NPC), and rise from approximately $15 per barrel in 1988 to nearly $19 in 1992. The NPC baseline volume of US oil imports rises from 7.2 million barrels per day (mmbd) in 1988 to an estimated 10.4 mmbd by 1992. For changes from this baseline caused by changes in US growth, an income elasticity of unity is applied, reflecting a lower income elasticity of demand combined with a stagnant volume of domestic production, so that incremental consumption comes entirely from imports. In the baseline projections, US oil imports rise from $39 billion in 1988 to $72 billion in 1992 (table 3.2), and thus grow in value terms at approximately twice the rate of nonoil imports (table 3.2).

The second adaptation addresses overprediction of trade prices in the original model, which called for 1987 dollar import prices to stand 14.7 percent higher than the levels that actually occurred, and overpredicted dollar export prices by 7.1 percent. Much of the divergence was attributable to the unusual lag of foreign wholesale prices behind consumer prices in 1986–87 (reflecting lower oil prices) and the model's use of the latter. The adjustment in the HHC model assumes that half of the gap between predicted and actual trade prices by 1987:4 is never closed, but that trade prices catch up to close the other half of the gap over a period of four quarters.

The EAG Model—Whereas the Helkie–Hooper model is among the more prominent of several models of the US external accounts, there are few existing models that provide trade and current account projections for major foreign countries and regions, or permit examination of the impact of US external adjustment on the economies of other countries. The External Adjustment with Growth (EAG) model divides the world into a total of 17 countries and multicountry groupings: the seven largest industrial countries individually; a group of Other Industrial countries; OPEC; Taiwan; Korea, Singapore, and Hong Kong; Argentina; Brazil; Mexico; a group of Other Latin American countries (i.e., excluding those in OPEC); a group of Other African countries; and a Rest of World grouping. All of world trade is incorporated in one or another of the cells of this 17 × 17 matrix, as shown for 1987 in table 4.1 (Chapter 4). Trade is defined as exports from one partner to another; imports are merely the partner's exports to the country in question.

The model separates oil trade implicitly. By identifying OPEC individually it isolates much of oil trade. In addition, the model divides the exports of Mexico and United Kingdom into oil and nonoil.

For each cell in the trade matrix (for example, US exports to Germany), there is a trade equation. This equation relates the real volume of trade to income in the importing area, the direct prices of the exporter relative to domestic prices in the importing area, and the cross-price competition of the exporter in question against all other exporters participating in the market of the importing area in question. Quarterly data for the period 1973–87, drawn from the International Monetary Fund's (IMF) *Direction of Trade Statistics,* are used to estimate the trade equations. Prices are the IMF's unit value export prices (which are uniform for a given exporting country or group in its trade with all of the other countries or groups). The domestic price term for the importing country is the country's wholesale price index divided by its exchange rate against the dollar. The estimation procedure sets upper and lower bounds on the acceptable elasticities (3.0 and 0.3, respectively, in absolute value). It applies nonlinear programming to minimize the sum of squared residuals in obtaining the estimates, subject to these constraints.

For oil trade, the price of oil is projected independently as discussed above. Oil import volumes depend on income growth in the importing area, with an income elasticity of 0.5 (except for the United States, where the elasticity is set at 1.0 as discussed above).

Imports of OPEC depart from the general model. They are determined by applying a fixed respending ratio out of export earnings, and distributing total imports across supplier countries according to past averages.

The EAG model includes a simple current account estimation for each country. Nonfactor services, such as shipping and insurance, are set proportional to merchandise trade (on both the import and export sides) in the base year 1987. Capital services are based on an "inherited" component reflecting the rate of net capital earnings in the base year, and an incremental component capturing the earnings on the cumulative current account balance over the period 1988–92.

Table 4.3 (Chapter 4) provides a summary view of the elasticities estimated in the EAG model. In general the elasticities are relatively high. The responsiveness to price is sufficient to meet the Marshall–Lerner conditions for exchange rate depreciation to improve the trade balance: the sum of the price elasticities, in absolute value, is greater than unity. Import income elasticities have a trade-weighted average of approximately 2.0. For some countries (United States, United Kingdom, France, Canada, and Argentina), the income elasticity for imports exceeds that for exports,[13] whereas for others (Japan, Brazil, Mexico, Taiwan, Korea–Singapore–Hong Kong) the reverse is true. Such divergences imply a tendency for the trade balance to deteriorate or improve over time, respectively.

EAG Backcasts and Model Adjustments—Table 4.1 shows the 1987 trade matrix for the countries and groups identified in the EAG model. The table shows the dominant role of the United States, Germany, Japan, and the blocs Other Industrial and Rest of World in total world trade. It also shows the large trade deficit of the United States and the large surpluses of Japan and Germany in the base year.

Figure 4.1 (Chapter 4) compares actual total imports and exports for each of the 16 countries or country groupings in the EAG model from 1975 through 1987 with the levels predicted or "backcast" from the EAG model.

---

13. This is the so-called "Houthakker–Magee" phenomenon identified for the United States in the late 1960s. Hendrik S. Houthakker and Stephen P. Magee, "Income and Price Elasticities in World Trade," *Review of Economics and Statistics*, 51, no. 2, May 1969.

Figure 4.2 shows EAG-predicted and actual bilateral trade between the United States and its nine largest trading partners. As the figures indicate, the model generally achieves a close fit with actual trade in the past. There is, nonetheless, a tendency for the model to underpredict US imports in 1987, and correspondingly to underpredict exports of Japan and certain other key countries (such as Taiwan) to the United States in that year. The impact of the 1986 decline in the dollar on 1987 US imports was less than predicted by the model for trade with some important countries.

To address these divergences and more generally to ensure that prediction errors in the important 1987 base year do not distort the medium-term forecasts, for projection purposes the EAG model is recalibrated to place estimated 1987 trade halfway between the actual levels and those predicted by the unadjusted model. In addition, to reduce the vulnerability of the projections to idiosyncrasies in the estimated elasticities for individual trade equations, the projection model applies in each case an average between the estimated specific elasticity and a "uniform" elasticity for the entire model, which in turn is equal to the trade-weighted average value for the elasticity in question (table 4.3).[14] A further adjustment imposes a consistency constraint across the substitution elasticities for the class of countries whose currencies are expected to appreciate in exchange rate simulations and all others, so that changes in US trade from the first group must offset changes from the second insofar as the substitution effect is concerned.

Baseline Projections

The base case economic assumptions are as follows (see tables 3.1 and 5.1). The United States is assumed to make little if any further progress in reducing its fiscal deficit.[15] The dollar is projected to remain constant at its real level against other currencies of the fourth quarter of 1987. The dollar had returned to approximately this level by early 1989, and its rise in 1988

---

14. A high estimated price elasticity for US exports to Canada in particular places a disproportionately large share of future US adjustment on trade with that country; dilution by averaging with the uniform elasticities yields more plausible results.

15. This assumption follows the Congressional Budget Office projections that the federal fiscal deficit, which stood at $155 billion in fiscal 1988, will be $155 billion in 1989, $141 billion in 1990, $140 billion in 1991, and $135 billion in 1992 (fiscal years). Although these forecasts nonetheless reflect a reduction in the deficit relative to GNP, from 3.2 percent in FY1988 to 2.2 percent in FY1992, they may be too optimistic, as they are based on "current services" and do not allow for likely program expansions. Congressional Budget Office, *The Economic and Budget Outlook: Fiscal Years 1990–1994* (Washington: Congressional Budget Office, January 1989), xv.

through August is likely to have been regarded by firms as transitory. Average real GNP growth in 1989–92 is placed at 2.6 percent annually for the United States and Canada, 2.5 percent for Europe, 4 percent for Japan, 8 percent for Taiwan and Korea, and 4½ percent in the rest of the world. World inflation is assumed to average 4½ percent annually in dollar terms.

Table 3.2 shows the baseline projections of the US trade and current accounts using the HHC model. Table 5A.4 (Chapter 5) shows the corresponding world trade matrix projected for 1992 using the EAG model. Table 5.4 in that chapter presents the summary projections of the two models, and figures 5.3 and 5.4 illustrate their projections for the trade and current account balances.

The model projections are from a 1987 base, and comparison of projected 1988 values against actual 1988 results indicates that actual US export and import values both lie approximately halfway between the respective estimates of the two models. The best estimate thus appears to be the simple average of the two projections.[16] On this basis, the central baseline projection is that the US trade deficit will drop no further than to $105 billion in 1989, and will then rise again to $125 billion by 1992. The current account deficit will similarly reach a trough of $119 billion in 1989, and then widen again to over $150 billion by 1992.

As indicated in table 5.4, the nominal values of trade rise briskly through 1992, especially in the HHC model. Based on the average of the two models' projections, US exports should rise by 110 percent from 1987 to 1992, and imports by 62 percent. As world inflation at 4½ percent annually accounts for increases of approximately 25 percent in nominal values over the period, real exports rise by 68 percent (an average of 11 percent annually), while real imports rise by 30 percent (5½ percent annually). Because of the rapid rise of the export base (especially in nominal terms), the current account deficit falls from 48 percent of exports of goods and nonfactor services in 1987 to 24 percent by 1992, even though by that year the nominal current account deficit is once again back up to the $150 billion range. Thus, in relative terms there is improvement even in the base case. Even so, the absolute current account deficit remains far too large for comfort about its sustainability and risks to the economy.

---

16. Note that although the absolute levels of both imports and exports tend to lie some $35 billion to $40 billion higher each year in the HHC model than in the EAG model, the two agree relatively closely on the size of the trade deficit. They show greater divergence with respect to the magnitude of the current account deficit, especially by 1991–92. As discussed in Chapter 3, the HHC model shows a persistently higher rate of return on US direct investment abroad than on foreign direct investment in the United States, and from this standpoint may introduce an upward bias of perhaps some $15 billion annually by 1991 in the current account estimate.

Table 3.3 (Chapter 3) reports projections of other forecasting entities, public and private. It is evident from the table that most of the forecasts identify the same inverse-U profile for the US current account balance that is found with both the HHC and EAG models. This pattern stems from the fact that, with the lagged effects of exchange rate change largely exhausted by the second year, 1989 should show the minimum US trade deficit following the end to the dollar's decline in 1987. Because there is still a $100 billion gap between exports and imports at that point, when proportionate growth in response to domestic and foreign income growth resumes, the absolute size of the trade deficit begins to widen again. World inflation at 4½ percent annually (in dollar terms) also causes the nominal deficit to swell after 1989. For the current account deficit, the renewed widening is augmented by the growing burden of interest payments on rising net external liabilities. As indicated in table 3.2, net US external liabilities reach $1.1 trillion by 1992 in the base case.

Overall, the baseline projections of the HHC and EAG models, and of several other private and official organizations, indicate that in the absence of policy change the US trade and current account deficits will not fall below $100 billion and will begin to increase again after 1989. The policy implication of these projections is that far more needs to be done to reduce the US external deficits to sustainable levels that can forestall the economic and protectionist risks outlined above.

In late 1988, the US Treasury issued a report challenging the conventional models that show results such as those summarized here. The Treasury authors argued that, because of fundamental changes US industry has made in recent years to cut costs and improve quality, there would be a more positive response of US exports than standard models predict from past experience. They added that the increased presence of foreign investment should mean a partial replacement of imports by goods produced by foreign firms in the United States.[17]

It is unclear what basis the Treasury had in mind for anticipating a stronger response of exports than predicted by models estimated from past performance. Although it is true that US labor costs have fallen sharply relative to those of competing nations, this improvement should already be taken into account in the relative price terms of the models.[18] As for direct

---

17. US Department of Treasury, *Report to Congress on International Economic and Exchange Rate Policy* (Washington: US Department of Treasury, 15 October 1988). The report also stated that the Group of Seven countries stood ready to adjust policies to ensure reduction of trade imbalances, but the baseline projections here assume no policy change so that the needed scope of policy adjustment can be analyzed.

18. In a rare attempt to quantify these effects, Hooper has examined indicators of absolute unit labor costs and found that the higher competitive position of US

investment effects, the most important sector is automobiles. There, the presence of voluntary export restraints in Japan meant the existence of an economic rent that could be reduced without necessarily changing the volume of Japanese exports to the United States, so that new "transplant" autos could replace primarily US production rather than imported cars from Japan. Moreover, the transplant firms have a high import content, and their expansion may be expected to increase imports of components.[19] For policy purposes it would thus appear dangerous to take a complacent attitude about large projected external deficits on grounds that effects absent in the models will provide a major improvement.

Distortions in International Payments

As set forth in Chapter 5, the baseline projections in the EAG model reveal important distortions in the medium-term outlook for international payments balances that go well beyond an excessive US deficit. The counterpart of this deficit is not distributed evenly. Instead, the foreign surpluses are highly concentrated in Japan and Germany. The pattern of 1992 trade balances bears a close resemblance to the existing structure of high concentrations of surpluses in these countries. Moreover, the absolute size of these surpluses rises over time in the base case, reaching $136 billion in Japan and $85 billion in Germany by 1992 (table 1.1).

At least four adjustment problems emerge from the baseline projections. The first is the need for the United States to reduce its prospective external deficit. The second is the need for Germany and Japan to reduce their exceptionally large surpluses. Third, the United Kingdom faces a large prospective external deficit. Fourth, some of the intermediate industrial countries face emerging external deficit problems, in considerable measure as the counterpart of the rising German surplus. Surprising weaknesses develop, not only for the United Kingdom but also, to a lesser degree, for

---

manufacturing by late 1987 might yield a higher trade balance than predicted by the conventional models, by as much as nearly $60 billion by 1993. This outcome would still leave the current deficit at a plateau of approximately $100 billion. However, Hooper's estimate of these supply-side effects has an extremely wide variance. Moreover, in subsequent work Hooper raises new doubts about the prospects for such effects, particularly in light of the strengthening of investment growth in Europe and slackening of that in the United States. Peter Hooper, "Exchange Rates and US External Adjustment in the Short Run and the Long Run," *Brookings Discussion Papers in International Economics* 65 (Washington: Brookings Institution, October 1988); also William L. Helkie and Peter Hooper, "U.S. External Adjustment: Progress and Prospects" (Washington: Federal Reserve Board, February 1989).

19. W.V. Bussmann, "The Trade Deficit in Autos with Japan: How Much Improvement?" *Business Economics*, April 1988, 20–25.

Table 1.1 Trends in trade and current account balances, 1987–92
(billions of dollars except as noted)

Country/group	Trade balance 1987	Trade balance 1992 Base case	Trade balance 1992 FAP	Current account 1987	Current account 1992 Base case	Current account 1992 FAP	CA as % of XGS 1987	CA as % of XGS 1992 Base case	CA as % of XGS 1992 FAP
United States	−160.2	−124.5	−44.3	−153.9	−168.0	−48.4	−48	−26	−6
United Kingdom	−16.4	−70.8	−32.7	−3.4	−76.1	−22.5	−2	−29	−7
France	−7.5	−16.4	−13.0	−1.5	−6.7	0.4	−1	−2	0
Germany	70.2	89.8	41.0	45.2	84.8	15.7	14	16	3
Italy	−0.5	−14.2	−4.2	−0.7	−20.9	−6.3	0	−9	−2
Canada	8.8	13.7	12.5	−6.3	−11.8	−14.2	−6	−6	−7
Japan	96.4	129.3	80.8	86.6	136.4	63.4	34	34	16
Argentina	1.0	3.8	4.8	−3.7	−3.5	−2.3	−51	−22	−13
Brazil	11.2	26.7	30.1	1.2	15.5	19.1	4	28	31
Mexico	9.6	11.9	12.9	3.9	3.9	5.0	14	9	10
Taiwan	20.7	6.2	1.9	18.0	−1.6	−9.3	32	−2	−11
OPEC	36.0	25.6	25.9	−5.0	−34.8	−34.9	−4	−24	−24
Other Industrial	−8.9	−22.7	−69.1	−6.2	−22.9	−83.1	−1	−2	−8
Korea–Singapore–Hong Kong	6.5	−18.4	−36.8	11.0	−6.9	−27.5	8	−3	−10
Other Latin America	−1.7	4.1	9.2	−9.1	−8.3	−2.0	−30	−14	−3
Other Africa	4.7	1.4	10.5	−4.7	−20.5	−10.2	−8	−21	−9
Rest of World	−37.5	4.5	21.8	−8.0	63.5	89.2	−3	13	16

FAP = Feasible Adjustment Package.
XGS = exports of goods and nonfactor services.
Note: EAG model estimates for the United States.

Table 1.2 Trends in US bilateral trade balances, 1987–92
(billions of dollars)

Bilateral US trade balance with:	1987	1992 Base case	1992 FAP
United Kingdom	−4.1	3.9	3.9
France	−2.5	−1.7	−0.5
Germany	−16.1	−22.0	−17.1
Italy	−5.6	−6.8	−6.2
Canada	−13.4	−10.8	−1.9
Japan	−56.8	−60.5	−30.0
Argentina	0.1	0.4	0.6
Brazil	−3.6	−8.1	−7.8
Mexico	−4.1	−0.6	0.3
Taiwan	−17.2	−10.1	−3.2
OPEC	−11.4	−16.6	−16.4
Other Industrial	2.2	24.3	39.7
Korea–Singapore–Hong Kong	−22.8	−28.0	−14.5
Other Latin America	0.0	1.8	2.2
Other Africa	−1.3	0.4	1.2
Rest of World	1.6	10.8	14.4

Source: tables 4.1, 5A.4, and 5A.8.
Note: these data are from the EAG data base, and contain minor differences from the data converted to a balance of payments trade data basis (as in table 1.1).

France, Italy, and the Other Industrial countries. Moreover, these weaknesses emerge even in the absence of US external adjustment. If the United States were to achieve a major reduction in its external deficit in the absence of other measures to affect the developing distribution of trade and payments balances among other nations, the potential difficulties faced by the weaker industrial countries would be intensified.

Table 1.1 provides a summary view of the trends in external accounts for each of the 17 major countries and country groupings examined in the EAG model. The table reports actual 1987 and projected 1992 trade and current account balances. The 1992 estimates include not only the base case discussed above, but also a Feasible Adjustment Package (FAP) case, developed below. Table 5A.4 shows the projected baseline trade matrix for 1992, and thus indicates the detailed composition of the trade balances that lie behind the summary in table 1.1. Table 1.2 summarizes the corresponding bilateral US trade positions, and indicates the persistence of large US bilateral deficits with Japan, Germany, and the East Asian NICs in the base case of no policy change. It is evident from the tables that the major trading nations and groupings divide into several distinct tiers with respect to the medium-term strength of their external accounts.

Germany and Japan

In the strongest tier, Germany and Japan further increase their already large external surpluses. Thus, Germany's trade surplus rises from $70 billion to approximately $90 billion, while that of Japan increases from $96 billion to $129 billion in the base case with no additional policy adjustment. The bilateral US deficit with Japan reaches $60 billion by 1992, threatening intensified pressure for protection against imports from that country. The corresponding current account surpluses rise from $45 billion to $85 billion in Germany, and from $87 billion to $136 billion in Japan. Even so, because of a rising nominal export base, the current account surpluses of Germany and Japan are more stable in relative terms, as the German surplus edges up from 14 percent of exports of goods and nonfactor services in 1987 to 16 percent in 1992, while that of Japan remains constant at 34 percent.

The rising absolute surpluses of the two countries may be illustrated as follows. In both, the trade balance remains in strong surplus by 1989. Thus, Japan's exports for this year are estimated at $234 billion, while its imports are projected at $138 billion (EAG model). With lagged effects of the dollar's decline through 1987 broadly exhausted in 1989, thereafter normal import and export growth resumes. Annual dollar inflation contributes 4½ percent each year, and if export and import volumes both rose at 6 percent, nominal trade values would rise by some 30 percent from 1989 to 1992. The large 1989 gap between exports and imports means that in this simple example the proportionate rise boosts Japan's trade surplus to $125 billion by 1992 (the actual model estimate is $129 billion; table 1.1). In addition, the growing surplus on capital income (from rising net external assets) swamps Japan's traditional deficit on nonfactor services, and adds several billion dollars more to the 1992 current account surplus.

East Asian NICs

Although the newly industrializing countries (NICs) of East Asia, Taiwan and Korea–Singapore–Hong Kong, are a second strong tier with high current account surpluses in the base year ($18 billion, or 32 percent of exports of goods and services, and $11 billion, or 8 percent, respectively), the two areas show a rapid decline in their surpluses over the five-year period even in the base case without policy adjustment (and at 1987:4 real exchange rates). Thus, Taiwan's current account falls to a deficit equal to 2 percent of exports of goods and services by 1992, while that of Korea–Singapore–Hong Kong turns to a deficit of 3 percent.

For these two areas, the standardized adjustments used in the EAG forecasting model probably introduce a downward bias in future trade and current account balances. In the past the two areas have enjoyed a strong positive difference between the income elasticity of demand for their exports and that for their imports. Thus, for both Taiwan and Korea–Singapore–Hong Kong, the import elasticity is approximately 1.3 whereas the export elasticity is twice as large at 2.7 (table 4.3). Such a divergence is typical for high-growth countries, which otherwise would tend to require persistent real depreciation to avoid rising trade imbalances.[20]

The EAG forecasting model dilutes this favorable elasticity asymmetry by averaging the country-specific elasticities with uniform elasticities for all countries on a trade-weighted basis (as discussed above). Although this technique appears to provide more stable projections for the key case of the United States (and especially Canada), it may bias the Taiwan and Korea–Singapore–Hong Kong projections downward by failing to allow sufficient income elasticity asymmetry in view of their growth rates (8 percent annually), which are much higher than the average for other countries (some 3 percent).[21] Nonetheless, the projections do suggest that, if the two areas maintain exceptionally high growth rates, their high external surpluses could well diminish substantially over the medium term even without specific policy action.

Intermediate Industrial Countries

In contrast to the strong baseline trends for external balances in Germany and Japan, the trends are weaker for a tier of intermediate industrial

---

20. For recent empirical documentation of this international pattern, see Paul Krugman, "Differences in Income Elasticities and Trends in Real Exchange Rates," *NBER Working Paper* 2761 (Cambridge, Mass.: National Bureau of Economic Research, 1988).

21. Thus, when country-specific elasticities are applied, the baseline trade balance for Korea–Singapore–Hong Kong in 1992 stands at a surplus of $20 billion rather than a deficit of $11 billion. For Taiwan, the corresponding divergence is between a surplus of $5.3 billion and one of $1.4 billion. The potential bias from averaging country-specific and uniform elasticities thus appears considerably smaller for Taiwan.

countries. The current account balance declines[22] from -1 percent of exports of goods and services in 1987 to -2 percent by 1992 for France, from 0 percent to -9 percent for Italy, and from -1 percent to -2 percent for the Other Industrial countries; it remains at a relatively weak -6 percent in Canada.[23] In absolute terms the corresponding current account balances all show widening deficits, with 1992 deficits of approximately $21 billion in Italy, $12 billion in Canada, $7 billion in France, and $23 billion in the Other Industrial countries.[24]

Comparison of tables 4.1 and 5A.4 shows that much of this prospective weakness is associated with widening trade imbalances with Germany. Thus, the bilateral trade deficit of France with Germany rises from approximately $12 billion in 1987 to $20 billion by 1992; that of Italy with Germany from $4 billion to $6 billion; and that of the Other Industrial countries with Germany from $31 billion to $38 billion.[25]

United Kingdom

The weakest external sector outlook is for the United Kingdom, which stands in a class by itself. In the absence of special policy adjustments, the country's current account deficit rises from $3 billion in 1987 to $76 billion in 1992, or from 2 percent of exports of goods and services to 29 percent. Several factors contribute to this outcome. The country has a relatively large adverse asymmetry between income elasticities for exports and imports (even after dilution by averaging with uniform elasticities). Oil accounts for 10 percent of its exports, and oil exports grow slowly in value terms. The United Kingdom has already entered a new cycle of declining external accounts, as the trade balance shifted from surplus in 1980–82 of approxi-

---

22. All references to changing positions on trade or current account "balances" are used in an algebraic sense. An increase in the balance refers to a rise in a surplus or a decline in a deficit. A decline in a balance indicates a reduction in a surplus or an increase in a deficit.

23. For Canada the model actually shows a declining trend, because it substantially overpredicts the level of the current account balance (at zero) in the base year 1987.

24. Note that the Other Industrial country grouping, which includes Australia, Austria, Belgium, Denmark, Finland, Iceland, Ireland, the Netherlands, New Zealand, Norway, Spain, Sweden, and Switzerland, accounts for a large bloc of international trade. Its exports and imports of nearly $500 billion each exceed those of the United States and especially, Germany or Japan.

25. In contrast, bilateral trade with Japan contributes practically nothing to the external sector erosion for France and Italy, although its contribution is comparable to that from trade with Germany in the case of the Other Industrial countries.

mately 7 percent of merchandise exports to deficits of 2.6 percent in 1983–85 and 9.5 percent in 1987. Even if the average percentage changes in imports and exports for other European countries from 1987 to 1992 are applied to the 1987 UK trade base, the adverse initial gap is such that the 1992 trade deficit reaches $31 billion. In addition, UK export prices in dollar terms have risen relatively rapidly since 1986.

Other Countries

Among the other country groupings, there is notable strength in the baseline trend for the Rest of World group, which includes Asia apart from Japan and the NICs (and thus incorporates such countries as China and India); the middle-income countries of Europe (such as Turkey and Portugal); the non-oil-producing nations of the Middle East; and the Eastern bloc countries. Many countries in this area have held real exchange rates against the dollar relatively constant since 1985, and have thus depreciated in real terms against high-income Europe and Japan.[26] The trends are even stronger for Brazil, although that country's unusually low income elasticity for imports probably causes an upward bias in the trend for the trade surplus. Mexico shows moderate external strength but a declining trend.

The levels of current account balances relative to exports, or their baseline trends, or both, tend to be weak for the other groups in the model: Argentina (in the extreme), OPEC, Other Latin America, and Other Africa. These countries are in no position to absorb any of the counterpart of a potential adjustment of the US external deficit.

Early Evidence

The EAG model projections use 1987, the most recent year for which data are available for detailed intercountry trade flows, as the base year. The

---

26. The baseline projection shows the Rest of World current account rising from a deficit of $8 billion in 1987 to a surplus of $63.5 billion in 1992. If it is assumed instead that this developing region spends the potential surplus on increased imports, and that its 1992 baseline current account balance is held to zero, then on the basis of 1992 supplier shares in Rest of World imports (excluding those from other Rest of World countries) the impact would be an increase of current account positions by approximately $7 billion each for the United States, Germany, and Japan; by $9 billion for Korea–Singapore–Hong Kong; and by $12 billion for the Other Industrial countries. This reallocation does not alter the qualitative conclusions of the analysis, as the reduction in the US external deficit is modest and smaller in proportional terms than the corresponding increase in the external surpluses of Germany and Japan.

estimates for 1988 are thus projections rather than historical data. By early 1989, initial data on aggregate trade and current account balances for 1988 were becoming available, and they provide a basis for early evidence on the validity of the baseline trends identified in the model.

Salient trends in the baseline projections include persistence and widening of the large surpluses in Germany and Japan, and a large emerging deficit in the United Kingdom. In 1988, Germany's actual trade surplus rose from $70 billion to $79.5 billion, and its current account surplus rose modestly from $45 billion to $49.1 billion.[27] These surpluses are actually larger than the 1988 estimates in the EAG model ($68 billion and $39 billion, respectively), suggesting that the future projections do not exaggerate the surpluses. In Japan, the trade surplus was almost unchanged in 1988 (at an estimated $93 billion versus $96 billion in 1987), whereas the current account surplus declined only modestly (from $87 billion to $79 billion).[28] The EAG projections for 1988 called for a trade surplus of $93 billion and a current account balance of $86 billion, suggesting that the future projections are on track for trade but may be modestly too high for the current account surplus. In the United Kingdom, the deterioration identified in the EAG model was already apparent in 1988, as the trade deficit rose from $17 billion to an estimated $33 billion and the current account deficit from $4 billion to $23 billion (in part because of a cyclical boom in private domestic demand). The EAG projections for 1988 were actually more modest: a trade deficit of $25 billion and a current account deficit of $20 billion.

The Impact of Policy Measures

The severe distortions in international payments in the baseline projections indicate the need for decisive policy adjustment to reduce international imbalances over the medium term. The key measures for the United States are reduction of the fiscal deficit and some further depreciation of the dollar in real terms. The adjustment measures needed abroad, especially in the high-surplus countries, are the expansion of domestic demand and real exchange rate appreciation.

The Role of Fiscal Adjustment and Exchange Rate Change

The root causes of the US external imbalance are the rise in the fiscal deficit and erosion of personal saving, as discussed above. The first and foremost

---

27. International Monetary Fund, by communication.

28. The 1987 and estimated 1988 results are from *OECD Economic Outlook,* December 1988.

corrective policy should be full achievement of the Gramm–Rudman–Hollings targets, which would result in elimination of the federal deficit by 1993.[29] Under this act the deficit would be cut by approximately $40 billion annually in each of the next four years.[30]

The national accounts identities (and the resource balance discussed above) establish a direct accounting relationship between the fiscal deficit and the external deficit.[31] It is unlikely, however, that elimination of a fiscal deficit of $150 billion would automatically eliminate an external deficit of the same size in the absence of other influences. A significant portion of the reduced fiscal deficit would tend to be offset by induced increases in domestic investment, as lower government borrowing reduces interest rates and encourages investment ("crowding in"). Lower interest rates could also raise private consumption, although if the fiscal deficit is reduced by higher taxes, private consumption would tend to decline as the result of lower disposable income.

Reduction of the fiscal deficit by $150 billion could thus reduce domestic demand (consumption plus investment plus government spending, $C + I + G$) by perhaps $75 billion to $100 billion. The marginal propensity to import (the fraction of each additional dollar of total demand that is spent on imports) in the United States is approximately one-fifth.[32] The reduction in domestic demand associated with elimination of the fiscal deficit would thus translate into a cutback in imports by some $15 billion to $20 billion, much less than the full $150 billion reduction in the fiscal deficit.

On the export side, lower interest rates in the United States could encourage other countries to lower their own interest rates, and could thus increase

---

29. If policy instruments existed that could reliably raise personal savings rates, they too would be appropriate. Unfortunately, experience has shown savings rates to be stubbornly resistant to policy measures, including such instruments as Individual Retirement Accounts.

30. The revised act of 1987 sets the following deficit targets: fiscal 1988, $144 billion; 1989, $136 billion; 1990, $100 billion; 1991, $64 billion; 1992, $28 billion; 1993, zero. Congressional Budget Office, *The Economic and Budget Outlook*, xv.

31. From the final product side of gross national product, $Y = C + I + G + X - M$, where Y is GNP, C is consumption, I is investment, G is government spending, X is exports, and M is imports. From the factor payments side of national accounts, $Y = C + S + T$, where S is saving and T is taxes. Subtracting the second equation from the first, and rearranging, $X - M = (S - I) + (T - G)$. The external balance thus equals the excess of private saving over private investment, plus the excess of tax revenue over government spending. The final bracketed term, the fiscal balance, thus has a direct accounting impact on the external balance.

32. The average propensity to import, or the ratio of imports to GNP, is approximately 10 percent. The income elasticity of imports is approximately 2 (table 4.3). The marginal propensity to import equals the income elasticity multiplied by the average propensity to import.

growth of foreign demand and stimulate US exports. In addition, lower domestic demand would tend to release some resources for increased exports. It is unlikely, however, that these indirect export effects would be as large as the direct import effects. Liberal allowance for export effects might boost the total impact of the fiscal adjustment on the trade balance to a range of $25 billion to $35 billion. By implication, with domestic demand down by $75 billion to $100 billion and the trade balance up by only $25 billion to $35 billion, respectively, domestic production would decline by $50 billion to $65 billion, or by 1 to 1½ percent of GNP.[33]

In short, fiscal adjustment is a necessary condition for US external adjustment, but by itself it is likely to be inadequate. As developed below, the US current account deficit needs to be cut from its prospective 1992 level of approximately $150 billion to some $50 billion. Reduction in the external deficit by some $25 billion to $35 billion as the result of elimination of the fiscal deficit alone would achieve only one-fourth to one-third of this objective. Two other measures will be required: real depreciation of the exchange rate, and acceleration of foreign growth from the baseline outlook. This would essentially require merely the maintenance of high 1988 growth rates in key countries, as discussed below.[34]

Exchange rate change is fortunately a natural counterpart of fiscal adjustment. In the mainstream macroeconomic analysis for an open economy (for example, the Mundell–Fleming framework), fiscal contraction reduces the interest rate, which in turn reduces the inflow of capital from abroad. Lower capital inflows mean less foreign exchange bidding for dollars, and the exchange rate of the dollar declines.[35]

---

33. This discussion (but not necessarily the quantitative magnitudes) follows John Williamson, "Achieving a Sustainable Payments Position," Testimony before the Joint Economic Committee, US House of Representatives, 9 February 1989.

34. The need for exchange rate cnange to supplement fiscal adjustment (even when matched by fiscal expansion abroad) is forcefully argued in Paul Krugman, "Adjustment in the World Economy," *Occasional Paper* 24 (New York: Group of Thirty, December 1987) The issue is essentially the classic transfer problem. The home country has a lower marginal propensity to spend on imports than on its own goods, as does the foreign country. Only a modest portion of fiscal contraction in the home country thus translates into lower imports, and a limited portion of fiscal expansion abroad translates into higher imports from the home country. The net reduction in demand in the home country and expansion abroad creates excess supply at home and short supply abroad. A change in the relative price, the exchange rate, is necessary to clear the markets.

35. Market sentiment might initially react to a firm announcement of US fiscal correction in just the opposite way, by bidding up the dollar on the grounds that the central flaw in economic policy was now being corrected. Eventually the influence of lower interest rates would be likely to dominate, however.

Just as fiscal adjustment without exchange rate adjustment is likely to be inadequate, so would be the reverse. Even if the exchange rate could be independently depreciated without fiscal adjustment, the results would be unfavorable. In this case, the resulting upward pressure on net exports without a reduction in domestic demand would cause an acceleration in inflation, risking a vicious circle of depreciation, inflation, and more depreciation in the attempt to maintain the real decline of the dollar. (This process has been witnessed in several Latin American countries that have attempted to adjust externally without adequate fiscal adjustment.) In contrast, a balanced package of fiscal adjustment and exchange rate reduction can help avoid the negative output impact of fiscal contraction alone. In the illustration above, US GNP declined by 1 to 1½ percent. By adding dollar devaluation to the policy package, higher exports and lower real import volume can provide additional demand so that production need not fall.

In sum, a policy package containing US fiscal adjustment, real depreciation of the dollar, and some economic expansion abroad is likely to be required to achieve US external adjustment, and can permit adjustment without a slowdown in domestic growth or a recession.

Model Simulation of Policy Changes

The HHC and EAG models provide a basis not only for projecting the baseline outlook for US and foreign external accounts, but also for simulating the impact of policy changes.

Conceptual Issues—Three main variables drive both projection models: US GNP, the real exchange rate of the dollar, and foreign GNP. Neither model explicitly incorporates fiscal policy. Instead, it is implicitly assumed that the fiscal stance changes in a way that is consistent with the changed income and exchange rate variables applied in alternative policy simulations. In particular, there must be sufficient fiscal adjustment so that the postulated real depreciation of the dollar is not frustrated by rising inflation, which neutralizes nominal exchange rate changes.

In the HHC and EAG models, US GNP affects the US external accounts on the side of demand for imports. Faster growth spurs faster import expansion. Foreign GNP affects exports, as faster growth abroad increases demand for US exports. In terms of the impact of fiscal adjustment as outlined above, the models capture the reduction of the fiscal deficit (at an unchanged exchange rate) only insofar as the net reduction in domestic demand translates into reduction in GNP (production) and therefore imports.

Similarly, they capture any non-exchange rate effects of fiscal adjustment on exports only through higher foreign growth (in response to lower world interest rates).

In practice, the "growth" variables in both models serve as proxies for a mixture of production ($C + I + G + X - M$, or GNP) on the one hand and domestic demand ($C + I + G$) on the other. A portion of imports is closely related to production: intermediate inputs into the manufacturing process. Another portion is more closely related to domestic demand: final goods (C) and capital goods (I). Empirical estimates over time estimated on the basis of GNP tend to capture both influences. Similarly, policy simulations that change "growth" to influence imports implicitly can change the mixture of output growth and domestic demand growth. Thus, if Japan increases government spending and Japanese consumption rises as the result of shorter work weeks and more leisure time, Japanese demand for US exports can rise even with an unchanged level of GNP in Japan. In this regard, the policy simulations that call for higher growth rates abroad should be interpreted to include higher growth of domestic demand instead of or as well as higher GNP. This interpretation is important, because it means that "growth" acceleration that might appear implausible in terms of actual output (because of capacity constraints) is feasible when understood in terms of domestic demand expansion.

The other central variable, the exchange rate, also raises questions of interpretation. The model simulations apply changes in the exchange rate independently (but, as noted, with the implicit assumption that fiscal policy changes in a compatible way). Some would ask whether it makes any sense in a floating rate world to consider the exchange rate as an independent variable. At a proximate level, the answer is affirmative. Especially since the Plaza Agreement of 1985 and the Louvre Accord of 1987, the industrial countries have in practice reverted to a system of central exchange rates with, apparently, relatively narrow bands. At successive meetings the Group of Seven (G-7) determines whether to reaffirm the existing exchange rates or change the targets. The system is essentially an unannounced target rate regime. Under these circumstances, the exchange rate has again become de facto a direct policy variable, in contrast to its benign neglect under more freely floating rates in the first half of the 1980s.

At a deeper level, however, the answer to whether the exchange rate can be treated as a policy variable for model simulation is that underlying fiscal and monetary policy are telescoped into the exchange rate variable. Despite the G-7 agreements, any alignment of exchange rates sharply at odds with interest rate differentials and inflationary expectations would be likely to collapse soon, as central bank intervention would be insufficient to sustain it. At this more fundamental level, then, the direct use of the real exchange rate variable in the policy simulations once again reaches back to the assumption that underlying fiscal (and monetary) policy is compatible with the real exchange rate specified.

Policy Impact Estimates—Table 5.5 (Chapter 5) shows the estimated impact of each "policy instrument"—exchange rate, foreign growth, and US growth—on the US trade and current account balances by 1992. The policy simulations used to derive the parameters are a 10 percent real depreciation of the dollar phased in over the four quarters of 1989, and a change in baseline 1989–92 annual growth by 1 percentage point.

Real depreciation of the dollar by 1 percent against all foreign currencies increases the 1992 US trade balance by $7.5 billion in the EAG model and by $5.2 billion in the HHC model. The larger impact in the EAG model stems from its higher price elasticities for trade than in the HHC model. The corresponding effects for the current account are $10.2 billion and $7.8 billion. Thus, one-fourth to one-third of the total effect arises in the service sector—a point often missed by trade models. The HHC model in particular captures such effects as the change in valuation of direct foreign investment income resulting from a change in the exchange rate.

Because most developing countries are not in a position to allow their currencies to appreciate against the dollar, the simulations also examine exchange rate change against "strong" areas only, defined to include all of the industrial countries (including or excluding Canada), Taiwan, and Korea–Singapore–Hong Kong. A 1 percent real depreciation of the dollar against the strong countries including Canada increases the 1992 US current account balance by $8.9 billion in the EAG model and by $6.4 billion in the HHC model. (The special role of Canada is most evident in the EAG model.)

One-percentage-point higher growth for one year in the strong countries including Canada increases the 1992 US trade balance by $6.5 billion in the EAG model and by $6.9 billion in the HHC model. The corresponding current account effects are $9.1 billion and $13.3 billion, with the larger HHC estimate attributable primarily to higher earnings on US direct investment abroad when foreign growth accelerates.

The two models show practically identical effects of 1-percentage-point lower growth for one year in the United States: an increase in the 1992 trade balance by approximately $11 billion and in the current account balance by $15 billion.

These parameters provide an initial basis for gauging the dimension of the policy actions required. For example, if it is desired to reduce the 1992 US current account deficit from the base case estimate of $153 billion to only $50 billion, and if the average parameters for the two models are applied, acceleration of growth from the baseline by ¾ percentage point annually in 1989–92 in the strong countries including Canada would contribute $33 billion (¾ × 4 × $11 billion), and the remaining $70 billion could be obtained from real depreciation of the dollar against the same areas by 9.1 percent ($70 billion/$7.65 billion per percentage point). Acceptance of some reduction in US growth would permit either less growth acceleration abroad or a smaller dollar depreciation.

Unbalanced Distribution of Adjustment Abroad—As might be suspected from the emerging distortions in external balances of countries other than the United States, discussed above, a uniform application of exchange rate and growth policies places undue burdens on the weaker foreign countries, even when foreign adjustment is limited to the industrial countries (including Canada) and the East Asian NICs. Indeed, one of the most striking findings of the simulations using the EAG model is that if exchange rate or growth changes abroad are adopted uniformly across countries, the large surpluses of Germany and Japan essentially fail to decline; instead the full burden of the counterpart of lower US deficits is absorbed by declining external balances of the intermediate and weaker foreign countries.

Thus, with an across-the-board 10 percent appreciation of foreign currencies against the dollar by the strong countries,[36] Germany's 1992 trade balance remains unchanged from the baseline level at $107 billion, and that of Japan declines only marginally (from $128 billion to $122 billion); meanwhile the trade deficit of France rises from $13 billion to $20 billion, that of Italy from $7 billion to $13 billion, and that of the Other Industrial countries from $62 billion to $83 billion (tables 5A.4 and 5A.5, Chapter 5). This outcome is partly attributable to low price elasticities in Germany, but principally to what may be called the "balloon effect." Because Germany and Japan have sizable trade surpluses against the intermediate industrial countries in the baseline projections, even at unchanged trade volumes with these other countries a rise in the dollar price of German, Japanese, and other European goods due to the decline in the dollar causes the dollar value of the preexisting trade imbalances to balloon. The swelling of the dollar value of the German and Japanese surpluses against industrial countries other than the United States thus largely or fully offsets the decline in the surpluses of these two countries with the United States (and other dollar-area countries) resulting from the exchange rate change. In contrast, for the intermediate countries a rising deficit with Germany and Japan adds

---

36. The uniform policy simulations exclude Canada from the adjustment.

to the declining surplus with the United States to cause a twofold deterioration in their trade balances.

The balloon effect also applies to changes in foreign growth rates, although in this case it is trade volumes rather than nominal values that swell. Thus, when all strong countries (excluding Canada) adopt an increase in their annual growth rates of 1 percentage point over four years, the 1992 trade balances of Germany and Japan remain virtually unchanged from their baseline levels, while the trade balance of France falls by $9 billion, that of Italy by $3 billion, and that of the Other Industrial countries by $16 billion. The German and Japanese surpluses with the intermediate countries in the base case mean that when relatively similar proportional increases in trade volumes occur as the result of uniform growth acceleration, the volume of the trade deficit expands. Once again, the balloon effect vis-à-vis the intermediate industrial countries neutralizes the trade balance reduction of Germany and Japan against the United States and the dollar-area countries, while compounding the deterioration of the intermediate countries against the dollar area.

Thus, exchange rate appreciations against the dollar and acceleration of growth rates (and/or increases in domestic demand) from baseline trends need to be differentiated by country if disparities between high-surplus Germany and Japan, on the one hand, and the intermediate countries, on the other, are to be avoided as a consequence of US external adjustment. Another important issue in the foreign impact of adjustment measures concerns the alternative of US growth reduction as the means of adjustment rather than exchange rate change or foreign growth acceleration. An obvious drawback of this option is the loss of GNP in the United States. An additional disadvantage, however, is the sideswiping of the developing countries. When US adjustment takes place through reduced growth, US imports decline not only from strong areas but also from the developing countries. If instead adjustment is achieved through exchange rate appreciation and higher growth in the strong areas, the developing countries obtain a windfall gain by improving their competitiveness as their exchange rates with the dollar remain unchanged. For example, the trade balance of the non-OPEC Latin American countries declines by $5 billion from its 1992 baseline when the United States grows more slowly by 1 percentage point over four years, whereas the region's trade balance rises by $7 billion from the baseline value when the strong countries (excluding Canada) appreciate by 10 percent, and by $6 billion when, alternatively, the strong countries accelerate growth above baseline by 1 percent over four years (tables 5A.4 through 5A.7).

Because of the potential for US external adjustment to aggravate already emerging imbalances among other countries, it is important that an overall international adjustment strategy differentiate prospective policy action among various countries. In general, the most energetic measures in terms of exchange rate change and growth demand changes need to be focused on the countries with the largest surpluses. In the absence of such concentration, the burdens imposed on intermediate countries as a consequence of US external adjustment could incite resistance in these countries to that adjustment. In particular, these countries could oppose exchange rate appreciation and could resort to increased protection as the result of new balance of payments pressures.

An International Adjustment Program

The EAG projection model provides a basis for design and simulation of a package of policy measures to reduce the US external deficits in a manner that is compatible with an appropriate distribution of the counterpart adjustment by surplus countries, and thus with sustained global growth.

US Current Account Target

The first decision to be made in designing an international adjustment package is the appropriate level for the US external balance. The baseline deficit of some $150 billion by 1992 is almost certainly too high in view of the risks already outlined. Thus, Marris and Bergsten have both argued that a target of zero should be set for the current account balance.[37]

The analysis that follows indicates that even a less ambitious adjustment target would involve substantial real exchange rate appreciation and the maintenance of high rates of growth by Germany, Japan, and such countries as the Netherlands, Switzerland, and Belgium. The need to concentrate adjustment on these countries poses limits on the magnitude of adjustment that are less apparent when the extent of adjustment is considered under uniform foreign measures.

At the same time, there are reasons to believe that a current account deficit in the range of $50 billion could be sustainable. Williamson argues that the target should be set at approximately 1 percent of US GNP by 1992, or $60 billion. He notes that, with US demographic growth higher than that in Europe and Japan, there is a case for capital inflow into the United States (although the more traditional position is that as a high-income country the

---

37. Stephen Marris, *Deficits and the Dollar* (1987 revision), 203; C. Fred Bergsten, *America in the World Economy*. Marris also notes that by the early 1990s the United States could be in current account surplus, but only if the dollar falls beyond its equilibrium level and the economy enters into recession (p. xxvii).

United States should be a provider of capital to the rest of the world rather than a net user). With nominal GNP growing at 7 percent, holding the annual increment of net external debt to 1 percent of GNP would eventually stabilize the ratio of net external debt to GNP at 14 percent.[38]

A range of $50 billion for the 1992 current account deficit would also be consistent with relatively modest investment patterns by foreign investors. In 1987 and the first three quarters of 1988, gross US capital outflows amounted to an average of approximately $70 billion annually.[39] After allowance for inflation, these outflows by 1992 might be in the range of $85 billion annually. Foreign earnings on assets held in the United States are projected at $146 billion (table 3.2, Chapter 3). With a current account deficit of $50 billion and gross capital outflows of $85 billion, total financing requirements would amount to $135 billion annually. On this basis, passive reinvestment by foreigners of their annual earnings on assets held in the United States would be sufficient to cover US financing requirements.[40] Under the assumption that the overall portfolios of foreign investors would be growing at a rate at least as high as reinvestment of earnings, the share of US assets in their portfolios would hold steady or decline, avoiding the risk of satiation.

In sum, although a target closer to zero for the current account deficit might be more certain to dispel the risks of macroeconomic crisis, persistent interest rate pressure, and protectionism, an outcome in the range of $50 billion by 1992 should be broadly manageable and might have some justification in view of demographic trends. The analysis of this study adopts this objective for the external sector.

Program Design

The international adjustment program should take into account the fact that there are at least three adjustments that need to take place: reduction of the US external deficit, moderation of a large emerging deficit in the United Kingdom, and limitation of emerging deficits of intermediate European

---

38. If dD is the change in foreign debt, dY the change in income, and Y income, then $dD = .01Y$, $dY = .07Y$, and $dD/dY = .14$. Thus, at the margin, new foreign debt is 14 percent of increased GNP. Under the adjustment scenario, 1992 net external debt is $843 billion (table 5A.9), or approximately 14 percent of GNP. With the marginal rate equal to the average, the ratio would stabilize at this level. John Williamson, "Achieving a Sustainable Payments Position."

39. *Commerce 1988:3 Current Account.*

40. Note that the specific HHC model projections call for a larger gross capital outflow in 1992, but still the rate of accumulation of foreign holdings in the United States (8.8 percent) remains close to the rate of passive reinvestment.

countries resulting largely from trade with Germany (and other high-surplus European countries: Belgium, the Netherlands, and Switzerland). The adoption of adjustment measures should be as broadly dispersed as possible, to obtain the largest possible scope for US adjustment, while recognizing the different tiers of strength of external accounts. In particular, the adjustment program is designed to ensure that no country is pushed into a current account deficit in excess of 10 percent of exports of goods and nonfactor services as a consequence of US external adjustment.[41]

Another principle of the adjustment program is that, if possible, adjustment through reduction in US growth should be avoided. The sacrifice of growth is a costly way to improve the external balance, and the baseline growth rate for the United States (2.8 percent in 1989 and 2.5 percent thereafter) is not so high as to call for reduction solely for anti-inflationary purposes.

Numerous simulations of the EAG model following these principles and seeking a $50 billion current account deficit target for the United States by 1992 yielded the Feasible Adjustment Package (FAP) set forth in table 5.7 (Chapter 5). The FAP involves a sharp appreciation of the German mark (23 percent) and the Japanese yen (28 percent) against the dollar in real terms from the base levels of 1987:4, to nominal rates of 1.33 DM/$ and 102 yen/$ by the end of 1989 (table 5.10, Chapter 5) or, at the latest, equivalent real rates by the end of 1990 (as discussed below). The two countries would also accelerate their domestic economic growth (or at least the growth of domestic demand) by 1 percentage point annually from the baseline levels (from 2½ percent to 3½ percent for Germany and from 4 percent to 5 percent for Japan). In practice, the two countries would need only to sustain their high growth rates of 1988 over the next four years, rather than increase growth still further. The currencies of the two East Asian NIC areas, Taiwan and Korea–Singapore–Hong Kong, would also appreciate in real terms against the dollar, by 12 and 14 percent, respectively, although in view of their already high growth rates these countries would not accelerate domestic growth.

The Other Industrial countries would appreciate their currencies by an average of 13.5 percent in real terms, but in two subgroups: the currencies of the surplus European countries (the Netherlands, Belgium, and Switzerland) would appreciate by the same amount as Germany (23 percent), while those of the other industrial countries not individually analyzed (such

---

41. In view of the decline of the US current account deficit to 6 percent of exports of goods and services in the FAP adjustment program proposed below, it would be anomalous to expect other countries to accept far higher external deficits as the counterpart of US adjustment, thereby potentially creating a new group of countries with deficit problems.

as Sweden and Australia) would appreciate by only 5 percent. Similarly, growth would accelerate by 1 percent annually for the three stronger countries, and by only ½ percent annually for the weaker ones; the average increase in the growth rate for the Other Industrial countries would be 0.75 percent.

France and Italy would also appreciate their currencies by only 5 percent in real terms against the 1987:4 dollar, and accelerate growth by only ½ percent annually. As a result of divergent appreciation, there is a major realignment within the European Monetary System, with a rise of some 17 percent in the currencies of a strong deutsche mark bloc against the other member currencies. In the absence of this realignment, the German surplus tends to remain high, and the deficits of the intermediate European countries become large as the United States adjusts. The implications of EMS realignment are considered below.

Table 5.7 also shows exchange rate changes for the other areas identified in the EAG model. Because of their strong baseline trends, Brazil and the Rest of World group are able to match the currency appreciation and growth acceleration of the intermediate group; Canada and Mexico can make more modest adjustments in the same direction. All the other developing countries have underlying trends too weak to permit absorption of any of the counterpart to US adjustment, and therefore they keep their real exchange rates against the dollar and their baseline growth rates unchanged. The only country that should depreciate in real terms against the dollar is the United Kingdom, to address the severe negative trend in its external accounts.

The changes in growth rates in the FAP are spread evenly over 1989–92. The exchange rate changes are all implemented in 1989, with one-fourth of the change introduced in each of the four quarters. Alternative simulations indicate that the exchange rate changes could instead be spread over two years (1989–90), to moderate the pace of their change, without major jeopardy to US external adjustment; the cost in terms of the 1992 current account deficit would be only $4 billion. However, further delay would cause a serious shortfall from the adjustment goals by 1992, in view of the two-year lags in the trade effects of exchange rate changes.[42]

---

42. Spreading the exchange rate changes evenly over three years raises the 1992 US current account deficit by $38 billion from the unadjusted FAP program. Note that some models identify an adverse trend for US trade over time even when external accounts begin from approximate equilibrium, so that additional subsequent real depreciation might be required. There is no such adverse trend in the HHC model, and in the EAG projection model the unfavorable asymmetry between the trade-weighted, specific/uniform averaged income elasticities on the import and export sides (2.2 and 1.8, respectively) is more than offset by the differential in base case growth rates (2.6 percent annual average for the United States versus 3.7 percent abroad weighting by US exports).

Table 5.10 (Chapter 5) reports the real exchange rate changes on a trade-weighted basis. For the United States, the FAP depreciation amounts to 10.7 percent. For Germany, there is a trade-weighted real appreciation of approximately 15 percent; that for Japan is 21 percent. These changes are less traumatic than might be inferred from the larger appreciations of the mark and yen against the dollar in the package (23 and 28 percent, respectively). Trade-weighted real exchange rates actually depreciate by 4 to 5 percent for France and Italy, because of the importance of Germany and the stronger European countries in their trade. For Taiwan and Korea–Singapore–Hong Kong, trade-weighted appreciation is limited to a range of 3 to 5 percent, reflecting the importance of trade with Japan, whose currency appreciates by more than those of the East Asian NICs. The Other Industrial countries' currencies appreciate by 5 percent on a trade-weighted basis, but this figure results from averaging higher appreciation by the strong payments bloc and real depreciation by the intermediate countries.

Table 5.10 also reports the implied nominal exchange rates for 1989 corresponding to the targets for real exchange rate change. These estimates take account of differential inflation between the United States and each country. The nominal value of the German mark by the end of 1989 is set at 1.33 per dollar, and for the yen at 102 to the dollar. As indicated in the table, if the mark had stayed at its stronger level at the end of 1987, the required change in the nominal rate against the dollar would have been only 19 percent. Instead, because of the weakening of the mark against the dollar in 1988, the required change from the late March 1989 nominal rate amounts to 40 percent. Among the various countries, only Korea and Canada experienced exchange rate movements in 1988 that placed their rates at approximately the desired levels.

Impact of Adjustment Measures on External Balances

As Table 1.1 indicated, the Feasible Adjustment Package reduces the 1992 US current account deficit to $48 billion, meeting the $50 billion ceiling. This deficit amounts to 6 percent of US exports of goods and services. Because the baseline current account deficit in the EAG model is $168 billion in 1992, the amount of the correction is $120 billion, rather than the rounded adjustment of $100 billion from a broad range of $150 billion (the average of the HHC and EAG models) to the $50 billion target.

The reduction of the 1992 US current account deficit by $120 billion is the result of a trade-weighted real exchange rate depreciation by 10.7 percent and a weighted-average acceleration of foreign growth by 0.41 percentage point annually from baseline (or by 1.64 percentage-point-years). Application of the policy parameters of table 5.5 to these changes yields a current account change of 10.7 × $10.2 billion + 1.64 × $11.5 billion = $128 billion. The divergence is attributable to alteration in the policy parameters when the measures are not uniform but concentrated in the surplus countries. These calculations indicate that, of the total adjustment, 85 percent is from real exchange rate change and 15 percent from acceleration of foreign growth and/or domestic demand.[43]

A natural question is why an additional depreciation of the dollar by only some 10 percent, along with modest acceleration of foreign demand, would suffice to cut the external deficit to $50 billion when previous depreciation of the dollar had achieved far less adjustment. The dollar declined in real terms by almost 40 percent from its peak in 1985:1 through 1987:4 (against currencies of 18 major countries, using multilateral trade weights and deflating by foreign consumer prices and US export-weighted wholesale prices). The main answer is that if the dollar had remained at its real 1985:1 level, by 1992 the US current account deficit could have reached over $400 billion, on the basis of simulations with the HHC model. Most of the dollar's decline so far has served merely to prevent explosive growth of the deficit.

The difference between the trade and current account deficits for the United States in the adjustment scenario ($44 billion and $48 billion, respectively; table 1.1) is surprisingly small; in the base case, the current

---

43. Note that this decomposition leaves no room for an additive, independent effect of fiscal adjustment, although it was suggested above that the partial-equilibrium effect of a reduction in the US fiscal deficit by $150 billion could be a trade balance improvement of up to $35 billion (if domestic demand fell by $100 billion). The harmonization of the two approaches is as follows. The $15 billion increase in US exports hypothesized from the induced foreign interest rate reduction and resulting faster growth abroad may be seen as contained in the $19 billion increase in exports from foreign growth acceleration in the FAP simulation of the EAG model (suggesting that a major portion of this acceleration could occur automatically from lower interest rates abroad rather than require increased fiscal stimulus). The $20 billion reduction in imports hypothesized for lower US "domestic demand" from fiscal adjustment should probably be seen as half associated with lower imports of intermediate inputs because of declining US production under fiscal contraction without exchange rate change, and half attributable to reduced domestic demand at constant output. Because addition of the 10 percent exchange rate decline reduces the real trade deficit by more than enough to prevent a decline in production, the first half of this partial-equilibrium fiscal effect on the import side disappears. The only remaining additive impact of the fiscal contraction per se, in the FAP scenario, is the $10 billion import cutback associated with reduced domestic final demand. In broader terms, however, the contribution of fiscal adjustment is far more important. By reducing domestic demand by $100 billion, it essentially makes room for the increase in the trade balance by approximately the same amount when the 10 percent real exchange rate depreciation is added. Otherwise the depreciation would cause overheating of the economy, rising inflation, and less external adjustment.

account deficit exceeds the trade deficit by $35 billion (EAG model). The explanation is that, for the United States, nonfactor service exports are higher relative to merchandise exports (29 percent) than are nonfactor service imports relative to merchandise imports (18 percent). Hence, when the merchandise trade gap narrows, there is a growing surplus on nonfactor services that largely offsets the deficit (of approximately $45 billion in the FAP case) on transfers and capital services.

Application of the FAP to the HHC model generates closely similar results for the trade deficit, which stands at approximately $40 billion in both models. However, the current account deficit resulting from the FAP in the HHC model is considerably smaller at only $18 billion (table 5A.9). Nonetheless, if account is taken of possible upward bias in the capital services projections in the HHC model because of the persistence of a large differential in the rates of return on new US direct investment abroad and foreign investment in the United States (as noted above), the two models generate similar current account estimates, both within the $50 billion target range.

Table 1.2 shows the distribution of adjustment in US trade by individual trading partner. The largest absolute improvements in US bilateral balances occur with Japan and the Other Industrial countries. The reduction of the US deficit with Japan from $60 billion in the base case in 1992 to only $30 billion augurs well for the potential of the adjustment package to relieve political pressure in the United States for protection against that country.[44] Large absolute contributions to improved US trade also come from Taiwan, Korea–Singapore–Hong Kong, Canada, and the Rest of World group. The most disappointing bilateral trend is in trade with Germany: the FAP actually widens the bilateral deficit from $12 billion to $17 billion, a reflection of the low price elasticities in US–German trade. However, protectionism against Germany has not been an issue, and bilateral balances per se have little importance except insofar as they fuel such political pressure.

The FAP has far more success than any of the uniform policy measures in reducing the outsized surpluses of Germany and Japan. Thus, by 1992 with the FAP Germany's current account surplus falls from a baseline $85 billion to only $16 billion, or from 16 percent of exports of goods and services to 3 percent. Japan's surplus is more resistant but nonetheless

---

44. Note that a $30 billion US bilateral trade deficit is close to the range identified by Bergsten and Cline as a structural equilibrium rate, in view of triangular trade and a more normal surplus position for the Japanese current account overall. C. Fred Bergsten and William R. Cline, *The United States–Japan Economic Problem*, POLICY ANALYSES IN INTERNATIONAL ECONOMICS 13 (Washington: Institute for International Economics, October 1985), 40.

declines from the baseline $136 billion to $63 billion, from 34 percent of exports of goods and services to 16 percent.

For intermediate countries France and Italy, the FAP actually increases the 1992 current account balance from the baseline level, because of the trade-weighted depreciation of their currencies. The package thus addresses the emerging intra-European imbalance. In contrast, the East Asian NICs experience deterioration, although again their current account levels may be understated by dilution of their individually favorable trade elasticities through averaging with uniform elasticities. Even so their 1992 deficits remain at approximately the permitted limit of 10 percent of exports.

The developing countries generally experience increases in their current account balances relative to the base case as a result of the FAP, because their fixed real exchange rates against the dollar and absence of growth acceleration above baseline mean that increased competitiveness in third-country markets more than offsets reductions in trade balances against the United States (as a result of US substitution for other country supply).

The FAP broadly achieves the intended concentration of the current account reductions in the high-surplus countries. Except for a small reduction in the position of Canada, only five countries or country groups experience lower surpluses or higher deficits compared with the baseline outcome: Japan ($-$73 billion), Germany ($-$69 billion), the Other Industrial countries ($-$60 billion), Taiwan ($-$7 billion), and Korea–Singapore–Hong Kong ($-$20 billion). The principal shortfall from the extent of adjustment that might be desired is in the case of Japan, as discussed above (and some would argue that the persistence of a significant surplus in Japan is not inappropriate, on grounds that surplus savings from this high-savings country contribute to capital availability for global growth).[45]

---

45. Note that the proportionate distribution of surplus reduction in the FAP resembles that recommended by a group of 33 economists in late 1987. In both cases, Germany absorbs approximately 30 percent of the total surplus reduction, and Korea and Taiwan together account for 12 to 14 percent. The principal differences are for Japan (32 percent in the FAP, versus 52 percent in the earlier study), and the Other Industrial countries (26 percent in the FAP versus none). The Japanese surplus is thus more resistant than had previously been anticipated, while there is a considerably larger role for such surplus European countries as the Netherlands, Switzerland, and Belgium than identified before. In addition, the absolute magnitude of the total surplus reduction is much larger (some $230 billion versus $125 billion), because of the addition of the objective of reducing a large emerging deficit in the United Kingdom (and to a lesser extent Italy and France) to the underlying goal of reducing the US external deficit, on the one hand, and because of the larger baseline surpluses in Japan and Germany than in the 1987 base used in the earlier study, on the other hand. Institute for International Economics, *Resolving the Global Economic Crisis: After Wall Street*, SPECIAL REPORT 6 (Washington: Institute for International Economics, December 1987), 17.

If a more ambitious program to achieve zero US external deficit by 1992 is pursued, further dollar depreciation and/or foreign growth acceleration (or US growth deceleration) will be required. Because large currency appreciations are already called for in the more moderate FAP for Germany, Japan, Belgium, the Netherlands, and Switzerland, it is implausible that the additional necessary adjustment to reach a zero US external balance could similarly be concentrated in these countries. Instead, the Zero Balance Package (ZBP) increases the amount of currency appreciation by all countries appreciating in the FAP (except Mexico) by a flat 4 percentage points, and in addition increases the annual growth acceleration by ¼ percentage point beyond the FAP increment over four years in all the industrial countries. The resulting calculations show a heavy burden of adjustment on Canada in particular, but relatively modest further adjustment beyond the FAP case for other intermediate countries such as France and Italy. Nonetheless, several countries might consider the ZBP to impose excessive adjustment on them (for example, the yen would experience real exchange rate appreciation against the dollar of 32 percent).

Another alternative approach would seek to moderate the realignment of exchange rates within the European Monetary System, and moderate the large appreciations of the German and Japanese currencies with respect to the dollar, while still accomplishing the US external adjustment called for in the FAP. Political reaction in Europe and Tokyo could well be expected to push in this direction. For this purpose, a Second-Best Adjustment Package (SBAP) limits the appreciation of the yen to 20 percent in real terms against the 1987:4 dollar, and that of the mark to 18 percent. In contrast, the SBAP raises the appreciation of the currencies of the intermediate European countries from 5 percent in the FAP to 8 percent, and adds another percentage point appreciation beyond the FAP for Canada, Mexico, Rest of World, and Brazil. Other measures remain unchanged from the FAP.

The result of the SBAP is a 1992 US current account deficit that only slightly exceeds the target (at $52 billion), but much larger current account surpluses in Germany ($32 billion) and Japan ($87 billion) than under the FAP, and considerably larger deficits in the intermediate countries ($9 billion for France, $18 billion for Italy, and $77 billion for the Other Industrial countries); there is also serious trade deterioration for Canada compared with the FAP outcome. As expected, this lesser concentration of the policy adjustment results in poorer achievement of the objective of concentrating the counterpart of US adjustment in the high-surplus countries.

Implications for International Adjustment Policy

These simulation results have several major policy implications. For the United States:

☐ An appropriate policy target is to reduce the US current account deficit to $50 billion by 1992. Complete elimination of the deficit could require adjustment beyond the degree acceptable to other, especially high-surplus, countries. A $50 billion deficit would represent less than 1 percent of GNP; would permit a stable or falling foreign debt-to-GNP ratio; would probably require only the passive reinvestment of foreign earnings on investments in the United States rather than additional inflows beyond this amount; and, if used for capital investment, could be an appropriate use of international savings in view of relatively high US demographic growth.

☐ Fiscal adjustment that meets the goals of the Gramm–Rudman–Hollings legislation, which calls for reduction of the federal deficit by $40 billion annually over four years, is the sine qua non for US external adjustment. In its absence, exchange rate depreciation will tend to raise inflation, undermining the extent of real exchange rate decline.

☐ Both models used in this study (HHC and EAG) indicate that further real depreciation of the dollar by approximately 10 percent beyond its 1987:4 level will be required to achieve the $50 billion current account target, as well as moderate acceleration of growth abroad (or maintenance of recent high growth rates, in Germany and Japan).

☐ Once the United States has cut back its external deficit to this range, the current account deficit should not greatly exceed the trade deficit, as a surplus on nonfactor services offsets the sizable deficit on transfers and investment income.

☐ Political pressure for protection against Japan—a considerable threat with a baseline bilateral deficit of $60 billion by 1992—should be ameliorated by the reduction of this deficit by half under the FAP, as should protectionism more generally with reduction of the overall trade deficit to $44 billion.

For foreign countries:

☐ An appropriate set of measures can achieve reduction of the US current account deficit to $50 billion by 1992 without imposing severe strain on the external accounts of other individual countries (and with any resulting deficits limited, in most cases, to no more than 10 percent of exports of goods and services).

□ For this purpose, however, it is necessary to concentrate foreign adjustment measures heavily in the high-surplus countries: Germany, Japan, Belgium, the Netherlands, and Switzerland, and to a lesser extent, Taiwan and Korea. Otherwise, there will be an undue burden on countries in intermediate payments positions.

□ Even with such concentration (including 28 percent appreciation of the yen), Japan's current account surplus in 1992 remains at a relatively high $60 billion, and appropriate financial recycling of this surplus (ideally including more lending to developing countries) remains of particular importance for this country.

□ The need for larger appreciation by Germany and Japan than by intermediate countries means that a realignment of up to 17 percent is called for between a strong deutsche mark bloc within the European Monetary System (EMS) including Germany, Belgium, and the Netherlands, on the one hand, and other members such as France and Italy, on the other. Otherwise external sector pressures on the intermediate European countries will be burdensome as the United States seeks to adjust. A second-best policy limiting the intra-EMS realignment to 10 percent could still permit the United States to meet its external adjustment target, but would imply larger imbalances within Europe and the need for greater financial flows from surplus to deficit countries in the EMS.

□ The United Kingdom faces special problems of severe external sector deterioration and cannot contribute to US adjustment. The United Kingdom can instead take advantage of exchange rate realignments and depreciate modestly against the dollar, and thus sharply against the mark and the yen, to reduce its external deficit trend dramatically (table 1.1).

□ The developing countries can safely weather, and indeed benefit from, US external adjustment by keeping real exchange rates unchanged against the dollar and becoming more competitive in third markets. The trade gains under international adjustment are prospectively the largest for those developing countries with export markets concentrated in Europe (especially Germany) and Japan.

For international policy coordination among the G-7 industrial countries:

□ Both models show that foreign growth matters importantly to US adjustment, contrary to those who argue that foreign expansion has so little effect on US external accounts that policy coordination cannot contribute much to US adjustment.[46]

☐ G-7 exchange rate stabilization efforts beginning with the Louvre Accord in 1987 were premature because the dollar remained overvalued in real terms. The failure of US and Japanese authorities to intervene energetically against the brisk rise in the dollar following the Toronto summit in mid-1988[47] was highly questionable, in view of the fact that the dollar had already risen after the end of 1987 and the need instead for a trade-weighted decline of the dollar by approximately 10 percent from its 1987:4 level (or 5 percent from its December 31, 1987, level).

☐ G-7 exchange rate policy has tended to set relatively narrow ranges around current exchange rates (after the Louvre Accord). The need for a much more sharply differentiated set of exchange rate changes means that this policy should allow for wider changes and facilitate substantially differing changes of individual currencies against the dollar, rather than implicitly expect all industrial country currencies to move in tandem against the dollar.

Two final issues of policy strategy warrant special discussion. The first concerns second-best strategy in the United States; the second, the role of the European Monetary System in international adjustments. The central policy package includes both fiscal adjustment and additional exchange rate depreciation for the United States (as well as increased growth abroad). Skeptics about the political feasibility of US fiscal adjustment must ask whether, in its absence, the second-best policy package should nonetheless include dollar depreciation along the lines proposed here. The Federal Reserve by early 1989 was clearly opposed to further dollar depreciation in the absence of fiscal correction, and indeed by moving toward higher interest rates out of fear of an overheating economy, the Fed showed itself prepared to allow the dollar to rise further rather than seek its decline.

If the painful choice posed by this "second-best" question cannot be avoided, the conventional answer would be that the Federal Reserve is right to fight inflation at all costs and allow the US dollar and American external deficits to rise. However, relegation of the external deficit to a minimal policy priority in the past, far behind price stability and growth, has already placed the US economy in potential jeopardy for the reasons set forth at the outset. At some point US authorities may find it necessary to revise their

---

46. For example, Martin Feldstein, "The End of Policy Coordination," *Wall Street Journal,* 9 November 1988.

47. *Wall Street Journal,* 28 June 1988, 3.

policy weights on growth, inflation, and external balance, or else risk far greater recessionary and inflationary shocks in the future because of failure to act promptly on the external imbalance.

With respect to the European Monetary System, some observers note an increasing determination among countries with weaker payments positions, such as France, to maintain an essentially fixed exchange rate with the German mark. In this perspective, these countries have enjoyed macroeconomic gains from adherence to a German-led "zone of stability" that they do not want to jeopardize. Some even contend that the intra-EMS exchange rate realignment suggested here would "destroy" that system. The move toward more complete integration in Europe by 1992 contributes to this insistence on unchanged parities, as it implies not only possible strengthening of monetary integration but also an increasing tendency to view intragroup payments imbalances as of no greater concern than, for example, imbalances between individual states within the United States.

The analysis of this study, and particularly the simulation applying uniform appreciation of exchange rates by other industrial countries against the dollar, indicates that, if members of the EMS are firmly determined to avoid exchange rate realignment among each others' currencies, the surplus countries (especially Germany) will have to be prepared to provide large amounts of financing on an ongoing basis to the members with deficits. Although a case might be made that such transfers are desirable for European economic growth, the central point from a global standpoint is that pursuit of these intra-EMS objectives should not impose a roadblock to international adjustment, and to US external adjustment in particular.

Real Adjustment in the United States and Abroad

The analysis presented in this study indicates that, with decisive but reasonable policy action in the United States and other major countries, it should be possible to achieve reduction in the US external deficit to sustainable levels over the medium term. However, it is important to go beyond the financial analysis to examine the implications of deficit reduction for real magnitudes of trade, production, and consumption. It is these real volumes that affect employment and production.

Real Versus Nominal Adjustment

As analyzed in Chapter 6, real trade and economic changes associated with US external adjustment are likely to differ from nominal dollar changes. Because some 25 percent cumulative inflation is likely from the base year 1987 through 1992, from this standpoint real changes should be smaller than nominal changes. However, because of adverse changes in the terms of trade—that is, in the ratio of export prices to import prices—as the dollar declines, the real changes can considerably exceed the nominal changes. In particular, the nominal dollar value of imports is unlikely to change much even as the volume of imports is reduced by higher dollar prices, because the same rise in the dollar price that stimulates the reduced purchases also raises the unit price and tends to leave the total dollar outlay on imports unchanged. Although there is some offsetting gain from a rise in dollar prices of exports, this induced price rise tends to be smaller than that on imports. In broad terms, most of the work of external adjustment must be accomplished on the side of increased export volume. In real terms, this increase must be added to the reduction in import volume (which is largely invisible in financial terms because of the rise in the dollar price of imports) to gauge the total shift in real resources that must be mobilized to accomplish external adjustment.

A simple model of the relationship of real to nominal external adjustment shows that, given the empirical trade elasticities and tendencies to pass through exchange rate changes into prices, the real trade balance must rise by almost twice as much as the nominal trade balance when adjustment is accomplished by exchange rate depreciation.[48] An objective of reducing the nominal external deficit by $100 billion through exchange rate adjustment thus requires a combination of real import volume reduction and real export volume expansion amounting to nearly $200 billion at constant prices, or some 4½ percent of US GNP.

Real Effects of Trade Imbalances in the 1980s

External adjustment thus can serve as a major source of demand for the US economy over the medium term. The opposite was true through much of the 1980s. From 1980 to 1986, the real trade balance on goods and services

---

48. Specifically:
$$Z = [-Hda - eb]/\{[-Hda - eb] + [H(1 - a)(1 - dar) - b(1 + ebr)]\}$$
where Z is the ratio of real to nominal adjustment, H is the base period ratio of exports to imports, a is the pass-through ratio from dollar depreciation to dollar import prices, b is the pass-through ratio for export prices, d is the price elasticity of foreign demand for US exports, e is the price elasticity of US demand for imports, and r is the proportionate change in the exchange rate (Appendix F). Note that as a rises from zero to unity, the exchange rate change impact rises from zero effect on the dollar price of imports to complete effect. As b rises from zero to unity, a given dollar depreciation causes a full corresponding rise in dollar export prices (none of the benefit of lower foreign currency price of the dollar is passed through to foreign purchasers) to zero rise (complete pass-through of this benefit). Applying the average values in the HHC and EAG models for the trade elasticities and price pass-through ratios, Z has an average value of 1.9.

declined from a surplus of $57 billion to a deficit of $138 billion (at constant 1982 prices; table 6.1, Chapter 6). The decline of the real external balance thus reduced external demand during this period by an amount equal to 6 percent of 1980 GNP.[49] Over the same period, the real balance on nonoil, nonagricultural trade declined by an amount equivalent to 23 percent of 1980 manufacturing value added. Despite offsets by domestic consumption and rising defense expenditure, manufacturing production and especially employment suffered during the 1980s as the result of the collapse of net demand from the external sector. Indeed, these adverse real trends mounted the pressure for protection that eventually forced the Reagan administration to shift its approach from commending the strong dollar to seeking its reversal, as formalized in the 1985 Plaza Agreement.

The reverse side of the coin was a large stimulus from US demand to the economies of major trading partners. From 1980 to 1986, the rise in Japan's real trade balance accounted for 26.3 percent of Japan's total increase in real GNP, and for Germany trade contributed 52 percent of growth. The rise in the real bilateral trade balance with the United States in this period accounted for approximately one-half of the total trade contribution to growth for both countries. More specifically, the rise in the real trade balance with the United States from 1980 to 1986 amounted to 2.0 percent of 1980 GNP for Germany and 3.4 percent for Japan (table 6.2, Chapter 6). The corresponding figure for Canada was 10.5 percent, and the impact was even higher in Taiwan and Korea. For the world as a whole, the rise in real trade balances against the United States from 1980 to 1986 amounted to 2.1 percent of 1980 non-US global GNP. A central challenge of US external adjustment over the medium term is whether the reversal of US demand for the rest of the world's goods, from a positive to a negative stimulus, can be absorbed by other countries without a serious reduction in their growth rates.[50]

Prospective Real Adjustment in the United States

The simulations of FAP adjustment using the HHC and EAG models confirm that real US external adjustment through 1992 to achieve the $50 billion

---

49. Calculated from Council of Economic Advisers, *Economic Report of the President,* February 1988, 250, 261, 271.

50. An important ameliorating factor in the challenge foreign countries face because of the large shift from positive to negative demand stimulus from trade with the United States is the accompanying reversal of US fiscal–monetary mismatch. In the mid-1980s, high US interest rates spilled over into foreign economies and acted as a drag, partially offsetting the stimulus from rising real trade surpluses with the United States. US fiscal correction could moderate world interest rates and help offset the adverse demand impact on other countries from US external adjustment.

nominal current account deficit target amounts to approximately $200 billion at 1987 prices (table 6.3, Chapter 6). This adjustment of 4½ percent of 1987 real GNP over four years means that domestic demand will have to be restrained relative to growth of production, with the growth in demand lagging that of GNP by approximately 1 percentage point annually.[51] With production growing at a rate of 2½ percent annually, domestic demand for consumption, investment, and government spending should rise by only 1½ percent each year.

Because investment should grow at least as fast as GNP (to maintain capital stock relative to GNP) and perhaps faster (to the extent that external adjustment requires a reallocation of the economy toward tradeable goods, which tend to be more capital intensive than nontradeables such as retail sales and other services), consumption and government spending should probably grow by only about 1 percent annually.[52] As the population is growing at this rate as well, per capita consumption and government spending per person should remain frozen in real terms over the next four years to accommodate external adjustment. This freeze, after rapid growth in the 1980s (by 2.3 percent annually from 1980 to 1987, for both real per capita consumption and real per capita government spending),[53] is in many ways the principal "burden" of US external adjustment. It represents a period of correction after what amounted to a spree of private and public consumption during the 1980s, financed by foreigners.

Although the real external adjustment implies domestic belt-tightening, it also signifies dynamism in precisely the sectors of the economy that were under the greatest pressure from faltering external demand in the earlier years of the decade. Most of the increase in the trade balance will have to occur in the manufacturing sector. If the entire rise took place in manufacturing, it would amount to approximately 16 percent of 1987 manufacturing GNP. With 4 percent annual manufacturing growth over 1989–92 needed to meet external demand and another 1½ percent annually for rising domestic demand, the sector should grow at over 5 percent annually, or more than twice its 2.5 percent average rate from 1980 to 1986. This pace is sufficiently brisk to raise the question of whether manufacturing capacity will be

---

51. This useful formulation appears in C. Fred Bergsten, *America in the World Economy*, 7–8, 84.

52. With gross investment equal to 16 percent of GNP, if investment grows at 3 percent annually and domestic demand (consumption plus investment plus government spending) can only grow at 1½ percent, then growth of consumption and government spending must be limited to 1.2 percent [.015 − (.16 × .03)]/.84 = .012.

53. Council of Economic Advisers, *Economic Report of the President*, January 1989, 310–311.

sufficient, but with trend capacity growth at 2½ percent and some initial excess capacity in 1988, capacity shortages should not be a major problem (although they could be a constraint in some specific sectors such as rubber, chemicals, aerospace, and paper).[54]

By 1987 and 1988 the process of positive demand stimulus from a declining real trade deficit had already begun in the United States. In 1987 the real nonagricultural, nonoil trade deficit declined from $124 billion to $116 billion, and in 1988 the deficit fell further to $79 billion (at 1982 prices).[55] This trend illustrated the divergence between real and nominal adjustment, as the real deficit declined in 1987 even as the nominal deficit continued to rise. It also was an early indication of the demand stimulus that could be anticipated for manufacturing if US external adjustment continued. In the two years, the decline in the real nonoil, nonagricultural trade deficit amounted to approximately 5 percent of 1987 manufacturing GNP. Nonetheless, it was an ominous sign that the decline in the real trade deficit stopped by the second quarter of 1988 (when the nonoil, nonagricultural trade balance at 1982 prices stood at an annual rate of $74.4 billion), and began a small reversal thereafter (to $76.3 billion by the fourth quarter).

The Global Impact of US Adjustment in Real Terms

Table 6.5 (Chapter 6) provides estimates of the impact of real external adjustment on the economies of other countries that may be expected in the base case and under successful US external adjustment as called for in the FAP. As shown, the real impact is negligible for Germany and Japan in the base case, but large in the case of the FAP. Successful US external adjustment by 1992 along the lines developed here would mean a reduction in the real trade balance of Germany amounting to 7.3 percent of 1987 GNP, and in that of Japan by 4.1 percent. The negative real demand effect would also be high in the Other Industrial country group (− 7.3 percent), and even higher in Taiwan and Korea–Singapore–Hong Kong.[56] The impact of real

---

54. Robert Z. Lawrence, "The International Dimension," in Robert E. Litan, Robert Z. Lawrence, and Charles L. Schultze, eds., *American Living Standards* (Washington: Brookings Institution, 1988), 23–65.

55. US Department of Commerce, *Gross National Product: Fourth Quarter 1988 (Preliminary)*, BEA-89-05 (Washington: US Department of Commerce, 28 February 1989).

56. Although in the East Asian NICs the relative impact tends to be exaggerated because the base should ideally include imported intermediate inputs (which are particularly important for comparisons with manufacturing alone) as well as GNP. Note also that the US figure of 3.7 percent of GNP real adjustment in the table is lower than the 4½ percent discussed above because it refers to merchandise trade alone and excludes nonfactor services.

adjustment abroad is especially high if compared to manufacturing production, reaching − 23.9 percent in Germany and − 13.5 percent in Japan.

The real impact of the adjustment program on the high-surplus countries
is pronounced. In real quantities Germany's imports rise by 34 percent in
the base case from 1987 to 1992, but by 57 percent under the FAP, while
Germany's export expansion falls from 24 percent in the baseline to 11
percent. Real imports rise by 54 percent over the period in the base case for
Japan, but increase by 85 percent under the FAP, while Japan's real export
expansion declines from 24 percent in the base case to − 1 percent under
the FAP.

For the United Kingdom, the international adjustment program works in
the opposite direction, and prevents what otherwise would be a baseline
reduction of the real trade balance equal to 7.2 percent of GNP. Real
correction through the adjustment program is thus proportionately larger
for the United Kingdom than for the United States.

It is evident from table 6.5 that relatively large negative real demand
effects must be anticipated in other countries (especially the high-surplus
countries) as the United States carries out external adjustment. It will be
necessary for these countries to replace their export-led growth of the early
1980s with growth led by domestic demand. Since 1986 there have been
initially encouraging signs that this transition is under way. Thus, whereas
Japan's GNP growth exceeded that of its real domestic demand by 0.9
percentage point in 1985, by 1986–88 domestic demand growth exceeded
that of GNP by an average of 1.4 percent annually. In Germany, the
corresponding shift was from − 1.1 percentage point (domestic demand
growth less GNP growth) in 1985 to 1.3 percent annually in 1986–87,
although the differential slowed to 0.3 percent in 1988. The danger is that
these trends toward international adjustment will stall as the pipeline effects
of dollar devaluation become exhausted, as implied by the minimal real
adjustment for these surplus countries over the 1987–92 period in the base
case (table 6.5).

Policy Implications

The analysis of this study indicates that the United States is far from being
on an acceptable course of correction of its external deficits, despite the
reduction of the trade deficit by some $30 billion in 1988 and the prospects
of a substantial further reduction in 1989. The trade and current account
deficits are likely to remain above $100 billion in 1989 and then, absent
policy change, to begin to widen again, with the current account reaching
a deficit of approximately $150 billion again by 1992. This outlook threatens
a macroeconomic crisis from an eventual collapse of confidence by foreign

investors, with a hard landing for both the dollar and the economy. It condemns the economy to high interest rates to attract foreign financing, and thus prospectively low investment and growth. And it runs the risk of a renewed outbreak of protectionism. Moreover, the outlook in the absence of policy action is for further aggravation of existing distortions in international payments, with current account surpluses of nearly $140 billion in Japan and $85 billion in Germany by 1992, while deficits emerge in such intermediate countries as France, Italy, and especially the United Kingdom.

United States

Correction of the US deficit must begin at home, with a new phase of restrained private and government consumption following the consumption binge of the 1980s. A coordinated package of fiscal policy, for spending restraint, and exchange rate policy, to provide the proper price signals for expenditure switching, is required.

Fiscal Policy—The single most important measure for the United States to adopt is the actual fulfillment of the Gramm–Rudman–Hollings targets, which call for reduction of the fiscal deficit by $40 billion annually to zero by 1993.

Exchange Rate Policy—In addition to fiscal measures, to reduce the current account deficit to a sustainable $50 billion by 1992 it will be necessary to reduce the real trade-weighted value of the dollar by approximately 10 percent from its level as of the fourth quarter of 1987, which was approximately the same as its level at the end of 1988 and in early 1989. US and foreign officials missed an important opportunity when they supported a rebound of the dollar from its low of December 31, 1987, and presided over a counterproductive rise of the dollar through the third quarter of 1988. From its end-1987 level, the dollar would have needed to decline by only about an additional 5 percent.

Macropolicy Mix—Reduction of the fiscal deficit will exert a contractionary influence on the economy, while dollar depreciation and the increase in the real trade balance will exert an offsetting expansionary influence. On the basis of 16 leading macroeconomic models of the United States, Bryant, Helliwell, and Hooper (BHH) calculate that reduction of the US fiscal deficit by 1 percentage point of GNP causes a 2 percent decline in the real value of the dollar, as the consequence of lower interest rates and reduced capital inflows bidding for dollars. They also find that a 1 percent rise in the stock of money causes a real decline in the dollar by 1 percent. They estimate that a fiscal contraction amounting to 1 percent of GNP cuts real GNP by 1 percent by the third year, and that a 1 percent rise in the stock of money increases GNP by ¼ percentage point.[57]

On this basis, a macroeconomic mix broadly consistent with the FAP strategy for reducing the US external deficit to $50 billion by 1992 would be as follows.[58] Implementation of Gramm–Rudman–Hollings amounts to a fiscal cut of approximately 3 percent of GNP. This measure should thus reduce the real value of the dollar by 6 of the nearly 11 percentage points called for in the FAP, while at the same time exerting a potential contractionary effect of 3 percent on GNP. To obtain the remaining real dollar depreciation of approximately 5 percentage points, and to provide an expansionary effect to help offset fiscal contraction, it would be appropriate to increase the money stock over 4 years by 5 percentage points more than would otherwise be the case, for example by raising the target for annual money growth from a range of 5 to 6 percent to a range of 6¼ to 7¼ percent.

The combined impact would be contractionary, based on the BHH parameters $[(-3\% \times 1) + (5\% \times 0.25) = -1.75\%]$, and GNP would decline from its baseline by approximately 0.4 percent annually over four years. However, as discussed above, the real effect of the FAP on US production is in the range of $200 billion (at 1987 prices), or more than the fiscal cutback rather than less, and the BHH relationships may be biased toward contraction. In practice, the fiscal–monetary mix just outlined could appropriately be altered in the direction of greater monetary expansion if the signs of inflationary trends in early 1989 proved to be transitory and fiscal contraction appeared to be reducing growth, whereas monetary expansion could be cut back if the inflationary danger turned out to be serious and persistent. The central thrust of the macroeconomic mix over

---

57. Ralph C. Bryant, John F. Helliwell, and Peter Hooper, "Domestic and Cross-Border Consequences of US Macroeconomic Policies" (Washington: Brookings Institution, Conference on Macroeconomic Policies in an Interdependent World, December 12–13, 1988).

58. Note, however, that as illustrated by the sharp decline in the dollar from 1985:1 through 1987:4 without massive fiscal and monetary adjustment, the relationship of the dollar to macropolicies is less than ironclad. If the policy mix indicated here failed to bring the dollar down sufficiently (for example, because of a short-term boost to confidence because the United States was finally correcting its fiscal imbalance), it seems likely that a policy of "jawboning" would be adequate to set the dollar in the proper range. If necessary, US authorities could reinstate a withholding tax on foreign earnings in the US capital markets to back up its verbal guidelines.

the next four years, however, should be to return policy toward a more normal configuration, after several years of an unusual (and, for the external sector, damaging) combination of loose fiscal policy and tight monetary policy.

Germany, Japan, and the Surplus European Countries

The two largest surplus countries, Germany and Japan, need to follow essentially two policies to fulfill their role in international adjustment: first, they should maintain over the next four years relatively high rates of growth of GNP and, especially, domestic demand similar to those they achieved in 1988; second, they should facilitate rather than oppose real appreciation of their currencies against the dollar by about 23 and 28 percent, respectively (and on a trade-weighted basis by 15 and 20 percent, respectively), as analyzed in this study. The other high-surplus European countries—Belgium, the Netherlands, and Switzerland—should follow policies parallel to those of Germany. These growth and domestic demand policies would essentially boost the rates of expansion by 1 percentage point annually above the baseline that could otherwise be expected.

To some extent these objectives could be facilitated by the package of US measures outlined above, which would tend to reduce US interest rates. There would be some induced reduction in interest rates in other countries as a result, contributing to maintenance of brisk domestic growth.

It is quite possible, however, that maintenance of buoyant growth of production and domestic demand will require greater fiscal expansion than currently planned in these countries. On balance there has been no movement toward fiscal stimulus in Japan, where the cyclically adjusted fiscal stance actually tightened by 0.7 percent of GNP in 1986, loosened by 0.5 percent in 1987, and tightened again by 0.2 percent in 1988.[59] The boost to Japanese demand and growth in 1987 from real wealth effects of the rising yen and the stock market boom cannot be expected to persist. The monetary expansion in Germany and Japan, which in part reflected coordinated support of the dollar, could be the object of increasing concern by monetary authorities because of its possible inflationary consequences. In view of the major contractionary effects to be expected in the high-surplus countries as the counterpart of the US external correction, policymakers in these countries may find it necessary to turn to fiscal stimulus not only to play their part in international adjustment but also to avoid a domestic downturn.

---

59. *OECD Economic Outlook,* June 1988, 24.

East Asian NICs

Taiwan and Korea can fulfill their role in international adjustment by sustaining high domestic growth rates (in the range of 8 percent annually) and accepting the substantial real appreciations of their exchange rates suggested in the adjustment program reviewed above. As indicated in table 5.10, by late 1988 Korea had already largely accomplished the appropriate real appreciation of its exchange rate, although Taiwan had not.

The likelihood is that the surpluses of Taiwan and Korea will remain somewhat higher than projected in the EAG model, for reasons discussed above (higher export elasticities and lower import elasticities than used in the model's central projections). If the surpluses do persist, aggressive liberalization of imports would be the appropriate response, followed by additional exchange rate appreciation if necessary.

Although Hong Kong and Singapore are included in the same country grouping with Korea in the EAG model, it is unlikely that corresponding real appreciation of exchange rates would be appropriate for at least Singapore. Neither has incurred large current account surpluses in recent years of proportions comparable to those of Taiwan and Korea.[60]

Intermediate Industrial Countries

Perhaps the principal policy breakthrough needed in countries such as France and Italy is reassessment of the strongly held view that the existing fixed exchange rates in the European Monetary System are inviolable. As discussed above, a major realignment of rates within the EMS between the weaker members and the stronger bloc (Germany, Belgium, the Netherlands) appears necessary if severe pressure on the weaker members is to be avoided as the United States adjusts externally. If a lesser realignment (limited to 10 percent, for example) is all that is feasible politically, it will have to be accompanied by larger financing from the surplus members. It is imperative that Europe not turn toward protection as the consequence of insistence on maintenance of existing EMS exchange rates despite their prospective incompatibility with payments equilibrium for the weaker European countries, especially in an environment of US external correction.

---

60. Although there may be a case for some real appreciation in Hong Kong; see Chapter 5.

The Latin American and other debtor countries stand to gain from the program of international adjustment outlined here. Their export opportunities should rise if they hold real exchange rates constant against the dollar and thus gain in competitiveness in the European and Japanese markets. Importantly, the debtor nations stand to gain from the lower international interest rates that should result from US fiscal correction. Real interest rates could drop from recent levels of some 5 percent to historically more normal levels of approximately 3 percent. A decline of 2 percentage points in international interest rates would save approximately $10 billion annually on the variable-interest debt of the developing countries. They could be expected to respend more than one-third of these savings on purchases of exports from the United States.

In addition, measures to reverse partially the large swing toward negative resource transfers from the debtor countries following the debt crisis could contribute to their economic growth as well as to international adjustment.[61] Simulations with the EAG model indicate that the provision of an additional $20 billion annually in effective finance (or cash flow relief from appropriate voluntary debt relief) at 1987 constant dollars would permit an improvement in the US current account by approximately $10 billion (nominal) by 1992.

---

61. Although the debt crisis probably played only a moderate role in the deterioration of the US external accounts in the 1980s, ranging from a trade balance deterioration of $12 billion (most probable) to a maximum of $25 billion on the basis of comparison against alternative benchmarks for what otherwise could have been expected of US trade with debtor countries.

2

Origins of the Problem

The United States today faces serious economic risks from internal and external imbalances: the fiscal and trade deficits. The Reagan administration restored economic growth and reduced inflation, but it is increasingly dangerous to delay corrective action on these two adverse side effects of the Reagan era.

The Economic Legacy of the 1980s

In 1980 Ronald Reagan campaigned on a promise to cut income taxes by 30 percent. The new president essentially sought to limit the role of government by reining in its resources. Supply-side enthusiasts invoked the "Laffer curve" to argue that the reductions in tax rates would be more than compensated by the resulting rise in economic activity, so that tax revenue would not decline. Many were concerned at the time that lower taxes would lead to fiscal deficits, which would risk higher inflation.[1] The second oil price shock in 1980 had already boosted US inflation to 14 percent, and fiscal deficits risked adding demand pressure to cost-push inflation.

Congress enacted the Reagan tax cuts in the Economic Recovery Tax Act of 1981.[2] As it turned out, the real danger was high interest rates rather than inflation. Steady erosion of oil prices brought relief on cost pressures,

---

1. As I warned in testimony before the Joint Economic Committee, Hearings on International Economic Policy, 4 May 1981.

2. The reform cut marginal tax rates from a prospective 32 percent by 1984 to 25 percent for median-income families, and from 49 percent to 38 percent for those at twice the median income. Council of Economic Advisers, *Economic Report of the President*, February 1982 (Washington: Council of Economic Advisers, 1982), 120.

while the Federal Reserve intensified the monetary contraction begun in 1979 to squeeze inflation out of the economy. The Fed felt impelled to act even more forcefully because of the prospect of fiscal deficits, and interest rates reached unprecedented levels of nearly 20 percent. The result was the recession of 1982, the worst since the 1930s. Only after the depths of the 1982 recession became clear, and after Mexico had suspended payment on its debt, threatening the international financial system, did the Federal Reserve relent and permit interest rates to decline.

In the next five years the US economy experienced an expansion based in fact, if not in intent, on old-fashioned Keynesian fiscal stimulus. The phasing in of the tax cuts and the relaxation in monetary policy lifted the economy out of recession in 1983 and especially 1984. Lower taxes brought a boom in consumer spending, while rapid expansion of defense spending raised demand from the public sector. Oil prices eased further and fell sharply in 1986, providing additional relief on inflation. Interest rates also fell, although as they lagged behind declining inflation they remained high in real terms (at some 4 to 5 percent, compared with real rates close to zero and frequently negative in the 1970s).

In the 1984 election and again in 1988, the Reagan–Bush administration was able to ask the American public whether it felt better off than before, confident of an affirmative reply. The public had bitter recollections of stagflation and gas lines in the 1970s. In contrast, although the Reagan years had brought the 1982 recession, they subsequently brought growth as high as 6.8 percent in 1984 and 3 to 4 percent thereafter, a reduction of inflation from double digits to the range of 3 to 5 percent, and 17 million new jobs during a decade in which Europe created none.[3] There were even some positive results in the fiscal area, as the decline in marginal tax rates improved the incentives for effort and risk-taking.[4] But these economic gains came at the price of massive fiscal and external deficits. The central question today is whether the economic progress of the Reagan era can be retained while redressing its negative legacy of internal and external imbalances.

---

3. Civilian employment rose from 99.3 million in 1980 to 116.7 million in August 1988. Of the total increase, 4.3 million occurred in 1988 alone, suggesting that the economy was nearing capacity or even flirting with overheating. *Economic Report of the President*, February 1988, 287; *Survey of Current Business*, September 1988, S-9.

4. However, the incentive gains from an improved tax structure (including the 1986 reform, which removed loopholes and lowered rates) could have been achieved at a somewhat higher average level and, with the help of more restraint on spending, thereby reduced or eliminated the fiscal deficit.

Fiscal Deficits

The central flaw in the Reagan macroeconomic policy was its failure to close the fiscal gap once the economy had recovered. In 1980–81 the federal budget deficit averaged $60 billion, or 2¼ percent of GNP. In the recession year of 1982 the deficit rose to $150 billion, or 4¾ percent of GNP. That deficit could be justified as proper macroeconomic policy to pull the economy out of recession. But during the 1983–85 recovery the deficit continued to rise to an average of $190 billion annually, or 5 percent of GNP.[5] No economic theory justifies an increase in the fiscal deficit when the economy is recovering.[6] Fiscal balance or even surplus is required when the economy is healthy, to avoid excessive stimulus and to leave room for maneuver when stimulus is truly needed during a future recession.

There was some improvement in the federal deficit in 1987, as it eased to about $160 billion, or 3½ percent of GDP. But it is widely recognized that the deficit remains far too high. Congress acknowledged as much in 1985, when it passed the Gramm–Rudman–Hollings (GRH) Act.[7] The law calls for deficit cuts of about $40 billion annually during 1989–92 to eliminate the deficit by 1993. It provides for deep proportionate cuts in domestic and defense spending, excluding Social Security, if Congress does not otherwise meet the targets by specific expenditure and tax measures. The key political question is whether the new president and Congress will take the difficult decisions required to meet these targets. Candidate George Bush's repeated pledge in the 1988 campaign that he would not raise taxes placed potentially serious limitations on the room for maneuver in achieving fiscal adjustment. By early 1989, with the release of the new administration's budget based on the principle of a "flexible freeze," the hard task of reducing specific programs to hold spending totals in broadly defined categories remained to be accomplished, and there was predictable opposition to those few areas where the new president did specify spending cuts.[8]

---

5. For the federal deficit. The combined deficits of federal, state, and local government (table 2.1) were somewhat smaller because of surpluses at the state and local levels.

6. Although the "neo-Ricardian" school argues that deficits do not matter in any event because they induce households to save more against the future day when taxes will be raised to achieve fiscal adjustment, this assumption about household behavior makes implausibly high demands on personal clairvoyance and is contradicted by the simultaneous decline of personal savings rates and rise of fiscal deficits in the 1980s. R. Barro, "Are Government Bonds Net Wealth?" *Journal of Political Economy*, November–December 1974.

7. Although the original formulation was found unconstitutional in its mechanism for implementing automatic spending cuts, a revised bill with new targets became law in September 1987.

8. The largest cuts in the proposed budget were $5 billion in Medicare, $4.4 billion

A large and persistent fiscal deficit is costly to the economy. A major reason is that, as the government competes with the private sector for savings to finance the deficit, the pressure on credit markets drives up the interest rate. A high interest rate discourages investment. Yet investment is the key to productivity growth and long-term expansion of productive capacity. If government spending were primarily in physical investment, the diversion of funds from private credit markets might not matter. But the bulk of government spending is for current consumption, including national defense and transfers (much of which goes to the middle class, for example in Social Security).[9]

The US fiscal deficit has preempted an increasingly large share of private savings. In 1980–81, personal saving was approximately 5 percent of GNP and net business saving (after depreciation) 1½ percent of GNP. In recent years the consumer has gone on an extraordinary spending binge, and personal saving has declined to 2½ to 3 percent of GNP (first two graphs in figure 2.1). However, a rise in net business saving (after depreciation) held total private saving at about 6 percent of GNP through 1983–86. By then the fiscal deficit (including state and local) had ballooned to absorb approximately two-thirds of net private saving. Under these circumstances it was no accident that the real interest rate remained extremely high.

The fiscal deficit also places a burden on future generations as the interest on the resulting debt will have to be serviced year after year. In the past, economics textbooks downplayed this burden, noting that because government debt was also held by Americans as assets, we "owed it to ourselves." But as government borrowing has overburdened domestic credit markets and (along with falling personal saving) forced increased total borrowing from foreigners, this argument is no longer valid. Even for a country without net external debt, increased government debt poses issues of distributional equity not only among generations but also across income classes. Asset ownership tends to be more concentrated in the hands of upper-income groups than is the burden of taxes, so that the real cost of servicing

---

in retirement and health benefits for government employees, and several billion dollars in reduced farm price and income supports. *Wall Street Journal,* 10 February 1989.

9. Moreover, the share of investment in government spending has been declining. Thus, from 1963 to 1987 federal investment outlays (on defense and nondefense equipment, structures, and research and development) fell from 6 percent of GNP to 4 percent (reaching as low as 3.2 percent in 1978), even as total federal spending rose from 19 percent of GNP to 24 percent. In recent years the share of defense spending going to investment (e.g., weapons systems) has, however, reversed an earlier declining trend. Council of Economic Advisers, *Economic Report of the President,* January 1989, 80–82.

Figure 2.1 US private consumption, private saving, and government dissaving, 1979–87

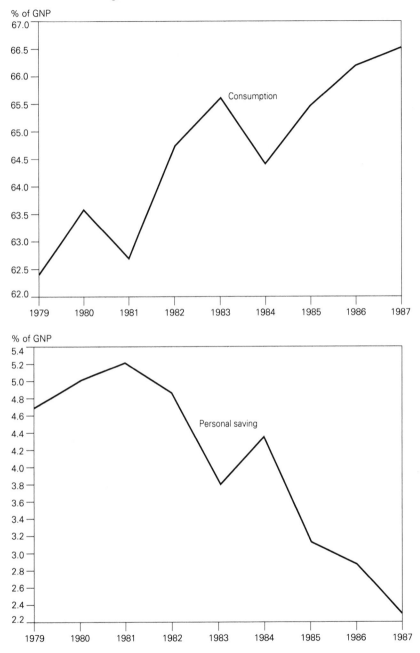

Figure 2.1 (continued)

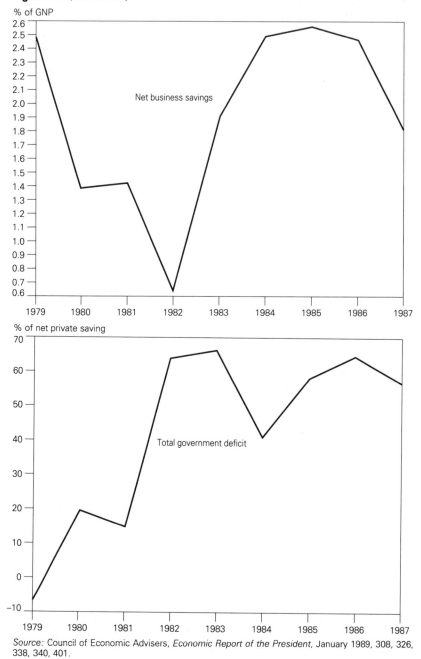

Source: Council of Economic Advisers, Economic Report of the President, January 1989, 308, 326, 338, 340, 401.

domestically held debt can involve a net transfer from lower- to upper-income classes, a cost that is magnified if high deficits and debt raise real interest rates.

Figure 2.2 shows the growth of fiscal deficits and the resulting accumulation of government debt since 1979. The figure shows that federal revenue declined by about 1 percentage point of GNP from 1980 to 1984 (to approximately 19 percent of GNP), while federal spending rose briskly (from about 21 percent of GNP in 1979 to approximately 24 percent in 1987, although about half of this rise occurred before the Reagan administration took office). The gap between the two trendlines represents the federal deficit. The corresponding public-sector shares in GNP, including state and local governments, showed a somewhat narrower but persistent gap as well (with revenue at about 31 percent of GNP and spending at 34 to 35 percent). The uppermost trendline in the figure indicates that the federal debt (end of fiscal year) rose from approximately one-third of GNP in 1981 to over one-half by 1987 as the consequence of the cumulative deficits of the Reagan era.[10]

Beyond their burden in the form of future debt servicing, fiscal deficits also are a classic source of inflationary pressure. Falling oil prices and excess capacity masked this strain in the early 1980s, but the US economy is now nearing full capacity, and the deficit risks imposing inflationary excess demand on the economy. The inflation rate has already returned to the range of 4 to 5 percent, high by historical standards, and higher rates threatened at the beginning of 1989.

External Imbalance

The external deficit is the second dangerous legacy of the Reagan era, and it is closely related to the internal imbalance. Figure 2.3 shows the explosion of the US trade and current account deficits in the 1980s. Even when evaluated relative to the trade base rather than in absolute dollar terms, the current account showed enormous erosion, falling from a surplus of 2 percent of exports of goods and nonfactor services in 1980 to a deficit of 48 percent in 1987.[11]

---

10. All data are from *Economic Report of the President 1988*, 337, 341; and *Survey of Current Business*, July 1988, 57.

11. Comparison of the external deficit to the export base provides a sense of the extent to which exports must be increased to achieve equilibrium. The alternative basis for comparison, GNP, gauges the external deficit relative to total income and production; however, it may not fully convey the dimensions of the external deficit

Figure 2.2 US fiscal deficits and debt, 1979–87

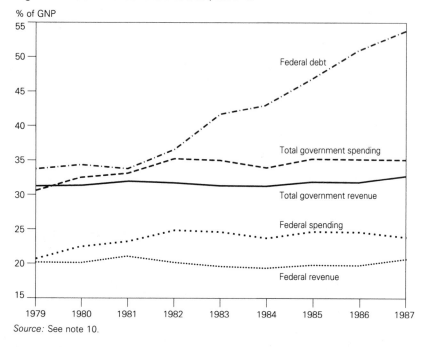

Source: See note 10.

The current account deficit on exports and imports of goods and services reached $154 billion in 1987, and in 1988 it amounted to $135 billion (Chapter 3), or some 3 percent of GNP. The rising fiscal deficit and declining private saving are the root causes of the external imbalance.

The external balance equals the difference between domestic use and domestic availability of resources. When resource use exceeds availability, the shortfall of goods and services must be imported from abroad. With rising government spending, lagging government revenue, a boom in private consumption, and some rise in investment, the US economy has been using far more resources in recent years than it has been producing. Inflows of foreign capital have been required to pay for the imports not covered by US export earnings. The capital inflow in turn means that US liabilities abroad have been rising much more rapidly than US foreign assets.[12]

---

problem in a relatively closed economy in which exports are low relative to GNP, and in which it is not necessarily the case that a large nontradeables sector can be smoothly converted to tradeables production.

12. In technical terms, from the national accounts equation $M - X = I - S$, where

Figure 2.3 US trade and current account balances, 1980–87

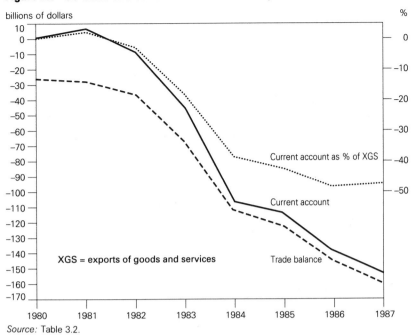

billions of dollars

%

Current account as % of XGS

Current account

XGS = exports of goods and services

Trade balance

Source: Table 3.2.

Table 2.1 presents the resource balance for the United States in the 1980s. Gross investment and saving in the private sector are shown in the first two columns. Investment has been relatively constant at approximately 16 percent of GNP, although it experienced boom levels of approximately 18 percent in 1979 and 1984 as well as recession levels of 14 to 15 percent in 1982–83. For most of the period, private saving was more than adequate to finance investment, and the excess of private saving over investment reached approximately 3 percent of GNP in 1982–83.

For 1979–81, the total government deficit was in the range of 1 percent of GNP or less, so that the excess of private saving over investment was

---

M is imports and X exports of goods and services, I is investment, and S is total saving. Primarily because of government dissaving (fiscal deficits), total domestic saving has been inadequate to cover investment ($S < I$), and imports have exceeded exports by the shortfall ($M > X$). Some have argued an opposite direction of causation: that large autonomous inflows of capital were the driving force, and that the domestic investment–saving gap merely widened in response to the inflow. But for this direction of causation to have been correct, real interest rates in the 1980s should have been unusually low rather than high, as the supposed shift in the foreign capital supply curve would have reduced the going price of capital.

Table 2.1 United States: Resource and current account balance, 1979–87
(percentages of GNP)

Year	Invest-ment[a] (A)	Private saving[a] (B)	Private saving minus invest-ment (C)	Govern-ment saving[b] (D)	Resource balance (E)	Current account balance (F)
1979	18.1	17.8	−0.4	0.5	0.1	0.0
1980	16.0	17.5	1.5	−1.3	0.3	0.1
1981	16.9	18.0	1.1	−1.0	0.2	0.2
1982	14.1	17.6	3.5	−3.5	0.0	−0.3
1983	14.7	17.4	2.6	−3.8	−1.1	−1.4
1984	17.6	17.9	0.2	−2.8	−2.6	−2.8
1985	16.0	16.6	0.6	−3.3	−2.7	−2.9
1986	15.7	16.1	0.4	−3.4	−3.0	−3.3
1987	15.7	14.7	−1.1	−2.3	−3.4	−3.4

a. Gross.
b. Federal, state, and local.
Note: C = B − A; D = government revenues − expenditures; E = C + D.

Sources: Council of Economic Advisers, *Economic Report of the President,* February 1988, 248, 280, 364; *Survey of Current Business,* July 1988, 40, 71, 72.

sufficient to cover the government's financing needs. Beginning in 1983, however, the government deficit reached such high levels (in the range of 3 to 4 percent of GNP) that the private saving surplus was no longer adequate to cover government dissaving, and the nation's resource balance turned negative. The result was a need to obtain net resources from abroad. The final column of the table reports the US external current account balance for goods and services. As shown, the actual current account deficit as a percentage of GNP rose almost identically with the resource imbalance.[13]

It is sometimes argued that the external deficits of recent years have been justified because they were used to finance a boom in investment that increased the nation's productive capacity and thus its ability to service external debt in the future (as was the case in the United States in the 19th century). However, the data on investment in table 2.1 indicate that there has been no such trend. Indeed, the average ratio of investment in the two

13. In national accounts terms the two are identical, but there are small accounting divergences between the balance of payments and national accounts concepts.

Figure 2.4 Government purchases of goods and services, 1979–87

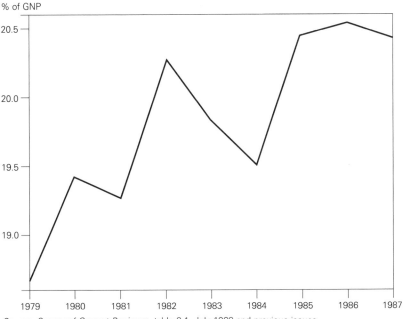

% of GNP

Source: Survey of Current Business, table 3.1, July 1988 and previous issues.

years prior to the Reagan period (1979–80) stood at 17.0 percent of GNP, whereas the average ratio for 1981–87 was only 15.8 percent. If the seven-year period 1974–80 is used for comparison (to provide a span of equal length to the 1980 years), the average investment rate was 16.0 percent, practically the same as in the 1980s and again contradicting the thesis that the external deficits of recent years have stemmed from an investment boom. Instead, foreign resources were used to finance a boom in government spending and private consumption, as suggested by figures 2.1 and 2.2. Figure 2.4 confirms the surge in government spending, this time reporting government purchases of goods and services in the national accounts (and thus omitting outlays on transfer payments and interest, included in figure 2.2).

For most of the 1980s the causal mechanism that led to the translation of the resource imbalance into the external deficit was as follows. The fiscal gap caused pressure on credit markets, boosting the interest rate. A high US interest rate induced an inflow of foreign capital responding to attractive yields. This inflow meant that foreign currencies were bidding for dollars, pushing up the price of the dollar. Broadly based measures showed a rise in the dollar in real terms by some 35 to 40 percent from 1980 to the first

Figure 2.5 Real dollar exchange rates, 1979–89

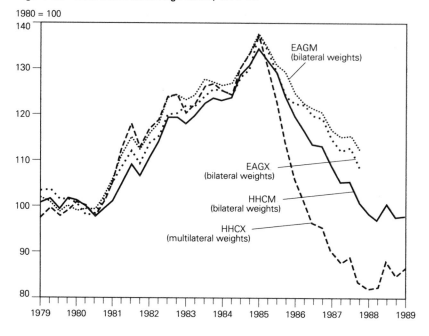

1980 = 100

quarter of 1985 (figure 2.5), and the increase was even greater against key currencies such as the German mark and the Japanese yen.[14] The rise in the dollar acted like a 40 percent tax on exports and an equal subsidy to imports. As a result, from 1980 to 1985 exports stagnated at approximately $225 billion annually, whereas imports rose by almost 50 percent, even though the cost of oil imports fell by half.

In this period, it was the capital market that was driving the dollar's exchange rate. Traditionally, a deteriorating trade balance has been expected to cause a decline in the country's exchange rate. But in this case the dollar kept on rising even as the US trade deficit grew, because the force driving the dollar was the movement of capital entering the country rather than the trade balance. Only after the dollar bubble burst in 1985 did the dollar start to fall into the more normal pattern of a weakening currency in response to a serious trade deficit problem. By then the damage had been done, and trade orders were on the books that would keep the trade deficit rising right through 1987. More fundamentally, even after the turnaround in the

14. The real exchange rates of figure 2.5 are discussed below.

dollar, the external deficit was bound to stay high as long as the imbalance between domestic resource use and availability was not corrected.[15]

The US current account balance moved from near zero in 1980 to a deficit of $100 billion by 1984, and the deficit continued climbing. The cumulative effect was to turn the United States from the world's biggest creditor into its largest debtor. In 1981 net foreign assets peaked at $130 billion. By the end of 1987, external liabilities exceeded US assets abroad by $450 billion (table 3.2). Although the level of net liabilities was exaggerated because US direct investment abroad was worth much more than historical book value, there was no ambiguity about the sharp negative trend in the US net position, and by early 1988 US net earnings on capital had turned negative.[16]

Dangers of the US External Imbalance

Some argue that the external deficit and debt are no cause for alarm. They contend that it does not matter to the typical American whether he owes money (directly or indirectly through government debt) to other Americans or to foreigners. They argue in addition that accumulating foreign debt is not undesirable if the borrowing is being used to invest in productive capacity that can be used to service the debt in the future.

Large external deficits and rising net debt are dangerous, however, and US policymakers cannot afford to be nonchalant about adjustment of the external imbalance. The fact is that borrowing from abroad has not been used to increase US investment; instead, it has mainly financed fiscal deficits and a rise in consumption, as discussed above.

---

15. The resource imbalance could of course be "corrected" by a sharp reduction in investment or, more desirably, by a decline in private consumption, so that reduction of the external deficit would be possible even in the absence of adjustment of the fiscal deficit. However, an investment collapse would jeopardize future growth. Although some analysts have argued that most of the external deficit will be eliminated by a rebound of personal saving to more normal levels, it would be risky for policymakers to wait for this felicitous resolution of the problem. Gross personal saving fell from 5.1 percent of GNP in 1980–81 to 4.4 percent in 1982–84, 3.0 percent in 1985–86, and 2.3 percent in 1987. Although the rate edged upward again to 2.9 percent in the first three quarters of 1988, it remained far below its level of the beginning of the decade. Council of Economic Advisers, *Economic Report of the President,* January 1989, 308, 340.

16. Some analysts argue that the net US external liability figure is not overstated because failure to incorporate past errors and omissions into the estimate of US liabilities approximately offsets understatement of US direct investment abroad by historical accounting. However, the capital services account does not show the sizable deficit that would be expected if the true net liability position were as high as reported, and until 1988 there was a significant surplus on capital services.

More ominously, the large external deficit imposes an ongoing risk of a macroeconomic crisis.[17] At some point a loss of confidence on the part of foreign investors could choke off the inflow of foreign capital. Foreigners discouraged over the absence of any sign of serious US action to correct the fiscal deficit could give up on the dollar, or foreign investors' portfolios could simply become saturated with dollars after the unusual buildup of recent years. For fear of taking large capital losses on dollar assets, they could stop lending to the United States, and begin withdrawing some of their $1.3 trillion in portfolio claims on the US government and private sector. They might even be joined by US citizens in a generalized flight from the dollar.

Under these circumstances the dollar would plunge, and there could be a "hard landing" for both the dollar and the economy. The Federal Reserve could be forced to step in with forceful monetary restriction, which could cause a rise in interest rates by several percentage points (and the underlying shortage of capital could force the interest rate increase even if the Fed did not adopt tight restraint).[18] The rise in the interest rate in turn would precipitate a recession. Both the dollar and the economy would suffer severe shock. Worse, the dollar's collapse would impose cost-push pressure from higher import prices, threatening stagflation.

From one standpoint the risk of this macroshock scenario may have lessened in 1988. The hard-landing scenario assumes that foreign investors will tend to jump on a bandwagon in betting against the dollar, and thus that their expectations are "extrapolative" (simplistically projecting the most recent trends) and unstable. If such excessive overreaction were not a threat, pressure in the exchange markets to drive down the dollar would not be undesirable as long as the dollar remained above the equilibrium rate required to reduce the external deficit to a sustainable level. With extrapolative, unstable expectations, however, a developing decline of the dollar would feed on itself and intensify, causing a seriously excessive decline in the dollar's value beyond the level needed to correct the external deficit.

However, the experience since the dollar's decline began in early 1985 has shown a relatively civilized retreat rather than a rout of the dollar. At each successively lower level of the dollar, there were foreign investors who

---

17. For the first and definitive statement of the macroeconomic risk, see Stephen Marris, *Deficits and the Dollar: The World Economy at Risk*, POLICY ANALYSES IN INTERNATIONAL ECONOMICS 14 (Washington: Institute for International Economics, December 1985).

18. Faced with the *fait accompli* of a sharply lower dollar, the Fed could conclude that higher interest rates were required to dampen domestic investment and consumption, for fear that otherwise the prospective rise in net exports would push the economy into inflationary excess demand.

considered it now to be a good investment, suggesting that expectations are stabilizing and look toward some long-term "normal" value, rather than being extrapolative and destabilizing (bandwagon). The upward turnaround of the dollar in the first three quarters of 1988 was particularly important in this regard, because it served notice to all investors that the dollar's decline was not a safe one-way bet. This experience made it less likely that a further decline would turn into a collapse that would trigger the hard-landing scenario.

From other standpoints, however, the risk of a hard landing for the dollar (defined as a major decline of the dollar well beyond its equilibrium level) may have increased. The longer the large external deficit persists, and the larger the net external liability position, presumably the greater the risk of a sharp decline in the dollar. Similarly, the growing signs of renewed inflation by early 1989 threatened an erosion of foreign confidence, as did the financial fragility associated with the savings and loan crisis.[19] In sum, the scenario of the hard landing for the dollar (and possibly for the economy) remained a significant risk in early 1989. Although the chances for such an event were not necessarily high, its probability when weighted by the economic costs of the scenario meant relatively high "expected costs" that warranted close policy attention.

There have already been storm warnings that such a macroeconomic shock could occur. In early 1987, pressure on the dollar (as well as a revival of inflationary expectations after the abnormally low inflation of 1986) induced a sharp rise in long-term US interest rates.[20] US and foreign monetary authorities responded in an attempt to stabilize the dollar through a lowering of foreign interest rates, in the Louvre Accord of February. Even so, US bond markets experienced a serious decline by the second quarter of 1987. Then in the third quarter of that year a renewed round of higher US interest rates geared toward defense of the dollar triggered the October crash in the stock market. These warnings cannot be ignored.

Although there is some probability of a sudden macroshock from the external imbalance, it is almost certain that even if the abrupt hard landing is avoided the US economy will suffer prolonged adverse effects until the

---

19. Another possible safeguard against the hard-landing scenario has been that foreign central banks would be reluctant to see their currencies rise so sharply against the dollar and would tend to intervene in support of the dollar. However, these central banks are themselves becoming relatively saturated with dollar holdings, as they already had to finance the great bulk of the US external deficit in 1987.

20. Thus, yields on AAA corporate bonds rose from 8.4 percent in January 1987 to 9.3 percent by May (and reached 10.5 percent in October). *Survey of Current Business*, March 1988, S-16.

imbalance is corrected. Chinese water torture is better than the guillotine, but not much. In order to continue attracting capital from abroad, the United States would have to offer high interest rates on an ongoing basis. High interest rates would discourage investment and future growth. The external deficit would also impose a rising burden on the public in future years, as the debt service paid to foreigners would rise continuously. Although less directly of concern to Americans, failure to adjust would mean a continuation of the perverse channeling of global savings to the leading industrialized country, in contrast to the opposite net flow of resources (to the developing world) usually considered normal.

A major danger of failure to adjust the external imbalance is that protectionism could intensify in the United States.[21] It should be recalled that the proximate cause of the reversal of official US policy toward the dollar in the 1985 Plaza Agreement to bring the US currency down from its excessively strong level was the threat that Congress would impose protective legislation. Treasury Secretary James A. Baker III offered intervention to make US goods more competitive through a lower dollar, to defuse the explosive atmosphere among US legislators and business interests. If after several years the macroeconomic solution of exchange rate adjustment were seen to have failed to bring down the trade deficit, demands for aggressive protectionist action could prevail.

Despite the Plaza Agreement and a declining dollar, in 1988 Congress nearly passed the Gephardt amendment, which would have imposed retaliatory protection against high-surplus countries such as Japan and Korea that failed to reduce their surpluses at a prescribed rate. The instinctive public view is that American markets are open whereas foreign markets are closed, and it is an easy leap to conclude that the large and persistent external deficit is attributable to unfair trade abroad rather than to US policy mismanagement. Yet the imposition of new protection out of frustration would risk a spiral of retaliation and counterretaliation such as occurred in the 1930s. In sum, trade policy risks reinforce the dangers from failure to adjust the external imbalance.

The Rise and Fall of the Dollar

In view of the risks of macroeconomic shock, long-term growth reduction, and protectionist outbreak posed by the high external deficit, it is fortunate

---

21. Bergsten in particular has emphasized the protectionist risk and presents further analysis of the role of fiscal imbalances in the US external deficit, and of the hard-landing scenario. C. Fred Bergsten, *America in the World Economy: A Strategy for the 1990s* (Washington: Institute for International Economics, 1988).

that the dollar did begin to decline after early 1985. If it had not done so, the prospective current account deficit would have been far larger (see Chapter 3).

Figure 2.5 presents alternative measures of the real, trade-weighted exchange rate of the dollar, with a base of 1980 = 100. The two series extending through the first quarter of 1989[22] are the real exchange rates implied by the modified Helkie–Hooper (HHC) model (Chapter 3); the two series ending in 1987:4 are those obtained from the External Adjustment with Growth (EAG) model (Chapter 4). In each case, there is one real exchange rate pertaining to imports and another to exports (indicated in the figure by M and X, respectively).

The real exchange rate for imports in the HHC model is calculated as the bilateral, nonoil import-weighted exchange rate of the 18 largest US trading partners, deflated by the corresponding weighted consumer price index for the same countries and, on the US side, by the GNP deflator. These are the exchange rates and price deflators applied for the import equations in the HHC model. For exports, the real exchange rate from the model applies the same 18 exchange rates but with multilateral trade weights. Once again it deflates by consumer prices on the foreign side, but on the US side it uses the export-weighted US wholesale price index as the deflator.

The real exchange rate from the EAG model is different in concept. It is the ratio of dollar unit value trade prices to the dollar equivalent of domestic prices as measured by wholesale price indexes. Thus, the series EAGM refers to the bilateral nonoil import-weighted dollar unit values of imports from the 15 non-OPEC trading partners identified in the EAG model, deflated by the US wholesale price index.[23] The series EAGX is the ratio of the US export unit value to the bilateral US export-weighted index of foreign domestic wholesale price indexes (translated to dollar indexes by applying the exchange rate). As ratios of actual trade and domestic prices, the EAGM and EAGX series incorporate not only exchange rate change but also the extent of pass-through in pricing behavior by firms.

Five salient patterns are apparent in figure 2.5. First, by all four measures (with surprising unanimity) the real strength of the dollar rose by some 35 to 40 percent from 1980 to 1985:1. Second, thereafter the actual relative trade prices of the United States declined substantially, back to only about 12 percent above the 1980 level by 1987:4. However, their decline was not as great as that of the real exchange rate, as was to be expected from the lag of pass-through behind exchange rate change. Third, the real exchange

---

22. Estimated on the basis of February 1989 exchange rates.

23. And then inverted, to show a decline as the strength of the dollar declines.

rate based on domestic prices and exchange rates (rather than actual trade unit values) had fully returned to the 1980 level by the first quarter of 1988, and indeed by the export-based measure the dollar had declined substantially below its 1980 level. Fourth, there was a substantial divergence between the real decline of the dollar on the export side and on the import side, based on the HHC measures. Fifth, on a quarterly basis the real dollar reached its trough in 1988:2, and there was a significant rebound thereafter.

The divergence between the HHC export and import real exchange rates during the decline of the dollar after 1985:1 is driven by two factors. First, because the US GNP deflator rose by 8.0 percent from 1985:1 to 1987:4 while the export-weighted wholesale price index rose by only 0.4 percent, the real dollar as measured on the export side (applying the latter as the deflator) declines by almost 8 percent more than that measured on the import side (applying the former). The HHCM index declines from 134.9 in 1985:1 to 101.0 in 1987:4, or by 25 percent, whereas the HHCX index declines from 137.0 to 83.9, or by 38.8 percent. If the GNP deflator were used on the export side, the dollar's decline would be 33.9 percent,[24] closing approximately 40 percent of the gap between the dollar's decline on the import measure and the export measure. Second, bilateral weights in the HHCM index give far more weight to Canada, and less to Germany and other European countries, than the multilateral weights in the HHCX index.[25] Because the real dollar fell much more during this period against the European currencies (for example, by 47.8 percent against the German mark, using the HHCX deflators) than against the Canadian dollar (only 6.4 percent), the weighting difference is important.

Because US exports are in the first instance affected by direct competition in bilateral markets, and the role of some markets (particularly the intra-European) is less important in US export sales than in shares of total world trade, a more appropriate measure on the export side would be an average of bilateral and multilateral weights, perhaps with the weights tilted toward bilateral US exports. For this reason the HHCX index probably overstates the decline of the dollar since 1985. In addition, from another standpoint both indexes overstate the decline of the real dollar. For the foreign price variable, both use consumer prices, which in this period have risen considerably more than foreign wholesale prices (Appendix C). Because foreign export prices are more likely to move closely with foreign wholesale than with consumer prices, US competitiveness by 1987–88 is overstated (that

---

24. That is: $83.9 \times 1.08 = 90.6; (90.6/137.0) - 1 = -0.339$.

25. Thus, the weight of Canada is 24 percent for bilateral imports and only 6 percent for multilateral exports; the corresponding weights for Germany are 8.7 percent and 16 percent, respectively.

is, the decline of the real dollar is exaggerated). The best overall measure of the real dollar is thus probably a simple average of the HHCM and HHCX measures,[26] and because of the bias just noted the true measure may be closer to HHCM.

Based on the average between the two HHC real exchange rates, by 1987:4 the dollar was approximately 7½ percent below its 1980 level. The real rate fell even further by December 31, 1987 (not shown in the figure), to an average index of 87.7. Thus, the real exchange rate fell by 5 percent from the 1987:4 average to the December 31, 1987, trough. As shown in the figure, the dollar then rebounded in 1988, especially in the third quarter. As developed in Chapters 3 and 5, the recovery of the dollar was a missed opportunity to obtain a significant portion of the further real depreciation of approximately 10 percent beyond the 1987:4 level that, together with correction of the US fiscal deficit, is required to bring the US external deficit down to a sustainable level.

A fundamental question remains about the decline in the dollar. If by late 1987 the real dollar was already below its level of 1980 when US external accounts were in approximate balance (table 3.2), why would any further dollar decline be necessary to achieve US external balance today? The principal reason is that the accumulated current account deficits of the 1980s have turned a large net external asset position into a net external debt. The swing in net US external assets from 1980 to 1992 (base case projections, Chapter 3) amounts to nearly $1.2 trillion. Even applying a low nominal interest rate of 6 percent (to allow for a differentially higher return on US investment abroad than on foreign investment in the United States; Chapter 3), the corresponding deterioration in the capital services balance should be on the order of $70 billion. Applying the parameters estimated in Chapters 3 and 5, on average the EAG and HHC models indicate that a 1 percent movement in the real exchange rate generates an impact of $9 billion on the current account by 1992. To offset a deterioration of $70 billion in the capital services account, it is reasonable to expect a decline in the real dollar of approximately 8 percent (70/9), or to approximately the level

---

26. Alternative real exchange rate measures confirm this conclusion. Thus, with 1980 = 100, the International Monetary Fund (IMF) series of real exchange rates for the dollar behaved as follows. They peaked in 1985:1 at 155.7 based on relative labor costs (manufacturing) normalized for the business cycle; 140.1 based on relative GNP deflators; 146.5 using relative wholesale prices; and 156.3 using relative export unit values. By 1987:4 they had returned to 96.9, 83.7, 93.4, and 110.3, respectively. Excluding the unit value trade measure (which reflects pass-through lags), by 1987:4 the three other IMF measures were back to an average of 91.3. By comparison, the average of HHCM and HHCX stood at 92.4. IMF, *International Financial Statistics*, November 1987 and February 1989.

attained by 1987:4 (and at less optimistic interest rate assumptions the required decline is greater). In addition, the real price of oil has declined sharply since 1980. Because the United States is relatively more self-sufficient in oil than are Europe and Japan, lower oil prices tend to strengthen the external positions of those areas relative to that of the United States, requiring further real depreciation of the dollar as an offset.

Inadequacy of US External Adjustment to Date

Despite the broad decline in the dollar, through 1987 there was no sign of correction in the external deficit, which instead worsened. Even though in real terms the dollar had fallen once again to approximately its level of 1980, in 1987 the nominal trade deficit rose from $145 billion to $160 billion. The real trade deficit did decline (from $168.6 billion to $158.9 billion at 1982 prices; Chapter 1), but the J-curve phenomenon, whereby the initial change in real trade volume is too small to offset the rising dollar price of imports, meant a widening of the trade gap in nominal terms. Although the pace of import expansion moderated in 1987 and export expansion rose, so that the two rates were identical (at 11 percent in nominal terms), the import base remained far higher than that of exports, so that the absolute increase in imports exceeded that in exports. The markets registered their disappointment as private capital inflows largely dried up, foreign central banks were forced to bear the bulk of the financing of the US external deficit, and US officials were forced to boost the interest rate to support the dollar (with resulting jolts to financial markets).

The despair of 1987 was premature. There are long lags in trade performance. It takes time for firms to recognize that the exchange rate has really changed, especially in view of the wide fluctuations that occur under the floating rate regime. It takes time for importers to place orders and for deliveries to reach destinations. A lag of two years between the exchange rate signal and the actual trade result is not unusual. On this basis, the markets should not have been surprised that the trade deficit peaked in 1987, because the dollar peaked in 1985.

Market sentiment then shifted excessively in the other direction. In early 1988 the trade figures began to show significant improvement, as monthly trade deficits fell from a range of $12 billion to $13 billion to as low as $9 billion (figure 2.6). Moreover, the central banks showed strong determination at the end of 1987 to place a floor under the dollar, and they reaffirmed at the Toronto summit in June that the currency was about right, even though it had strengthened. There was a sense that the Reagan administration (and even key foreign governments) sought a stable or strengthening dollar to

Figure 2.6 US monthly trade, seasonally adjusted, 1986–88

billions of dollars

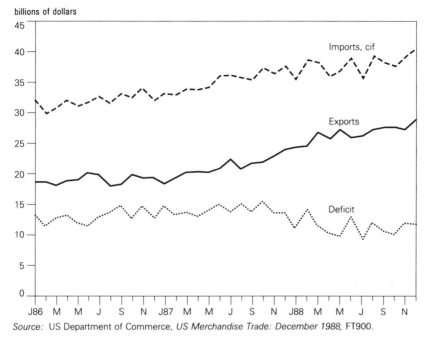

Source: US Department of Commerce, *US Merchandise Trade: December 1988,* FT900.

avoid any financial crisis that might worsen the chances for the election of Vice President George Bush. The market then proceeded to search for a ceiling, and a phase of false euphoria ensued as, by August, traders bid up the dollar some 12 percent or more above its level at the end of 1987 (figure 2.5 and Chapter 3; HHC export basis). By November much of the summer rally in the dollar had been given up, but precious time had been lost in the path toward external adjustment.

In the third quarter of 1988 there was intense debate over whether it was necessary for the dollar to fall back to its end-1987 level or lower. At the Berlin annual meetings of the International Monetary Fund (IMF), Managing Director Michel Camdessus criticized the rise of the dollar during 1988 as contrary to US adjustment, while US Treasury Secretary Nicholas Brady insisted that dynamic factors not captured by the IMF's statistical models would call forth a buoyant response of US exports without further devaluation.[27] The debate raged even within the circles of the Republican Party,

27. *Wall Street Journal,* European Edition, 29 September 1988. See Chapter 1 for a discussion of the US Treasury position.

as former Council of Economic Advisers chief Martin Feldstein argued that a further decline of some 30 percent was necessary for the dollar, while other officials insisted that Feldstein did not speak for the Bush campaign on these issues.

Much depends on how far into the future one projects the trend toward trade improvement in 1988. For that year the trade deficit was declining at a rate of about $30 billion annually. If that rate of change could be continued, the trade deficit would disappear by 1992 without further dollar depreciation. As summarized in Chapter 1 and developed in Chapters 3 and 5, this study finds instead that far more will have to be done to bring the external deficit down to sustainable levels, with fiscal adjustment paramount and a need for further dollar depreciation as well.

There are several reasons why policy measures, including the past decline of the dollar, remain inadequate to achieve external adjustment. First, because the lags from exchange rate to trade change tend to become exhausted after two years, it would be wrong to make a straight-line projection of the trade improvement in 1988 over the next four years. The trade benefits already in the pipeline may be expected to end in 1989, as the decline of the dollar halted in 1987.

Second, there is a "gap" effect that makes the deficit tend to widen over time if it is not successfully closed. The projections in Chapters 3 and 5 indicate that exports will still be about $100 billion below imports in 1989 (at $380 billion versus $480 billion). With the lagged effects of dollar depreciation largely exhausted at that time, normal growth of both imports and exports in response to foreign and domestic GNP growth may be expected to resume. Proportionate growth of both imports and exports causes a widening trade deficit when an absolute gap remains.

Third, in the past the United States enjoyed a surplus on capital service income, because of its positive position on net international assets. In the future, the capital services account may be expected to be in deficit by several billion dollars annually, because of the shift of the United States to a net debtor position (of at least $800 billion and perhaps more than $1 trillion by 1992).

Many would add a fourth consideration: in the past, there has been a tendency toward an adverse trend in US trade. Some formulations interpret this trend as a higher responsiveness of US imports to domestic income growth than of US exports to foreign income growth. Others interpret it as essentially the outcome of rapid growth in productivity and technical change in countries such as Japan, with the implication that the adverse trend could disappear in the future as Japan, Germany, and even countries such as Korea enter more normal phases of growth. The projections of this study take the latter view.

For these reasons, the return of the dollar to its 1980 level in real terms is unlikely to be sufficient to correct the US external imbalance. US fiscal adjustment and some additional depreciation is likely to be required, and still further depreciation would be necessary over time if an underlying adverse trend were expected to persist. In addition, some contribution to international adjustment from increased demand abroad is likely to be required.

The Need for Symmetrical Adjustment Abroad

The mirror image of reduction in the US external deficit is a decline in the aggregate surpluses abroad. These surpluses are concentrated in Japan ($86.6 billion in 1987), Germany ($45.2 billion), Taiwan ($18.0 billion), and Korea ($9.9 billion), with smaller but significant surpluses in Belgium ($2.9 billion), the Netherlands ($4.2 billion), and Switzerland ($5.9 billion).[28]

Some argue that the high surpluses of countries such as Japan and Germany are to be applauded rather than criticized, because they represent domestic savings that these countries are making available to a capital-starved world. According to this view, there should be no special action in the high-surplus countries to reduce their external surpluses, least of all measures to stimulate consumption at the expense of saving.

As summarized in Chapter 1 and developed in Chapter 5, this study formulates a policy package that concentrates the reduction in foreign current account positions—the necessary counterpart of reduction in the US external deficit—in the high-surplus countries. Although the advocates of high saving and (by implication) external surpluses abroad would no doubt agree with the arithmetic of international payments adjustment in the aggregate, some might question the policy objective of concentrating the foreign adjustment in the high-surplus countries. Instead, it might be argued that the surpluses of countries such as Germany and Japan could appropriately continue while the present current account balances of other countries instead move into larger deficit to absorb the counterpart of the US external correction.

In a world with perfect capital mobility and no creditworthiness constraints, this position would be tenable. In particular, from the viewpoint of global development there is much to be said for up to $50 billion annually of the counterpart of a declining US current account deficit emerging as a rising current account deficit in the troubled debtor countries of Latin America and Africa, with most of the rest distributed across other developing

---

28. Table 1.1 above and IMF, *International Financial Statistics*, March 1989.

areas and industrial countries (such as France and Italy) in widening current account deficits, instead of being focused in declining surpluses in Japan and Germany.

In practice, however, there are severe creditworthiness constraints in the Third World debtor countries that rule out this type of global adjustment (even in the presence of accelerated market-based debt reduction programs). Moreover, countries such as France have had relatively recent experience with frustration of domestic growth programs because of increases in their external deficits to magnitudes considered unsustainable. Under these circumstances, attempts to freeze the high surpluses of countries such as Japan and Germany in the face of sharply lower US external deficits would almost certainly mean pressure toward global contraction and protectionism. Countries already in substantial deficit could feel compelled to take measures to contract domestic demand as their deficits began to increase further, and could experience political pressures to deal with rising imports through increased protection.

To a large degree, normal market processes should send the appropriate signals to determine the allocation of the foreign counterpart of the US external adjustment. Thus, once pressure on US credit markets is eased by US fiscal correction and the dollar declines further, the inconsistency of current high surpluses in Japan and Germany with other countries' external positions would be likely to exert disproportionately larger pressure for appreciation on the yen and the deutsche mark than on currencies of intermediate countries. It is important, however, that policymakers not impose obstacles to these market processes. Moreover, it is likely to be helpful to the international adjustment process to have in addition some differential domestic demand policies abroad related to individual countries' external balance positions, as developed in Chapter 5.

The prospective impact of US external adjustment on real trade flows and demand for production abroad underscores the possible need for active demand policies abroad. For the next few years the United States must pursue export-led growth. In the 1980s Europe and Japan have received a major demand stimulus from rising trade surpluses. Thus, from 1980 to 1986 the rise in Japan's real trade balance accounted for 26.3 percent of the total increase in real GNP, whereas in Germany the corresponding contribution of trade to growth amounted to 52.0 percent of the total.[29] The rest of the world can no longer count on growth stimulus from a rising trade surplus with the United States, however. On the contrary, as those surpluses decline, other countries will have to find alternative sources of demand.

---

29. Calculated from the *OECD Economic Outlook* data base.

Otherwise the net impact on the world economy will be contractionary. Viewed in this light, policies to expand domestic demand in other industrial countries (especially the high-surplus countries) may be seen not as a favor to the United States to facilitate its external adjustment, but as a prerequisite if other industrial countries are to avoid a slowdown in their growth (box 2.1).[30]

Conclusion

In sum, the day of economic reckoning has arrived. The Reagan period brought growth and lower inflation, but it has left severe domestic and external imbalances that must be corrected if the risk to the world economy of severe new rounds of recession and inflation is to be reduced.

The United States must do its part, especially through reducing its fiscal deficit and depreciating the real exchange rate. But Europe, Japan, Canada, and the newly industrializing countries of Asia must undertake their share of the international adjustment as well, through the expansion of domestic demand to replace the elimination of artificial export demand associated with the unsustainable US external deficit and by permitting exchange rate appreciation to occur.

Policy formulation will require care, or else severe strains could arise in several countries as the process of US external adjustment develops, especially in the United Kingdom (Chapter 5) but also in other countries such as France. Fortunately, the development of international economic policy coordination since the Plaza Agreement in September 1985 has laid the groundwork for a cooperative approach that, if energetically pursued, can help ensure that the resulting adjustment of international imbalances is achieved while retaining economic growth and high employment.

---

30. Bergsten suggests that foreign industrial countries should seek growth in domestic demand that exceeds growth in GNP by some 1 to 1½ percent annually. In Japan, domestic demand would grow at 6 percent annually while GNP grows at 5 percent. In Europe and Canada, the two rates would average 4 percent and 3 percent, respectively. C. Fred Bergsten, *America in the World Economy*, 19–20.

Box 2.1 US External Adjustment and Global Aggregate Demand

The need for foreign countries to replace demand previously provided by trade surpluses with the United States by domestic demand may be illustrated using the Keynesian diagram of income determination, familiar from introductory textbooks. In graph A of figure 2.7, the United States initially achieves equilibrium income (where the total demand curve, DD, intersects with the total supply curve, the 45 degree line along which demand on the vertical axis equals output on the horizontal axis) through a combination of high domestic demand ($C + I + G$, consumption plus investment plus government spending) and negative external demand ($X - M$, where X is exports and M imports and $X < M$). After fiscal adjustment and reduction in

Figure 2.7 Keynesian income equilibrium before and after US external adjustment

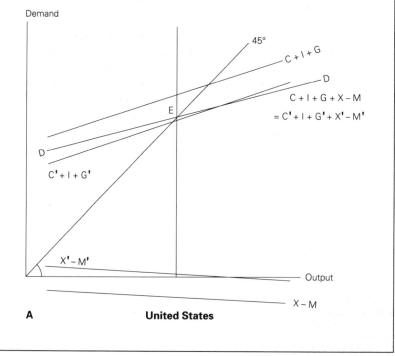

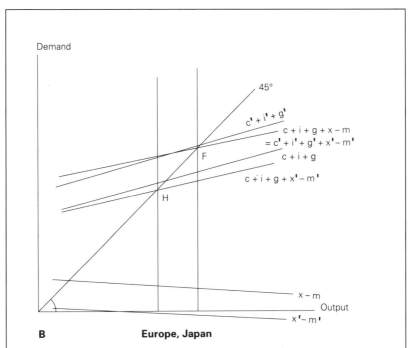

Demand

45°

$c' + i' + g'$

$c + i + g + x - m$
$= c' + i' + g' + x' - m'$

$c + i + g$

$c + i + g + x' - m'$

F

H

$x - m$

Output

$x' - m'$

B **Europe, Japan**

consumption ($G' < G$ and $C' < C$) combined with external sector adjustment ($X' > X$, $M' < M$, $X' > M'$), the economy is once again at the full-employment equilibrium E, but now positive net exports make up for the shortfall that would exist if the only sources of demand were domestic (demand curve $C' + I + G'$ intersects the 45 degree line at a point below full employment).

In graph B of figure 2.7, the foreign economy starts at equilibrium F. Its initial domestic demand ($c + i + g$) is inadequate to reach full employment, but it enjoys an initial trade surplus corresponding to the US trade deficit (curve $x - m$ exceeds zero), so that total demand equals full-employment supply. When the United States adjusts, the net export curve for the foreign country turns negative. If the country increases domestic demand to curve $c' + i' + g'$, it can regain full employment, because total demand (including $x' - m'$) then intersects the 45 degree line at F. Otherwise, its new equilibrium will be where the total demand curve with unchanged domestic demand ($c + i + g + x' - m'$) then intersects the 45 degree line, at point H below full employment.

3

Medium-Term Prospects for the US External Accounts

The future growth and stability of the US economy and the world economy more generally will depend importantly on whether the United States can reduce its external deficit. The outlook for the US external balances under current and alternative policies is a matter of intense debate. One contentious issue is whether the dollar has declined enough to bring about the needed correction over time once fiscal adjustment is on track. Another is the role that can be played by growth policy in other countries, and thus in markets for US exports.

Analysis of the likely future course of US external accounts requires an economic model. One of the most widely recognized foreign sector models is that prepared by William L. Helkie and Peter Hooper of the Federal Reserve Board. This chapter examines the Helkie–Hooper (HH) model, suggests modifications, and then applies the modified model to make projections of the US current account through 1992. The analysis includes evaluation of the implications of alternative paths for exchange rates and economic growth in the United States and abroad. The multicountry model developed in Chapter 4 provides a basis for verification of the projections of this chapter.

The Helkie–Hooper Model

The model constructed by Helkie and Hooper contains 431 equations. It provides quarterly estimates of the principal components of the US balance of payments. The two authors have published the central features of the model elsewhere.[1] The model begins with merchandise trade, divided into

---

1. William L. Helkie and Peter Hooper, "An Empirical Analysis of the External Deficit, 1980–86," in Ralph C. Bryant, Gerald Holtham, and Peter Hooper, eds., *External Deficits and the Dollar: The Pit and the Pendulum* (Washington: Brookings Institution, 1988), 10–56.

agricultural exports, nonagricultural exports, oil imports, and nonoil imports. The volume of nonagricultural exports is a function of foreign income, the US nonagricultural export price relative to the foreign consumer price index translated to dollars through an exchange rate index (with lags distributed over nine quarters), the ratio of US to foreign private fixed capital stock, and a variable for periods affected by dock strikes.

The income and relative price variables are standard elements in the demand for exports. The relative capital stock variable seeks to capture the adverse time trend in US trade that many studies have noted. Empirical analyses frequently pick up this trend through wide differences between the income elasticities of US demand for imports, on the one hand, and foreign demand for US exports, on the other.[2] Helkie and Hooper argue that the existing price indexes do not adequately take account of the introduction of new product lines, such as the entry of Japan into exports of automobiles and consumer durables in the 1960s and early 1970s. They contend that, as a result, standard import demand equations often spuriously attribute to US income growth much of long-term import growth that instead is caused by outward-shifting foreign supply. Their trade equations seek to incorporate these supply effects through the relative capital stock variable.

The volume of nonoil imports is estimated as a function of US income; the nonoil import price deflator as adjusted to take account of tariffs, relative to the US GNP deflator (with lags distributed over eight quarters); the relative capital stock variable; the ratio of foreign to US manufacturing capacity utilization; and a dock strike variable. The volume of agricultural exports is estimated as a function of foreign income, the ratio of the agricultural export price deflator to an index of foreign consumer prices translated into dollars through an exchange rate index (with lags), the ratio of the US GNP deflator to the agricultural export price deflator (with lags), and a dock strike variable. The volume of oil imports equals oil consumption plus oil stock change plus oil exports minus oil production; oil consumption in turn is a function of US income and the ratio of the oil import price deflator to the US GNP deflator (with long lags).

---

2. The classic empirical study that first identified a seeming structural disadvantage for US trade because of a higher income elasticity for imports than for exports was by Hendrik S. Houthakker and Stephen P. Magee, "Income and Price Elasticities in World Trade," *Review of Economics and Statistics* vol. 51, no. 2 (May 1969). Whether such a structural divergence does exist has been the subject of a long controversy. For example, Haynes and Stone find that when cyclical influences are taken account of separately, the disparity in long-term income elasticities disappears. Stephen E. Haynes and Joe A. Stone, "Secular and Cyclical Responses of U.S. Trade to Income: An Evaluation of Traditional Models," *Review of Economics and Statistics* vol. 65, no. 1 (February 1983), 87–95.

Current dollar values of trade require multiplication of the volume estimates by estimates of prices. Nonagricultural export prices are estimated as a function of US sectoral wholesale price indexes weighted by shares in exports, and the foreign consumer price index as deflated by an index of exchange rates (with lags). The second term means that, when the dollar depreciates, there is a positive feedback effect to US export prices in dollar terms. The basis for such feedback is that exporters are in a better position to raise dollar prices when the foreign demand curve facing them shifts outward as the result of dollar depreciation (although most studies show that US export prices tend to be set primarily in dollars and show relatively little response to the exchange rate).

On the side of import prices, the model estimates nonoil import prices as a function of foreign consumer prices, an index of foreign exchange rates (with lags distributed over eight quarters), and an index of world commodity prices (with lags over four quarters). In turn, the model estimates world commodity prices as a function of income of the 10 largest industrial countries, an index of exchange rates, the difference between the US Treasury bill interest rate and the time trend of commodity prices, and the lagged commodity price.

The principal elements of the rest of the model are as follows. In factor services, income on direct investment abroad depends on foreign income, foreign capacity utilization, and the stock of US direct investments abroad. Payments on foreign direct investment in the United States depend on US income, US capacity utilization, and the stock of foreign direct investment in the United States. Other investment receipts from abroad depend on the rate of return on US portfolio assets abroad and on the stock of those assets. The rate of return is estimated as a function of the US Treasury bill rate and the rate of return in the previous period. Payments on other investments depend on the rate of return on foreign portfolio holdings in the United States and on the stock of those holdings, with the rate of return similarly dependent on the Treasury bill rate and the lagged rate of return.

Nonfactor service exports (deflated) are a function of foreign income and the ratio of the service export price to foreign consumer prices translated to dollars through the exchange rate index (with lags over eight quarters). Similarly, real nonfactor service imports are a function of US income and the ratio of the price of these services to the US GNP deflator.

The trade balance is the sum of agricultural and nonagricultural export values less oil and nonoil import values. The current account balance equals the merchandise trade balance plus the balance on factor and nonfactor services plus net transfers. The model then requires that the change in net foreign assets equal the current account balance.

The core trade equations of the HH model warrant replication here. Prices of nonagricultural exports are estimated as:

$$(1) \quad \ln P_x = -0.150 + 1.046 \ln P_{xw} + 0.214 \ln (P_{18}/E_{18})$$

where ln is the natural logarithm, P_{xw} is the average of US sectoral wholesale price indexes weighted by shares in exports, P_{18} is an index of foreign consumer prices in 18 countries (bilateral US nonagricultural export weights), and E_{18} is the exchange rate index for the same countries (multilateral trade weights). The coefficient on the final term is the sum of lagged coefficients over a four-quarter lag period. The coefficient on wholesale product prices shows that export prices vary almost directly with domestic wholesale prices for the products in question, but with a slight magnification of changes. The coefficient on the foreign price term indicates that when foreign prices rise by 10 percent, or when the dollar declines by 10 percent, there is feedback causing US export prices to rise by approximately 2 percent.

The volume of nonagricultural exports (at 1982 prices) is estimated as:

$$(2) \quad \ln XQ = -7.256 + 0.785 \ln D_x + 2.198 \ln Y_w + 1.358 \ln k_{t-1}$$
$$- 0.822 \ln (P_x/[P_{18}/E_{18}])$$

where D_x is the dock strike variable, Y_w is an index of world GNP with bilateral US nonagricultural export weights (1982 = 100), k is the ratio of an index of US capital stock to an index of foreign industrial country capital stock, the subscript $t - 1$ refers to the previous period, and the final term refers to the variables in equation 1. The coefficient shown here for the final term is the sum of individual lag coefficients over eight quarters.

The price of nonoil imports is estimated as:

$$(3) \quad \ln P_m = 4.291 + 0.862 \ln P_{18} - 0.903 \ln E_{18} + 0.166 \ln P_c$$

where P and E refer as before to foreign consumer prices and exchange rates, respectively (but in this case using bilateral nonoil import weights), the subscript 18 again refers to the 18 large trading countries, and P_c is an index of commodity prices. The coefficient shown for the exchange rate index is the sum of lagged coefficients covering seven quarters.

The volume of nonoil imports (at 1982 prices) is estimated as:

$$(4) \quad \ln MQ = -2.291 - 0.286 \ln u_{t-1} + 0.810 \ln D_m$$
$$+ 1.098 \ln Y + 0.992 \ln Y_{t-1} - 0.837 k_{t-1}$$
$$- 1.147 \ln (T P_m/P_d)$$

where u is the ratio of capacity utilization in 10 major industrial countries to capacity utilization in the United States, D_m is the dock strike variable, Y is US GNP, k is as in equation 2, T is the influence of the tariff on import prices, and P_d is the US GNP deflator. The coefficient shown for the final term (relative price of imports) is the sum of lagged coefficients over seven quarters.

Several important features of the model emerge from these equations. The Marshall–Lerner condition for devaluation to improve the trade balance is met: the sum of the absolute values of the price elasticities for exports (0.82) and imports (1.15) substantially exceeds unity. (For very low elasticities, the quantity changes would be too small to offset the increased dollar price of imports, and depreciation would actually increase the dollar value of the trade deficit.)

The Houthakker–Magee asymmetry between income elasticities for imports and exports (note 2 above) is absent in these equations. The reason is probably not only that the relative capital stock variable removes the distorting influence of outward-shifting foreign supply, as Helkie and Hooper suggest, but also that incorporation of the relative capacity utilization variable in the import equation tends to purge the income variable of cyclical effects. For exports, the income elasticity is approximately 2. For imports, the sum of the current and lagged income elasticities is also approximately 2.

There is a feedback effect from dollar depreciation to dollar prices of US exports of approximately 20 percent. This effect, combined with the fact that the price elasticity of demand for US exports is less than unity, means that there is some assistance from the price side that adds to export value to supplement the quantity expansion resulting from dollar depreciation.

There is nearly complete "pass-through" of exchange rate changes to price changes on the import side, as shown by the coefficient of 0.90 for the impact of exchange rate change on import price. The estimated lag on the price effect is relatively short. Within the first four quarters, 83 percent of the impact of exchange rate change on import price has taken place. It seems likely that this lag structure changed in the second half of the 1980s, causing overprediction of import price increases by late 1986 and early 1987 as discussed below.[3]

The HH model implies that, in nominal dollar terms, all of the adjustment in the US external deficit must come on the side of exports. The reason is that the price elasticity of imports is approximately unity, so that the reduction in import quantity resulting from higher import prices after

---

3. Note that whereas in early 1987 Helkie and Hooper considered that their model was correctly predicting the course of the US trade balance, by late in the year they had concluded that there was a delay of adjustment (persistence of the trade deficit) that by then could not be fully explained by the model, and the delay was concentrated in the slower-than-expected impact of exchange rate change on trade prices. Peter Hooper and Catherine L. Mann, "The U.S. External Deficit: Its Causes and Persistence," *International Finance Discussion Papers* 316 (Washington: Federal Reserve Board, November 1987).

depreciation may be expected to be offset almost exactly by the rise in dollar prices of imports. The model also provides at least a partial explanation of the delay of adjustment in the trade deficit. On the export side, where the correction must occur in nominal terms, there are relatively long lags from exchange rate change to quantity change. The elasticity of 0.82 (equation 2) is fully obtained only after eight quarters, and in the first year only 41 percent of the total effect takes place.

If there is a bias in export price elasticity in the HH model, it is probably toward understatement. As indicated in Chapter 4, the total price elasticity for exports (including substitution effect) in the multicountry EAG model developed in this study is 1.74, more than twice as high. Some would also question whether the increase in US competitiveness in the late 1980s (and resulting increases in investments in exports) is fully captured by the elasticity, and whether lags of two years are sufficient to obtain the full effect of responses to changed prices.

Nonetheless, in broad terms the HH model achieves a good explanation of the external accounts in the past, and for the future its overall projections provide results qualitatively similar to those of the EAG model. Among five international models of the US external sector used by Bryant and Holtham in summary analysis (including models of Data Resources, Inc., and the Economic Planning Agency of Japan), the HH model achieved the best explanation (as indicated by the allocation of an accuracy-based weight of 36 percent to the HH model in the Bryant–Holtham calculations, as opposed to an average weight of only 20 percent for each model).[4]

The accuracy of the model declines somewhat in the period 1985–86, which postdates the sample period for which the model is estimated (1968–84). The model's price equations overpredict the level of both import and export prices by the fourth quarter of 1986, with predicted import prices 5 percent above actual levels by 1986:4. The volume equations for nonoil imports and nonagricultural exports continue to perform as well in the postsample period as before, but the model substantially underpredicts oil import volume and overpredicts agricultural export volume for 1985–86.[5] The predictions for services in the postsample period are relatively accurate, except for underprediction of receipts on US direct investment abroad.

---

4. Ralph C. Bryant, "The US External Deficit: An Update," *Brookings Discussion Papers in International Economics* 63 (Washington: Brookings Institution, January 1988), 29.

5. The authors attribute underprediction of oil imports to stock-building in mid-1986 in anticipation of a recovery of oil prices, and relate depressed agricultural exports in 1986 to expected changes in US farm support programs.

Modifications

The purpose of the present study is to conduct projections of the US current account through 1992, and to explore the impact of alternative exchange rate and growth scenarios on the outcome. Two types of modifications of the HH model are appropriate for this objective. First, the analysis here streamlines the model to facilitate use in simulation. It is possible to condense the HH model to 130 equations[6] by eliminating many equations that involve agricultural exports and oil imports as well as numerous equations that deal with estimation residuals. This approach requires that special assumptions about agricultural and oil trade replace those blocs of the HH model for forecasting purposes. Second, it is necessary to modify the model to deal with the prediction errors that had developed by late 1986.

Application of the HH trade equations to data for 1987 yielded the following prediction errors. For the year as a whole, the predicted index for prices of nonagricultural exports stood 7.1 percent above the actual level. Predicted prices for nonoil imports were 14.7 percent above the actual level. The predicted level of nonagricultural export volume was 5.9 percent above the actual level. (Note that in this case the model prediction was based on application of the actual, not the model-predicted, export price.) The predicted level of nonoil import volume was 11.5 percent below the actual level. For both exports and imports, then, the model overpredicted the extent of US external adjustment by 1987, although on the import side the shortfall did not matter much, because a smaller-than-expected cutback in import volume was largely offset by a smaller increase in import prices than predicted.[7]

The combined effects were that the model predicted 1987 nonagricultural exports of $249.7 billion, or 13.5 percent above actual, and nonoil imports of $372.2 billion, or 1.4 percent above actual, for a predicted nonagricultural, nonoil trade balance of − $122.5 billion versus − $146.9 billion actual.

The economic information contained in these divergences between model and reality is that, by 1987, fully two years following the peak of the dollar,

---

6. Note that most of these equations are in the services sector, particularly the numerous equations concerning capital income and net external assets. In the trade sector, the streamlined model condenses to only five equations: the four listed above and one for commodity prices.

7. From the viewpoint of the real burden of adjustment, this outcome may even be regarded as favorable, because approximately the same dollar value of imports was achieved with less cutback in the availability of imported goods and services in real terms.

the dollar prices of traded goods had risen by considerably less than had been widely expected on the basis of historical experience of the relationship of trade prices to the dollar. On the export side, US exporters had raised their dollar prices by less than would have been predicted from the feedback relationship of exchange rate to price discussed above.[8] On the import side, foreign suppliers had not raised their dollar prices by as much as implied by the rise in the number of dollars per unit of foreign currency, but instead had cut their profit margins in their own currencies in order to avoid or delay loss of market share. Although as noted, the HH model incorporates lags from exchange rate change to import price change, the rise in import prices by 1987 had been considerably less than predicted even allowing for these lags. Various authors have focused on the shortfall of price increases from their expected levels, and on the question of whether there has been a structural shift that should make forecasts of US trade performance more pessimistic than would be expected on the basis of historical patterns.[9]

In the case of the HH model, a major additional cause of the divergence between predicted and actual trade prices is the model's use of foreign consumer rather than wholesale prices as the basis for expected US import prices and feedback to US export prices. As discussed in Chapter 4 and Appendix C, in 1986–87 an unusual gap emerged between wholesale and consumer prices in major foreign countries. Declining oil prices and the falling dollar caused goods prices at the wholesale level to rise much more slowly than consumer prices (and actually to decline in important countries), thereby breaking the generally close relationship between the two series in the past. Indeed, if foreign wholesale prices are applied directly to the model in the place of consumer prices (without reestimating the parameters), the predicted US import price by 1987 stands at only 6.4 percent above the actual level, rather than 14.7 percent.

The basic strategy adopted in the projections of this study is to assume that the shortfall of trade price movements from patterns predicted by the original model will be only partially closed over the medium term. In particular, it is assumed that, over a period of four quarters, there will be a phased-in elimination of one-half of the gap between actual and model-

---

8. In addition, as noted above, the volume of exports was lower than predicted applying actual export prices to the model. However, in view of the boom in export volume in 1988, when the real volume of nonagricultural exports rose by 23.7 percent, the 1987 overprediction was only temporary. US Department of Commerce, *Gross National Product: Fourth Quarter 1988 (Final)*, BEA-89-10 (Washington: US Department of Commerce, 23 March 1989).

9. Paul R. Krugman and Richard E. Baldwin, "The Persistence of the U.S. Trade Deficit," *Brookings Papers on Economic Activity*, 1987, no. 1, 1–45; Hooper and Mann, "The U.S. External Deficit: Its Causes and Persistence."

predicted trade prices. Thus, in 1987:4 actual export prices were 7.8 percent lower than predicted by the HH model. For the bulk of the 1988–92 forecast period, then, the modified model estimates export prices at the HH model level less 3.9 percent, following a phase-in period so that the shift from actual to adjusted-predicted is not unduly abrupt. A similar but larger adjustment is made in the projection model on the side of import prices, where, after phase-in the future, model-predicted prices are reduced by 8.7 percent (because of a 17.5 percent shortfall of actual from predicted prices in the base period, 1987:4).[10]

The economic implication of these adjustments is that half of the missing price change that should have occurred by 1987:4 will indeed arrive, although behind schedule, whereas the other half is simply given up as lost. The logic for delay beyond past experience is essentially that the rise in the dollar's strength through early 1985 was so much greater than in past experience that it is reasonable to expect a longer period than in the past to be required before full price adjustments take place. The basis for dismissing the other half of the price gap as gone for good is primarily that it seems imprudent to count on elimination of the gap entirely. Higher export and import prices mean a lower nominal trade deficit, and it could be risky for policy purposes to overstate the expected reduction in the deficit.[11] Moreover, the analysis using wholesale prices suggests that there is less of an enigma in the trade prices than appears on the basis of the model when applying consumer prices, suggesting that a lesser rather than greater share of the gap between predicted and actual prices will simply never be closed.

An economic justification for assuming that half of the price gap remains

10. Note that there is no corresponding adjustment imposed on the export and import volumes. Instead, the changes in the price feed through the trade equations to induce corresponding changes in volume.

11. The elasticity of nonoil imports with respect to price is -1.15, so that, after lags are completed, a higher import price means lower volume and slightly lower nominal dollar levels of imports (as the percentage decline in volume modestly exceeds the percentage increase in price). On the export side, if the dollar price of exports rises, the dollar value of exports rises somewhat, because demand is slightly price-inelastic (-0.82). Of course, this fact does not mean that dollar depreciation fails to raise dollar export earnings. If US goods become more competitive as the result of a lower dollar price (for example, through cost reduction), the slight inelasticity of demand means that dollar export earnings decline modestly. But if US competitiveness improves because of depreciation of the dollar, the dollar value of export earnings will rise. In this case the dollar price of foreign goods rises as the result of the currency translation of a given yen price (for example) of the foreign product, so that the US exporter gains competitive advantage and increases export volume without having to reduce his dollar price (and indeed, with some room for increasing the dollar price).

permanently unclosed is again that the exchange rate swings of the early 1980s were so much greater than before that the historical relationship between trade price and exchange rate could have been altered. In particular, with such a large rise in the dollar through early 1985, foreign suppliers probably adjusted to a greater extent than in the past by enjoying windfall profits rather than expanding the volume of their exports to the United States. As a result, a proportionately larger share of the subsequent decline of the dollar would have been translated into greater squeezing of those profit shares (and thus a lesser increase in dollar prices) than in the past.

In sum, the modified HH model used in this study limits the changes to two: streamlining of the number of equations, and modification of the import and export price predictions by a proportion set to eliminate half of the difference between the HH model's predictions and actual price levels found in 1987:4. This "changed" HH model, referred to below as HHC, serves as the basis for projections and policy simulations.

Medium-Term Projections

With the projection model in hand, it is possible to project a base case path for the US trade and current accounts over the next five years, and to conduct experiments to determine the impact of alternative exchange rate and growth scenarios on the accounts. First it is necessary to postulate the central outlook for the economic variables required by the forecasting model. The central policy premise of the projections is that economic policies remain unchanged. In particular, it is assumed in the base case that there is no further progress in reducing nominal fiscal deficits (as discussed in Chapter 1), and that the real exchange rate remains unchanged.

Table 3.1 reports the economic assumptions for the base case projection. The projections for 1988 and 1989 are taken from the International Monetary Fund (IMF).[12] Economic growth in the United States is projected at 4.0 percent in 1988, assumed to slow down to 2.8 percent in 1989, and then assumed to hold at a steady 2.5 percent level. In Japan, growth is placed at 5.8 percent for 1988, falling to 4.2 percent in 1989 and 4 percent for 1990–92. European growth averages 2.9 percent for 1988 and 2.5 percent thereafter. In view of the absence of demographic growth in Europe, a higher long-term rate seems unlikely, although rates higher than these could be achieved in the near term through catch-up growth reducing currently high unemployment. Real GNP is assumed to grow at 5.0 percent in the rest of the

---

12. IMF, *World Economic Outlook*, October 1988, 60.

world, which includes high-growth Asian countries as well as Latin America, where gradual emergence from the debt problem should permit restoration of higher growth rates. OPEC is the exception; growth of only 2 percent is assumed for its members.

It is possible that in practice a recession will interrupt the relatively smooth growth paths assumed here. However, the implicit assumption is that any such further reductions in growth will be offset by subsequent above-average growth, and that the cumulative effects of fluctuating as opposed to steady growth are small. A justification for the relatively favorable growth rates projected here, and in particular for continuation of US growth at 2½ percent or more, is that the major causes of recession in the last 15 years—oil shocks and the need to reduce high inflation—are unlikely to be a problem in the next five years, in view of the soft oil market and the relatively low level to which inflation has declined in most industrial countries. Alternative growth assumptions, including a scenario for low US growth, are examined below.

US inflation is projected at an average level of 4.5 percent through 1992 for consumer prices, 4.0 percent for the GNP deflator, and 4.5 percent for wholesale prices of export goods. The rates projected here could be somewhat understated if the inflationary signals of early 1989, associated with relatively low unemployment, rising capacity utilization, and relaxation of price-competitive pressure on some markets as the result of prior dollar depreciation, prove to be more than transitory.

The projections assume that inflation will continue to be lower in Germany and Japan than in the United States, as in recent years. The rate for Germany is projected at 1.5 percent, and for Japan at 2 percent. Other national inflation rates are projected at their rates of the 1985–86 period, except for Mexico and Brazil, where rates have been extremely variable (and where the 150 percent rate for both probably overstates for Mexico and understates for Brazil).

The baseline forecast assumes that the dollar is fixed in constant terms at its real level of the fourth quarter of 1987. The rebound of the dollar in 1988 is thus considered transitory, and it is essentially assumed that firms treat it as such in their production and trading decisions. As will be shown, the United States remains in fundamental disequilibrium even at the exchange rate of 1987:4, and the dollar revival of the first three quarters of 1988 can only be viewed as an aberration caused by excessive intervention in support of the dollar at the end of 1987, rising US interest rates, and premature optimism on the part of traders at the first signs of improving trade figures in 1988.

To leave the real exchange rate unchanged at its 1987:4 level, for each country the exchange rate against the dollar moves by the difference between

Table 3.1　Assumptions for medium-term projections
(annual percentages)

Variable	Assumptions		
	1988	1989	Average 1990–92
GNP growth[a]			
United States	4.0	2.8	2.5
Japan	5.8	4.2	4.0
Germany	2.9	1.9	2.5
France	2.9	2.4	2.5
Italy	3.0	2.4	2.5
United Kingdom	4.0	2.5	2.5
Other Europe	2.9	2.3	2.5
Canada	4.2	3.2	2.5
OPEC	2.0	2.0	2.0
Rest of World	5.0	5.0	5.0
Consumer price inflation (1989–92 average)			
United States			4.5
Japan			2.0
Germany			1.5
France			2.5
United Kingdom			3.5
Italy			3.5
Canada			4.6
Belgium			4.4
Netherlands			1.9
Sweden			7.2
Switzerland			2.9
Brazil			150.0
Mexico			150.0

national consumer price inflation and US consumer price inflation. For example, for Germany with inflation at 1.5 percent versus US inflation at 4.5 percent annually, the nominal DM/$ exchange rate appreciates by 3 percent annually.

For the influence of outward-shifting foreign supply as captured by the relative capital stock variable, it is assumed that capital stocks continue to grow at their rates in the two years from 1985:1 to 1987:1, or at 3 percent in the United States, 2.3 percent in the industrial countries as a whole, and 6.3 percent for the developing countries. With a weight of 77 percent for

Variable	Assumptions		
	1988	1989	Average 1990–92
Hong Kong			3.9
Korea			2.9
Malaysia			1.7
Philippines			34.8
Singapore			0.8
Taiwan			−0.1
US wholesale price inflation, exports			4.5
US GNP deflator			4.0
Increase in capital stock			
United States			3.0
Industrial countries			2.3
Developing countries			6.3
US Treasury bill rate			7.0
US agricultural exports			
Volume increase			4.0
Price increase			3.0

a. For more country detail, see table 5.1.
Additional assumptions: Real dollar exchange rates are assumed to remain constant at the 1987:4 level; changes in nominal rates are then calculated as country CPI change (%) minus US CPI change (%). Relative capacity utilization, defined as the ratio of capacity utilization in the foreign G-10 countries to that in the United States, is assumed to remain unchanged at 1.209. See Appendix D for baseline projections for US oil imports.

industrial country capital stock and 23 percent for developing countries, the world capital stock grows at 3.2 percent annually, virtually the same as the US capital stock, and the relative capital stock variable (world/US) becomes neutral over the forecast period.

Thus, in these projections one major source of past deterioration in US external accounts, an adverse trend factor beyond any caused by income or price elasticities, is wholly absent. At the operational level of the model, the reason is essentially that, by 1985–86, US capital stock was growing as fast as that of the rest of the world. At a broader level, the reason is essentially that the major shifts of the past associated with the rise of such nations as Japan and Korea as new exporters were concentrated in a particular historical period and are unlikely to be continued, at least with the same intensity, into the future.

Relative capacity utilization is frozen at its level of the first quarter of 1987, in the absence of sharp divergence of relative growth rates from past trends. However, this assumption may somewhat overstate foreign relative to US capacity utilization in the future, as expansion of US manufacturing output to meet export demand pushes the US rate up, while weakening demand for European and Japanese exports to the United States presses in the opposite direction.

The US Treasury bill rate is projected at 7.0 percent, or 2.5 percent above the inflation rate. The projections thus assume that the excesses of both the negative real interest rates of the period 1973–80 (when the spread averaged −1.8 percent) and the high real rates of the period 1981–86 (when the spread averaged a remarkable +5.2 percent, at first because of tight money and later because of the lag of interest rates behind declining inflation) are avoided.[13] By 1987 the spread had declined to 1.4 percent, and in the years immediately before the inflationary boom of 1973 it had been positive but only about 1 percent (1970–72). A real rate of 2.5 percent for the Treasury bill would appear to be a more realistic medium-term level in view of continuing budget deficits. At the same time, the projection makes the crucial assumption that a "hard landing" involving a severe rise in interest rates is avoided.

Market developments by early 1989 suggested that if there is a direction of bias in the interest rate projections, it is toward understatment. Thus, by March, Treasury bill rates stood at 8.7 percent, two-year Treasury obligations at 9.5 percent, and 30-year Treasury bonds at 9.1 percent.[14] Although the inverted yield curve indicated that the market considered the high short-term rate a temporary consequence of tighter monetary policy by the Federal Reserve to avert rising inflation, the absence of fiscal adjustment in the base case does imply pressure on the financial markets. Higher rates than projected here could have a self-reinforcing adverse effect. By 1992 foreign holdings of government and private portfolio investments (that is, excluding direct investment) exceed those of US private and government portfolio holdings abroad by $1.17 trillion (table 3.2), so that a 2-percentage-point increase in

---

13. Calculated from Council of Economic Advisers, *Economic Report of the President,* February 1988, 317, and *International Financial Statistics,* Yearbook 1986 and March 1988.

14. *Wall Street Journal,* 10 March 1989.

the interest rate could cause additional net payments abroad of approximately $24 billion annually. There could be negative indirect effects as well, as the consequence of a stronger dollar resulting from the greater attraction to capital inflows. A rising dollar would further erode the trade outlook.

The projections here apply exogenous forecasts of US agricultural exports and oil imports, for purposes of simplifying the model. The baseline projection for US oil imports is developed in Appendix D. Variations from that baseline occur only in the simulations altering US growth, in which an income elasticity of unity is applied to calculate the resulting changes in oil imports (as discussed in the appendix).

Agricultural exports are projected to grow at a steady rate of 4 percent in volume, but to increase in price at a rate of only 3 percent, below US inflation at 4.5 percent. The decline of the dollar and a modest trend toward international trade liberalization provide the basis for relatively buoyant volume growth, whereas the recent trend toward recovery in agricultural prices suggests that any further real deterioration will be limited. The 1988 base for agricultural exports is from the US Department of Agriculture.[15]

The principal results of the projections for the base case appear in table 3.2. The table shows actual values through 1987. The base case projections estimate 1988 exports at $339.0 billion, for a nominal increase of 35.8 percent. Although this increase, which to a considerable degree is driven by the "catch-up" phase-in of recovery of half of the gap between expected and actual export prices, as discussed above, proved somewhat excessive, actual experience bore out the potential for an increase almost this rapid. Thus, total US exports rose in 1988 by 28.2 percent in nominal terms.[16]

Imports are projected by the HHC model to rise to $466.9 billion in 1988, or by 13.9 percent. This estimate, too, reflects the phase-in of the catch-up on import prices, which, when combined with time lags for quantity response, can balloon the nominal value of imports in the short term (the J-curve effect). Actual data for 1988 indicate an increase in the nominal value of imports by 8.9 percent to $446.4 billion.[17] Of the total, oil accounted for $39.4 billion, almost exactly the same as projected here (table 3.2).[18]

The base case projection calls for a reduction of the trade deficit by $32.4

---

15. Which estimated fiscal 1988 agricultural exports at $34 billion; by communication.

16. US Department of Commerce, *Summary of US International Transactions: Fourth Quarter and Year 1988*, BEA-89-09 (Washington: US Department of Commerce, 14 March 1989), hereafter referred to as *Commerce Balance of Payments 1988*.

17. *Ibid.*

18. US Department of Commerce, *Gross National Product: Fourth Quarter 1988 (Final)*, BEA-89-10 (Washington: US Department of Commerce, 23 March 1989).

Table 3.2 US balance of payments, actual and projected (HHC, base case), 1980–92 (billions of dollars)

	1980	1981	1982	1983	1984	1985
Merchandise exports	224.27	237.08	211.20	201.82	219.90	215.93
Agricultural	42.16	44.03	37.23	37.14	38.40	29.57
Nonagricultural	182.11	193.05	173.97	164.68	181.50	186.36
Volume	201.81	198.23	173.97	167.60	184.29	195.60
Deflator	90.27	97.42	99.98	98.25	98.50	95.28
Merchandise imports	249.78	265.09	247.67	268.90	332.42	338.08
Oil	79.41	77.79	61.27	54.99	57.31	50.39
Nonoil	170.37	187.29	186.40	213.91	275.11	287.69
Volume	173.06	184.96	186.38	219.20	285.24	307.44
Deflator	98.49	101.28	100.01	97.62	96.47	93.57
Trade balance	−25.51	−28.00	−36.47	−67.08	−112.52	−122.15
NONA	11.75	5.76	−12.43	−49.23	−93.60	−101.33
Services exports	118.22	139.42	138.37	132.72	140.87	144.64
Factor	72.51	86.41	83.55	77.25	85.91	88.84
DI income	37.15	32.55	21.38	20.50	21.22	33.20
Other private	32.80	50.18	58.05	51.92	59.46	50.13
Gov't	2.56	3.68	4.12	4.83	5.23	5.50
Nonfactor	45.71	53.00	54.83	55.47	54.96	55.80
Services imports	83.27	97.09	101.65	102.41	123.32	122.59
Factor	42.12	52.33	54.88	52.38	67.42	62.90
DI income	8.64	6.90	3.16	5.60	9.23	6.08
Other private	20.89	28.55	33.44	28.95	38.42	35.52
Gov't	12.59	16.88	18.28	17.83	19.77	21.31
Nonfactor	41.15	44.76	46.76	50.03	55.90	59.69
Services balance	34.94	42.32	36.72	30.31	17.55	22.05
Factor services	30.39	34.08	28.67	24.87	18.49	25.93
Unilateral transfers	−7.59	−7.46	−8.96	−9.48	−12.10	−15.01
Current account	1.84	6.86	−8.70	−46.25	−107.08	−115.11
As % of GNP	0.07	0.23	−0.26	−1.36	−2.84	−2.87
Net external assets	95.10	129.99	125.73	78.48	−7.46	−122.97
Claims on foreigners						
DI	215.38	228.35	207.75	207.20	211.48	229.75
Other private	301.19	392.73	508.63	553.45	564.81	588.78
Gov't	79.37	87.60	97.39	102.14	108.70	119.75
Foreign claims on US						
DI	83.05	108.71	124.68	137.06	164.58	184.62
Other private	270.12	313.32	391.39	462.18	511.83	633.92
Other on gov't	147.67	156.66	171.98	185.07	216.03	242.72

DI = direct investment; NONA = nonagricultural, nonoil.
Note: 1980–87 are actual, 1988–92 projected figures.

1986	1987	1988	1989	1990	1991	1992
223.97	249.57	338.98	404.24	445.84	496.06	553.64
27.36	29.52	29.11	31.21	33.46	35.88	38.46
196.61	220.05	309.87	373.03	412.38	460.18	515.17
212.99	237.42	315.74	353.05	371.80	395.22	421.47
92.33	92.66	97.99	105.63	110.89	116.41	122.20
368.52	409.85	466.86	505.14	553.21	611.71	670.07
34.39	42.88	38.96	46.21	56.18	63.91	72.36
334.13	366.97	427.90	458.93	497.03	547.80	597.72
346.35	365.40	379.24	359.19	375.53	392.19	411.20
96.44	100.40	112.99	127.77	132.33	139.66	145.33
− 144.55	− 160.28	− 127.88	− 100.90	− 107.37	− 115.65	− 116.43
− 137.52	− 146.91	− 118.03	− 85.90	− 84.65	− 87.62	− 82.54
151.09	175.26	178.90	189.92	202.19	216.02	232.40
90.11	103.76	100.93	103.99	109.69	117.07	126.63
38.42	52.31	46.45	54.76	63.20	72.45	82.77
45.27	46.12	50.51	45.46	42.70	40.71	39.85
6.42	5.33	3.96	3.77	3.78	3.91	4.01
60.98	71.50	77.97	85.93	92.51	98.95	105.77
130.06	155.50	176.22	190.30	205.02	221.10	238.78
66.97	83.38	104.37	114.15	123.44	133.91	145.50
5.38	10.51	18.55	21.16	23.46	25.93	28.72
38.98	48.83	61.58	68.80	74.71	81.38	88.89
22.61	24.05	24.25	24.19	25.27	26.60	27.89
63.09	72.11	71.84	76.15	81.58	87.18	93.28
21.03	19.76	2.68	− 0.38	− 2.83	− 5.07	− 6.38
23.14	20.37	− 3.45	− 10.16	− 13.76	− 16.84	− 18.87
− 15.31	− 13.44	− 13.00	− 13.59	− 14.21	− 14.86	− 15.54
− 138.83	− 153.97	− 138.20	− 114.87	− 124.41	− 135.59	− 138.36
− 3.28	− 3.43	− 2.83	− 2.19	− 2.22	− 2.26	− 2.15
− 274.63	− 453.46	− 591.65	− 706.52	− 830.93	− 966.52	− 1,104.88
259.89	261.02	303.93	345.24	384.42	423.36	463.11
670.03	711.87	582.73	538.08	509.82	490.93	488.57
126.90	116.59	116.59	116.59	116.95	116.95	116.59
209.33	251.31	272.91	297.99	326.91	360.32	398.59
831.36	966.37	1,019.50	1,105.40	1,202.19	1,311.27	1,434.19
290.76	325.27	302.49	303.04	312.66	325.82	340.37

Source: US Department of Commerce, 1980–87.

billion in 1988, to an estimated $127.9 billion. In the event, the actual deficit amounted to $126.5 billion.[19] Thus, although the HHC model overstates both exports and imports for 1988 by approximately $20 billion, its trade balance projection is highly accurate.

The lagged effects of dollar depreciation through 1987 cause additional improvement in the trade deficit over the medium term. By 1989 the trade deficit declines to $100.9 billion. However, as the lagged effects of depreciation end, the trade deficit widens again from an ongoing gap effect, as imports still exceed exports, and comparable percentage increases in both (associated with income growth) widen the absolute difference between them. By 1990 the trade deficit rises again to $107.4 billion, and by 1992 it reaches $116.4 billion.

The outlook for the current account in the base case is even worse. The rising net external debt causes continued deterioration in the factor services accounts, as the United States makes increasing payments on investment income to foreigners. Thus, in 1988 for the first time the factor services balance turns negative, and swings from a surplus of $20.4 billion in 1987 to a deficit of $3.5 billion. By 1992, the factor services deficit reaches $18.9 billion, for a total swing of $39.3 billion from 1987.

The combined impact of the exhaustion of lagged exchange rate effects on the trade side and a mounting factor services deficit is that the current account deficit shows a pronounced U shape. In 1988 it declines by $15.8 billion, to $138.2 billion. The deficit falls another $23.3 billion, to $114.9 billion, in 1989. But thereafter it rises again and reaches $138.4 billion by 1992—only 10 percent less than in the peak deficit year of 1987. In a word, the baseline projection for the US current account shows a deceptive initial improvement but no net gain by 1992.

Because the dollar value of US trade and GNP increases over time, this outcome does mean some improvement in relative terms. The current account deficit declines from 48 percent of exports of goods and nonfactor services in 1987 to 21 percent by 1992, and from 3.4 percent of GNP to 2.1 percent. Even so, continuation of external financing needs in the range of $100 billion to $150 billion annually would risk macroeconomic shocks, and even if these could be safely navigated, their imposition of heavy debt-servicing burdens on the public in the future means that such an outcome is simply irresponsible and unacceptable in terms of policy objectives.

Table 3.2 also reports the projected path of US net external assets in the base case. From the end of 1987 until the end of 1992, the model indicates that US foreign assets should decline from $1,090 billion to $1,068 billion.

---

19. *Commerce Balance of Payments 1988.*

US foreign liabilities rise from $1,543 billion to $2,173 billion. Net foreign liabilities thus rise from $453 billion to $1,105 billion, or by $652 billion. Thus, the $39 billion deterioration in the net factor services balance from 1987 to 1992 is consistent with the decline of the net asset position combined with a marginal rate of return of approximately 6 percent.

In sum, with real exchange rates at their 1987:4 level, the US trade balance can be expected first to improve to only a $101 billion deficit by 1989 but then to rebound to $116 billion by 1992, while a deterioration of over $39 billion in factor services will mean the current account deficit falls no lower than to $115 billion by 1989 and then widens again to $138 billion by 1992, showing little improvement in nominal terms against the record-poor outcome for 1987. This prospective outcome can only be judged as discouraging and dangerous from the standpoint of economic stability. There is reason for concern that the outcome may be even worse, as the dollar strengthened in the first three quarters of 1988. The prospective impact of this perverse movement of the dollar, if sustained, is examined below.

Factor Services

A further word about the factor services account is warranted. The net balance by 1992 is not as unfavorable as might be expected from simple application of a market interest rate to the net external asset position. Thus, the net deficit on factor services in 1992 stands at $19 billion. In contrast, a 7 percent return on the net foreign liabilities outstanding at the end of 1991 ($966 billion) would yield a factor services deficit of $68 billion for 1992, over three times as large.

The reason for the surprisingly modest capital service deficit is that the average rate of return on US foreign assets exceeds that on assets held by foreigners in the United States. Thus, in 1992 US earnings on foreign assets amount to $126.6 billion, for an average rate of return of 12.3 percent on end-1991 assets abroad ($1.03 trillion). Foreign earnings on assets held in the United States in 1992 are $145.5 billion, representing an average yield of 7.3 percent on end-1991 foreign holdings in the United States ($2.0 trillion).

With the average rate of return 68 percent higher on US holdings abroad than on foreign assets in the United States, the effective burden of the US net external liability position is less severe than might be anticipated. However, this disparity does raise the question of whether the HHC model is too optimistic on factor services. Although there are good reasons why the rate of return on US foreign assets in the past has exceeded that on foreign holdings in the United States, it may be asked to what extent this asymmetry should be projected into the future.

Two factors account for the higher return on US assets abroad. First, the rate of return on direct foreign investment has been considerably higher for US investment abroad than for foreign investment in the United States. Bergsten and Islam calculate the two average rates at 13.1 percent and 6.2 percent, respectively, for 1980–85.[20] The usual explanation for the difference is that US direct investment abroad tends to be of older vintage, and thus relatively understated as measured by book value. Second, even the rate of return on private portfolio assets is higher for US holdings abroad (11.4 percent versus 8.1 percent in the 1980–85 period, according to Bergsten and Islam), largely because foreign holdings in the United States tend to be more oriented toward stocks whereas US holdings abroad tend to be more heavily placed in interest-bearing assets, and unrealized capital gains on stocks are not reported in earnings. The only category in which US foreign assets have a lower return than foreign assets in the United States is that of government assets, where the US government tends to hold low-yielding foreign assets such as claims on international organizations, whereas US government obligations to foreigners pay market rates.

It is appropriate to ask whether the differential return on direct investment in particular should be projected into the future. For new claims of identical vintage, it is reasonable to expect rates of return to be more symmetrical. In the HHC projections, the 1992 rate of return on end-1991 direct investment amounts to 19.6 percent for US holdings abroad, and only 8.0 percent on foreign direct investment in the United States (calculated from table 3.2). The corresponding rates on actual income in 1987 against end-1986 capital stock were 20.1 percent and 5.0 percent, respectively. The differential thus remains high.[21]

As a test of the plausibility of these estimates, direct investment stock and earnings by 1992 may be divided into the amounts from investment already in place by end-1987 and those from new investment in 1988–91. US direct investment abroad stood at $261 billion at the end of 1987 (table 3.2). Allowing for 4½ percent annual inflation, the nominal value of this stock should have grown to $311 billion by the end of 1991. Similarly, applying the inflation rate, nominal income from this investment stock should have risen from $46.5 billion in 1988 (table 3.2) to $55.7 billion by 1992. Subtracting these amounts from the totals at the end of the period,

20. C. Fred Bergsten and Shafiqul Islam, *The United States as a Debtor Country* (Washington: Institute for International Economics, forthcoming).

21. Note that the 1992 rate of return is composed of an especially high rate on investment in the oil sector (38.8 percent), and a lower rate in manufacturing and other direct investment (13.7 percent). The high rate in oil reflects the older vintage of investments and the sharp rise in oil prices since the early 1970s.

newly installed investment by end-1991 should amount to $112 billion, and the 1992 income from this investment to $27.1 billion, for a marginal rate of return of 24.2 percent.

The marginal investment thus shows a continuing high rate of return. A more conservative estimate might place the rate of return on newly installed investment at, say, 10 percent (still above the average return on direct investment by foreigners in the United States). On this basis, the contribution of the new direct investment to 1992 investment income would amount to $11.2 billion rather than $27.1 billion, and the estimate for 1992 direct investment income abroad would be reduced by approximately $16 billion, to $67 billion.

Otherwise the HHC capital service projections appear reasonable. For 1992, the rate of return on US portfolio holdings abroad is 8.1 percent, versus 6.8 percent on foreign portfolio assets in the United States (table 3.2, comparing 1992 income against the corresponding end-1991 capital stock)— not an inordinate divergence. On government assets, the US earns only 3.4 percent in 1992 whereas foreign holders of US government obligations earn 8.6 percent.

An alternative broad-brush means of examining the plausibility of the capital services projections is to make a single large adjustment for the base period value of net US foreign liabilities. By the first quarter of 1988, factor services had turned slightly negative in the US accounts. For practical purposes, then, it might be argued that the true net US external asset position at the end of 1987 was zero (rather than − $453 billion). Indeed, in 1987 a relatively large factor services surplus of $20 billion might have suggested that the US foreign asset position was still positive and sizable, but that outcome largely reflected one-time revaluation of capital associated with depreciation of the dollar during 1987, and by 1988 the balance on capital services fell to only $2.6 billion.[22]

If one assumes that "effective net external debt" was zero at the end of 1987, then the capital services account for 1992 would simply represent a reasonable rate of return as applied to the deterioration in the net foreign asset position from the end of 1987 to the end of 1991 (noting that each year's payments are based on the capital stock at the end of the previous year). This deterioration amounts to $513 billion in the base case (table 3.2). If one applies a rate of return of 7 percent, the capital services account in 1992 would be expected to stand at − $36 billion. This estimate is somewhat larger than the HHC estimate, essentially because it denies comparative advantage in international financial intermediation (a higher

22. *Commerce Balance of Payments 1988.*

return on assets than on liabilities) at the margin. Yet it is much closer to the HHC base case projection than would be a simple application of a market rate of return to the full nominal value of net foreign liabilities by 1992.

In sum, there are valid reasons why the future factor services deficit should not be as large as the nominal net external liability position might imply. Closer examination shows that higher returns on US foreign investment than on foreign investment in the United States do have justification. There may nonetheless be some bias toward optimism in the projections, and more conservative estimates enforcing more symmetrical returns on new capital assets acquired in the 1988–91 period could trim the factor services income projection by some $17 billion by 1992, raising the deficit in factor services from an estimated $19 billion to $36 billion (and the current account deficit to $155 billion). Moreover, as noted above, the capital services deficit could also be larger than projected because the assumption of 7 percent for the Treasury bill rate may be understated.

Alternative Projections

The medium-term projections here are consistent with several other major forecasts. Table 3.3 reports recent current account projections by various groups. The table also reports the projections of the EAG model (Chapters 4 and 5). As discussed in Chapter 5, the "best estimate" of this study is a simple average between the HHC and EAG projections.

In October of 1988, the IMF projected that the US current account deficit would stand at $129 billion in both 1988 and 1989. Projections by the Organization for Economic Cooperation and Development (OECD) published in December 1988 placed the 1988 deficit at $132 billion and that for 1989 at $116 billion. The actual outcome for 1988 was a current account deficit of $135.3 billion, extremely close to the HHC and EAG projections. For 1989, the HHC and EAG projections are within the same range as the IMF and OECD projections.

Projections by private analysts provide an outlook through 1992. In the third quarter of 1988, Wharton Econometric Forecasting Associates (WEFA) projected that under existing policy the current account deficit would fall no lower than $138 billion, and would rise again to $161 billion by 1992. In early 1988, Ralph Bryant projected a similar U-shaped profile, with the trough occurring at $108 billion in 1989 and a more moderate increase thereafter (on the basis of a Brookings Institution survey of five major macroeconomic models). Working with the Data Resources, Inc. (DRI), model, in September 1988 Nigel Gault projected baseline deficits that reached

Table 3.3 Alternative projections of the US current account balance
(billions of current dollars)

Study	Date	Real exchange rate basis	Projections 1988	1989	1990	1991	1992
IMF	October 1988	August 1988	−129	−129			
OECD	December 1988	November 2, 1988	−132	−116	−108		
DRI-Gault	December 1987	July 1988					
Excluding trend term[a]			−137	−134	−154	−177	−201
Including trend term			−133	−138	−169	−204	−243
DRI-business	October 1988	Rate not fixed	−134	−126	−96	−83	−92
WEFA	September 1988	Rate not fixed	−143	−137	−138	−156	−161
Bryant	January 1988	December 22, 1987	−125	−108	−113	−127	
Cline	November 1988	1987:4					
HHC			−138	−115	−124	−136	−138
EAG			−137	−122	−135	−151	−168
Average			−137	−119	−130	−143	−153

a. The DRI forecasts are made with and without a term to incorporate the past adverse trend in the current account.

Sources: International Monetary Fund (IMF), World Economic Outlook, October 1988, 92; Organization for Economic Cooperation and Development, OECD Economic Outlook, December 1988, 71; Nigel Gault, "The Outlook for the US Current Account Deficit," Testimony before the Joint Economic Committee, US Congress, 13 September 1988, and by communication; Ralph C. Bryant, "The US External Deficit: An Update," Brookings Discussion Papers in International Economics 63, January 1988, Table 3; WEFA Group, US Macro Model: Medium-Term Forecast (Bala Cynwyd, Penn.: WEFA, 1988); DRI, International Business and Financial Outlook: Third Quarter 1988 (Lexington, Mass.: DRI, 1988:3), 42.

$200 billion by 1992 (and over $240 billion if the past adverse trend term was included), although in the actual DRI business forecast, which incorporates expected exchange rate changes as well as adjustment factors, the 1992 deficit was estimated at only about $90 billion.

Although the specific dates and assumptions of these projections vary, their broad pattern is relatively uniform and coincides with that identified in this study. The principal official and private forecasts place the US current account deficit in a range of $100 billion to $150 billion through 1992, and in most cases the forecasts identify an initial reduction followed by a subsequent rebound in the size of the deficit (with the low point typically in 1989). The pattern of initial improvement reflects further exchange rate effects in the pipeline. The subsequent worsening is caused by the fact that, after the corrective effects of US dollar depreciation through 1987 are exhausted in 1989, a large absolute gap remains between imports and exports. As normal income growth causes both imports and exports to grow at relatively similar rates in 1990 and after, the absolute gap between the two widens. In addition, there is a deterioration in the balance on capital services because of growing net external debt.

The DRI–Gault projections highlight a major issue: whether there is a strong long-term trend that is adverse to US trade. As indicated above, the HHC model incorporates the secular trend in a variable for relative capital stock. Because the projections here show no further change in relative US capital stock through 1992 (based on extrapolation of the trend since 1985 as discussed above), a secular adverse effect is absent in the projections here. Bosworth has conducted statistical tests that tend to confirm the view that any adverse long-term trend has declined to practically nil in recent years.[23]

Impact of Exchange Rate Depreciation

The logical question to ask in view of the inadequacy of the external adjustment already in the pipeline for the United States is, what further measures are necessary? At a proximate level, the two possible sets of measures are exchange rate changes and changes in the growth paths of the United States and its trading partners. At an underlying level, the key policy change is reduction of the US fiscal deficit. Although the HHC model does not explicitly incorporate fiscal policy (which, for example, is absent in

---

23. Barry Bosworth, "Comments and Discussion," *Brookings Papers on Economic Activity*, 1987, no. 1, 46–47.

equations 1 through 4 above), it implicitly assumes that broader fiscal and monetary policy is consistent with implementation of changes in the variables directly in the model, and with exchange rate change in particular.

The mainstream formulation of the relationship between fiscal policy, the exchange rate, and the external accounts is the Mundell–Fleming frame-work.[24] It provides that, in a world with capital mobility and floating exchange rates, fiscal expansion drives up both income (and hence import demand) and interest rates, thereby attracting capital inflows and bidding up the value of the dollar. The rise of the dollar reduces net exports, partially offsetting the output expansion from fiscal expansion but reinforcing the impact on external accounts. In the case of the needed US adjustment, in this formulation fiscal restraint would reduce domestic demand and imports, and further cut the trade deficit by leading to further dollar decline.

An alternative tradition assigns a potentially more independent role to fiscal policy. The "absorption approach" of Sidney Alexander[25] starts with the national income accounting identity that states that the current account balance equals the excess of domestic saving (including fiscal revenue) over domestic expenditure (including government spending). Alexander stressed the reduction of domestic expenditure ("absorption") relative to production as the key to correcting an external deficit. He was skeptical that exchange rate changes alone (pursuing the "trade elasticities approach") would accomplish adjustment in the absence of a cut in absorption. At the operational level, the IMF for years has applied the absorption approach in insisting in its stabilization programs that fiscal correction accompany exchange rate changes.

A recent restatement of the elasticities–absorption debate has arisen from the insistence of Ronald McKinnon (and Robert Mundell) that, in a world with capital mobility, exchange rate changes are both unnecessary and unlikely to correct the US external deficit, whereas by implication fiscal adjustment would do so.[26] Krugman has disputed the McKinnon view by invoking the simple difference in expenditure propensities between coun-tries: any country tends to spend a larger fraction of additional income on its own goods than on imports, so that a fiscal cutback in the United States matched by a fiscal expansion in Europe and Japan will leave excess supply of US goods and excess demand for European and Japanese goods that can

---

24. See, for example, John Williamson, *The Open Economy and the World Economy* (New York: Basic Books, 1983), 217–24.

25. *Ibid.*, 156–60.

26. Ronald McKinnon, *An International Standard for Monetary Stabilization*, POLICY ANALYSES IN INTERNATIONAL ECONOMICS 8 (Washington: Institute for International Economics, March 1984).

only be eliminated by a change in their relative prices, and thus a change in the exchange rate. Thus, depreciation should accompany fiscal correction.[27]

At the policy level, the issue remains whether further depreciation of the dollar would provide additional correction of the US external deficit in the absence of further reductions in the budget deficit. The mainstream answer is in the negative. The essential reason is that, as the economy nears capacity, further depreciation and export expansion tend to generate domestic inflation that erodes the real depreciation and competitiveness, unless room is made for increased exports through reduction in demand from the fiscal side. Because the induced inflation would tend to be less than the initial exchange rate depreciation, there would still be some real depreciation and correction of the external deficit even without fiscal adjustment. The change in the relative price of tradeables and nontradeables would cause some expenditure switching, and the tendency for real wages to decline from rising inflation would contribute some adjustment from expenditure reduction. Overall, however, the consequences of depreciation without fiscal correction would be higher inflation and limited external adjustment.

The model simulations that follow examine the impact of further dollar depreciation on the US external balance. As the foregoing discussion indicates, however, the assumption is that fiscal adjustment is consistent with further depreciation, so that it is not thwarted in its potential impact.[28] The absence of more explicit treatment of fiscal policy in the model is one of the limitations of any partial-equilibrium external sector forecasting model.[29]

Table 3.4 reports the simulation estimates of the HHC model for alternative degrees of additional depreciation of the dollar beyond its real level in the

---

27. Paul Krugman, "Adjustment in the World Economy," *Occasional Paper* 24 (New York: Group of Thirty, December 1987).

28. An important ambiguity that arises even within the framework of the now-standard Mundell–Fleming model is how to interpret the likely coordination of exchange rate and fiscal policy once expectations are taken into account. In particular, a reversal of expectations played a large role in the decline of the dollar from its February 1985 peak to its end-1987 level. In the Mundell–Fleming model, the decline of the dollar could only have occurred as the result of a sharp decrease in the US fiscal deficit (or increase in the money supply), which would be an overly generous description of the fiscal adjustment to date.

29. For further discussion of the justification for direct application of the exchange rate and the growth rate as policy variables, rather than the underlying fiscal deficit and monetary targets, see the section on "The Impact of Policy Measures" in Chapter 1. For translation of the simulated policy package into corresponding fiscal and monetary policy, see the discussion of "Policy Implications" for the United States in Chapter 1.

fourth quarter of 1987. These additional depreciations are phased in evenly during the course of 1989.

It is important to recognize that the depreciation is in real terms, as measured by the nominal exchange rate deflated by the Consumer Price Index. There is no feedback in the model from depreciation to increased US domestic consumer price inflation (although export prices are affected), nor from appreciation of the Japanese yen (for example) to reduced domestic consumer price inflation in Japan. Because such feedback does exist, in general the real depreciation rates examined in table 3.4 will correspond to somewhat larger nominal depreciation rates.

The simulation results shown in the table indicate that the US current account deficit is sensitive to the exchange rate. A 5 percent further real depreciation against all currencies would cut the US current account deficit from $138 billion in 1992 to $100 billion. A depreciation of 10 percent would reduce the deficit by 1992 to $61 billion and one of 15 percent to a deficit of $20 billion. A 20 percent real depreciation would bring the 1992 current account to a surplus of $22 billion.

The table shows the composition of this improvement. Consider the case of a 10 percent real depreciation against all currencies. The total improvement in the current account by 1992 is $77 billion. Of this amount, $44 billion, or approximately three-fifths, comes from the increased dollar value of exports. Only $8 billion, or about one-tenth, comes from a reduction in the dollar value of imports. This small reduction in nominal imports reflects the fact that the price elasticity of demand for imports is only marginally larger than unity.

That the trade value adjustment will have to come mainly on the export side is widely recognized. What is less commonly perceived, however, is that a large portion of the external adjustment to exchange rate change comes on the side of services. Within services, the largest gains come in factor services (net income on capital assets). Thus, in the case of the 10 percent depreciation, the factor services balance improves by $18 billion by 1992, accounting for 23 percent of the total current account improvement against the base case. Nonfactor services contribute the remaining improvement of $7 billion. (As in the case of merchandise trade, the improvement in nonfactor services comes primarily on the side of exports.)

As a check on the plausibility of these estimates, it is useful to consider the implied total "value" (as opposed to quantity) elasticity of merchandise trade with respect to the exchange rate. By 1992 the increase in nominal dollar export value resulting from the 10 percent depreciation is 7.9 percent ($44 billion/$554 billion), whereas the reduction in nominal imports is 1.2 percent. The implied value elasticity is 0.79 for exports and 0.12 for imports.

Table 3.4 Impact of real dollar depreciation on US external accounts, 1988–92

(billions of current dollars)

	1988	1989	1990	1991	1992
Current account					
Base case	−138	−115	−124	−136	−138
After depreciation					
Against all countries					
5%	−138	−112	−110	−105	−100
10%	−138	−109	−95	−74	−61
15%	−138	−106	−80	−42	−20
20%	−138	−103	−64	−10	22
Against strong countries[a]					
5%	−138	−113	−114	−114	−111
10%	−138	−110	−103	−92	−83
15%	−138	−109	−93	−70	−55
20%	−138	−106	−82	−47	−26
Including Canada					
5%	−138	−112	−113	−111	−107
10%	−138	−110	−101	−85	−74
15%	−138	−107	−89	−60	−42
20%	−138	−105	−77	−34	−9
Exports					
Base case	339	404	445	496	554
After depreciation					
Against all countries					
5%	339	406	456	515	576
10%	339	407	467	535	598
15%	339	409	478	555	622
20%	339	410	489	576	646
Against strong countries					
5%	339	405	454	511	571
10%	339	407	462	526	589
15%	339	408	471	542	607
20%	339	409	479	558	625
Including Canada					
5%	339	405	455	512	572
10%	339	407	464	529	591
15%	339	408	473	545	611
20%	339	409	482	563	631

	1988	1989	1990	1991	1992
Imports					
Base case	467	505	553	612	670
After depreciation					
Against all countries					
5%	467	508	554	609	666
10%	467	510	555	607	662
15%	467	512	557	604	658
20%	467	515	558	602	653
Against strong countries					
5%	467	507	554	610	667
10%	467	508	555	609	665
15%	467	509	555	608	662
20%	467	511	556	606	660
Including Canada					
5%	467	507	554	660	666
10%	467	509	555	608	663
15%	467	511	556	606	660
20%	467	513	557	604	656
Factor services					
Base case	− 3	− 10	− 14	− 17	− 19
After depreciation					
Against all countries					
5%	− 3	− 7	− 10	− 11	− 10
10%	− 3	− 3	− 7	− 5	− 1
15%	− 3	1	− 3	1	9
20%	− 3	4	1	7	19
Against strong countries					
5%	− 3	− 8	− 12	− 13	− 13
10%	− 3	− 6	− 10	− 10	− 7
15%	− 3	− 4	− 8	− 6	− 2
20%	− 3	− 1	− 6	− 3	4
Including Canada					
5%	− 3	− 7	− 11	− 13	− 12
10%	− 3	− 4	− 9	− 8	− 5
15%	− 3	− 1	− 6	− 4	2
20%	− 3	2	− 3	1	10

a. Strong countries = industrial countries (including or excluding Canada), Korea, and Taiwan.

These overall parameters would appear reasonable.[30] Nonetheless, as indicated above and as evident in the comparison of "policy parameters" for the HHC and EAG models (table 5.5), the relatively low export elasticity in the HHC model may understate the responsiveness of the trade balance to exchange rate change.

The important contribution of the factor services account to the improvement resulting from depreciation warrants further investigation. The basic influence in this result is that depreciation of the dollar causes an increased valuation of the dollar equivalent of foreign assets (denominated in deutsche marks, yen, and so forth), without any corresponding increase in the valuation of foreign holdings of dollar-denominated assets in the United States.

Consider the HHC equation[31] for income from US direct investment abroad in the manufacturing sector, excluding capital gains:

$$(5) \qquad \ln X_{Kdm} = 6.278 \ln (Y_f/Y_f^*) + 0.0565 \ln (K_{dm,t-1} P_{18}/E_{18}) + H$$

where Y_f is foreign GNP (investment-weighted) and Y_f^* the corresponding potential foreign output, X_{Kdm} is the investment income in question, K_{dm} is real direct investment abroad in manufacturing, $t-1$ refers to the previous period, P is the foreign consumer price index, E is the foreign exchange rate, the subscript 18 refers to 18 large trading partners (with investment weights for both the price and exchange rate indexes), and H is a set of constants for the various quarters and a dummy variable for 1981. Here, the exchange rate in yen per dollar (for example) enters in the denominator of the second term on the right hand side, so that when the dollar depreciates,

---

30. Note that in approximate terms these value elasticities may be derived directly from equations 1 to 4 above. A 1 percent exchange rate depreciation causes dollar prices of exports to rise by 0.21 percent (equation 1). The relative US export price thus declines by 0.79 percent (a 1 percent depreciation partially offset by a 0.21 percent dollar export price rise). From equation 2, this change causes an increase in export volume by 0.649 percent (that is, $0.822 \times 0.79 = 0.649$). Adding the volume change to the dollar price change, the overall value elasticity of exports with respect to the exchange rate is 0.86 (that is, $1.00649 \times 1.0021 = 1.0086$). On the import side, a 1 percent depreciation raises import prices by 0.903 percent (equation 3). This change reduces import volume by $0.903 \times 1.147 = 1.036$ percent (equation 4), for a net decline in value of about 0.13 percent.

31. Note that while the trade equations listed above are precisely the same as those in the original Helkie–Hooper study, all other equations in the HHC model may have slight variations. For facility of entry into the MODLER simulation program, they were simply reestimated for the same time period as the original HH model, but revisions in the data sets meant slight changes in parameters. Also note that most of the factor service equations are estimated with an ending period of 1986:4 rather than 1984:4 (the endpoint for the trade equations), in keeping with the most recent available version of the HH model.

the dollar value of foreign investment earnings increases. This valuation effect contributed handsomely to the profits of US multinationals in 1987.

In contrast, there is no exchange rate valuation effect on US earnings on portfolio investments abroad. These earnings merely equal the estimated rate of return multiplied by the stock of portfolio claims on foreigners. The rate of return for its part is determined by the US Treasury bill rate and the lagged value of the rate of return. The absence of valuation effects on US portfolio claims abroad reflects the fact that a considerable portion of these claims are denominated in dollars, as in the case of Eurodollar deposits. To the extent that US citizens hold foreign stocks and other nondollar assets in their portfolios, there is a bias toward conservatism in the model's estimation of the impact of dollar depreciation on the factor services account.

There is a deeper economic significance to the improvement on the factor services account that arises from further dollar depreciation. Essentially, foreigners have accumulated claims against the United States in dollar-denominated assets, whereas an important part of US claims abroad are in foreign currency-denominated assets (direct investment). The United States is thus in a position to grant itself debt relief by dollar depreciation. That is, depreciation does not increase the capital payments to foreigners because there is no exchange rate valuation effect to incorporate, whereas depreciation does increase the income from foreign assets of US citizens. In contrast, for debtor countries such as Brazil, foreign claims on the country tend to be denominated in foreign currencies (dollars, deutsche marks, yen), and so Brazil cannot lighten its debt burden by depreciation of its own currency.

There are presumably limits to this process of external adjustment through the asymmetrical effects of depreciation on the factor services account. Depreciation tends to be inflationary, and thus to raise the inflation premium in the domestic interest rate, and along with it the interest rate paid to foreigners on their holdings of US portfolio assets. However, at least so far US inflation and interest rates have shown only moderate feedback from dollar depreciation. A more fundamental limit to adjustment in this dimension would arise if foreigners began to insist that further claims on the United States be denominated in the currencies of the foreign holders (as in the case of the Carter bonds of the late 1970s). In that event, depreciation would begin to cause an adverse valuation effect on factor services, because the dollar value of obligations on such instruments would rise as the dollar depreciated.

Returning to the central results of table 3.4, the broad finding is that real depreciation of the dollar by somewhat less than 15 percent against all other currencies, beyond its level of 1987:4, would be required to bring the 1992 current account deficit into what would appear a sustainable range (modestly under $50 billion annually). Although such a depreciation is by no means small, to some degree this finding may nonetheless seem surprising in its implication that an intermediate range of further depreciation would deal with the deficit even though a seemingly large depreciation through 1987 had failed to do so.

By late 1987 there was an atmosphere of despair that the external deficit could ever decline substantially as the result of dollar depreciation, and many questioned its potential effectiveness. Ironically, by the third quarter of 1988 there had been a major shift in sentiment, at least as implied by the strength of the dollar. The dollar's rebound (for example, from 1.58 DM on December 31, 1987, to 1.88 DM on August 15, 1988) suggested that market actors suddenly became overly enthused about the prospects for US adjustment, as they began to see monthly trade deficits decline. Specifically, the deficits had been in the range of $12 billion monthly through most of 1987. When an initial report placed the March 1988 deficit at only $9 billion (with imports on a c.i.f. basis), optimism stirred. Simplistic straight-line projections of the trend could have led some to conclude that the deficit was on its way to full elimination in the not-too-distant future.

As analyzed below, the increase in the dollar's value in the following months could have proved to be extremely damaging to adjustment prospects, if it had persisted. Instead, as might have been expected based on models of the type examined here, this episode became what could be called the bubble of 1988, as the dollar had lost most of its gains by late in the year. Nonetheless, rising US interest rates provided a new boost to the dollar in early 1989, and there was some risk that the result would be the bubble of 1988–89.

It is useful, then, to return to the prevalent attitude of the last quarter of 1987, when the central questions were whether trade adjustment could ever occur, and why there had been so little improvement despite the massive depreciation of the dollar since its peak in 1985:1. More specifically, it may be asked why a further depreciation of the dollar in real terms by less than 15 percent from its 1987:4 level would be sufficient to bring the US current account deficit down to a tolerable level if the large preceding depreciation had done so little.

The reasons for this seeming paradox are the following. First, the observed US external deficit during 1986–87 was considerably lower than what would have occurred if the dollar had not begun its descent after the first quarter of 1985, and the deficit that could have been expected by the early 1990s was correspondingly much higher than that projected here with end-1987 real exchange rates. Marris has estimated that if the dollar had stayed at its real level of 1984:4–1985:1, by 1990 the current account deficit would have reached $320 billion.[32] Simulation of the HHC model at constant real exchange rates of 1985:1 gives even more dramatic results: the current account deficit would have mushroomed to $339 billion by 1990 and $437 billion by 1992 if the dollar had not declined from its peak. On this basis, the total adjustment already taking place is much greater than suggested by the path of the actually observed US current account deficit, and accordingly the additional adjustment that may be purchased by 15 percent further real depreciation of the dollar is less surprising in proportional terms.

Second, there is an important "gap factor" at work that makes the improvement nonlinear (box 3.1). A given percentage depreciation brings a certain percentage increase in export value and another, much smaller percentage reduction in import value. At the beginning of the process when imports are extremely high relative to exports, the small proportionate change is working on the large base (imports) while the large proportionate change is affecting a smaller base (exports). Later, as some adjustment has taken place, the larger percentage change on the export side works on an export base that is now considerably larger than before relative to imports.

Specifically, the simulations here indicate that the value elasticity of exports with respect to exchange rate depreciation is 0.79 and that of imports −0.12. In 1986 when exports were $224 billion and imports $369 billion, a 10 percent depreciation applying these summary elasticities would have meant an increase of $18 billion in exports and a reduction of imports by $5 billion. By 1992 when the export base should stand at $550 billion and the import base at $670 billion, the same percentage depreciation and value elasticities imply an export increase of $43 billion and an import reduction of $8 billion.

Third, ongoing dollar inflation balloons the dollar amounts of trade correction that may be obtained by a given percentage depreciation. In the numerical example given above, both import and export values had risen in part because of inflation. Specifically, with US inflation at 4½ percent annually, by 1992 all dollar magnitudes rise by approximately 25 percent solely from US inflation. The dollar size of the trade correction achievable by 1992 from a given percentage change in the exchange rate tends to escalate correspondingly.

Fourth, a 15 percent real depreciation of the dollar against all currencies is relatively large compared to the depreciation that had already taken place by 1987:4. Thus, as discussed in Chapter 2, from the dollar's peak in the first quarter of 1985 to 1987:4, the real exchange rate of the dollar against 18 large trading partners (multilateral trade weights, foreign consumer price

---

32. Stephen Marris, *Deficits and the Dollar: The World Economy at Risk*, POLICY ANALYSES IN INTERNATIONAL ECONOMICS 14 (Washington: Institute for International Economics, 1987 edition), 86.

Box 3.1 The Impact of Exchange Rate Changes on Imports and Exports: The Gap Factor

The gap factor may be illustrated by a diagram relating the exchange rate to the level of exports and imports. In figure 3.1, the vertical axis shows nominal trade values. The horizontal axis shows the exchange rate (dollars per unit of foreign currency). The X curve indicates the dollar value of exports at a given exchange rate, and the M curve the dollar value of imports. Their slopes and curvatures reflect the greater impact of the exchange rate on export value than on import value.

Figure 3.1 The gap factor

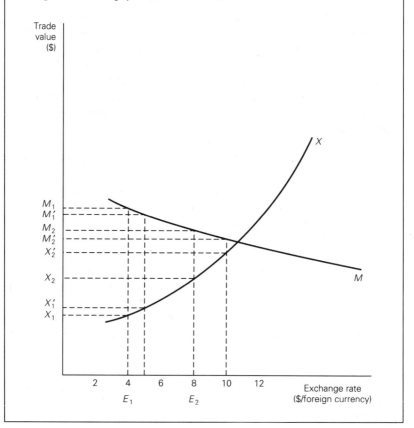

At a strong level of the dollar, E_1, a given proportionate change in the exchange rate (in the illustration, by one-fourth) causes export value to rise by the vertical distance X_1 to X_1' and imports to decline by the distance M_1 to M_1'. At a weaker dollar level, E_2, where the export base is much larger relative to imports, the same proportionate depreciation causes a much larger absolute rise in exports (distance X_2 to X_2') while the decline in imports remains small (distance M_2 to M_2'). In short, the impact of a given percentage depreciation on the trade balance is nonlinear and rises as the export base comes closer to the import base.

The gap factor disappears if the value elasticities of imports and exports with respect to the exchange rate are identical. In that case, the X and M curves are symmetrical. The smaller initial base for exports is fully offset by the larger initial import base, which now makes a proportional contribution to trade deficit reduction equal to that of exports (because of equal value elasticities). When exports have risen and imports have declined, the relative sizes of their contributions to improvement change places, but the total improvement does not. Note, however, that identical value elasticities would imply the unlikely situation that the volume elasticity for imports exceeded (in absolute value) that for exports by unity, to offset the impact of rising price on the import side.

and US export-weighted wholesale price deflators) declined from an index of 137.0 to 83.9 (with 1980 = 100). In real terms, then, the dollar lost 38.8 percent of its value, and using the real exchange rate for imports the reduction was only 25 percent against these currencies. Another 15 percent real depreciation would thus extend the decline of the dollar that had occurred already by another two-fifths to three-fifths.

It is only against such currencies as the yen and the deutsche mark that the percentage changes have been much greater. Thus, over the same period the dollar fell from 3.26 DM to 1.71 DM, a reduction of 47.5 percent, while it fell from 257.7 yen to 135.8 yen, or by 47.3 percent.[33] Because of the

---

33. IMF, *International Financial Statistics*, March 1988.

importance of Canada and developing country trading partners whose currencies have not appreciated against the dollar, the overall real depreciation of the dollar has been only one-half to three-fourths as large (depending on the use of the HHC import or export real exchange rate). In short, an additional 15 percent depreciation of the dollar in real terms against all trading partners would be relatively large compared to the depreciation that had already taken place by the fourth quarter of 1987.

The final reason why an extra 15 percent real depreciation causes a more complete solution to the external deficit than some might believe is that the depreciation is real, not nominal. As noted above, a significantly larger nominal depreciation might be required for the same real depreciation. In reviewing various studies of the feedback from dollar depreciation to consumer prices in the United States, Marris settles on a coefficient of 0.15; for the feedback of dollar depreciation to consumer prices in foreign countries, he places the coefficient at 0.10.[34] On this basis, to achieve a 15 percent depreciation in real terms would require nominal depreciation of the dollar by 18.75 percent (with the extra 3.75 percent necessary to offset the 1.5 percent reduction in foreign consumer prices and the 2.25 percent increase in US consumer prices).

A central thrust of these findings is nonetheless that the US external accounts are closer to adjustment through further depreciation of the dollar than at least some observers contend, but much further from adjustment than the ebullient course of the dollar in the first three quarters of 1988 would imply. Some leading economists have argued that the dollar may have to fall by as much as an additional 30 percent.[35] The results here suggest that a real depreciation of 15 percent from the 1987:4 level, or a nominal depreciation of 18¾ percent, would be sufficient, even without further measures such as acceleration of foreign growth or deceleration of US growth, to bring the current account deficit to a manageable range by

---

34. Stephen Marris, *Deficits and the Dollar*, 276.

35. Feldstein in particular is associated with the 30 percent figure. Martin Feldstein, "A Self-interested Way to Avoid Death in Venice," *Financial Times*, 20 May 1987, 27. Note, however, that the dollar had already fallen by 8 percent from May to the end of 1987 (in real terms against the 18 currencies examined in this study). Moreover, Feldstein was referring to the nominal exchange rate against the mark and the yen, and he anticipated 3 to 4 percentage points annual depreciation to be necessary just to compensate for the lower inflation in Germany and Japan than in the United States. Allowing 15 percent for this factor (3 to 4 percent inflation over three to five years, in his terms), Feldstein was implicitly calling for only a 15 percent real devaluation over three to five years, of which half has already taken place (abstracting from the dollar's rebound in early 1988). The remaining 7 percent in real terms is actually smaller than the amount identified here as the further real depreciation required.

1992. This outcome would, however, require implementation of fiscal and monetary policy adjustment consistent with achievement of the 15 percent real depreciation of the dollar.

Table 3.4 also reports the results of a depreciation of the dollar only against areas that are in relatively strong current account positions and thus more likely to be able to appreciate than other regions. This subgroup includes all the industrial countries except Canada, as well as Taiwan and Korea. It excludes Canada because of that country's sizable current account deficit in 1987 ($7 billion, or approximately 6 percent of exports of goods and nonfactor services). It also excludes Latin America, other developing countries, and OPEC. As indicated in the table, limitation of the real depreciation to change against this subgroup of stronger countries reduces the impact on the US external accounts. In this case, a 10 percent real depreciation of the dollar causes the US current account deficit to decline by $55 billion in 1992 from the base case outcome, rather than by $77 billion when the depreciation is against all foreign currencies. Thus, restriction of foreign appreciation to the countries with relatively stronger external accounts still permits 71 percent of the impact achieved when all foreign currencies appreciate. By implication, the required extent of real depreciation (from 1987:4) rises from the 15 percent range to about 20 percent, which when stated in nominal terms translates to some 25 percent.

The table also reports the impact of depreciation when the strong-country group is expanded to include Canada. In this case, a 10 percent real decline in the dollar against this group of countries (from 1987:4 levels) causes the 1992 current account deficit to decline by $64 billion, raising the magnitude of the adjustment by approximately 16 percent and bringing the total for the strong-group case to 83 percent of the amount obtained when the dollar depreciates against all foreign currencies. As expected from its large role in US trade, Canada's inclusion makes a major difference to the scope for US adjustment.

Impact of Differential Growth

Beyond, or instead of, exchange rate depreciation, the level of aggregate demand is an alternative variable that can affect the external account. Whereas the exchange rate is an intermediate variable that policymakers can to some extent affect directly through intervention and jawboning, but that nonetheless reflects underlying fiscal and monetary policies, domestic demand and especially growth are one step further removed from the fundamental policy variables. As in the case of postulated real exchange rate changes, in analyzing the impact of changes in domestic demand and/

or growth it is necessary to assume that fiscal and monetary policy is being modified in a way that is consistent with the specified change.

The basic influence of aggregate demand, or economic growth, on the external accounts occurs through its impact on imports. Thus, in equations 2 and 4 above, the HHC model relates US export volume positively to foreign real GNP (Y_w) and import volume to US real GNP (Y). Higher growth abroad contributes to adjustment of the deficit on the export side, and lower US growth can further adjustment on the import side.[36] Adjustment of an external deficit through reduction in demand is sometimes referred to as adjustment through "expenditure reduction," in contrast to the adjustment through "expenditure switching" that occurs as exchange rate change causes a change in the relative price between tradeables and nontradeables. Expenditure switching tends to have either a positive or a neutral effect on domestic growth (as the production of exports and import substitutes expands but with some cutback in the production of nontradeables), whereas expenditure reduction tends to have negative growth effects (unless the cutback in domestic components of demand can be exactly offset by rising demand for exports).

There is an important conceptual distinction between domestic demand and economic growth that is not captured in the HHC model applied here. In the absorption approach, it is domestic demand that determines imports. Growth itself, and thus total production, actually have the opposite effect on the trade balance. That is, if output rises with no change in absorption, there is a greater surplus to be exported and a rise in the trade balance.

At a more operational level, there is another distinction between growth and domestic demand that is relevant. For a country in which imports are primarily intermediate inputs into the production process, imports would tend to be a function of GNP growth. In an economy in which imports are primarily final consumer goods, imports would depend on domestic demand rather than output.[37]

---

36. Note that the cyclical state of the economy could also affect the other sides of the trade flows, respectively. Slower growth in the United States would tend to mean lower capacity utilization and greater scope for "vent for surplus" exports; similarly, faster growth abroad could reduce foreign supply and thus US imports. Statistically significant terms in these directions are found for equations estimated for bilateral US–Japan trade in C. Fred Bergsten and William R. Cline, *The US–Japan Economic Problem*, POLICY ANALYSES IN INTERNATIONAL ECONOMICS 13 (Washington: Institute for International Economics, October 1985), 153–54.

37. Note that Hooper and Mann have reestimated one version of the HH model using the alternative formulation of domestic demand rather than GNP growth. They have doubts about the estimates because of simultaneity problems, and conclude that the best variable may be a hybrid attributing a weight of one-half to domestic demand and one-half to GNP. Hooper and Mann, "The U.S. External Deficit: Its Causes and Persistence."

In the dimension of "growth" the absence of explicit incorporation of fiscal policy into partial-equilibrium analysis of the external accounts once again causes problems for policy interpretation. With output (GNP) as the variable assumed to influence imports, the means of influencing the trade balance through fiscal policy implicitly becomes reducing the growth of GNP through fiscal contraction. If imports were instead a function of domestic demand, fiscal contraction could be interpreted as the means of reducing domestic demand and thus imports but without necessarily having a major (or, conceivably, any) adverse effect on output and growth.[38]

In sum, simulations of the trade effects of changes in growth rates must be interpreted with caution, and as imperfect proxies for trade changes resulting from domestic demand variations that result from fiscal (and monetary) policy measures. In particular, it is essentially counterproductive for global economic welfare to recommend adjustment through imposition of low growth rates in the deficit area at levels well below potential growth. Yet when fiscal contraction is combined with monetary ease, the result should be a reduction in the real exchange rate that boosts net exports and thus the contribution of the foreign sector to demand even as domestic demand is cut back from the fiscal adjustment. With this change in policy mix, there can be reduction in domestic demand without reduction in growth of GNP. Correspondingly, recommendations for high growth in surplus areas may appear implausible to critics but actually overstate the increases in growth rates required for adjustment in view of the fact that it may be domestic demand in those countries that drives imports rather than growth, and domestic demand can rise by much more than production (because of capital and other constraints on the latter).

When the real exchange rate is held constant, domestic demand and growth move together. Thus, if fiscal policy tightens and reduces domestic demand, in the absence of an offsetting increase in foreign demand from an exchange rate change, domestic production will tend to decrease as well. In the policy simulations that follow, the intent is to examine the influence of changing domestic demand and growth with all else held constant, and the "variable" driving the change in trade may be viewed interchangeably

---

38. It is clear that, if the exchange rate is allowed to vary, the stimulus to exports and import substitution from relative price change can neutralize the growth-reducing impact of fiscal contraction from the side of domestic demand. It requires more extreme, essentially "small country," assumptions to avoid growth reduction when fiscal contraction is applied and the exchange rate is held fixed. In that case this adjustment is, however, possible. Foreign demand curves are infinitely elastic, and the slightest incipient decline in the relative price of the home country's product causes an increase in exports that completely offsets the reduction in domestic demand.

Table 3.5 Impact of growth on US external accounts, 1988–92
(billions of current dollars)

Case	Dollar	Assumptions Foreign growth	US growth	1988	1989	1990	1991	1992
				Current account				
1	B	B	B	−138	−115	−124	−136	−138
2	B	H	B	−138	−106	−99	−87	−59
3	B	B	L	−138	−109	−104	−97	−78
4	B	H	L	−138	−100	−78	−49	1
5	D	H	B	−138	−100	−68	−21	26
6	D	B	L	−138	−103	−75	−37	−1
7	D	H	L	−138	−93	−47	17	86
8	D_s	H_s	B	−138	−107	−91	−68	−43
9	D_s	H_s	L	−138	−100	−71	−30	16
10	B	H_s	B	−138	−111	−113	−113	−102
11	B	H_{sc}	B	−138	−109	−108	−103	−85
12	D_{sc}	H_{sc}	B	−138	−104	−83	−51	−17
13	D_{sc}	H_{sc}	L	−138	−98	−62	−13	43
				Exports				
1	B	B	B	339	404	446	496	554
2	B	H	B	339	410	461	523	596
5	D	H	B	339	413	483	564	644
8	D_s	H_s	B	339	409	469	539	608
12	D_{sc}	H_{sc}	B	339	410	474	548	621
				Imports				
1	B	B	B	467	505	553	612	670
3	B	B	L	467	500	537	583	626
6	D	B	L	467	505	540	578	618
9	D_s	H_s	L	467	503	539	580	621
13	D_{sc}	H_{sc}	L	467	504	539	579	619
				Factor services				
1	B	B	B	−3	−10	−14	−17	−19
2	B	H	B	−3	−7	−5	2	14
3	B	B	L	−3	−9	−11	−10	−7
4	B	H	L	−3	−7	−2	8	26
5	D	H	B	−3	0	3	15	36
6	D	B	L	−3	−2	−4	2	12
7	D	H	L	−3	1	6	22	48
8	D_s	H_s	B	−3	−4	−5	0	11
9	D_s	H_s	L	−3	−3	−2	7	23
10	B	H_s	B	−3	−9	−9	−7	−2
11	B	H_{sc}	B	−3	−8	−8	−4	4
12	D_{sc}	H_{sc}	B	−3	−2	−2	6	20
13	D_{sc}	H_{sc}	L	−3	−1	1	13	32

B = base case; L = low; H = high (1% additional annual growth, 1988–92); D = real depreciation by 10%; S = with respect to strong countries (industrial countries, Korea, and Taiwan) only; SC = with respect to strong countries and Canada.

as "domestic demand" or "growth." The calculations here simply vary the growth rates themselves, without attempting to incorporate parallel changes in other variables of the HHC model (in particular, capacity utilization, capital stock, or trends in agricultural exports and oil imports). For this reason, the impact on trade accounts should be a minimum statement of the actual magnitude to be expected. Specifically, in equation 4 import volume depends not only on US GNP but also on the relative state of capacity utilization. If US growth declines, imports decline not only because of a smaller rise in GNP but also because US capacity utilization declines; however, only the direct GNP effect is captured here.

Table 3.5 reports the simulation results for variations in foreign and US growth, and growth changes in combination with dollar depreciation. The growth changes are specified as an increase in the annual growth rate by 1 percentage point, sustained over the four-year period 1989–92 in the case of higher growth abroad (H), and a reduction in US growth by 1 percentage point annually over the same period in the case of lower US growth (L). In the case of dollar depreciation, the dollar depreciates in real terms by 10 percent. In the final six cases, any higher foreign growth or dollar depreciation is limited to changes for the stronger countries (the industrial countries plus Korea and Taiwan), both excluding and including Canada.

Higher growth for all foreign countries (case 2) is sufficient by itself to cut the current account deficit from $138 billion in 1992 to $59 billion. Four years of 1-percentage-point higher foreign growth thus reduces the current account deficit by $79 billion. Four years of 1-percentage-point lower growth in the United States also has a major impact (case 3), and cuts the current account deficit in 1992 from $138 billion to $78 billion, for a swing of $60 billion.

The corresponding rates of improvement per year-percentage point are $19.8 billion on the side of foreign growth and $15 billion for US growth (as discussed below). The result that higher foreign growth is more powerful by one-fourth than lower US growth does not stem primarily from the trade side but from factor services. As indicated above, the HHC model has symmetrical long-term growth elasticities for US exports and imports. And in the component changes shown in table 3.5, high foreign growth increases US exports by $41 billion by 1992 (or $10.25 billion per year-percentage point growth) against the base case projection, whereas low US growth reduces US imports by $42 billion ($10.5 billion per year-percentage point), approximately confirming the elasticity symmetry.

In contrast, high growth abroad improves the balance in net factor services by $33 billion in 1992 (case 2 in the final portion of table 3.5), whereas low US growth improves it by only $12 billion (case 3). Higher foreign growth increases US direct investment earnings abroad in two ways. The equations specifying new flows of direct investment to foreign countries have a variable for foreign GNP (as faster growth abroad makes investment more attractive), so that higher foreign growth increases the stock of direct investment abroad over time. In addition, the rate of return on direct investment abroad is higher when foreign GNP is higher relative to foreign potential GNP. Although similar influences cause foreign earnings on direct investment in the United States to decline in response to lower US growth, the asymmetry in the size of the two direct investment stocks means that the impact of foreign growth on US earnings from abroad exceeds the impact of US growth on foreign earnings in the United States. (Thus, from table 3.2, US direct investment abroad exceeds foreign direct investment in the United States by about $51 billion at the end of 1986, rising to $65 billion by the end of 1992.)

The combination of high growth abroad and low US growth (case 4) eliminates the US current account deficit (and brings a $1 billion surplus by 1992). Addition of a general 10 percent real dollar depreciation to higher foreign growth alone (case 5) causes a surplus of $26 billion in that year. Dollar depreciation by 10 percent combined with lower US growth alone (case 6) places the current account at a deficit of only $1 billion by 1992. When all three instruments are combined in case 7—higher foreign growth, lower US growth, and 10 percent real depreciation of the dollar from the 1987:4 level—the US current account reaches a massive surplus of $86 billion by 1992.

Two central points emerge from these simulations. First, growth does matter. Some authors have tended to play down the potential effects of higher growth abroad.[39] Second, adding a sustained reduction in US growth to the instruments of higher foreign growth and dollar depreciation would amount to overkill. The US current account balance could shift into large surplus, and the loss of US production would be broadly unnecessary.

---

39. Thus, Krugman estimates that it would require a minimum increase of 8 percent in GNP in the rest of the world, beyond trend, to eliminate the $150 billion US current account deficit. He argues that this increment greatly exceeds excess capacity. (Paul Krugman, "Adjustment in the World Economy.") Krugman places non-US world GNP at $8 trillion and estimates the foreign marginal propensity to import from the United States at 0.12. An increase of foreign GNP by 1 percent thus raises US exports by $9.6 billion. Arguing that foreign countries would at most be able to raise GNP by 2 percentage points (cumulative) without overheating, he implicitly concludes that higher foreign growth can only reduce the US deficit by about $20 billion, so that "faster growth can play at best a distinctly secondary role in correcting external imbalance" (p. 26). However, as shown in table 3.6 below, while the HHC model also identifies a trade impact of only about $10 billion per year-percentage point from higher foreign growth, inclusion of services boosts the total current account impact to approximately $19.8 billion, so that 2 percent higher foreign GNP would add $40 billion to the US current account balance.

Table 3.5 reports additional simulations that may more accurately portray the potential of growth policies. These cases limit the growth increase to higher growth just in the countries with relatively strong balance of payments positions: the industrial countries (including and excluding Canada) and Korea and Taiwan. Similarly, they specify combinations of higher foreign growth and a decline in the dollar as involving a depreciation only against these areas.

When higher foreign growth by 1 percentage point over four years is limited to the narrowly defined strong areas (case 10), the favorable shift in the US current account by 1992 from the base case amounts to $36 billion. The fact that increased growth limited to the strong countries achieves only 46 percent of the impact of increased global foreign growth reflects these countries' share in US exports (49.8 percent in 1987; see table 4.1). When Canada is included in the higher foreign growth (case 11), the gain for the 1992 current account balance rises to $53 billion, or two-thirds of the total potential from higher growth in all foreign countries. (The corresponding 1987 share of the strong countries plus Canada in US exports was comparable, at 72.7 percent.)

Adjustment concentrated in the strong countries thus provides an impact roughly proportional to their shares in US exports, with respect to higher foreign growth. The share of total potential impact is even higher in the case of dollar depreciation. Thus, as noted above, the strong countries plus Canada account for 67 percent of the total potential gain from higher foreign growth, but 83 percent of the total from dollar depreciation. The higher share for exchange rate change reflects the greater weight of these countries in the HHC model's variable for the relative price effect facing US exports and imports. Thus, use of the HHC model for partial-area simulations (as employed here but not in the original Helkie–Hooper analysis) appears to impart a modest upward bias for the impact of strong-country action in the calculations regarding exchange rate changes, and a small downward bias for the corresponding impact of higher foreign growth.[40]

For his part, Feldstein considers the potential impact of higher growth abroad to be so small that he regards macroeconomic policy coordination as having only minor significance. He contends that a doubling of real GNP growth rates in Europe and Japan would raise US exports by only $5 billion. (Martin Feldstein, "The End of Policy Coordination," Wall Street Journal, 9 November 1988.) Feldstein states no time dimension, but even for only one year the impact of going from 2.5 percent growth in these countries to 5 percent would be approximatley $15 billion for the US current account in 1992, on the basis of the HHC model (see table 3.6), of which about 40 percent would come from factor services rather than exports.

40. Thus, in the index for foreign prices in the US export equation P_{18}/E_{18} in equation 2 above), the Group of 10 countries (industrial) have a share of 78 percent. Adding

If in addition to higher growth in the strong areas (excluding Canada) the dollar depreciates by 10 percent against the currencies of these same areas (case 8), the adjustment rises to $95 billion (for a 1992 deficit of $43 billion). If slower US growth is added (case 9), the current account deficit turns to an unnecessarily strong surplus of $16 billion. The corresponding cases of combined policies including action by Canada (cases 12 and 13) place the 1992 current account at a deficit of $17 billion and a surplus of $43 billion, respectively.

In short, the qualitative conclusions remain valid even when the growth effects are limited to the areas with stronger balance of payments positions: foreign growth matters, accelerated foreign growth combined with exchange rate movement is considerably more powerful, and the addition of a sustained US slowdown unnecessarily sacrifices output and overshoots the current account objective. These qualitative results hold whether or not Canada is included in the group of strong countries appreciating their currencies and accelerating growth.

Policy Parameters

The simulations conducted here provide a basis for identifying useful rules of thumb for the impact of alternative policy instruments on the current account balance. Table 3.6 summarizes these relationships, and in addition presents the corresponding estimates in Bryant's synthesis of five forecasting models as well as the DRI model. The Bryant and DRI parameters, like those here, are for "partial equilibrium" impact. For example, a depreciation in the exchange rate is specified in real terms, with no offsetting effects from any induced domestic inflation or from stronger domestic income associated with export expansion.[41]

Based on the case of 10 percent real depreciation of the dollar, real depreciation by 1 percent against all currencies brings about an increase in

---

Korea and Taiwan brings the total to over 80 percent, even though the shares of the broadly defined strong group of countries in 1987 exports and imports were only 72.7 percent and 78.6 percent, respectively. In contrast, in the growth variable, world GNP is weighted by nonagricultural US exports. On this basis the strong countries including Canada account for a weight of 65 percent (smaller than the overall export share because of the greater weight of agricultural goods in US exports to industrial than to developing countries). Note that the simulations here do not vary agricultural exports in response to changes in foreign growth and exchange rates.

41. Potential leakage associated with these general equilibrium effects is the reason why this study stresses the need for fiscal adjustment to accompany exchange rate change, to create room for increased external demand.

Table 3.6 Policy parameters for US external accounts, 1992
(billions of dollars)

Instrument	Change in 1992 current account deficit	Of which:[a]		
		Exports	Imports[b]	Factor services
This study				
Exchange rate depreciation of 1%	7.8	4.4	0.8	1.8
Against strong areas only	5.6	3.5	0.5	1.2
Including Canada	6.4	3.7	0.7	1.4
Increased foreign growth				
(1% for 1 year)	19.8	10.5		8.3
In strong areas only	9.2	4.5		4.3
Including Canada	13.3	6.8		5.8
Decreased US growth				
(1% for 1 year)	15.0		11.0	3.0
Other studies				
Bryant (Brookings)[c]				
Exchange rate depreciation of 1%	4.4			
Increased foreign growth				
(1% for 1 year)	9.2			
Decreased US growth				
(1% for 1 year)	8.2			
Gault (DRI)				
Exchange rate depreciation of 1%	7.7			
Increased foreign growth				
(1% for 1 year)	9.8			
Decreased US growth				
(1% for 1 year)	11.8			

a. Excludes nonfactor services.
b. Decrease.
c. Estimates are for 1991.

Sources: Ralph C. Bryant, "The US External Deficit: An Update," 33–34; Nigel Gault, "What Would Eliminate the Current Account Deficit?" *Data Resources U.S. Review,* December 1987, 24.

the nominal US current account balance of $7.8 billion by 1992. The table summarizes the composition of this improvement; as discussed above, export gains and an improved balance on factor services dominate the increase. If the real depreciation occurs only against the currencies of the industrial countries excluding Canada, plus Taiwan and Korea, the current account gain by 1992 is $5.6 billion; including Canada, it reaches $6.4 billion.

The growth impact is stated in terms of year-percentage points. The estimates of table 3.5 showed the effects of changes in growth rates by 1 percent sustained over four years. The parameter reported in table 3.6 divides these effects by four to estimate the impact of a single year's change in growth by 1 percentage point. (This procedure involves a small overstatement of the effect of a single year's change, because the growing export base in the case of higher foreign growth, for example, means the cumulative effect over four years is somewhat larger than four times the effect in the first, or an average, year.)

One year-percentage point additional foreign growth increases the 1992 US current account balance by $19.8 billion. If higher foreign growth is limited to areas with strong payments positions, the gain is still $9.2 billion, and if Canada is included the impact reaches $13.3 billion. One year-percentage point of lower US growth causes an improvement of $15.0 billion in the 1992 current account balance.

The weighted-average results of the five forecasting models surveyed in the Brookings study yield the parameters shown in table 3.6. One percent depreciation of the dollar reduces the 1991 current account deficit by $4.4 billion; 1 year-percentage point of higher foreign growth improves it by $9.2 billion; and 1 year-percentage point of lower US growth improves it by $8.2 billion.

All of the Brookings estimates are smaller than those estimated with the HHC model here. For the exchange rate, Bryant takes the average impact of depreciation against all currencies and depreciation just against the yen and the European Community currencies, and so his estimate should be compared to an average of the two estimates shown in the top part of the table. Even so, his impact is smaller. In part this divergence comes from a higher sensitivity to the exchange rate in the original HH model (which, as one of the models surveyed by Bryant, was reported in his study as having an exchange rate impact 39 percent larger than the weighted average). In part it derives from the use of 1991 as the terminal date, allowing one year less for cumulative effects.

With respect to growth impacts, the averages calculated by Bryant are approximately half as large as those estimated from the HHC model for increased foreign growth, and only 55 percent as large for reduced US growth. These divergences arise primarily from the greater growth sensitivity of the HH model than of the weighted model averages in the Brookings survey (by 59 percent for impact of foreign growth and 35 percent for the impact of US growth, as reported by Bryant). Again the use of an earlier terminal year explains part of the difference.[42]

The policy parameters in the DRI model are somewhat closer to the estimates here. Thus, Gault places the impact of 1 percent depreciation of the dollar at an increase in the current account balance by $7.7 billion in 1992, slightly larger than identified here. However, the DRI estimate of the impact of higher foreign growth, $9.8 billion for 1 year-percentage point, is close to the Brookings estimate and only 50 percent as large as the estimate here. On the side of US growth, DRI estimates that reduction by 1 year-percentage point cuts the 1992 current account deficit by $11.8 billion, or 79 percent of the figure in the HHC model.

It seems likely that an important reason for the smaller growth impacts in both the Bryant survey and the DRI model than in the HHC model is the pronounced influence of growth on the factor services balance in the HHC analysis, as examined above. This impact requires substantial depth in the development of the factor services bloc of the model, and many models focus primarily on the trade accounts and apply only accounting-type equations for factor services. Thus, whereas the HHC model specifically relates the rate of return and of new accumulation on direct investment to the growth rate, models with less detail in the services account tend to apply an unchanged rate of return to the cumulating stock of net external debt resulting from annual current account deficits.[43]

It should be noted that for policy purposes the most germane growth impact figures are probably those limiting higher foreign growth to the strong areas. Many other nations are not in a position to expand growth above base case rates because of external balance constraints. To the extent that the DRI model and the Bryant synthesis of five forecasting models tend to use growth in the principal industrial countries as a proxy for "foreign" growth, without attention to such areas as Latin America and OPEC, their growth effects may correspond more to the case here in which growth changes are limited to strong areas than to the case in which there is increased global foreign growth.[44]

---

42. Thus, from table 3.5, if 1991 is considered as the final year, 1 year-percentage point higher foreign growth contributes $16.3 billion to improvement in the current account balance (instead of $19.8 billion), and 1 year-percentage point lower US growth contributes $13.0 billion (instead of $15.0 billion).

43. The DRI model in particular omits any sensitivity of the rate of return on direct investment (or the rate of accumulation of direct investment) to the growth rate. By communication.

44. For example, Bryant's study asked five forecasting models to simulate the impact of higher growth in all foreign countries "in the system." For some, this scope may

In sum, a reasonable range for the rules of thumb applicable to alternative policy instruments would be as follows. One percent real depreciation of the dollar against all currencies provides an improvement of approximately $7½ billion on the current account in 1992 (based on the HHC and DRI estimates). One percent depreciation against just the industrial countries (including Canada) plus Korea and Taiwan provides some $6 billion.

One year-percentage point higher foreign growth improves the 1992 current account balance by a range of $10 billion to $19 billion, with the high end of the range representing greater attention to favorable effects on earnings on direct foreign investment (and, conceivably, more complete attention to OPEC and developing countries). One year-percentage point higher growth in just the industrial countries (including Canada) plus Korea and Taiwan improves the balance by some $13 billion (or as little as $6½ billion on a proportional basis using the DRI and Brookings average results). One year-percentage point lower US growth cuts the 1992 current account deficit by some $12 billion to $15 billion, with the higher figure again reflecting incorporation of effects on the return to direct investment.

Sensitivity

Despite the resemblance of the HHC model here and the DRI model with respect to changes at the margin, the two models give widely differing estimates of the baseline outlook for the US current account balance. As indicated in table 3.3, the most extreme estimate (the DRI model applied by Gault to unchanged policy, with no model adjustment factors and including the adverse time trend) yields a 1992 current account deficit of $243 billion, far greater than the base case HHC estimate of $138 billion. (The Bryant synthesis model gives results much closer to those of the HHC model, at $127 billion versus $136 billion for 1991; the same is true of the WEFA projection, at $161 billion for 1992.) These divergences highlight the great sensitivity of projections over the medium term to the particular parameters and structure of the individual model, as well as to the assumptions about the economic environment (box 3.2).

The sensitivity of current account projections raises a fundamental policy question: what should be the stance of policy under uncertainty? On the basis of the projections developed here and those prepared by other authors, the doubt about the US current account balance is not whether it will be

---

have excluded some important world areas. Bryant, Holtham, and Hooper, *External Deficits and the Dollar*, 109.

Box 3.2   Variability in Trade Balance Projections

Bryant has formally explored sensitivity in the five forecasting models he surveyed by calculating the outcome with parameters set 1 standard deviation above and below their central values. (A parameter estimate is a random variable with a probability distribution around its mean. For an estimate that is statistically significant at the 5 percent level, the chances are 95 percent that the true parameter value lies in a range starting at 1 standard deviation below the mean estimate for the parameter and extending to 1 standard deviation above it.) He finds that the weighted-average synthesis of five forecasting models yields a range of the estimated current account deficit for 1991 from $207 billion, if parameters are set at unfavorable limits by subtracting 1 standard deviation, to as low as $47 billion, if they are set optimistically by adding 1 standard deviation. This range is even larger than that between the DRI projection and the projection here for 1992.

The current account deficit is highly variable because it is a residual between underlying magnitudes that themselves are subject to error of prediction. Consider just the trade balance. With imports and exports in the broad range of $500 billion to $600 billion by 1992, an error of 5 percent in one direction for imports and in the other direction for exports will cause an error of $50 billion to $60 billion in the trade balance. Then consider the services account. With foreign assets in the range of $1.1 trillion and foreign liabilities of some $2.0 trillion by the end of 1991 (table 3.2), an error understating the return on foreign claims by just 2 percentage points and overstating the return on US foreign assets by 2 percentage points (that is, error amounting to about one-fourth of the level of rates of return) generates an overstatement of the factor services balance by approximately $60 billion. A swing of over $100 billion to $120 billion can thus arise in the current account deficit from errors that are far from egregious.

positive or negative under current exchange rates and growth prospects, but whether it will be in deficit at the low end or the high end of a range from some $140 billion to over $200 billion by 1992.[45] Even though the consensus centers much more closely on the lower range, both figures are so high that there should be little scope for uncertainty about whether a major problem on the external accounts remains. There is more room for doubt about the extent of additional measures required to correct the trade deficit.

The Bubble of 1988

This interpretation is strongly reinforced by the unfortunate exchange rate developments of 1988. The dollar reached a low point at the end of December 1987. It then proceded to strengthen, especially at mid-year. Thus, the dollar rose by nearly 20 percent against the German mark, French franc, and Italian lira from December 31, 1987, to August 15, 1988, and by 7 percent against the Japanese yen over the same period (table 5.10). The only important countermovement was against the Canadian dollar, which appreciated by 6 percent.

On the basis of the 18-country real exchange rate used on the export side in the HHC model, the path of the dollar was as follows. The real exchange rate for exports, which had risen from 100 in 1980 to a peak of 137.0 in 1985:1, stood at 83.9 for the fourth quarter of 1987 as a whole (the real level applied in the baseline projections). By December 31, 1987, it had declined by 4.9 percent to 79.8. But by August 15, 1988, it had risen again to 89.4, or 6.5 percent above the 1987:4 level and 12.0 percent above the December 31, 1987, level.[46]

---

45. The range of estimates if the two outliers (Gault with trend and DRI business) are excluded, and extrapolating the deterioration in the Bryant projection. Note that the OECD projection through 1990 might imply a deficit below the range, but it is more likely that the OECD forecast would show a reversal to a higher deficit by 1992 as well if its published time horizon reached that far.

46. As shown in figure 2.5, the decline and subsequent rebound were more moderate for the import side, where bilateral weights give greater influence to the Canadian dollar. However, as the great bulk of adjustment must occur on the export side (because price changes tend to cancel out volume changes on the import side), the real exchange rate for exports is the more relevant measure of the policy problem caused by renewed strength of the dollar in 1988. Even averaging the import and export real exchange rate indexes, however, the pattern is essentially the same. Thus, from the 1987:4 average to December 31, 1987, the real dollar declined by 5 percent. From then until 1988:3 it rose by 7.9 percent, placing the averaged index 2.3 percent higher by 1988:3 than in 1987:4.

Application of the HHC model to these alternative exchange rates shows the important opportunity that was lost by the revival of the dollar in 1988. If the real dollar had remained at its December 31, 1987, level, the baseline projection indicates that the 1992 current account deficit would have stood at $90.6 billion, a substantial improvement over the $138 billion deficit expected at real 1987:4 exchange rates. But in a scenario that applies the actual exchange rates for the first and second quarters of 1988 and then freezes the real exchange rate at its August 15, 1988, level, the 1992 current account deficit balloons to $179.0 billion. Thus, the rebound of the dollar from the end of 1987 until August of 1988, if it proved to be permanent, could have cost as much as $90 billion on the US current account deficit by 1992.

By the first quarter of 1989, the real exchange rate was approximately back to where it had been in 1987:4, the exchange rate base period used throughout this study. Although the real export exchange rate in the HHC model (discussed further in Chapter 2) had risen by 3.5 percent, the real import exchange rate had declined by 2.8 percent, leaving the average index virtually unchanged from 1987:4 at 92.5 (with 1980 = 100). The divergence (which may be seen in figure 2.5) was largely associated with the real depreciation of the dollar during this period against the Canadian dollar (which has a large influence on the bilaterally weighted real exchange rate for imports) and real appreciation against the German mark (which, together with other strong European currencies, has a large weight in the multilaterally weighted real exchange rate for exports). If there was any net change, it was probably toward some lingering real appreciation of the dollar above its 1987:4 level, considering the greater role of the exchange rate in achieving adjustment on the export side (as volume effects largely neutralize price effects on the import side).

Conclusion

The thrust of the analysis of this chapter is that, although in the absence of further measures the US external imbalance will remain dangerously high for several years, plausible further steps would sharply reduce the deficit and leave it within manageable bounds. The estimates of this chapter suggest that, even given uncertainty, the following guidelines seem appropriate for policy. First, once the United States has adopted a firm program for reduction of its fiscal deficits, policymakers should change monetary and exchange rate intervention policies to facilitate a reduction in the value of the dollar, rather than intervene to support the currency as was done in early 1988. (The extent of needed depreciation, and its differential degree across individual key foreign currencies, are discussed in Chapter 5.) It would be a mistake to lock the dollar in at its real rate of early 1989. This conclusion is sharply reinforced if the more pessimistic projections among the major existing models are accepted.

Second, higher foreign demand growth can make an important contribution to the adjustment. In the Feasible Adjustment Package developed in Chapter 5, acceleration of foreign growth by approximately ½ percentage point annually over four years contributes $40 billion to US external adjustment by 1992 (HHC model), or one-third of the total (although this share in the EAG model is smaller).

Third, there is sufficient scope for correcting the US external deficit through depreciation and plausible temporary growth acceleration abroad that it would be a mistake to pursue conscious growth reduction in the United States for purposes of correcting the external deficit. Such a slowdown could become necessary for other reasons, including normal business-cycle dynamics, but policymakers would be wrong to cause an intentional slowdown of GNP growth for the sake of external adjustment. This conclusion is reinforced if the distinction is drawn between adjustment in demand, which indeed should grow more slowly, and the growth rate of production, which should not (at least not on account of external balances).

Fourth, and perhaps most important, US fiscal correction remains imperative to validate the potential effects of dollar depreciation and higher foreign growth. There is a major risk that, in the absence of a further correction in the US fiscal deficit, additional dollar depreciation would tend to generate inflation rather than external adjustment.

4

A Multicountry Model of International Trade

Sooner or later the United States will have to reduce its external deficits to much smaller levels. When it does, there could be new strains on other countries as their trade balances correspondingly decline. There has been little attention paid to the prospective impact of US adjustment on other countries, yet there is no guarantee that the corresponding process of foreign adjustment will be smooth or that it will be consistent with current policy tenets (such as the relative rigidity of exchange rates among countries within the European Monetary System).

Chapter 3 considered the prospects for US adjustment, and the impact of changes in exchange rates and growth on US external accounts. The model applied in that analysis provides considerable depth for examination of the US current account balance, but does not disaggregate among foreign countries. This chapter develops a multicountry trade model to explore the implications of US adjustment for individual major foreign countries and areas. Although several forecasting models exist for the US current account (table 3.3), few permit joint projections for other countries.[1]

The following analysis sets forth the model structure, reviews the issues involved in assembling the data base, and presents "backcasts" comparing model estimates to actual trade results for the past two decades. Chapter 5 then applies the model in forward-looking policy simulations to examine the prospects for individual countries under alternative paths for US external sector performance through 1992. Chapter 5 also extends the analysis to

---

1. Important exceptions are found in Jaime Marquez, "The Global Repercussions of Reducing the US Trade Deficit: An Econometric Analysis" (Washington: Federal Reserve Board, mimeographed, June 1987); and Paul Masson, Steven Symansky, Richard Haas, and Michael Dooley, "Multimod: A Multi-Region Econometric Model," *Staff Studies for the World Economic Outlook* (Washington: International Monetary Fund, July 1988), 50–104. Neither of these studies provides as great a degree of country detail as the model developed here, although the IMF model in particular places greater emphasis on macroeconomic relationships.

translate the projections of trade flows into corresponding results for current account balances (including services and transfers).

A Model of External Adjustment with Growth

The External Adjustment with Growth (EAG) model of this study relates trade flows among countries to real exchange rates and economic growth.

Geographical Detail

The model divides the world into 17 countries and blocs. The seven largest industrial countries—the United States (US), the United Kingdom (UK), France (FR), Germany (GE), Italy (IT), Canada (CA), and Japan (JA)—are treated individually. So are Argentina (AR), Brazil (BR), and Mexico (ME), the three largest Latin American debtor countries. The developing country with the largest surplus, Taiwan (TA), is also distinguished individually.

In addition to the 11 individual countries, there are six country blocs in the model. The oil-exporting countries (OP)[2] constitute one obvious grouping. All the Other Industrial countries (OI) not examined individually comprise another. Korea, Singapore, and Hong Kong (KS) form a third bloc. These three of the East Asian "gang of four" share the characteristics of outward orientation and rapid growth, but their surpluses remain more modest than that of Taiwan (some $20 billion annually). A fourth group, Other Latin America (OL), consists of Latin America excluding Argentina, Brazil, and Mexico, with Venezuela removed as well because of its inclusion in OP.[3] Other Africa (AN) is a fifth bloc, representing Africa excluding Algeria and Nigeria, which appear in OP. Finally, a Rest of World (RO) group accounts for all other countries, including the socialist nations. This large residual grouping includes all of Asia except for Japan, Taiwan, Korea, Singapore, and Hong Kong (and thus incorporates such major countries as China and India); developing countries in Europe (such as Portugal and

---

2. Defined by the International Monetary Fund as those countries for which oil accounted for at least two-thirds of exports in 1976–78. IMF, *International Financial Statistics*, June 1988, 14.

3. Technically Ecuador should similarly be removed from the Latin American data because it is already included in the oil-exporting countries. However, its trade flows are relatively small.

Turkey); non-OPEC nations of the Middle East; and Eastern Europe, including the Soviet Union.

In principle it would be desirable to distinguish product sectors in the model. In practice, the model is already large, as it involves 277 supplier–market trade flows (17 × 17 less the null entries for exports from any individual country to itself), and is applied to quarterly data (60 quarters from 1973 to 1987). Extension of the model into an additional dimension with several product sectors would considerably increase the data and estimation requirements. Except for oil, therefore, separate product sectors are not discriminated. Instead, the commodity composition of each country's trade is reflected indirectly in the estimated income and price elasticities of demand. Thus, countries with a heavy incidence of commodities in their export mix would be expected to have lower price and income elasticities of demand for their exports than would countries with exports concentrated in manufactures.

Petroleum Trade

Oil is an exception to the absence of product detail in the model. The properties of trade in oil are so distinct, and this trade is so large, that separate treatment of oil is especially desirable. The model accomplishes this separation indirectly. By treating the oil-exporting countries as a unit, it automatically treats separately a large portion of international trade in oil (essentially, that supplied by OPEC). In addition, two of the countries examined individually are major exporters of oil: the United Kingdom and Mexico. For each of these countries, oil is identified by creating an artificial exporting "country" that exports nothing but oil, and only to markets within the OECD.[4] These two artificial countries (UP and MP, respectively) have no imports; the imports remain attributed to the parent countries, as do all nonoil exports.

The basic structure of the model is thus a 19 × 17 trade matrix for any given period, with 17 importing areas (the countries and blocs enumerated above) and 19 exporting areas (the 17 plus the 2 artificial oil-exporting "countries," UP and MP). Separation of OP, UP, and MP captures the bulk of oil trade. Thus, in 1985, imports from OPEC (essentially group OP here), the United Kingdom, and Mexico accounted for 64.8 percent of total oil imports for the six largest industrial countries excluding the United King-

---

4. For reasons of data availability. As discussed below, exports to OECD countries encompass virtually all of UK oil exports and most of Mexico's. Data estimation for UP and MP is discussed below.

dom.[5] For the OECD as a whole, of $226.7 billion in oil imports in 1985, $149 billion, or 65.7 percent, was accounted for by the three suppliers separated here (OP, UP, and MP).[6]

The oil trade not captured through identification of exports from OP, UP, and MP tends to be from Rest of World suppliers. These include the USSR ($13.4 billion in exports to the OECD in 1985, c.i.f. [cost including insurance and freight]), China ($4.1 billion), and Singapore ($2.1 billion, largely refined products rather than crude). Among the industrial countries, the only large oil exporters besides the United Kingdom are the Netherlands ($10.0 billion, again in refined products) and Canada ($6.3 billion), although the United States also exports a nontrivial amount to the OECD ($3.1 billion).

For the specific supplier–market combinations of trade flows in the model, the largest potential distortion through failure to identify all oil trade is in the case of Canadian exports of petroleum to the United States, some $6 billion in 1985. However, this trade accounted for less than 10 percent of US imports from Canada in that year, and is thus unlikely to have a major influence on the measured influences of exchange rate and growth variables on Canada–US trade.[7] In general, the remaining presence of oil trade in a particular supplier–market trade combination will tend to bias downward the measured responsiveness (elasticity) of trade to exchange rates and income because of the large exogenous shifts in this trade associated with the two OPEC price shocks (in 1973–74 and 1979–80) and subsequent price erosion.

---

5. Using c.i.f. import data in category 33 (petroleum, petroleum products, and related materials) of the Standard International Trade Classification (SITC). Organization for Economic Cooperation and Development, *Foreign Trade by Commodities: 1985* (Paris: OECD, 1987), 150–52. Among the six, the lowest share of oil imports attributable to OP, UP, and MP was for Germany (52.8 percent), where sizable imports from the Netherlands and the USSR exist. Note that the share of OP–UP–MP was even lower for imports of oil into the United Kingdom (25.5 percent), where imports from Norway accounted for 23 percent, the Netherlands 10 percent, and other European OECD countries 25 percent.

6. Calculated from OECD, *Foreign Trade by Commodities: 1985*, and from the trade estimates of this study (adjusted to a comparable c.i.f. basis).

7. Similarly, the 1985 oil imports of some $4.8 billion from the Netherlands into Germany are small compared to the total trade flow from the Other Industrial countries to Germany (almost $60 billion); and UK imports of oil from Norway, the Netherlands, and the rest of the OECD excluding the six largest industrial countries are modest ($5.2 billion) relative to total UK imports from the Other Industrial countries (almost $40 billion on a c.i.f. basis).

Model Equations

The EAG model consists of quarterly estimates of the entries in the 19 × 17 trade matrix described above, for 1973:1 to 1987:4 in the backcasting period and for 1988:1 through 1992:4 in the forecasting period. Each cell in the trade matrix is a flow of exports from the supplier country (row i) to the purchasing country (column j). Imports are treated as being equal to the partner country's exports, and by definition the sum of all countries' exports must equal the sum of all countries' "imports."

The real volume of exports from country i to country j in a particular period depends on the income of the importing country, the price in the exporting country relative to the price in the market country, and the price in the exporting country relative to the prices of all alternative suppliers of imports into the market country. These three economic influences—income, direct price, and cross-price—all refer to the demand for exports from the supplying country. It is assumed that the supply curve for exports is horizontal (infinitely elastic), as should generally be the case for exports, which are only a fraction of total production (especially considering that the exports in question are only a fraction of the country's total exports— that is, the fraction sent to the purchasing market in question).

Time lags affect the direct and cross-price terms, as it takes time for traders to recognize new prices (recognition lag), to make changes in purchasing decisions on the basis of the new information (decision lag), and for actual deliveries of goods to take place (delivery lag). The basic equation for the volume of exports from country i to country j in time period t is thus:

$$(1) \quad \ln q_{ijt} = \alpha_{ij} + \beta_{ij}(\ln Y_{jt}) + \delta_{ij}\left(\sum_k w_k \ln [P_{i,t\text{-}k}/P_{j,t\text{-}k}]\right)$$

$$+ \sigma_{ij}\left(\sum_k w_k \ln [P^j{}_{Ni,t\text{-}k}/P_{i,t\text{-}k}]\right).$$

The elements in equation 1 are as follows. The term α_{ij} is a constant. The coefficient β_{ij} is the elasticity of demand for exports from country i with respect to income in country j. The coefficient δ_{ij} is the elasticity of demand for exports from country i into country j with respect to the direct relative prices of the two countries. The direct relative price term is a distributed lag variable stretching over eight quarters, with weight w_k applied to the kth previous quarter. The coefficient σ_{ij} is the elasticity of demand for exports from country i into country j with respect to the weighted price of all competitive foreign suppliers into market j, relative to the price of supplier *i*. As in the case of the direct price variable, this cross-price variable is a distributed lag measure, with weight w_k applied to the kth previous quarter.

For both the direct and cross-price variables the lag structure imposed is of uniform sign (so that there are no reversals from positive to negative moving from one period to the next). The structure is also symmetrical, an inverse-U shape that gives less weight to the current period and immediate past, rising weight to a peak at three or four quarters lag, and then symmetrically declining weight out through a lag of eight quarters (as discussed below).

The dependent variable q_{ijt} is the quantity (or real volume) of exports from country i to country j in period t.[8] The variable Y_{jt} is real income in purchasing country j in period t. The variable P_i refers to the dollar export price of country i, and its time dimension $t - k$ refers to the kth period before the current period (where k begins with zero, indicating the current period). The variable P_j is the price of the domestic good in the importing market, country j. Its time dimension is similar.

The cross-price term involves the calculation of the weighted-average dollar export price of all other countries competing in the market in question. Thus,

$$(2) \quad P^j_{Ni} = \left(\sum_h \Phi_h^j P_h \right) \bigg/ (1 - \Phi_i^j), \ h \neq i$$

where h refers to the hth other country, the superscript j refers to the market of country j, the subscript Ni refers to "not country i," the term Φ_h^j is the share of country h in the imports of country j, and the time dimension included in equation 1 is omitted for simplicity. The denominator normalizes the weighted shares of competitors by removing the share of the supplying country i in question. The share estimates refer to a 1980 base period.

The predicted quantities of trade shown in equation 1 are converted to dollar values at current prices by multiplying by the dollar export price of the exporting country in the period in question:

$$(3) \quad V_{ijt} = P_{it} q_{ijt}.$$

For oil trade, the model differs. There is no attempt to model the past values of oil trade; exogenous shocks in oil prices, and such influences as the development of new fields in Alaska's North Slope, make such an effort a major undertaking in itself. For the simulations of past trade flows (or

---

8. As discussed below, these quantity data are obtained by dividing value data by the unit-value export price index for the exporting country in question. These export prices, in turn, are assumed to apply uniformly to exports to all of the trading partners of the exporting country in question.

"backcasts"), the model simply imposes actual oil trade (exports from OP, UP, and MP) onto the trade matrix otherwise calculated according to equation 1. Similarly, exogenous shocks in oil prices and correspondingly large fluctuations in importing capacity have caused large shifts in the past in the imports of the OPEC countries, and there is no attempt to model these past imports.

For forecasting purposes, oil trade is calculated as follows. First, it is assumed that the dollar price of oil will follow the exogenous path set forth in Appendix D, based on the "low price" projection case prepared by the National Petroleum Council. Second, for the volume of oil imports by a particular country, the quantity growth of imports is related to the growth of real income in the country. Thus:

$$(4) \quad V_{ojt} = [V_{oj,t-1}][P^o_t / P^o_{t-1}]\{1 + [(Y_{jt}/Y_{j,t-1}) - 1]\beta_o\}$$

where V is the current dollar value of trade, subscript o refers to any one of the three oil-exporting countries (OP, UP, MP), j is the importing country, and P^o_t is the exogenous oil price. The income elasticity of oil demand, β_o, is set uniformly at 0.5 for all countries other than the United States. This estimate is based on the assumption that, for most countries, virtually all demand for oil is met through imports, and that conservation has limited the response of oil demand to income growth to an elasticity of only 0.5.

The oil imports of the United States differ from this equation. The baseline values of US oil imports are taken from the estimates presented in Appendix D. Explicit calculations then enter the forecasts only in alternative scenarios in which US growth differs from the baseline path. Thus, in the case of the United States:

$$(5) \quad V_{o1t} = V^*_{o1t} \{1 + [(Y_{1t}/Y^*_{1t}) - 1] \beta^U_o\}$$

where the subscript 1 refers to the United States (country 1) as importer, the asterisk refers to the baseline projection value (for oil imports and for income), and the income elasticity of oil imports for the United States β^U_o is set equal to unity.

The use of a higher income elasticity for US oil imports than for imports of such countries as Germany and Japan reflects the fact that the United States currently supplies about one-half of its consumption from domestic production, but this production is virtually constant (or declining), so that at the margin all increases in consumption translate into equivalent increases in imports. An income elasticity of consumption of one-half thus translates into an income elasticity of imports that is twice as large, or unity. That is, because imports are half of consumption, a given absolute change is twice as large proportionately for imports as for consumption. (See also the discussion in Appendix D.)

The model also treats the imports of OPEC (country OP) differently from those of other countries. The exports of another country to OPEC in a given period in the forecast simulations are determined by respending shares as applied to total OPEC exports. As may be seen in figure D.1 of Appendix D, the imports of the oil-exporting countries peaked in 1982 and have fallen substantially since then. This decline has closely followed the decline in dollar export earnings, which peaked in 1980. Since 1982, OPEC imports have averaged 77 percent of the export earnings of the oil-exporting countries. Application of the standard trade equations based on past relationships of OPEC imports to domestic income, domestic prices, and supplier country prices would tend to overstate OPEC imports in the future, as these equations do not explicitly take into account import-purchasing capacity based on OPEC exports.[9]

For exports of other countries to OPEC in the forecasting period, the model thus applies the following estimate:

$$(6) \quad V_{i,OP,t} = \Phi^o_i (0.77) \sum_j V_{OP,j,t}$$

where Φ^o_i is the share of country i in total exports to the oil-exporting group OP in the base period 1985–87.

Data

The quarterly data for the underlying 17×17 trade matrix, for 1973 to 1987, are from the International Monetary Fund's *Direction of Trade Statistics* (DOTS).[10] The export trade flow is used as the trade value. Thus, for US exports to Germany, for example, it is the IMF figure reporting US export

---

9. Note that the approach of allocating all export earnings to imports according to respending ratios could also be applied to non-OPEC developing countries on grounds that they too have imports constrained by foreign exchange availability. However, to do so would sacrifice important information about trade tendencies for these countries in the absence of exchange rate and growth changes. For example, when the dollar declines in real terms, those developing countries that maintain unchanged real exchange rates against the dollar experience increased trade balances as their competitiveness against third countries improves. It is more informative to model these gains explicitly, and to apply simulations involving offsetting real exchange rate appreciation and growth acceleration by the country in question if its current account trends are sufficiently strong, than to suppress the information on prospective trade gains by forcing the automatic respending assumption.

10. International Monetary Fund CD-ROM data base and selected published issues in 1987–88.

data rather than the figure reporting German imports from the United States that is applied as the trade flow in question. The two alternative measures are not necessarily the same, because of differences in timing of the reporting of transactions, and because the DOTS data express imports in c.i.f. values, whereas exports are free on board (f.o.b.).

Data for groupings of countries are obtained by summing their individual export data, in the case of Korea–Singapore–Hong Kong. As noted, exports of Other Latin America are obtained by subtracting the exports of Argentina, Brazil, Mexico, and Venezuela from the totals for Latin America, and for Other Africa by deducting exports of Nigeria and Algeria from the African totals.

The trade flows from the Rest of World group to a particular country are obtained residually. The DOTS data indicate total world exports to each country examined specifically. From total world supply to the country, the sum of exports from individually identified countries and blocs to the market country in question is subtracted to obtain imports from the Rest of World group. Similarly, exports of a particular country (such as the United States) to Rest of World are estimated by subtracting the sum of exports to individually identified markets from the total exports for the country in question.

The Rest of World grouping poses data difficulties. Its imports from a specific country are relatively firm, because the export data of the individual country are generally reliable. Similarly, Rest of World exports to a specific country tend to be relatively well behaved, as the DOTS estimates of total world exports to a given country appear close to the mark (and can be checked against that country's imports f.o.b.). However, estimated Rest of World exports to other broad groupings with data derived residually can be negative and thus unacceptable. Using the residual method, Rest of World exports are negative for trade with the Other Industrial countries in the early 1980s, and with Other Latin America and Rest of World itself in the 1970s. Thus, the DOTS data base appears to understate total world exports in these periods by the difference between these negative estimates and actual Rest of World exports.

The data base applies direct (rather than residual) estimates of Rest of World exports to OI, OL, and RO in 1981. These data refer to exports of the members of Rest of World: developing countries in Asia excluding Korea, Singapore, and Hong Kong; in the Middle East excluding OPEC members; in Europe; and from Russia and Eastern Europe. Rest of World export data to the OI, OL, and RO groups are then estimated for other years by extrapolating the 1981 estimates backward and forward using an average of indexes of Rest of World exports to "firm" countries (all excluding OL,

OI, and RO), on the one hand, and area imports from non-Rest of World sources, on the other.[11]

Trade data for Taiwan are included in the totals of the IMF DOTS data, but are not reported individually in the IMF source subsequent to 1980 in view of Taiwan's change to nonmember status. Total DOTS exports to a country thus include Taiwan's exports to the country, and total DOTS exports for a country include its exports to Taiwan,[12] but Taiwan-specific trade must be obtained from separate sources.[13] Any errors in the resulting Taiwan estimates have the effect of misallocating trade between Taiwan and Rest of World, the residual category.

Table 4.1 shows the trade matrix estimated for 1987. Each entry shows exports from the country listed in the row to the country listed in the column (for example, exports from Italy to Germany in 1987 were $21.17 billion). The total of world trade in 1987 amounted to $2.44 trillion. US exports accounted for 10.3 percent of total world exports. As the table indicates, German exports actually exceeded those of the United States, and Japan's exports were only slightly smaller. The largest exporting entity within the EAG trade matrix is the Other Industrial countries group, which in 1987 accounted for $458.9 billion in exports (including intratrade within the group), or 18.8 percent of world trade.

Table 4A.1 in the annex to this chapter provides a sense of the areas of dynamism in world trade. The table reports the average annual percentage growth rate of the nominal dollar value of exports in each cell of the trade

---

11. For any remaining instances of negative trade, which can arise in some of the residually estimated categories for periods of one quarter even though the annual totals do not have negative entries after the corrections just described, the constrained regression estimates of trade equations replace the negative observation with the average of the trade in question for the two previous quarters.

12. For example, in 1987 the DOTS shows total US imports c.i.f. at $424.1 billion, whereas it shows the three identified components as follows: industrial countries, $260.9 billion; developing countries, $136.1 billion; USSR and nonspecified, $0.7 billion. The total exceeds the sum of reported components by $26.4 billion. According to OECD data, US imports f.o.b. from Taiwan in 1987 amounted to $24.6 billion, which would correspond to the missing $26.4 billion figure in the DOTS data at the c.i.f. level. IMF, *Direction of Trade Statistics*, Yearbook 1988, 406–07; OECD, *Monthly Statistics of Foreign Trade*, April 1988, 50.

13. For 1979 through 1986, Republic of China, *Foreign Trade Development of the Republic of China, 1987* (Board of Foreign Trade, Ministry of Economic Affairs). For 1987, total Taiwan exports and imports are based on Central Bank of China, *Financial Statistics, Taiwan District, The Republic of China*, June 1988. For distribution across trading partners, OECD data are applied for industrial countries (with c.i.f. imports reduced by 10 percent to estimate f.o.b. imports). Taiwan's trade with OPEC is assumed to rise proportionately with OPEC's total exports and imports. For other countries, remaining trade is prorated according to 1986 shares.

matrix, from 1973 to 1987. Total world trade grew at 10.6 percent annually over this period, although because of rapid dollar inflation in the 1970s followed by slower inflation and declining dollar export prices in the early 1980s as the dollar strengthened, most of this growth had already occurred by 1980, and annual average growth for 1981–87 was only 3.1 percent in nominal dollar terms.

For the period as a whole, the countries with the fastest-growing exports were Taiwan (17.8 percent annually), Mexico (18.0 percent for nonoil, 19.9 percent for oil), and Korea–Singapore–Hong Kong (16.7 percent). Japan's exports grew at 13.1 percent, whereas those of the United States grew slightly more slowly than the world average, at 9.0 percent (and only 1.8 percent during 1981–87).

As indicated in table 4A.1, US imports grew much more rapidly over the period (at 12.8 percent annually) than US exports. Only Taiwan and Korea–Singapore–Hong Kong had higher import growth, reflecting increases in purchasing capacity from their rapid export growth. The market combination detail in the table indicates, however, that the US market was not the only one where exports from the East Asian NICs were growing rapidly. Exports from these countries grew almost as fast to the European and Japanese markets as to the US market. Thus, Taiwan's exports to the United Kingdom, Germany, and Italy grew in the range of 18 percent annually (and to France, at 28 percent annually), in the same range as in the US market (19 percent) and only moderately higher than in that of Japan (about 15 percent).

The slowest growth in trade occurred in the nominal value of exports from Argentina (4.8 percent) and Other Latin America (6.0 percent). Nominal export growth was also relatively low for OPEC (7.8 percent), and was much lower after 1975 as erosion in oil prices and volumes by 1987 had offset the second oil price shock of 1979–80. Imports grew slowly in Latin America (except for Mexico), as the result of import substitution to cope with the first oil shock and import compression after the debt crisis.

Because future adjustment of the US external imbalance is the driving force in the multicountry analysis of this chapter, it is important to examine whether the trade data base for the EAG model is compatible with US balance of payments statistics (and thus with the trade data base applied in the HHC model of Chapter 3). Table 4.2 compares total imports and exports for the United States for 1974–87, on the basis of the two alternative data bases.

As may be seen in the table, on the import side the DOTS data used for the EAG model have tended to be some 4 to 5 percent lower than the US balance of payments data for imports, although in 1987 the discrepancy was only 1.1 percent. It is perhaps not surprising that data based on the summation across all countries of their exports to the United States should

Table 4.1 Trade matrix, 1987 (billions of dollars)

Exporter	\<Importer\> US	UK	FR	GE	IT	CA	JA	AR
US	0.00	14.11	7.94	11.75	5.53	57.36	28.25	1.09
UK	16.26	0.00	11.31	13.61	6.22	2.57	2.39	0.02
FR	10.48	12.61	0.0	23.81	17.34	1.47	2.21	0.29
GE	27.88	25.75	35.48	0.00	25.71	2.65	5.90	0.94
IT	11.10	8.46	18.45	21.17	0.00	1.35	1.88	0.38
CA	70.78	2.26	0.81	1.23	0.63	0.00	5.25	0.08
JA	85.02	8.48	4.06	12.96	2.12	5.66	0.00	0.45
AR	0.96	0.08	0.14	0.41	0.25	0.07	0.23	0.00
BR	7.67	0.95	1.14	2.02	1.32	0.64	1.87	0.67
ME	13.96	0.24	0.28	0.37	0.04	0.75	0.18	0.15
TA	24.62	1.50	1.11	2.15	0.67	1.53	6.48	0.01
OP	21.95	2.40	5.65	5.44	9.27	1.06	25.19	0.05
UP	1.94	0.00	1.52	1.83	0.59	0.61	0.07	0.00
MP	4.70	0.12	0.33	0.00	0.09	0.14	1.32	0.00
OI	31.37	47.84	47.94	83.72	26.30	3.99	14.58	0.80
KS	38.89	4.54	2.04	5.54	1.43	2.73	13.50	0.11
OL	11.67	1.24	0.91	2.14	0.88	0.69	1.47	0.80
AN	4.61	2.43	5.02	3.74	3.65	0.35	3.30	0.05
RO	21.37	9.75	9.56	20.68	11.95	1.69	21.08	0.24
Totals								
Exports	250.39	131.24	148.53	294.17	117.99	97.03	231.33	6.40
Imports	405.21	142.76	153.69	212.56	113.98	85.31	135.15	6.12
Trade balance	−154.82	−11.52	−5.15	81.60	4.02	11.73	96.18	0.28

US, United States; UK, United Kingdom; FR, France; GE, Germany; IT, Italy; CA, Canada; JA, Japan; AR, Argentina; BR, Brazil; ME, Mexico; TA, Taiwan; OP, OPEC; UP, United Kingdom-oil; MP, Mexico-oil; OI, Other Industrial; KS, Korea–Singapore–Hong Kong; OL, Other Latin America; AN, Other Africa; RO, Rest of World.

yield a lower figure than the US figure for imports (f.o.b.). Incomplete data for trading partners would tend to bias the DOTS figure downward.[14] Fortunately this bias is almost completely absent in the data for 1987, the

14. A notorious example is that of the Mexican data. Mexican authorities consider goods imported duty-free and reexported after processing to be in their services sector rather than merchandise exports, and treat border trade similarly. Thus, their reported exports to the United States in 1985 (for example) amounted to only $13.3 billion, whereas the United States reported $19.4 billion in imports from Mexico (c.i.f.). *Direction of Trade Statistics*, Yearbook 1988, 283, 407.

				Importer				
BR	ME	TA	OP	OI	KS	OL	AN	RO
4.04	14.58	7.41	10.56	33.60	16.14	11.67	3.34	23.02
0.57	0.33	0.48	7.84	35.14	3.35	1.30	3.66	13.07
0.88	0.35	0.46	5.78	41.71	2.16	2.94	7.72	18.33
1.49	0.83	1.49	7.99	114.85	3.87	2.25	4.97	32.13
0.42	0.18	0.41	12.27	27.96	1.68	0.99	2.74	8.56
0.48	0.40	0.58	1.16	3.54	1.37	0.89	0.50	7.09
0.89	1.00	11.45	11.51	23.37	28.32	5.19	3.40	27.47
0.52	0.06	0.26	0.30	1.07	0.08	0.71	0.31	0.95
0.00	0.14	0.09	1.52	2.82	0.56	1.67	0.46	3.10
0.22	0.00	0.17	0.06	1.34	0.24	0.84	0.06	0.65
0.03	0.07	0.00	2.08	2.35	5.75	0.96	0.84	3.08
3.61	0.01	2.47	2.07	14.03	7.84	3.45	1.92	19.41
0.00	0.00	0.00	0.00	6.57	0.00	0.00	0.00	0.00
0.00	0.00	0.00	0.00	0.57	0.00	0.00	0.00	0.00
1.24	1.24	2.66	5.57	121.76	8.17	4.29	6.78	50.69
0.12	0.19	1.65	4.15	9.31	8.02	1.84	1.79	28.51
0.91	0.10	0.38	0.51	10.68	0.39	2.69	0.16	1.86
0.22	0.04	0.83	0.57	6.48	0.55	0.42	3.10	13.32
0.83	0.09	3.99	10.67	34.26	25.68	0.84	4.08	85.85
26.61	26.78	53.22	125.82	458.93	124.37	37.49	48.71	262.61
16.48	19.61	34.78	84.60	491.40	114.16	42.95	45.82	337.08
10.13	7.18	18.45	41.22	−32.46	10.21	−5.47	2.88	−74.47

base year given special weight in the projections (as discussed in Chapter 5). On the export side, the two data series diverge typically by less than 1 percent, and for 1987 are only 0.3 percent apart. This adherence is to be expected as the DOTS data are those submitted by the United States.[15]

---

15. Although the DOTS data are on an f.o.b. basis, whereas US balance of payments data are on a free-alongside-ship (f.a.s.) basis, which may account for the remaining minor discrepancy.

Table 4.2 Comparison of *Direction of Trade Statistics* to US balance of payments (BOP) data
(millions of dollars except as noted)

	Imports			Exports			Trade balance	
Year	DOTS	BOP	DOTS/ BOP ratio	DOTS	BOP	DOTS/ BOP ratio	DOTS	BOP
1974	97,850	103,811	0.942	98,524	98,306	1.002	674	−5,505
1975	91,402	98,185	0.931	107,655	107,088	1.005	16,253	8,903
1976	116,329	124,228	0.936	115,079	114,745	1.003	−1,250	−9,483
1977	143,186	151,907	0.943	121,169	120,816	1.003	−22,017	−31,091
1978	166,385	176,001	0.945	143,762	142,054	1.012	−22,623	−33,947
1979	202,468	212,009	0.955	182,003	184,473	0.987	−20,465	−27,536
1980	239,562	249,749	0.959	220,781	224,269	0.984	−18,781	−25,480
1981	250,871	265,063	0.946	233,739	237,085	0.986	−17,132	−27,978
1982	227,626	247,642	0.919	212,274	211,198	1.005	−15,352	−36,444
1983	256,142	268,900	0.953	200,528	201,820	0.994	−55,614	−67,080
1984	316,824	332,422	0.953	217,889	219,900	0.991	−98,935	−112,522
1985	325,759	338,083	0.963	213,146	215,935	0.987	−112,613	−122,148
1986	353,851	368,700	0.960	217,291	224,361	0.968	−136,560	−144,339
1987	405,206	409,850	0.989	250,390	249,570	1.003	−154,816	−160,280

Sources: International Monetary Fund, *Direction of Trade Statistics Yearbook* 1988, 1981 (world exports to US = US imports f.o.b.); Council of Economic Advisers, *Economic Report of the President,* February 1988, 364; US Commerce Department.

The final two columns of the table indicate the trade balance under the two alternative data sets. In the late 1970s, the DOTS data (used in the EAG data base) tended to understate the US trade deficit by some $8 billion annually. By the early 1980s the understatement had risen to some $10 billion to $12 billion (with the exception of the outsized discrepancy in 1982, probably related to that year's severe recession and timing lags in data).[16] By 1987, however, the DOTS trade deficit was only $5.5 billion (3.4

16. Import data based on partners' exports should tend to precede data based on home-country import records, by at least the time required for shipping. The plunge

percent) smaller than the balance of payments deficit. Thus, trade balance projections in the EAG model should be roughly comparable to the corresponding estimates under the US balance of payments trade concept, although any remaining bias from the data base standpoint tends to be toward under- rather than overstatement of the deficit.[17]

Data on petroleum exports from the United Kingdom ("country" UP) and Mexico (MP) are obtained from OECD statistics.[18] For UP exports, the exports in SITC category 33 (oil and oil products) from the United Kingdom to each specific partner country are directly available from these sources. For MP exports, it is necessary to use data on partner-country imports of oil from Mexico. These data are expressed in c.i.f. form, and accordingly are reduced by 10 percent to correspond to f.o.b. values. As indicated above, the UP and MP oil export data capture only the oil exports of the United Kingdom and Mexico to OECD countries. However, these exports accounted for 98.2 percent of total oil exports by the United Kingdom in 1985. For Mexico, estimated exports to OECD countries in that year ($12.1 billion) amounted to 82.2 percent of total oil exports.[19]

Export price data expressed in dollars are from the IMF. These data represent unit value export price indexes (1980 = 1.0), initially expressed in local currency and then converted at the exchange rate against the dollar for the period in question.[20] For country groupings, export price indexes are calculated using geometric averages of individual country indexes, weighting by 1980 shares of each country in the market in question.[21]

These dollar export prices are used for both the exporter's (country i) price and for the prices of the exporter's competitors from third countries (all $k \neq i$ and $k \neq j$) in a specific country market (country j). In the latter case, the cross-price term (P^j_{Ni}/P_i) is calculated weighting by shares of

---

in imports in 1982 would have shown up sooner in the partner-country export data than in the US import data.

17. Note, moreover, that the current account model developed in Chapter 5 incorporates a specific adjustment to translate from the EAG-DOTS data base to the balance of payments measure of trade.

18. OECD, *Foreign Trade by Commodities*, Series C, various issues.

19. OECD, *Foreign Trade by Commodities: 1985, Exports*, 161; *Imports*, 151; and Banco de Mexico, *Informe Anual 1986* (Mexico: Banco de Mexico, 1987), 228.

20. IMF CD-ROM data base, series 74 and rf, respectively.

21. Geometric averaging uses multiplication of the component indexes raised to powers equal to their respective weights, rather than weighted summation as in arithmetic averaging. The advantage of the former method is that, "unlike arithmetic means, geometric means are not unduly influenced by the few countries with extreme growth rates" (*International Financial Statistics*).

competing countries in total imports of country j from all sources except the exporter in question (i).

There is a single dollar export price for each country (or bloc) that applies to its exports to all other countries. The model does not provide for, nor does the data set permit examination of, discriminatory pricing among trading partners. Thus, when the Japanese yen (for example) rises against the dollar, Japan's dollar export prices are assumed to rise identically for its exports to all markets. It is possible that firms instead hold back the rise in their dollar prices to US customers to preserve market share, but allow dollar prices to rise in their sales to other areas. If so, a given observed average dollar export price will overstate the price charged in the US market (and presumably those of other dollar-area countries) and understate the dollar price in other (presumably non-dollar-area) countries. Considering that average dollar export prices have tended to track well with simple application of the exchange rate to domestic wholesale prices (see Appendix C), however, it seems unlikely that this distortion is serious. For it to be so, the Japanese firm in the illustration would have to be raising its dollar price in the German market (for example) by *more* than implied by the yen appreciation against the dollar, to average out against the lower-than-expected increase in the US market so that the average export price did reflect the expected change from yen appreciation.

For the domestic price in an importing market (that is, the denominator in the equation for direct competition between supplier and importing country, equation 1 above), the country's wholesale price is applied, as converted at the exchange rate against the dollar.

Export volume data (for the dependent variable in the trade equations) are obtained by deflating nominal dollar trade flows by the export price index in dollar terms (just described) for the exporter in question. Thus, they represent millions of dollars at 1980 trade prices.

Real income of each importing country is an index of the country's own national accounts estimates of GDP at constant prices, as reported by *International Financial Statistics* (with 1980 = 1.0). For country groupings, an aggregate index of GDP is obtained from the individual member indexes with a geometric average, weighting by shares in total GDP (converted at official exchange rates) for the group in question in 1980. In groupings of numerous countries, such as Other Africa or Rest of World, the GDP index is based on data for the largest 10 or 15 economies included in the group.

Estimation

For each of the 245 nonoil supplier–market combinations (16×16 less 11 because single-country sources do not export to themselves), the parameters of the model outlined above are estimated using constrained statistical regression. Except for the constant terms, which are unconstrained, the other parameters of the model are constrained to lie within acceptable bounds. The principal objective of the model is for use in policy simulation. Implausible parameters (especially those with the wrong sign) that could arise because of multicollinearity or other econometric difficulties would make the estimates useless for this purpose.

The constrained estimation technique applies nonlinear programming.[22] The program is set to minimize the sum of squared residuals of predicted from actual observations, and thus has the same statistical criterion (or objective function) as standard regression techniques. The programming approach permits direct specification of the upper- and lower-bound limits acceptable for the parameter estimates.

Although the nonlinear programming technique does not generate the familiar t statistics indicating the degree of statistical significance when the parameter is at its upper or lower bound, it is possible to obtain an idea of the extent to which the constraints imposed alter the estimates. An informal test is simply to examine the frequency with which the estimated coefficient lies at one extreme boundary or the other. Such estimates are constrained; all others are "estimated."

For each of the three elasticities in the trade equation (income elasticity, β; direct price elasticity, δ; and cross-price elasticity, σ), the absolute value is constrained to lie within the range of 0.3 to 3.0. (The algebraic value is negative for the direct price elasticity and positive for the other two.) These bounds permit a relatively wide range of estimates. Past empirical studies have tended to generate direct price elasticities in the vicinity of unity to 2, and income elasticities of unity to 3.[23]

The appropriate constraint range for the cross-price elasticity is somewhat more ambiguous. It may be shown that this elasticity is related to the elasticity of substitution in demand among suppliers.[24] Past estimates have

22. Using the GAMS (Generalized Algebraic Manipulation System) programs developed at the World Bank. Anthony Brooke, David Kendrick, and Alexander Meeraus, *GAMS: A User's Guide* (Redwood City, CA: Scientific Press, 1988).

23. See, for example, Robert M. Stern, Jonathan Francis, and Bruce Schumacher, *Price Elasticities in International Trade* (London: Macmillan, 1976). In the case of the Helkie–Hooper model for US trade, the aggregate export price elasticity is slightly below unity, whereas the income elasticity of exports is approximately 2 (see Chapter 3).

24. As shown in Appendix B the relationship is: $\sigma_i = -S/(1 + s_i/s_{Ni})$, where σ_i is the cross-price elasticity for exports from country i (to the market of country j), S is the elasticity of substitution in demand between goods from country i and goods from other suppliers, s is the share in the market in question, and subscript Ni refers to all supplying countries other than the exporting country in question (i). As the market share of exporting country i approaches unity, the cross-price elasticity

tended to place that substitution elasticity in the range of -2.5,[25] a value consistent with a range of 0 to 2.5 for the cross-price elasticity (which lies within the 0.3 to 3.0 range imposed here).

A word is in order concerning the lag structure imposed for the direct and cross-price elasticities. The estimates here apply weights that first rise and then fall again in a symmetrical, inverse-U structure over eight quarters.[26] The weight in the current quarter would tend to be modest because inadequate time has passed for recognition, decision, and delivery. The weight for the distant past is small because price influences become exhausted after a certain time. The midpoint of the lag structure, and thus its greatest weight, is set for quarters -3 and -4 (with the current quarter designated as zero). That is, on average, trade is assumed to respond to price with a one-year lag.

Estimation of the price terms applies the lag structure to create a weighted-average price; there is then a single parameter estimated for this weighted price. (Thus, in equation 1 above, the summation sign is within the parentheses, and the price elasticity itself, or δ_{ij}, does not vary by time period.) Because the same types of delays in terms of economic behavior are involved in the choice among alternative foreign suppliers as in the decision to import rather than purchase domestically, the same lag structure is applied to estimation of the cross-price elasticities.

Empirical Results

Trade Elasticities

Tables 4A.2 through 4A.4 of the annex to this chapter present the coefficients estimated for the trade equations: the income, direct price, and cross-price

---

approaches zero. As the exporting country's market share approaches zero, the cross-price elasticity approaches the full (absolute) value of the substitution elasticity. On this basis, with an elasticity of substitution of -2.5, the corresponding range for the cross-price elasticity would be 0 to 2.5.

25. See William R. Cline, *et al., Trade Negotiations in the Tokyo Round* (Washington: Brookings Institution, 1978), 60–1.

26. Beginning with the current quarter and working backward, the weights assumed are .067, .117, .150, .167, .167, .150, .117, and .067. This is the same general structure as for US exports in the Helkie–Hooper model of the US current account (see Chapter 3). Note that experimentation with US trade indicated that unconstrained lag structures often yielded individual lag parameters with signs shifting from positive to negative. Such parameters can achieve a close fit because they permit almost endless fine-tuning, but their economic meaning is nil. Thus, it is highly doubtful that a price increase of 10 percent in the first quarter can cause the quantity of imports to decline by 1 percent in the first quarter, rise again by 0.5 percent in the second, decline by 1.5 percent in the third, rise by 0.7 percent in the fourth, and so forth.

elasticities, respectively. These coefficients are estimated with quarterly data for 1973–87. Table 4A.5 reports the adjusted R^2 statistics (percentage of variation explained by the equation, adjusted for degrees of freedom).

As may be seen in table 4A.2, most of the unconstrained income elasticity estimates are highly significant, with t statistics well above the range of 2 associated with statistical significance at the 95 percent level. The constrained estimates (0.3 or 3.0) do not have t statistics, as they are imposed rather than statistically estimated. For the price elasticity (table 4A.3), the unconstrained estimates once again show relatively high statistical significance, although there is a higher incidence of imposed constraints as well as of insignificant estimates in unconstrained cases. The estimates for the cross-price elasticity (table 4A.4) show weaker results, as the majority of country combinations require imposed constraints, and the unconstrained estimates are approximately evenly divided between statistically significant and insignificant results.

The percentage of variation explained by the trade equations (table 4A.5) is generally relatively high for the major country combinations. US imports in particular indicate explanation within the range of 90 percent (except for a few of the developing regions). There are numerous instances of low $\bar{R}^2$s, but they typically arise in the small-country combinations.[27] The trade-weighted average $\bar{R}^2$ for the entire trade matrix is 0.703.

As noted above, one indication of the success of estimation is the frequency with which the elasticity is estimated directly as opposed to set at the upper or lower bound. For each parameter, the tables report the number of cases for which an unconstrained estimate is obtained (#UNC). These counts are stated for each country as an exporter (row), for each country as an importer (column), and for all 245 possible cases combined. The tables report corresponding figures for the percentage of trade accounted for by unconstrained estimates. For example, table 4A.2, reporting income elasticities, indicates that, for the United States as an exporter, 13 out of 15 possible trade cells (US to US does not exist) show unconstrained estimates, and these account for 96.9 percent of US exports (1986 trade weights). For the United States as an importer, only 5 out of a potential 15 equations show an unconstrained income elasticity, accounting for 38.3 percent of US imports. The lower incidence of unconstrained estimates for US income elasticities on the import side reflects the tendency toward high import growth and thus binding upper-bound constraints.

---

27. There are even some cases of negative $\bar{R}^2$s, which can arise if the equation is not even as successful as simply fixing the dependent variable as a constant at its average over the period. However, these cases account for only 1.72 percent of total trade in the world trade matrix.

For the income elasticity, the highest degree of estimation success without imposing a constraint occurs among the following exporters: United States, Germany, Canada, and Africa. An intermediate incidence of unconstrained estimates is obtained for exports by the United Kingdom, France, Argentina, Brazil, and Rest of World. In contrast, income elasticities typically tend to be constrained for exports by Italy, Japan, Mexico, Taiwan, Korea–Singapore–Hong Kong, and Other Latin America. In the first five of these cases, exports grow so rapidly that income elasticities tend to bump up against the upper-bound constraint; in the case of Other Latin America, the growth is so slow that the lower-bound constraint is frequently imposed. Overall, the income elasticities show unconstrained estimates for 148 of 245 cases, or 60.4 percent by number, accounting for 67.0 percent of total trade.

On the import side, the highest degree of success in achieving unconstrained estimates (for income elasticities) is found in the markets of Canada, Japan, Mexico, Taiwan, Korea–Singapore–Hong Kong, and Rest of World, all of which show 90 to 100 percent of import value covered by unconstrained estimates. Considering that four of these countries show primarily constrained estimates on the export side, this pattern reflects an asymmetry in which income elasticities are high (at the upper bound) for exports but intermediate (unconstrained) for imports. The opposite of this asymmetry is found in the cases of the United States, the United Kingdom, and France, where estimates tend to be at the upper bound for imports but not for exports. The only case of frequent lower-bound income elasticities is for the imports of Brazil.

Explanation without the aid of constraint is somewhat less successful for the price elasticity, and even less successful for the cross-price elasticity. Thus, for the direct price elasticity, 108 cases provide unconstrained estimates, accounting for 45.1 percent of total trade; for the cross-price elasticity, the corresponding results are 73 cases and 45.5 percent of trade. Whereas the upper bound tends to be the constraint in the income elasticities, for the direct and cross-price elasticities an imposed constraint is almost always at the lower bound.

Table 4A.2 shows the trade-weighted income elasticities for each country's imports and exports. The highest export elasticities are for Taiwan and Korea–Singapore–Hong Kong (both approximately 2.7). These estimates probably mix income elasticity on the demand side with the effect of rapidly outward-shifting supply not otherwise captured in the trade prices. For the industrial countries, trade-weighted income elasticities on both the export and import sides tend toward 2. The only notable exception is that of Japan, which has a trade-weighted income elasticity of imports of only 1.2.

It is important to consider whether the method of imposing upper and lower bounds causes a bias in the overall elasticity estimates. If the parameters were systematically at their upper limit, the suspicion would be that the estimates were biased downward, because left unconstrained they would tend to be higher. The opposite bias might be present if the parameters were systematically at their lower bound.

For the United States, on the export side there are few instances of constrained estimates. For imports, there are nine cases of upper-bound income elasticities and only one case of a lower-bound estimate. The average US income elasticity for imports may thus tend to be biased downward, although as discussed below a more complete model could result in typically lower, unconstrained import elasticities.[28]

Price elasticities for US exports are more frequently at the lower bound (five cases) than the upper (one case), but because the single instance of an upper limit is for the crucial trading partner Canada, total exports affected by constrained estimates are approximately evenly divided between upper- and lower-limit cases ($57 billion in 1987 exports to Canada, $69 billion to the five countries with lower-bound estimates). Similarly, the one instance of an upper-limit price elasticity for US imports (from Taiwan) covers approximately the same volume of trade as the three cases of lower-bound estimates (Argentina, Other Latin America, Rest of World), at $25 billion and $34 billion, respectively. The price elasticity constraints thus appear to show no pronounced direction (and thus suggest no particular bias) for the United States. However, they do tend to place a disproportionately high weight on the Canadian market in adjustment to US trade price changes.[29]

An important issue in empirical analysis of US trade has been whether the United States suffers from a secular bias against trade equilibrium because of a lower income elasticity of demand for its exports than for its imports. That is, if such an asymmetry exists, US imports will tend to rise faster than US exports when GNP grows at identical rates in the United States and its trading partners.

Houthakker and Magee presented the first empirical estimates suggesting that an adverse asymmetry existed for income elasticities of US trade.[30]

---

28. In particular, even with a high frequency of upper-limit income elasticities, the US shows an asymmetry in which the import elasticity exceeds the export elasticity. As noted below, this frequent finding for US trade probably reflects trend factors, which, if removed, would leave the income elasticities themselves more symmetrical.

29. Thus, Canada's share of US exports is 22.9 percent. With a price elasticity of 3, the sensitivity of US exports to Canada is 1.8 times as high as the average for US exports. The combined result of high share and high elasticity is that the Canadian market accounts for approximately 40 percent of any increase in US exports resulting from a generalized change in US export prices relative to prices in all other countries.

30. Hendrik S. Houthakker and Stephen P. Magee, "Income and Price Elasticities in World Trade," *Review of Economics and Statistics*, vol. 51 (May 1969).

Subsequent analysts have raised doubts about the validity of this result, however.[31] The essential problem is that there have been major structural changes in the postwar period involving rapidly outward-shifting supply from such nations as Japan and the newly industrializing countries. These strong trend factors tend to get picked up in income elasticities of the United States (and other market countries) if other variables are not explicitly included to remove the structural trend influences. When such variables are included, the income elasticity asymmetry can disappear.[32]

The EAG model does not directly incorporate trend variables for structural change,[33] and is thus susceptible to a measured income elasticity asymmetry. It is thus useful to examine whether the estimated elasticities do contain this adverse property. As noted, table 4A.2 shows that many of the US import elasticities are at the constrained upper bound of 3.0. This constraint applies to several of the most important suppliers, including Japan, Germany, Taiwan, and Korea–Singapore–Hong Kong. In contrast, on the export side the income elasticity is rarely at the upper bound. On the basis of trade-weighted averages (using 1987 trade), the overall income elasticity for US imports is estimated at 2.34, whereas that for exports is estimated at 1.7.[34]

The general range of the income elasticities for US trade approximates that in the HHC model (Chapter 3), where both of the elasticities have a value of approximately 2. However, unlike those elasticities, the estimates in the EAG model do show the adverse asymmetry. Thus, in the EAG estimates, a 1 percent increase in foreign income causes a rise of 1.7 percent in US exports, whereas a 1 percent rise in US income causes an expansion of US imports by 2.34 percent. Applying these percentages to the prospective levels of exports and imports, respectively, if the two elasticities were

---

31. See in particular Bela Balassa, "Export Composition and Export Performance in the Industrial Countries," *Review of Economics and Statistics*, vol. 61, no. 4 (November 1979), and Stephen E. Haynes and Joe A. Stone, "Secular and Cyclical Responses of US Trade to Income: An Evaluation of Traditional Models," *Review of Economics and Statistics*, vol. 65, no. 1 (February 1983).

32. As in the Helkie–Hooper model of the US current account (Chapter 3), which incorporates a variable for relative capital stock.

33. Note that experiments incorporating simple time trends gave highly unstable results.

34. The weighted averages exclude OPEC on the export side, because of the model's application of induced OPEC imports rather than direct trade equations for US exports to the oil-exporting countries. On the import side, the weighted income elasticity does include OP, MP, and UP supply, and applies an elasticity of unity, based on the marginal elasticity for US oil imports as discussed above. Note that the weighted import elasticity in table 4.2 differs because it excludes imports from OP, MP, and UP.

actually both 2.0, the model would bias projections toward a spurious trade balance deterioration by about $8½ billion annually, or some $45 billion over five years.[35]

In previous empirical analysis of US–Japan trade, I estimated that the income elasticity for US imports from Japan is approximately equal to that for US exports to Japan.[36] In contrast, the estimates here show the US elasticity for imports from Japan at 3.0 and the elasticity for US exports to Japan at only 1.23 (table 4A.2). Like the HHC model results, the earlier estimates for Japan suggest there may be some bias toward overstating the adverse elasticity asymmetry for the United States in the EAG model.

The price elasticities estimated in table 4A.3 show a substantial response of trade to price changes. For US imports, the trade-weighted import price elasticity is −1.36. This elasticity is relatively high and exceeds the import price elasticity of −1.15 in the HHC model of Chapter 3. The US price elasticity of demand for imports from Japan is high, at −1.6. This elasticity means that when the dollar depreciates against the yen, the dollar value of imports from Japan goes down as well as the physical volume of these imports. In contrast, the elasticity of near unity in the HHC model implies little change in dollar import values, as dollar depreciation causes a rise in dollar prices of imports that offsets the decline in volume.

The direct price elasticity on the export side is also relatively high for the United States, at a trade-weighted value of −1.09 (versus −0.82 in the HHC model). Moreover, the EAG model incorporates the additional influence of cross-price competition against third-country suppliers in a given market. The trade-weighted average cross-price elasticity for US exports is 0.65 (table 4A.4). When the dollar depreciates against all other currencies, this cross-price elasticity may be added to the direct price elasticity for exports

---

35. Suppose US and foreign income growth are both 3 percent. With income elasticities of 2, both exports and imports would grow at 6 percent annually. With the import income elasticity at 2.34 and the export income elasticity at 1.7, imports would grow at 7 percent annually and exports at 5.1 percent. Applied to a trade base of $400 billion for exports and $500 billion for imports (based on the projection results for 1990, the period midpoint), the divergence amounts to $3.6 billion on the import side and $5 billion on the side of exports.

36. In a model distinguishing secular from cyclical income elasticities, the estimates showed the US income elasticities for imports from Japan at 0.68 (long-run) and 1.62 (short-run), and the corresponding elasticities for Japan's imports from the United States at 0.78 and 1.81. Nonetheless, the model incorporated a term for Japanese industrial capacity (for Japan's exports to the United States) with an elasticity of 1.15, indicating a trend toward higher growth in US imports from Japan than based on income growth alone. C. Fred Bergsten and William R. Cline, *The United States–Japan Economic Problem*, POLICY ANALYSES IN INTERNATIONAL ECONOMICS 13 (Washington: Institute for International Economics, 1985), Appendix B.

to obtain the total export elasticity.[37] The estimates here place this total export price elasticity at 1.74, more than double the HHC export price elasticity. However, in most of the practical scenarios it is unlikely that the United States would depreciate against such weaker countries as most of Latin America, or perhaps even Canada, and so the effective export price elasticity would only add a portion of the cross-price elasticity to the direct price elasticity.[38]

Other notable patterns in the price elasticities include the following. Among the industrial countries, the United States and Canada appear to have the highest price elasticities of imports; demand is relatively price inelastic for other industrial countries. The exports of the Asian NICs tend to have a high price elasticity of demand, as might be expected to the extent that their competition tends to be on the basis of price rather than quality or product differentiation. For the cross-price elasticity, exports of Mexico appear to be highly sensitive to competition from third countries, especially in the US market; and exports of the Other Industrial countries tend to show a relatively high sensitivity as well.

Table 4.3 presents an overview of the estimated elasticities. For each country, it reports the trade-weighted elasticities on both the export and import sides (from tables 4A.2 through 4A.4). The table also reports two important measures: the difference between the average income elasticity for exports and that for imports; and the absolute sum of the price elasticities for exports, imports, and cross-price response. The first measure shows the direction and magnitude of any elasticity asymmetry of the Houthakker–Magee type (for income growth over time). The second shows whether trade is sufficiently responsive to price changes that devaluation will work to correct the trade imbalance. In particular, the Marshall–Lerner condition requires that the sum of export and import price elasticities (absolute value)

---

37. Thus, consider equation 1 above. When the United States depreciates the dollar, exports rise both from the direct price effect (applied to elasticity δ) and from the cross-price effect (elasticity σ) of greater competitiveness against third-country suppliers to the market in question. Both proportionate export volume increases apply to the same base trade volume $(q_{ij,t-1})$. Note that, on the import side, the cross-price elasticity is irrelevant, because it affects only the composition across suppliers of a given level of US imports (for example), not the level itself. Thus, in equation 1 the direct price term (applied to elasticity δ) changes when the dollar depreciates against all other currencies identically, but the cross-price term (applied to σ) does not (both the numerator and the denominator of the final price term move by the same proportion, so that the price ratio remains unchanged).

38. Moreover, as discussed in Chapter 5 and Appendix A, the central projections make a further correction to ensure consistency of the cross-price elasticities across all suppliers to a given market. This adjustment reduces the trade-weighted US export cross-price elasticity to 0.51 (table 5A.1).

Table 4.3 Country-specific trade elasticities and trade-weighted averages

Country/group	Import elasticities		Export elasticities			Difference of income elasticities[a]	Sum of price elasticities[b]
	Income	Price	Income	Price	Substitution		
United States	2.44	−1.36	1.70	−1.09	0.65	−0.74	3.10
United Kingdom	2.35	−1.04	1.79	−0.67	0.40	−0.56	2.11
France	2.68	−0.57	1.79	−0.42	0.32	−0.89	1.31
Germany	2.26	−0.48	2.04	−0.51	0.30	−0.22	1.29
Italy	2.48	−0.49	2.61	−1.10	0.49	0.13	2.08
Canada	2.01	−2.35	1.57	−1.01	0.37	−0.44	3.73
Japan	1.21	−0.69	2.24	−0.90	0.38	1.03	1.97
Argentina	2.42	−0.32	1.54	−0.36	0.33	−0.88	1.01
Brazil	0.42	−0.56	2.29	−0.61	0.53	1.87	1.70
Mexico	1.69	−0.51	2.92	−1.33	0.33	1.23	2.17
Taiwan	1.31	−0.42	2.70	−1.88	0.61	1.39	2.91
Other Industrial	2.26	−0.50	1.91	−0.60	0.54	−0.35	1.64
Korea–Singapore–Hong Kong	1.33	−0.32	2.66	−1.20	1.46	1.33	2.98
Other Latin America	1.62	−0.45	1.32	−0.50	0.31	−0.30	1.26
Other Africa	0.73	−0.32	1.00	−1.12	0.43	0.27	1.87
Rest of World	1.13	−0.47	1.80	−0.31	0.74	0.67	1.52
Trade-weighted average	1.97	−0.77	1.97	−0.77	0.55	0	2.09

a. Export minus import.
b. Absolute value; includes cross-price elasticity.

exceed unity. Otherwise, higher import prices will swamp lower import volumes (for example), and devaluation can actually reduce the trade balance.

As may be seen in table 4.3, there are relatively large adverse income elasticity asymmetries for the United States, the United Kingdom, Canada, and especially France and Argentina. For Canada and Argentina, the weight of agricultural goods in exports may be one reason. In contrast, there are large positive asymmetries for Japan, Mexico, Taiwan, Korea–Singapore–Hong Kong, and especially Brazil. To a considerable degree, these asymmetries may reflect past trends in technical and institutional change (for example, market closure and import substitution accompanied by export expansion in Brazil) rather than pure income elasticity differences.[39] Nonetheless, in the absence of strong reasons for these trends to end, it is meaningful to incorporate the asymmetry information in the elasticities for purposes of projection.

The table also shows that trade is generally price sensitive. The sum of price elasticities exceeds the Marshall–Lerner condition in all cases (although only barely so for Argentina), and it is in the range of 3 or higher for the United States, Canada, Taiwan, and Korea–Singapore–Hong Kong. As noted above, for at least the United States this outcome does not appear to be biased from the standpoint of incidence of lower rather than upper bounds in constrained estimates.

Among the industrial countries, trade is the least price sensitive in France and Germany, with Italy, Japan, and the Other Industrial countries at an intermediate level. Among developing countries, Other Latin America and Rest of World have the lowest price sensitivity. The large weight of commodities in their exports is consistent with this finding (although on this basis the price elasticities for Africa would have been expected to be somewhat lower).

Overall, the estimated elasticities in the EAG model show considerable responsiveness to income and prices. They thus provide a basis for encouragement that external adjustment can be carried out through proper exchange

---

39. Moreover, as Krugman points out, there is a strong inverse correlation between a country's growth rate and its observed income elasticity for imports. Thus, Japan tends to have low import income elasticities, yet its exports are to slower-growing countries that, by the inverse rule, have higher import income elasticities—giving Japan relatively high observed export income elasticities. This interrelationship between growth and elasticity is essentially necessary for growth differences to be compatible with relatively balanced trade. Otherwise high-growth countries such as Japan would have growing trade deficits over time. The implication is that the divergent elasticities are not intrinsic but, instead, would tend to converge if country growth rates did so as well. Paul R. Krugman, "Differences in Income Elasticities and Trends in Real Exchange Rates," *NBER Working Paper* 2761 (Cambridge, Mass.: National Bureau of Economic Research, 1988).

rate and demand policies. As discussed in Appendix A, additional modifications to the estimated elasticities are made prior to their use in the projection model.

Backcasts

Before turning to the projections and policy simulations of Chapter 5, it is useful to obtain a more complete sense of the model's accuracy. Figure 4.1 presents a graphical summary of the performance of the model over the period 1975–87. Each frame of the figure shows total actual and "predicted" (or "backcast") values for imports and exports of one of the countries or areas examined in the model (in billions of current dollars, annual totals). These totals are simply the sums of the country-specific trade flows (with exports the horizontal sum of the trade matrix of the type shown in table 4.1, and imports the vertical sum).

For the past 13 years as a whole, the fits of predicted to actual trade are extremely close for most of the industrial countries (including OI) and for Taiwan and Korea–Singapore–Hong Kong. There is some tendency to overpredict Canadian exports in the late 1970s and to underpredict them in the early 1980s. Otherwise the principal divergences between actual and predicted trade arise only for 1987, as discussed below. For the Latin American countries, the broad trends and turning points are captured by the model, although divergences between the absolute levels of actual and predicted trade are relatively wide for Argentina, Mexico, and Other Latin America. As a whole, nonetheless, the model achieves favorable accuracy. One reason is that these totals are the composite in each case of 16 trade equations, and errors that exist at the level of each individual equation tend to average out in the aggregation of their predictions.

There is one important pattern of error that is of particular concern, however: US imports tend to be underpredicted for 1987, whereas the exports of Germany, Japan, Taiwan, and (to a lesser degree) Korea–Singapore–Hong Kong tend to be underpredicted. Thus, 1987 predicted exports for the United States are 1.8 percent above their actual level, whereas predicted imports are 7.8 percent below actual. As a result, the predicted 1987 trade deficit of $118.5 billion is much lower than the actual deficit of $154.8 billion (EAG-DOTS data base). In contrast, for Japan predicted and actual imports coincide almost exactly over the full period 1975–87, but predicted exports begin to fall short of actual by 1984, miss the mark by 4.6 percent by 1986, and, most seriously, understate the true level by 12.8 percent or $29.5 billion in 1987. Of this shortfall, half is accounted for by underprediction of Japanese exports to the United States (at $69 billion

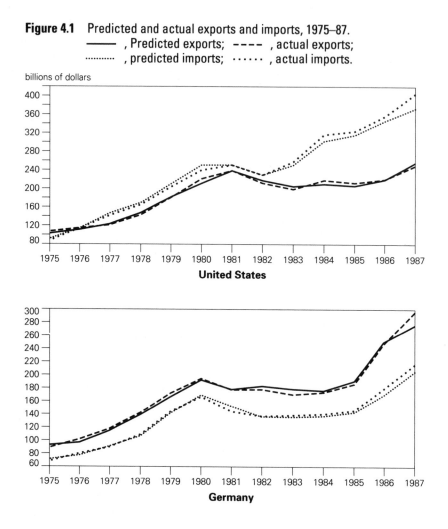

Figure 4.1 Predicted and actual exports and imports, 1975–87.
———— , Predicted exports; – – – – , actual exports;
·········· , predicted imports; ······ , actual imports.

billions of dollars

United States

Germany

instead of the actual $85 billion). Similarly, after almost perfect explanation through 1986, the backcasts for German exports fall short of actual 1987 results by 6.8 percent ($20 billion); for Taiwan, the 1987 export prediction shortfall is 21.9 percent ($11.6 billion). For Taiwan, as in the case of Japan, the divergence is concentrated in exports to the United States (understated by $6.4 billion), although the bulk of the prediction shortfall for Germany is in its exports to the Other Industrial countries and the Rest of World group.

The single major change underlying this shift in prediction performance is the sharp appreciation of the German mark and the Japanese yen against

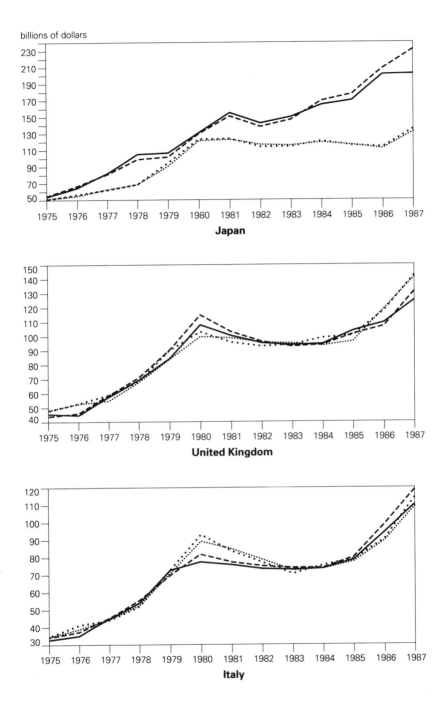

billions of dollars

Japan

United Kingdom

Italy

Figure 4.1 (continued)

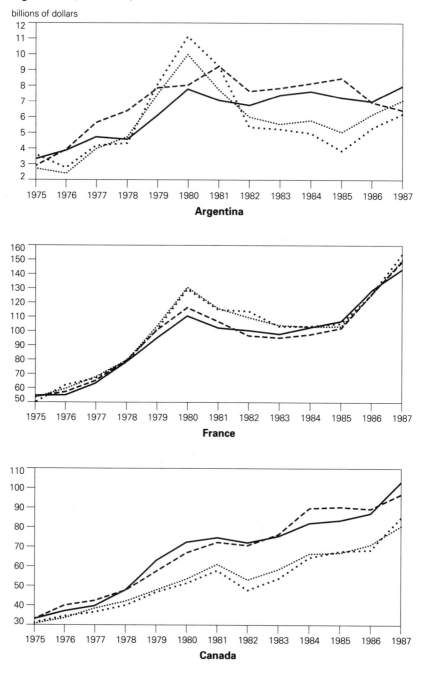

billions of dollars

Argentina

France

Canada

billions of dollars

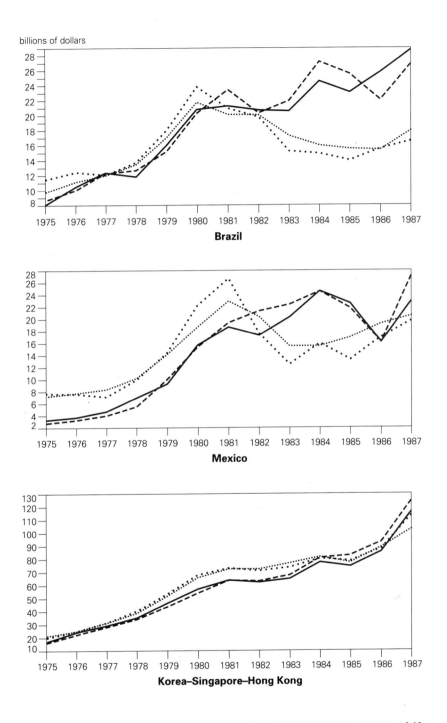

Brazil

Mexico

Korea–Singapore–Hong Kong

Figure 4.1 (continued)

billions of dollars

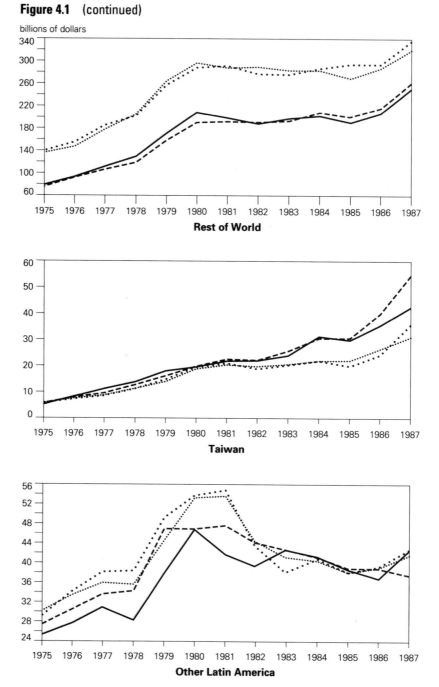

Rest of World

Taiwan

Other Latin America

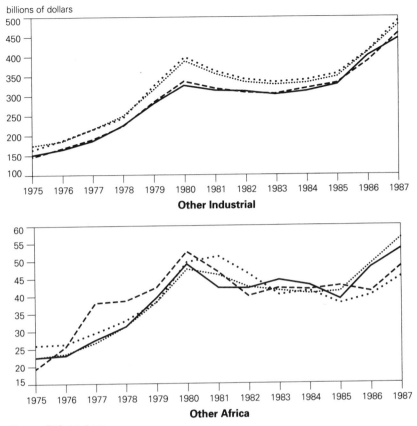

billions of dollars

Other Industrial

Other Africa

Source: EAG data base.

the dollar in 1986–87, which causes a predicted slowing or reduction of the dollar value of exports by 1987.[40] The problem is not that actual trade prices lag far behind predicted responses to exchange rates; on the contrary, as analyzed in Appendix C, the export unit values for Germany are almost precisely what is expected from application of the German wholesale price index to the DM/$ exchange rate, and in the case of Japan there appears to be only a modest lag. Instead, the divergence between predicted and actual values arises from the fact that application of the estimated direct and cross-

40. In addition, there may be an underlying tendency to underpredict the trend in Japanese and Taiwanese exports to the United States over time, as the income elasticity for both is constrained at the upper bound of 3.

price elasticities to the large actual rise in German and Japanese export prices yields a larger cutback in export growth than actually occurred.[41]

Figure 4.2 shows bilateral trade between the United States and each of the nine largest partners or areas in the EAG model, and indicates both actual and predicted exports and imports from 1975 through 1987. The same broad patterns emerge for US bilateral trade as for the country aggregates: the model generally tracks history well, but there are important shortfalls of predicted from estimated exports to the United States in 1987 in the cases of Japan, Taiwan, and to a lesser extent Germany. The overall results of the backcasts thus suggest two patterns. First, the EAG model replicates past trade trends relatively well, especially for the industrial countries and the East Asian NICs. Second, however, there is a tendency in 1987 to underestimate exports of some major countries (especially Japan, Germany, and Taiwan) and understate the imports of the United States. This tendency is almost certainly caused by the less-than-predicted response to the large change in the value of the dollar in 1986–87.

The EAG model thus confirms the finding by the Helkie–Hooper model and others that by 1987 US external adjustment seemed to be lagging somewhat behind schedule given the exchange rate changes that had taken place in 1985–87.[42] In the EAG model, however, the origin of this gap is not in a failure of trade prices to move as promptly as expected in response to exchange rates. The gap arises even though the model applies actually observed trade prices rather than predicted prices based on exchange rate changes. The implication, instead, is that in the 1986–87 experience the length of the lags from trade price to trade volume response became longer

---

41. Consider the case of Japan's exports to the United States. From 1985 to 1986, the dollar unit value of Japan's exports rose by 21.4 percent, while US domestic wholesale prices fell by 2.9 percent. The direct price term thus moved against Japan by 25 percent. With an elasticity of -1.6, and simplifying the trade response lag to one year, this effect meant an expected reduction in volume by 30.5 percent (note that for such a large change the exponential equation must be applied to obtain the percentage reduction, as simple multiplication of percentage price change by elasticity overstates the change). In addition, the cross-price term for other suppliers against Japan in the US market declined by 16 percent. With a cross-price elasticity of 0.3, this influence should have reduced export volume by an additional 5.1 percent. Against these forces, US income rose by 3.4 percent in 1987, and the income elasticity of 3 would have meant a 10.5 percent increase in the volume of imports from Japan. The net volume change should thus have been 26.6 percent. Allowing for the increase in the dollar export price, the dollar value of Japan's exports to the United States would have been expected to decline from 1986 to 1987 by 11 percent (or, more precisely in the full model, by 10.3 percent). Instead, they rose by 3.8 percent.

42. See, for example, Peter Hooper and Catherine L. Mann, "The US External Deficit: Its Causes and Persistence," *International Finance Discussion Papers* 316 (Washington: Federal Reserve Board, November 1987).

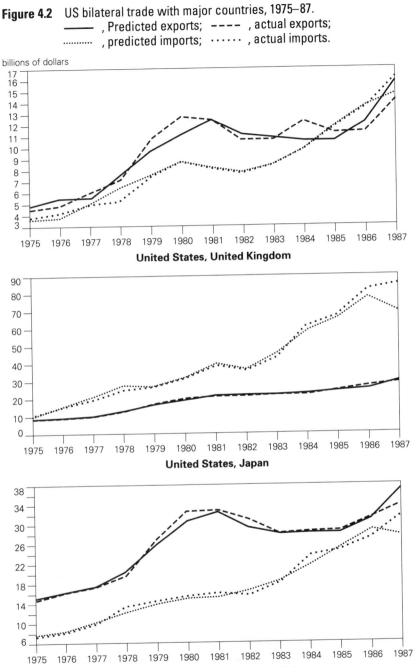

Figure 4.2 US bilateral trade with major countries, 1975–87.
——— , Predicted exports; ---- , actual exports;
·········· , predicted imports; ······ , actual imports.

billions of dollars

United States, United Kingdom

United States, Japan

United States, Other Industrial

Figure 4.2 (continued)

billions of dollars

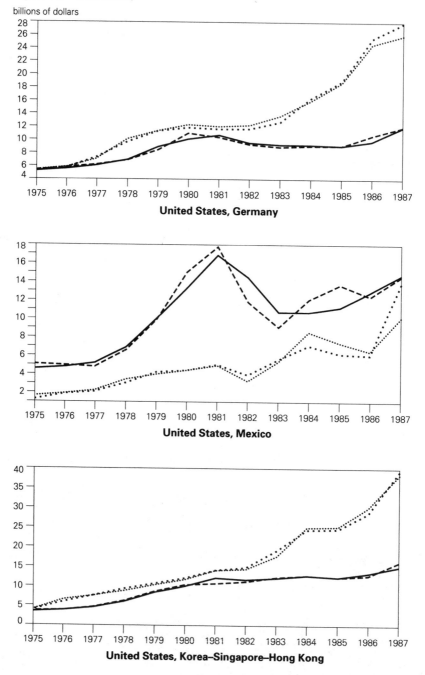

United States, Germany

United States, Mexico

United States, Korea–Singapore–Hong Kong

billions of dollars

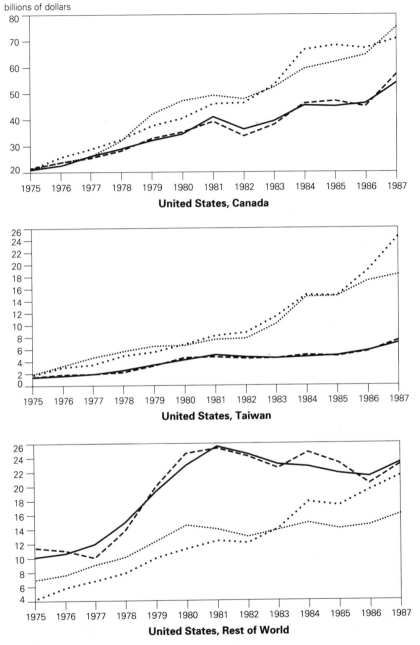

United States, Canada

United States, Taiwan

United States, Rest of World

Source: EAG data base.

A MULTICOUNTRY MODEL OF INTERNATIONAL TRADE 167

than for the 1973–87 period as a whole, or that there was a smaller total response (lower elasticities), or both.

The hypothesis of longer lags may be examined by considering the 1988 projections of the unadjusted EAG model against actual 1988 trade. Actual US exports rose in nominal terms by 11.2 percent in 1987 over 1986, and by 28.2 percent in 1988 over 1987.[43] The model prediction called instead for export value to rise by 17.0 percent in 1987 and then by 21.7 percent in 1988. The total increase from 1986 to 1988 was almost exactly the same for the actual and predicted results (42.6 percent and 42.4 percent, respectively), but the timing was later than anticipated. Export lags in response to the exchange rate change thus do appear to have been longer in the past three years than in the historically estimated model.

On the import side, the corresponding analysis indicates that actual nominal imports grew by 11.2 percent in 1987 and by 8.9 percent in 1988.[44] The unadjusted EAG model prediction called for growth rates of only 8.0 percent and 7.7 percent, respectively. There was thus little indication of a lengthening of the lag beyond model experience on the import side, but instead moderately less actual response to exchange rate change than predicted in both years.

In sum, the EAG model should provide a relatively sound basis for projection of trade effects of US external adjustment disaggregated by major trading partner. However, to ensure the most realistic projections possible, further refinement of the model is developed in Appendix A.

---

43. US Department of Commerce, *Summary of US International Transactions: Fourth Quarter and Year 1988*, BEA-89-09, and *Third Quarter 1987*, BEA-87-58 (Washington: US Department of Commerce, 14 March 1989 and 15 December 1987).

44. *Ibid.*

Statistical Annex to Chapter 4

Table 4A.1 Export growth rates, 1973–87
(percentages per year)[a]

Exporter	Importer								
	US	UK	FR	GE	IT	CA	JA	AR	BR
US	0.0	9.8	9.0	8.1	6.9	9.5	8.7	6.3	5.3
UK	10.6	...	13.8	14.2	13.5	6.7	9.0	−13.3	5.3
FR	13.0	12.1	...	8.8	10.1	10.9	11.7	8.6	8.8
GE	11.3	14.9	10.0	...	10.8	10.8	12.3	10.3	4.7
IT	12.6	14.5	12.5	10.6	...	13.0	13.7	7.4	4.7
CA	10.1	2.5	9.4	7.3	5.4	...	7.6	5.6	10.4
JA	15.6	13.1	17.3	16.6	13.8	12.4	...	4.2	2.7
AR	9.1	−7.4	1.1	3.1	−3.4	12.7	3.9	...	3.8
BR	13.7	8.0	12.1	9.2	9.4	15.9	10.6	8.7	...
ME	16.9	20.1	18.6	13.1	9.1	22.9	1.3	15.4	12.5
TA	19.1	18.5	27.5	16.5	18.1	15.7	14.7	24.8	12.0
OP	11.3	−2.8	3.5	4.8	7.0	1.0	10.0	−2.1	10.8
UP	24.3	...	27.2	24.3	34.0	40.8	...	...	...
MP	42.3	...	...	...	9.1	...	51.3	...	...
OI	10.4	10.1	11.0	10.3	11.6	9.2	8.1	7.8	3.1
KS	17.8	11.2	18.0	15.0	18.6	16.1	14.2	14.9	9.5
OL	7.0	5.7	9.0	7.3	8.7	9.0	6.0	9.2	13.4
AN	11.1	6.5	8.6	11.2	11.3	5.7	11.6	2.7	4.2
RO	13.0	6.3	11.0	11.2	10.3	8.2	9.1	...	13.0
Total imports	12.8	9.9	10.7	10.4	10.3	9.8	9.9	7.6	6.6

US, United States; UK, United Kingdom; FR, France; GE, Germany; IT, Italy; CA, Canada; JA, Japan; AR, Argentina; BR, Brazil; ME, Mexico; TA, Taiwan; OP, OPEC; UP, United Kingdom-oil; MP, Mexico-oil; OI, Other Industrial; KS, Korea–Singapore–Hong Kong; OL, Other Latin America; AN, Other Africa; RO, Rest of World.

a. Based on nominal dollar values.

| Importer | | | | | | | | Total exports |
ME	TA	OP	OI	KS	OL	AN	RO	
11.4	14.6	8.0	8.5	12.9	8.4	3.9	7.4	9.0
8.7	13.4	10.6	8.3	12.2	4.7	5.1	8.5	9.8
8.0	20.0	8.6	9.7	17.1	11.2	7.8	10.5	10.0
6.0	14.2	9.1	10.4	14.6	7.9	6.6	9.3	10.5
8.0	19.2	16.6	12.7	18.4	10.7	9.7	6.9	11.9
8.5	21.6	10.7	7.3	17.9	6.7	9.5	7.3	9.3
11.8	14.9	10.4	12.7	14.3	9.9	7.5	9.2	13.1
4.2	24.9	9.4	5.8	15.8	3.4	15.6	5.3	4.8
7.4	14.5	15.2	5.2	19.1	11.7	9.0	9.1	10.4
. . .	14.5	4.3	12.0	31.9	13.9	33.2	. . .	18.0
18.4	. . .	16.3	19.9	17.8	21.3	17.1	16.3	17.8
− 12.8	17.5	14.1	9.2	13.4	2.9	9.5	6.1	7.8
. . .	. . .	. . .	22.7	. . .	. . .	. . .	. . .	24.3
. . .	. . .	. . .	2.3	. . .	. . .	. . .	. . .	19.9
8.6	21.9	5.5	10.4	13.8	8.0	7.8	10.8	10.3
15.6	16.3	16.6	15.7	19.0	21.8	15.1	18.1	16.7
− 0.7	11.5	9.8	26.1	13.8	− 0.1	. . .	− 6.4	6.0
1.8	19.5	6.1	11.7	11.0	− 10.0	5.4	9.9	8.8
4.4	16.9	11.1	10.8	15.1	9.2	. . .	10.2	11.3
10.3	15.8	10.4	10.4	14.6	6.7	9.5	9.4	10.6

Table 4A.2 Matrix of income elasticities

Exporter	US	UK	FR	GE	IT	CA	JA	AR	BR
					Importer				
US	0 (—)	2.534 (6.0)	2.723 (9.3)	1.412 (7.3)	0.916 (2.8)	2.085 (14.8)	1.229 (18.0)	2.919 (3.7)	0.3 (*)
UK	2.424 (17.1)	0 (—)	3 (*)	3 (*)	3 (*)	1.887 (2.7)	0.342 (1.0)	3 (*)	0.3 (*)
FR	3 (*)	3 (*)	0 (—)	1.357 (8.4)	2.174 (11.5)	1.479 (6.2)	2.108 (17.6)	3 (*)	0.58 (2.9)
GE	3 (*)	3 (*)	2.288 (18.2)	0 (—)	2.51 (19.4)	1.618 (7.7)	1.818 (15.7)	3 (*)	0.3 (*)
IT	3 (*)	3 (*)	3 (*)	2.376 (8.3)	0 (—)	2.26 (11.8)	1.547 (9.1)	3 (*)	0.3 (*)
CA	1.774 (3.9)	0.3 (*)	2.426 (8.3)	0.823 (3.4)	0.3 (*)	0 (—)	0.679 (5.5)	2.739 (1.8)	1.25 (2.8)
JA	3 (*)	3 (*)	3 (*)	3 (*)	3 (*)	2.53 (17.6)	0 (—)	3 (*)	0.3 (*)
AR	3 (*)	0.3 (*)	0.3 (*)	1.748 (2.7)	0.3 (*)	3 (*)	0.449 (0.9)	0 (—)	0.539 (1.6)
BR	3 (*)	1.953 (3.6)	3 (*)	1.742 (3.6)	3 (*)	2.248 (4.4)	0.421 (2.1)	1.754 (2.1)	0 (—)
ME	3 (*)	3 (*)	3 (*)	3 (*)	3 (*)	3 (*)	0.765 (1.9)	0.3 (*)	1.269 (2.3)
TA	3 (*)	3 (*)	3 (*)	3 (*)	3 (*)	3 (*)	2.152 (18.0)	2.686 (2.0)	2.519 (8.6)
OI	1.79 (4.4)	1.577 (6.0)	3 (*)	2.256 (19.6)	2.824 (9.7)	0.959 (2.2)	0.826 (3.8)	3 (*)	0.3 (*)
KS	3 (*)	3 (*)	3 (*)	3 (*)	3 (*)	2.094 (5.8)	1.369 (7.9)	3 (*)	1.135 (4.1)
OL	0.3 (*)	0.44 (1.3)	2.348 (6.4)	1.129 (2.7)	1.953 (2.1)	1.476 (3.2)	0.73 (2.8)	0.3 (*)	0.708 (2.1)
AN	1.444 (3.1)	0.3 (*)	1.155 (2.9)	0.389 (0.8)	0.912 (2.2)	0.3 (*)	0.454 (2.6)	3 (*)	0.3 (*)
RO	1.269 (1.2)	3 (*)	2.077 (1.2)	3 (*)	3 (*)	0.3 (*)	1.211 (6.6)	3 (*)	0.3 (*)
WTDE	2.443	2.346	2.679	2.256	2.481	2.011	1.207	2.422	0.423
#UNC	5	4	6	9	6	10	15	4	7
%MUN	38.3	45.7	40.8	73.1	76.3	94.7	100	30.5	24.6

Numbers in parentheses are *t* statistics for unconstrained estimates. Asterisk indicates constraint is binding. (—) = no trade. WTDE = trade-weighted average elasticity; #UNC = number of country-pair equations for which the estimated elasticity is unconstrained; %MUN, %XUN = percentage of imports or exports, respectively, accounted for by countries for which elasticities are unconstrained. Country abbreviations are as in table 4A.1.

			Importer				WTDE	#UNC	%XUN
ME	TA	OI	KS	OL	AN	RO			
1.968	1.316	1.823	1.292	1.463	0.3	1.318	1.696	13	96.9
(12.2)	(22.5)	(9.1)	(19.2)	(17.7)	(*)	(8.1)			
0.3	0.363	1.281	0.915	1.071	0.485	0.578	1.794	9	70.9
(*)	(5.5)	(2.4)	(20.4)	(1.2)	(0.6)	(4.4)			
0.3	1.545	1.834	1.207	2.43	0.3	1.000	1.788	10	78.0
(*)	(12.1)	(10.7)	(9.6)	(12.7)	(*)	(10.4)			
0.852	0.934	2.066	1.181	0.482	0.3	0.49	2.044	10	67.2
(3.1)	(10.7)	(21.5)	(17.5)	(2.4)	(*)	(7.2)			
0.886	1.54	3	1.986	3	1.054	1.179	2.606	8	35.9
(2.3)	(19.6)	(*)	(23.8)	(*)	(3.9)	(2.8)			
0.443	2.271	1.089	1.735	1.651	0.993	1.014	1.571	13	97.0
(1.9)	(36.9)	(3.6)	(22.4)	(5.1)	(3.3)	(7.3)			
1.144	1.021	3	1.035	1.305	0.3	0.694	2.242	6	36.0
(3.6)	(15.8)	(*)	(21.0)	(6.8)	(*)	(6.8)			
0.3	2.642	1.705	1.324	1.13	0.867	1.405	1.536	9	74.4
(*)	(18.4)	(2.9)	(5.8)	(3.3)	(1.1)	(2.3)			
0.98	2.362	2.527	2.723	2.703	3	1.129	2.291	11	57.8
(2.2)	(10.3)	(7.5)	(19.9)	(9.6)	(*)	(3.5)			
0	2.128	3	3	3	3	2.645	2.921	4	6.20
(—)	(15.5)	(*)	(*)	(*)	(*)	(2.6)			
2.856	0	3	1.684	3	2.541	2.372	2.699	7	31.8
(8.5)	(—)	(*)	(27.3)	(*)	(15.6)	(7.5)			
1.013	2.284	2.147	1.176	1.799	1.544	0.725	1.912	13	85.9
(3.3)	(14.0)	(7.5)	(6.7)	(4.2)	(4.9)	(4.7)			
1.976	1.439	3	1.572	3	1.881	3	2.659	7	23.3
(4.7)	(14.8)	(*)	(25.4)	(*)	(7.9)	(*)			
0.3	2.191	3	2.987	0.3	0.3	0.3	1.317	9	24.3
(*)	(16.4)	(*)	(11.6)	(*)	(*)	(*)			
0.383	1.584	1.563	1.267	0.895	0.3	1.117	1.000	11	87.2
(0.4)	(22.1)	(5.7)	(11.5)	(0.9)	(*)	(2.0)			
0.3	1.231	3	1.554	1.217	0.521	1.171	1.796	8	68.5
(*)	(11.2)	(*)	(6.7)	(14.3)	(0.6)	(15.9)			
1.692	1.313	2.261	1.337	1.622	0.727	1.134	1.970		
10	15	9	15	11	8	14		148	
95.3	100	59.6	99.8	81.4	47.3	90.4			67.0

Table 4A.3 Matrix of price elasticities

Exporter	US	UK	FR	GE	IT	CA	JA	AR	BR
					Importer				
US	0	−0.889	−0.66	−0.53	−0.514	−3	−0.554	−0.377	−0.3
	(—)	(−4.2)	(−2.1)	(−5.2)	(−0.8)	(*)	(−4.4)	(−8.0)	(*)
UK	−0.677	0	−0.457	−0.3	−0.484	−0.3	−2.281	−0.3	−0.602
	(−5.7)	(—)	(−5.2)	(*)	(−2.9)	(*)	(−3.4)	(*)	(−0.6)
FR	−0.521	−0.499	0	−0.777	−0.3	−0.828	−0.3	−0.3	−0.3
	(−2.6)	(−5.0)	(—)	(−1.9)	(*)	(−4.0)	(*)	(*)	(*)
GE	−0.615	−1.462	−0.3	0	−0.3	−0.525	−0.3	−0.3	−0.3
	(−9.0)	(−19.0)	(*)	(—)	(*)	(−3.1)	(*)	(*)	(*)
IT	−1.365	−1.737	−0.367	−1.072	0	−1.378	−2.252	−0.3	−0.592
	(−7.3)	(−3.6)	(−2.2)	(−4.0)	(—)	(−6.5)	(−5.2)	(*)	(−1.0)
CA	−1.209	−0.3	−0.965	−0.79	−0.3	0	−0.374	−0.3	−0.3
	(−2.1)	(*)	(−5.6)	(−5.2)	(*)	(—)	(−2.2)	(*)	(*)
JA	−1.607	−1.719	−0.3	−0.3	−0.3	−1.43	0	−0.3	−0.749
	(−12.3)	(−11.7)	(*)	(*)	(*)	(−8.0)	(—)	(*)	(−0.9)
AR	−0.3	−0.3	−0.3	−0.647	−0.3	−0.3	−0.3	0	−0.3
	(*)	(*)	(*)	(−1.6)	(*)	(*)	(*)	(—)	(*)
BR	−1.084	−0.507	−0.3	−0.332	−0.3	−0.387	−0.39	−0.3	0
	(−9.9)	(−3.2)	(*)	(−1.2)	(*)	(−0.5)	(−1.9)	(*)	(—)
ME	−1.442	−2.285	−0.3	−0.3	−0.3	−2.962	−0.3	−0.3	−0.3
	(−6.5)	(−2.0)	(*)	(*)	(*)	(−1.4)	(*)	(*)	(*)
TA	−3	−2.031	−1.436	−0.673	−0.988	−1.107	−1.544	−0.775	−0.3
	(*)	(−7.1)	(−0.7)	(−2.2)	(−1.1)	(−2.1)	(−6.5)	(−9.8)	(*)
OI	−1.203	−0.949	−0.968	−0.3	−0.644	−0.704	−0.3	−0.3	−0.3
	(−4.1)	(−6.4)	(−3.5)	(*)	(−1.0)	(−1.8)	(*)	(*)	(*)
KS	−2.334	−1.176	−0.3	−1.095	−2.161	−0.87	−1.525	−0.677	−0.627
	(−15.6)	(−10.0)	(*)	(−6.4)	(−7.7)	(−1.7)	(−6.5)	(−8.2)	(−0.8)
OL	−0.3	−0.3	−0.543	−0.356	−0.431	−0.723	−0.384	−0.3	−0.739
	(*)	(*)	(−2.5)	(−1.4)	(−0.7)	(−1.6)	(−1.4)	(*)	(−1.4)
AN	−0.373	−0.3	−0.3	−0.509	−1.647	−0.3	−0.728	−0.3	−0.3
	(−1.4)	(*)	(*)	(−1.6)	(−2.0)	(*)	(−4.2)	(*)	(*)
RO	−0.3	−0.3	−0.3	−0.3	−0.3	−0.3	−0.3	−0.3	−3
	(*)	(*)	(*)	(*)	(*)	(*)	(*)	(*)	(*)
WTDE	−1.364	−1.036	−0.573	−0.482	−0.488	−2.346	−0.689	−0.322	−0.562
#UNC	11	10	7	10	7	10	9	3	5
%MUN	84.4	88.8	60.5	36.0	43.0	25.7	59.3	20.0	22.6

For an explanation of abbreviations see tables 4A.1 and 4A.2.

		Importer							
ME	TA	OI	KS	OL	AN	RO	WTDE	#UNC	%XUN
−0.381	−0.617	−0.3	−0.3	−0.3	−0.3	−0.676	−1.09	9	47.4
(−1.9)	(−2.0)	(*)	(*)	(*)	(*)	(−2.5)			
−0.722	−0.3	−1.053	−0.3	−0.869	−0.3	−0.3	−0.674	8	66.7
(−2.1)	(*)	(−3.1)	(*)	(−2.6)	(*)	(*)			
−0.3	−1.594	−0.3	−0.3	−0.3	−0.3	−0.3	−0.423	5	34.2
(*)	(−4.6)	(*)	(*)	(*)	(*)	(*)			
−0.488	−0.431	−0.3	−0.3	−0.3	−0.3	−0.3	−0.513	5	31.5
(−1.6)	(−2.0)	(*)	(*)	(*)	(*)	(*)			
−1.1	−0.3	−1.223	−0.3	−0.672	−0.3	−1.6	−1.097	11	95.1
(−2.2)	(*)	(−4.3)	(*)	(−4.2)	(*)	(−2.4)			
−1.026	−1.281	−0.582	−0.3	−0.643	−0.3	−0.3	−1.01	8	87.1
(−2.5)	(−3.1)	(−0.7)	(*)	(−3.9)	(*)	(*)			
−1.403	−0.3	−0.3	−0.3	−0.3	−0.3	−0.3	−0.896	5	46.0
(−3.5)	(*)	(*)	(*)	(*)	(*)	(*)			
−0.3	−0.3	−0.3	−0.3	−0.3	−1.002	−0.3	−0.358	2	11.7
(*)	(*)	(*)	(*)	(*)	(−5.2)	(*)			
−0.3	−0.447	−0.3	−0.3	−0.359	−0.329	−0.704	−0.614	9	73.5
(*)	(−1.2)	(*)	(*)	(−1.6)	(−1.1)	(−1.4)			
0	−0.478	−0.3	−3	−0.3	−1.689	−1.66	−1.33	6	81.3
(—)	(−1.1)	(*)	(*)	(*)	(−4.7)	(−1.1)			
−1.346	0	−0.3	−0.3	−0.3	−0.3	−0.3	−1.883	8	26.4
(−2.3)	(—)	(*)	(*)	(*)	(*)	(*)			
−0.933	−0.3	−0.3	−0.457	−0.3	−0.3	−0.3	−0.595	7	47.2
(−2.2)	(*)	(*)	(−0.9)	(*)	(*)	(*)			
−0.887	−0.3	−0.3	−0.3	−0.3	−0.335	−0.3	−1.203	10	57.3
(−1.1)	(*)	(*)	(*)	(*)	(−5.5)	(*)			
−0.3	−0.3	−0.3	−0.3	−1.901	−0.3	−1.144	−0.498	8	31.8
(*)	(*)	(*)	(*)	(−7.2)	(*)	(−0.5)			
−2.637	−0.3	−0.3	−0.3	−0.3	−0.3	−2.686	−1.117	6	59.6
(−1.8)	(*)	(*)	(*)	(*)	(*)	(−1.1)			
−0.3	−0.3	−0.3	−0.3	−0.3	−0.38	−0.3	−0.31	1	1.6
(*)	(*)	(*)	(*)	(*)	(−1.8)	(*)			
−0.508	−0.416	−0.497	−0.318	−0.448	−0.316	−0.474	−0.768		
10	6	3	1	5	5	6		108	
96.2	31.5	24.7	7.7	19.1	15.3	16.0			45.1

Table 4A.4 Matrix of cross-price elasticities

Exporter	Importer								
	US	UK	FR	GE	IT	CA	JA	AR	BR
US	0	0.393	0.349	0.3	0.49	0.544	0.3	2.651	1.564
	(—)	(1.4)	(0.9)	(*)	(0.7)	(3.6)	(*)	(11.0)	(5.9)
UK	0.3	0	0.3	0.3	0.3	0.3	0.3	3	1.7
	(*)	(—)	(*)	(*)	(*)	(*)	(*)	(*)	(1.4)
FR	0.612	0.3	0	0.3	0.3	0.3	0.3	0.3	0.3
	(1.3)	(*)	(—)	(*)	(*)	(*)	(*)	(*)	(*)
GE	0.3	0.3	0.3	0	0.3	0.3	0.3	0.3	0.3
	(*)	(*)	(*)	(—)	(*)	(*)	(*)	(*)	(*)
IT	0.388	0.503	0.3	0.346	0	0.3	0.3	0.66	0.3
	(1.0)	(0.6)	(*)	(0.7)	(—)	(*)	(*)	(0.7)	(*)
CA	0.3	0.97	0.3	0.3	1.768	0	0.3	3	0.571
	(*)	(3.3)	(*)	(*)	(5.1)	(—)	(*)	(*)	(0.4)
JA	0.3	0.3	0.3	0.3	0.3	0.3	0	0.3	0.3
	(*)	(*)	(*)	(*)	(*)	(*)	(—)	(*)	(*)
AR	0.3	3	0.3	0.3	0.3	0.3	0.3	0	0.3
	(*)	(*)	(*)	(*)	(*)	(*)	(*)	(—)	(*)
BR	0.3	0.3	0.871	0.3	0.653	1.141	1.69	0.798	0
	(*)	(*)	(4.2)	(*)	(2.3)	(1.3)	(7.3)	(3.7)	(—)
ME	0.3	0.3	0.3	0.3	0.3	0.691	0.3	1.929	0.3
	(*)	(*)	(*)	(*)	(*)	(0.3)	(*)	(2.4)	(*)
TA	0.3	0.3	0.59	0.3	0.3	1.947	0.3	0.3	0.3
	(*)	(*)	(0.2)	(*)	(*)	(2.6)	(*)	(*)	(*)
OI	0.3	0.47	0.338	0.342	0.3	0.3	1.123	0.3	0.3
	(*)	(1.4)	(0.6)	(1.7)	(*)	(*)	(2.4)	(*)	(*)
KS	1.431	0.3	3	0.3	0.3	2.12	1.291	3	0.3
	(2.6)	(*)	(*)	(*)	(*)	(2.4)	(1.8)	(*)	(*)
OL	0.3	0.3	0.3	0.3	0.3	0.3	0.3	0.59	0.3
	(*)	(*)	(*)	(*)	(*)	(*)	(*)	(1.5)	(*)
AN	0.3	0.3	0.616	1.267	0.565	0.3	0.3	0.3	0.3
	(*)	(*)	(1.7)	(2.1)	(0.4)	(*)	(*)	(*)	(*)
RO	0.3	0.3	1.473	0.3	0.707	0.3	0.3	0.3	1.26
	(*)	(*)	(1.0)	(*)	(0.8)	(*)	(*)	(*)	(0.6)
WTDE	0.428	0.392	0.447	0.339	0.379	0.567	0.558	0.967	0.831
#UNC	3	4	6	3	5	5	3	5	4
%MUN	16.1	51.8	49.7	52.9	22.2	75.4	27.6	50.9	46.0

For an explanation of abbreviations see tables 4A.1 and 4A.2.

| Importer | | | | | | | WTDE | #UNC | %XUN |
ME	TA	OI	KS	OL	AN	RO			
1.346 (5.1)	1.255 (6.9)	0.671 (5.2)	1.02 (5.6)	0.624 (7.7)	2.19 (7.3)	0.387 (1.1)	0.646	13	83.3
0.3 (*)	0.3 (*)	0.3 (*)	0.3 (*)	0.3 (*)	1.574 (2.0)	0.721 (3.8)	0.4	3	15.7
0.3 (*)	0.3 (*)	0.3 (*)	0.3 (*)	0.3 (*)	0.3 (*)	0.3 (*)	0.323	1	7.3
0.3 (*)	0.3 (*)	0.3 (*)	0.3 (*)	0.3 (*)	0.3 (*)	0.3 (*)	0.3	0	0.0
0.3 (*)	0.3 (*)	0.3 (*)	0.3 (*)	0.3 (*)	1.525 (1.8)	1.789 (0.9)	0.488	6	49.6
0.3 (*)	0.3 (*)	0.552 (0.5)	1.804 (4.8)	1.129 (3.1)	0.3 (*)	0.3 (*)	0.367	6	9.6
0.3 (*)	0.3 (*)	0.446 (1.3)	0.3 (*)	1.704 (4.7)	2.62 (7.0)	0.3 (*)	0.385	3	14.5
0.3 (*)	0.3 (*)	0.3 (*)	0.3 (*)	0.3 (*)	0.3 (*)	0.3 (*)	0.334	0	0.0
0.3 (*)	0.3 (*)	0.3 (*)	0.3 (*)	0.3 (*)	0.604 (0.7)	0.613 (1.3)	0.527	7	36.6
0 (—)	0.3 (*)	0.3 (*)	0.3 (*)	0.3 (*)	0.3 (*)	0.3 (*)	0.327	2	4.6
3 (*)	0 (—)	0.337 (0.3)	0.642 (1.0)	3 (*)	3 (*)	2.225 (2.2)	0.61	5	27.0
0.3 (*)	0.3 (*)	1.647 (2.6)	0.3 (*)	0.319 (0.5)	0.3 (*)	0.859 (1.5)	0.535	7	76.6
0.3 (*)	1.311 (2.3)	1.471 (6.1)	2.679 (6.3)	3 (*)	0.3 (*)	1.528 (1.3)	1.463	7	85.4
0.3 (*)	0.3 (*)	0.311 (0.6)	0.3 (*)	0.3 (*)	0.3 (*)	0.3 (*)	0.309	2	31.0
0.3 (*)	0.3 (*)	0.3 (*)	0.3 (*)	0.3 (*)	0.3 (*)	0.3 (*)	0.428	3	25.8
0.3 (*)	1.588 (5.3)	0.377 (4.8)	1.078 (1.7)	1.104 (11.6)	0.3 (*)	1.054 (7.9)	0.737	8	68.7
1.089	0.73	0.521	0.814	0.81	0.863	0.788	0.550		
1	3	8	5	5	5	8		73	
74.4	40.4	51.4	53.6	57.9	31.1	67.9			45.5

Table 4A.5 EAG trade equations: adjusted R^2

Ex-porter	Importer															
	US	UK	FR	GE	IT	CA	JA	AR	BR	ME	TA	OI	KS	OL	AN	RO
US	...	0.666	0.702	0.559	0.361	0.648	0.837	0.840	0.370	0.743	0.933	0.636	0.913	0.783	0.251	0.550
UK	0.848	...	0.708	0.818	0.799	0.057	0.170	0.027	0.282	0.153	0.261	0.176	0.836	0.381	-0.140	0.224
FR	0.916	0.887	...	0.624	0.727	0.675	0.875	0.320	0.092	0.508	0.840	0.699	0.673	0.668	0.250	0.659
GE	0.947	0.944	0.834	...	0.882	0.699	0.847	0.343	-0.074	0.182	0.767	0.894	0.865	-0.093	0.309	0.394
IT	0.887	0.786	0.743	0.703	...	0.803	0.868	0.244	0.259	0.080	0.871	0.751	0.916	0.367	0.236	0.163
CA	0.868	0.152	0.625	0.493	0.342	...	0.579	0.283	0.122	0.140	0.973	0.564	0.919	0.568	0.306	0.455
JA	0.949	0.875	0.691	0.742	0.697	0.910	...	0.007	-0.139	0.324	0.825	0.781	0.891	0.540	0.400	0.384
AR	0.551	0.049	0.594	0.185	0.490	0.433	-0.015	...	0.149	0.064	0.827	0.279	0.439	0.002	0.451	0.045
BR	0.918	0.667	0.784	0.558	0.679	0.875	0.944	0.653	...	0.106	0.873	0.624	0.876	0.723	0.593	0.664
ME	0.852	0.127	0.279	0.586	0.152	0.548	0.017	0.080	0.023	...	0.851	0.412	0.693	0.533	0.393	0.066
TA	0.931	0.789	0.114	0.677	0.525	0.908	0.940	0.729	0.553	0.663	...	0.571	0.940	0.788	0.884	0.485
OI	0.674	0.845	0.740	0.908	0.758	0.228	0.433	0.222	0.015	0.226	0.790	0.754	0.672	0.132	0.460	0.386
KS	0.966	0.900	0.747	0.854	0.857	0.953	0.924	0.672	0.251	0.329	0.913	0.908	0.966	0.658	0.789	0.742
OL	0.372	0.090	0.484	0.178	0.093	0.379	0.360	0.230	0.125	0.455	0.850	0.518	0.727	0.390	0.609	-0.080
AN	0.595	-0.171	0.603	0.686	0.807	-0.106	0.834	0.440	0.316	0.070	0.922	0.490	-0.745	-0.064	-0.245	0.162
RO	-0.004	0.010	0.036	0.106	0.210	0.195	0.560	0.145	0.097	0.312	0.896	0.955	0.666	0.897	0.070	0.899

The Impact of US External Adjustment on Trade and Current Accounts of Other Countries

Four years after the beginning of the decline of the dollar from its extremely strong levels of the early 1980s, it remains unclear whether the United States is on a course that will lead to correction of its external deficit. As the analysis in Chapter 3 shows, it is likely that in the absence of further correction of the fiscal deficit, dollar depreciation that goes well beyond reversal of the dollar's rise in the first several months of 1988, and faster growth abroad, the US current account deficit will fall no lower than about $115 billion in 1989 and then rebound to nearly $140 billion again by 1992.

With proper policy measures in the United States and abroad, it should be possible to bring the US current account deficit to a lower, sustainable level of some $50 billion or less by 1992. If these measures and this progress are realized, increasingly the emerging policy issue will be whether the rest of the world is prepared to adjust to the declining trade surpluses that US adjustment will imply. Surplus areas will be faced with the need to replace exports with domestic demand as the engine for growth in their economies. Although Japan has made considerable progress in this direction, Europe has not, and even Japan will need to sustain its growth effort.

In addition, other regions already under balance of payments pressure could face new export difficulties to the extent that US external adjustment reduces their sales to the American market. Intermediate European countries already experiencing growing imbalances with Germany could find their positions further burdened by US adjustment. Latin American countries experiencing debt difficulties could potentially be affected adversely, in view of the large share of the United States in their exports.

This chapter examines the prospective course of international trade flows through 1992. The analysis considers a range of scenarios, from a base case under current policies and exchange rates to alternative cases involving greater US adjustment. The fundamental policy issue at stake is whether the large US external deficit can be corrected while achieving favorable

179

economic growth in the international economy. For the United States, the question is whether serious recession will be necessary to reduce imports. For Germany, Japan, and other countries in strong balance of payments positions, the growth issue focuses on whether domestic demand can replace foreign. For other countries in weaker balance of payments positions, the challenge is to sustain growth despite potential constraints arising from lower exports to (and higher imports from) the United States.

Projection Variables

The EAG model developed in Chapter 4 provides the basis for projections of the 19 × 17 trade matrix over future years, under alternative assumptions about economic policies and performance. The initial projection is a baseline forecast under unchanged policies and base case assumptions. Baseline trends indicate whether the US external balance is on a sustainable path. Simulations for alternative policy scenarios then serve to show the extent to which underlying disequilibria can be corrected by changes in exchange rates and country growth rates, and it is possible to identify a "Feasible Adjustment Package" that achieves a target external US balance. The model permits analysis of the impact on other countries, both under the baseline forecast and under the alternative policy scenarios.

The information required for the EAG projections may be seen by referring back to equations 1 through 6 in Chapter 4. The calculations require estimates of future income in each importing country or area (Y), dollar export prices for each country (P_i and P^j_{Ni} in equation 1), domestic wholesale prices for each country (P_j in equation 1), and future oil prices (P^o in equation 4).

The projections assume specified rates of real economic growth for each country for the period 1988–92 to estimate the income variables. Domestic wholesale prices are projected on the basis of assumed inflation rates for each country. To obtain dollar export prices, it is necessary to apply future exchange rates. In the absence of specific scenarios changing exchange rates, it is assumed that the real exchange rate remains constant. On this basis, the nominal currency/dollar exchange rate is calculated as the rate in the previous period multiplied by the following ratio for the current period: country wholesale price divided by that price in the previous period, all divided by the US wholesale price divided by that price in the previous period. In addition, the exchange rate is further adjusted for any specified change in the real exchange rate. Thus:

(1) $E_{jt} = E_{j,t-1}\{[P^d_{jt}/P^d_{j,t-1}]/[P_{ut}/P_{u,t-1}]\}[1/(1 + e_{jt})]$

where E_j is the exchange rate of country j against the dollar (for example, DM/\$), P^d_j is the domestic wholesale price index for country j, P_u is the US Wholesale Price Index, and e_{jt} is any real depreciation of the dollar against the currency of country j imposed in the period in question.

Given the exchange rate, the dollar export price of the country is calculated as:

$$(2) \quad P_{jt} = P_{j,t-1}[P^d_{jt}/P^d_{j,t-1}]/[E_{jt}/E_{j,t-1}].$$

That is, dollar export prices for a given country increase proportionately with domestic wholesale prices of the country in question, and increase by the proportion of any nominal depreciation of the dollar against the currency in question.

This approach for projecting dollar export prices raises two issues. First, a proximate issue is whether time lags and incomplete exchange rate pass-throughs should be introduced. Second, a more underlying issue is whether some allowance should be made for the feedback of dollar depreciation to wholesale prices themselves in the partner countries.

On the proximate question, in the model as used for backcasting there is no problem presented by lags from exchange rate to trade price, or by incomplete pass-through from the one to the other, because the variable used for the calculations is the actually observed dollar export price, not the exchange rate. For forecasting purposes, however, the model must translate exchange rate changes into dollar export price changes. The approach adopted here assumes immediate and complete pass-through of exchange rate change to dollar export price change. The basis for this approach lies in the analysis of Appendix C, which shows that in the cases of most of the industrial country trading partners of the United States, there has been prompt and nearly complete translation of exchange rate change to dollar export price change, as tested by comparison of wholesale price multiplied by exchange rate as against actually measured dollar export price.

There are two exceptions: Japan and the United Kingdom. As may be seen in the graphs of Appendix C, their dollar export prices have tended to lag somewhat behind the exchange rate. For these two cases, then, there could be further changes in the dollar export price already in the pipeline from exchange rate changes that occurred in the base period. The projections of the initial values of their export prices take this consideration into account.[1] For other, future periods in the projections, the simplifying

---

1. Specifically, with 1987:4 as the base period quarter, the projections impose on the trends otherwise assumed for the dollar export prices of the United Kingdom and Japan an increase in 1988:1 gauged to capture one-half of the difference between the actual export price index in 1987:4 and the level expected on the basis solely of the domestic wholesale price index multiplied by the exchange rate.

approach of immediate and full pass-through of the exchange rate to export prices is retained. As indicated in Chapter 3, there is considerable evidence that the eventual pass-through of exchange rate change to the country's export price is complete or nearly so, and the projection model through 1992 is concerned with medium-term trends rather than the precise phasing of changes in the early quarters.

The more fundamental question of feedback from exchange rate change to domestic wholesale price change warrants separate study. As the graphs for wholesale and consumer prices in Appendix C show for Japan and other industrial countries, there is every reason to believe that the sharp appreciation of the yen against the dollar in 1986–87 contributed to a reduction in wholesale prices and an unusual divergence between consumer and wholesale prices. Depreciation of the dollar may be expected to have a feedback effect of reducing local currency prices in foreign countries and raising prices in the United States.[2]

The central point to bear in mind concerning the projections here is that they deal in changes in the real exchange rate, after these feedback effects have occurred, but do not attempt to model the nominal changes caused by these effects. Thus, in scenarios specifying a 10 percent dollar depreciation, the change is implemented in real terms—the US price declines by 10 percent relative to the foreign price. In practice this change would tend to come about only as the result of a larger nominal depreciation, followed by induced price reductions abroad and price increases in the United States.[3]

Beyond the additional equations just indicated, application of the EAG model for projection purposes requires further refinements to ensure more meaningful and reliable results. Appendix A sets forth these recalibrations. The model adjustments rebase the estimates for the base year 1987 so that half of the distance is closed between actual trade flows and the model's predicted values for that year. The recalibration adopts the average between the country-specific trade elasticities estimated in Chapter 4 and uniform elasticities applying to all country and trade combinations, to moderate the extreme results that can occur otherwise. The adjustments also include a technique to ensure that trade changes from the substitution effect are consistent, so that, within a given market, increases in purchases from the United States after dollar depreciation caused by replacement of imports

---

2. As noted in Chapter 3, a 10 percent depreciation of the dollar increases US consumer prices by an estimated 1.5 percent and reduces consumer prices in foreign industrial countries by 1 percent. The feedback at the wholesale price level would presumably be even greater.

3. Thus, as noted in Chapter 3, the feedback effects probably mean that a real dollar depreciation of 10 percent requires a nominal depreciation in the range of 12½ percent.

previously purchased from third countries are equal in size to the corresponding estimated reductions in those countries' exports to the market. Table 5A.1 reports the adjusted cross-price elasticities.

Current Account Model

An important expansion of the EAG model for forecasting purposes incorporates a whole new dimension rather than more refined parameters: calculation of the current account balance. The detailed trade flows by partner combinations constitute the core of the EAG model. But these estimates do not go far enough for policy purposes, as they generate trade balances but tell nothing about current account results. Yet it is a nation's overall balance on current account that determines its financing needs and the compatibility of its external trends with international balance among countries. Some countries have high surpluses or deficits in nonfactor services (such as tourism or shipping), capital services (interest and profits), or transfers (such as development assistance) that cause large differences between the trade and current account balances. For the United States, growing net external debt will mean that the current account deficit increasingly exceeds the trade deficit. In the past when US net external assets were high, the reverse was true, but the trend toward reversal is already apparent (figure 2.3).

To calculate the current account balances corresponding to the trade projections of the EAG model, it is first necessary to adjust the trade forecasts themselves for compatibility with the balance of payments estimates of exports and imports f.o.b. As indicated in Chapter 4, there are some discrepancies between the *Direction of Trade Statistics* (DOTS) data base used in the EAG model and the corresponding balance of payments estimates of trade, primarily on the import side because of the estimation of imports based on other countries' export data in the DOTS data base. Let γ_x be the ratio of balance of payments exports to DOTS exports in 1987, and γ_m the corresponding ratio for imports.

Second, it is necessary to incorporate services and transfers into the accounts. Nonfactor services such as shipping and insurance are the most easily added; they may be assumed to be proportional to merchandise trade, as the same price and income incentives operate on them. Let η_x be the ratio of nonfactor service exports to merchandise exports in the base year 1987, and η_m the ratio of nonfactor service imports to merchandise imports. Transfers may be projected exogenously at a specified nominal growth rate, so that if T_0 is the dollar value of net transfers in 1987, their value in the tth year after 1987 is $T_t = T_0(1 + g_T)^t$, where g_T is the (exogenous) growth rate of nominal transfers.

Capital services are more complicated. They may be divided into two parts: those stemming from the country's base year capital position, and those arising subsequently as the consequence of accumulated current account surpluses or deficits over the projection period. Suppose that in the base period capital services are F_0. They result from payments received on assets held against foreigners, net of payments made to foreigners on their assets held within the country in question. If the rate of return is i and is the same for both assets and liabilities, then the implicit (but probably unobserved and unmeasured) net capital stock inherited at the outset is $H_{-1} = F_0/i$. (The asset position refers to the end-of-year stock whereas the payments are the flow during the year, so it is assets at the end of the year preceding the base year, or $t = -1$, that generate the net capital services in the base year.)

For this first category of capital services, net income or payments on "inherited" net external assets or liabilities, it is sufficient to make the projection by applying the rate of return as the growth rate. Thus, $F_t = F_0(1 + i)^t$, where t again refers to the period.[4]

For the second category of capital services, payments resulting from cumulated current account results during the projection period, the basic notion is that a current account deficit (or surplus) raises the country's foreign debt (or assets) and a new capital service payment (or receipt) arises equal to the rate of return as applied to the change in the debt (or asset) position. Suppose that at the end of year t the cumulative net asset position originating from current account balances during the projection period, including interest and other capital service payments thereon, amounts to K_t. Then the current account balance for the year, C_t, is:

$$(3) \quad C_t = \gamma_x[X_t(1 + \eta_x)] - \gamma_m[M_t(1 + \eta_m)] + T_0(1 + g_T)^t + F_0(1 + i)^t + iK_{t-1}$$

where all variables are as just described, X_t is the current dollar value of exports predicted by the EAG model, and M_t is the model's prediction for the dollar value of imports.

---

4. More specifically, this capital income arises passively from the base period stock of net external assets. In year 1, $F_1 = i(H_0)$. But this income adds to the stock of assets, so that $H_1 = H_0 + F_1 = H_0 + iH_0 = H_0(1 + i)$. Thus, the stock of inherited assets grows passively at rate i, and $H_t = H_0(1 + i)^t$. With the underlying asset base growing at rate i, the net payments must also grow at this same rate. That is, $F_t = i(H_{t-1})$ grows over time at the same rate as H as long as the rate of return is constant at i.

For its part, the final element in the equation, the stock of assets accumulated from annual current account balances (and interest earnings on them) during the projection period, is calculated as:[5]

(4) $\quad K_t = \sum_{k=0}^{t} C_k(1 + i)^{t-k}.$

This current account model is simple and omits important influences included in the US current account model (HHC) in Chapter 3. In particular, the model here makes no allowance for the impact of exchange rate changes on capital asset valuation and therefore capital services, nor for the impact of economic growth on rates of return. Nonetheless, the formulation here permits estimation of broad patterns of current account balances that may be expected to arise as the consequence of the trade projections obtained with the EAG model. Importantly, it enables the analysis here to develop an adjustment policy package, which must be designed on the basis of target ranges of current account balances (as targets for trade balances would have little meaning).

Table 5A.2 in the annex to this chapter presents the estimates of 1987 current account balances for the 17 countries and areas examined in this study. The central sources for these estimates are the International Monetary Fund's (IMF) various publications. Some of the groupings require residual estimation, applying the IMF estimates for the geographical region but subtracting individual countries included elsewhere in the EAG data base. In some cases, ratios of nonfactor to merchandise trade must be estimated based on 1986 data because of incomplete data for 1987.[6] As indicated in the table, the world current accounts do not add up to zero as they should, and the statistical discrepancy amounts to $36.6 billion.[7] However, as

---

5. Consider the following progression: $K_0 = C_0$. $K_1 = C_0(1+i) + C_1$. $K_2 = C_0(1+i)^2 + C_1(1+i) + C_2$. In general, $K_t = C_0(1+i)^t + C_1(1+i)^{t-1} + C_2(1+i)^{t-2} + \ldots + C_t(1+i)^{t-t}$. Hence text equation 4. Note that the series begins with the base year current account, C_0, because it is not yet accumulated into the implicit debt at the beginning of the base year (H_{-1}) and therefore does not contribute to interest obligations in F_0.

6. The most difficult estimates are those for Rest of World. These are based on the IMF aggregates for Asia less the EAG estimates for Taiwan and Korea–Singapore–Hong Kong, as well as Indonesia; for European developing countries; IMF data for the major developing nonoil countries in the Middle East (Egypt, Israel, Jordan, and Syria); and for the Soviet Union and other non-IMF countries. For Rest of World, the ratio of nonfactor service exports to merchandise exports is arbitrarily set at 0.15, and the corresponding ratio for nonfactor service imports is obtained residually.

7. This discrepancy is smaller than the $44.6 billion estimated by the IMF only because of the somewhat lower US current account deficit reported by the US Commerce Department subsequent to the April 1988 IMF *World Economic Outlook*.

discussed in Appendix E, the best evidence suggests that any reallocation of the world current account discrepancy would not mean major changes for policy interpretation of existing payments balances and imbalances.

Annex table 5A.3 reports the corresponding model parameters and 1987 variable values required for implementation of the current account model in equations 3 and 4, for each of the countries or groups in the EAG model. As may be seen from the table, there are relatively large base year capital service receipts for the United Kingdom and Japan, whereas Germany has large outward transfers (of which two-thirds are official, a considerable portion no doubt associated with its European Community payments) but relatively modest capital income. Canada has large outflows on the capital services account, so that its current account position is considerably weaker than might be expected from the trade balance.

For the United States, the parameters suppress an actual capital services surplus of $20 billion that existed in the base year, 1987. The reason is that much of this net income was from a valuation effect on the stock of investment abroad as the dollar declined. By the first quarter of 1988 the capital services account had actually turned to a small deficit ($0.6 billion), so that it would be misleading to project the base year factor services account (F_0 in equation 3).

Base Case Projections

With refinements to close halfway the gap between actual and model-predicted trade in the 1987 base year, to moderate extreme elasticity estimates through the averaging of country-specific and uniform elasticities, and to impose consistency on the cross-price elasticities (Appendices A and B), the EAG model is ready for use in forward-looking policy simulations. The first projection sets forth the "base case," the outlook in the absence of changes in policy.

Baseline Assumptions

The assumptions on base case country growth and inflation for 1988–92 are shown in table 5.1 and are generally the same as those in the projections of Chapter 3. As discussed in Chapter 1, the growth variable may be interpreted as an increase either in domestic demand or in real domestic production. For 1988 and 1989, the growth estimates for industrial countries are those published by the IMF in late 1988.[8] The 1988 growth rates reflect the unexpectedly strong growth that was already becoming apparent by the

8. IMF, *World Economic Outlook*, October 1988, 60.

Table 5.1 Base case assumptions for projections
(annual percentages)

Country/group	Growth 1988	Growth 1989	Growth 1990–92	Inflation (1988–92)[a]
US	4.0	2.8	2.5	4.5
UK	4.0	2.5	2.5	3.5
FR	2.9	2.4	2.5	2.5
GE	2.9	1.9	2.5	1.5
IT	3.0	2.4	2.5	3.5
CA	4.2	3.2	2.5	4.6
JA	5.8	4.2	4.0	2.0
AR	4.5	4.5	4.5	150.0
BR	4.5	4.5	4.5	150.0
ME	4.5	4.5	4.5	150.0
TA	8.0	8.0	8.0	−0.1
OP	2.0	2.0	2.0	4.5
OI	2.0	2.3	2.5	4.5
KS	8.0	8.0	8.0	2.5
OL	4.5	4.5	4.5	100.0
AN	4.5	4.5	4.5	20.0
RO	4.5	4.5	4.5	20.0

US, United States; UK, United Kingdom; FR, France; GE, Germany; IT, Italy; CA, Canada; JA, Japan; AR, Argentina; BR, Brazil; ME, Mexico; TA, Taiwan; OP, OPEC; UP, United Kingdom-oil; MP; Mexico-oil; OI, Other Industrial; KS, Korea–Singapore–Hong Kong; OL, Other Latin America; AN, Other Africa; RO, Rest of World.

a. In wholesale prices.

fourth quarter of that year. For 1990–92, US growth is set at 2½ percent annually, a rate generally considered to be potential output growth for the United States on a basis that avoids accelerating inflation. Growth in Europe and Canada is also set at 2½ percent annually in this period. The baseline growth for Japan is higher, at 4 percent annually in 1990–92, in view of that country's persistent record of higher growth than in other industrial countries. The developing countries grow at 4½ percent throughout the period, with two exceptions: Taiwan and Korea–Singapore–Hong Kong grow at 8 percent annually, approximately their average growth rates actually experienced in the 1980s.[9]

---

9. From 1980 to 1986, real growth averaged 8.2 percent annually in Korea and 6.8 percent annually in Taiwan. World Bank, *World Development Report 1988* (Washington: World Bank, 1988), 225; Republic of China, *Taiwan Statistical Data Book 1987* (Taipei: Council for Economic Planning and Development, 1987), 23.

Inflation continues at recent levels in each country.[10] In the important case of US inflation, it is assumed that wholesale prices rise by 4.5 percent annually over the full period. Oil prices are as projected in Appendix D. Essentially, they rise in nominal terms but follow a path identified by the National Petroleum Council as a "low price scenario."

The baseline projections assume that the real exchange rate remains constant over the full period 1988–92 at its actual level of the fourth quarter of 1987. This assumption treats the reversal toward a stronger dollar in the first eight months of 1988 as transitory (and indeed by November the rise had been largely reversed). As will be seen, the base case projections are already pessimistic on US external adjustment even at the 1987:4 real exchange rate. As examined in Chapter 3, the outcome would be still more unfavorable if the higher dollar of mid-1988 were to persist.

Trade Projections

The results of the base case projection for the full trade matrix in 1992 appear in annex table 5A.4. As may be seen in the table, projected trade in that year bears an uncanny resemblance to actual trade in 1987 in terms of the persistence of the existing global imbalances. Thus, although as discussed below the US trade deficit at first declines to a low point of $102.4 billion in 1989 ($108.8 billion on a balance of payments basis for trade), it rebounds beginning in 1990 and by 1992 stands at $123.7 billion ($132.6 billion). The deficit is thus only modestly lower in nominal terms at the end of the period than in 1987 (although the reduction is greater in real terms because of an increase of 24.6 percent in US prices over 1988–92). As in 1987, there are enormous trade surpluses in 1992 for Japan and Germany.

Table 5.2 presents a summary of the trade changes predicted by the (adjusted) EAG model for the base case, from 1987 to 1992. The US trade deficit declines by only $13 billion over the period in nominal terms. Japan's trade surplus rises by $44 billion to $128 billion, and that of Germany rises by $30 billion to $107 billion in 1992. Brazil shows a surprisingly high trade surplus, which reaches $25 billion by 1992 (although this outcome is not wholly inconsistent with the country's 1988 surplus of approximately $19 billion, after taking future inflation into account). Only Taiwan and

---

10. The 150 percent inflation rates for Argentina, Brazil, and Mexico probably understate the rate in the first two cases and overstate it in the third. However, as the model neutralizes inflation and deals only with real exchange rates, the exact inflation rate does not affect the projections except in the translation of exchange rate changes into nominal terms, which is not attempted for these three high-inflation countries.

Korea–Singapore–Hong Kong show adjustment, as their trade surpluses decline substantially.[11]

The important surprise on the other side is the pattern of serious weakness in the trade accounts of several other industrial countries. Thus, by 1992 the United Kingdom has a trade deficit of $62 billion; France, $13 billion; Italy, $7 billion; and the Other Industrial countries, $62 billion. This weakness arises even in the absence of US trade adjustment, raising questions about the ability of some of these countries to absorb further trade erosion as the consequence of US trade correction.

In proportionate terms, the United Kingdom shows the most unfavorable baseline trend (box 5.1). Its trade deficit widens from 10.8 percent of exports in 1987 (model basis) to 32 percent in 1992, placing it in greater relative trade imbalance than the United States by the end of the period. This adverse trend reflects the divergence between the United Kingdom's high income elasticity of imports and lower income elasticity of demand for its nonoil exports (table 4.3), even after dilution of the difference through averaging with uniform income elasticities. In addition, there is slow growth in the value of oil exports, which accounted for 10 percent of total UK exports in 1987.

More generally, these baseline trends suggest that there are limits to the extent to which some of the weaker industrial country economies can bear the counterpart of the necessary reduction in the US trade deficit, as some will already be under pressure even without US trade correction. By implication, these trends suggest the need for concentration of the foreign counterpart of the US adjustment in a handful of large surplus areas: Germany, Japan, Taiwan, and Korea–Singapore–Hong Kong. The trade balance projections by themselves also suggest the potential for participation of some less likely countries in absorption of some of the counterpart of declining US deficits. Thus, the Canadian trade surplus is relatively large.[12] Similarly, Brazil should be able to contribute to international adjustment by converting the potentially large rise in its trade surplus into faster growth.

---

11. Experiments applying lower growth rates (4½ percent) for Taiwan and Korea–Singapore–Hong Kong show instead persistent large surpluses. The baseline projections using country-specific elasticities also show surpluses in 1992 for the two areas, especially for Korea–Singapore–Hong Kong (table 5A.10).

12. Note, however, that the size of the Canadian trade balance is overstated in these data by the use of US exports to Canada as the figure for Canadian imports from the United States. In recent years Canadian data have systematically shown imports from the United States at about $10 billion higher than indicated in the US export figure, and US statistical authorities undertook special corrections in 1988 to deal with underreporting of cross-border exports. See, for example, IMF, *Direction of Trade Statistics*, Yearbook 1987, 125 and 404.

Table 5.2   Baseline trends in trade, 1987–92
(billions of dollars except as noted)

Country	Exports				Imports			
	1987A	1987M	1992M	Change (%)	1987A	1987M	1992M	Change (%)
US	250.30	252.55	500.92	98.34	405.20	389.26	624.65	60.47
UK[a]	131.20	128.30	195.00	51.99	142.70	142.14	257.37	81.07
FR	148.50	145.79	244.99	68.05	153.60	151.70	257.70	69.87
GE	294.10	283.98	455.68	60.47	212.50	206.85	348.53	68.49
IT	117.90	114.00	183.64	61.09	113.90	111.69	190.46	70.53
CA	97.00	100.06	169.67	69.56	83.30	82.93	150.71	81.72
JA	231.30	216.65	363.18	67.63	135.10	133.07	235.44	76.94
AR	6.40	7.14	13.69	91.66	6.10	6.55	11.17	70.53
BR	26.60	27.69	51.80	87.11	16.50	17.13	26.63	55.47
ME[a]	26.80	24.69	43.54	76.35	19.60	19.90	37.28	87.31
TA	53.20	47.38	77.51	63.60	34.80	32.72	76.12	132.64
OP	125.80	125.82	143.50	14.05	84.60	84.60	110.49	30.61
OI	458.90	452.39	752.17	66.27	491.30	486.60	814.15	67.31
KS	124.30	120.17	236.26	96.60	114.10	108.29	247.38	128.45
OL	37.40	40.41	73.21	81.14	42.90	42.39	72.28	70.49
AN	48.70	50.90	84.61	66.24	45.60	51.21	86.04	68.02
RO	262.60	257.88	501.73	94.56	337.30	328.76	544.72	65.69

A = actual; M = predicted by EAG model. Country abbreviations are as in table 5.1.
a. Includes oil exports.

Table 5.2 (Continued)

Country	Trade balance (billions of dollars)				Trade balance as % of exports			
	1987A	1987M	1992M	Change	1987A	1987M	1992M	Change
US	-154.90	-136.71	-123.73	12.98	-61.89	-54.13	-24.70	29.43
UK[a]	-11.50	-13.85	-62.37	-48.52	-8.77	-10.79	-31.99	21.19
FR	-5.10	-5.92	-12.71	-6.80	-3.43	-4.06	-5.19	-1.13
GE	81.60	77.12	107.16	30.03	27.75	27.16	23.52	-3.64
IT	4.00	2.32	-6.82	-9.13	3.39	2.03	-3.71	-5.74
CA	11.70	17.13	18.96	1.83	12.06	17.12	11.18	-5.94
JA	96.20	83.58	127.73	44.15	41.59	38.58	35.17	-3.41
AR	0.30	0.59	2.52	1.93	4.69	8.30	18.41	10.11
BR	10.10	10.56	25.17	14.61	37.97	38.13	48.59	10.46
ME[a]	7.20	4.79	6.26	1.47	26.87	19.39	14.38	-5.01
TA	18.40	14.66	1.40	-13.26	34.59	30.94	1.80	-29.14
OP	41.20	41.22	33.00	-8.21	32.75	32.76	23.00	-9.76
OI	-32.40	-34.22	-61.98	-27.77	-7.06	-7.56	-8.24	-0.68
KS	10.20	11.89	-11.11	-23.00	8.21	9.89	-4.70	-14.60
OL	-5.50	-1.98	0.93	2.91	-14.71	-4.90	1.27	6.17
AN	3.10	-0.31	-1.42	-1.11	6.37	-0.60	-1.68	-1.08
RO	-74.70	-70.88	-42.99	-27.89	-28.45	-27.48	-8.57	18.92

Box 5.1 Adverse Trends in the United Kingdom

The trend toward deterioration is not new for the United Kingdom. The country experienced a serious external deficit in the mid-1970s, with a trade deficit averaging 17 percent of exports in 1973–76 (EAG-DOTS data base). After reestablishing balance in 1977–79 (+0.2 percent) and, with the help of higher oil prices, surplus by 1980–82 (+6.7 percent), the UK then experienced a new cycle of decline (to −2.6 percent in 1983–85 and −9.5 percent in 1987). Simple extrapolation of the 1980–87 trend would place the trade balance deficit at 23 percent of exports by 1992.

Besides the adverse asymmetry in income elasticities and the drag from oil exports, two additional factors explain the sharply unfavorable trend for the United Kingdom. First, the country begins with a relatively adverse trade base: 1987 imports stand at 12.1 percent above exports (and by 1988 the divergence had widened to 25 percent). Thus, even if the percentage changes in trade values from 1987 to 1992 for other intermediate European countries (France, Italy, Other Industrial) are applied (at an unweighted average of 65.1 percent for exports and 69.2 percent for imports) to the 1987 UK trade base (excluding oil), the 1992 trade deficit reaches $30.7 billion. Second, dollar export price increases (based in the UK case on wholesale prices) are relatively high for the United Kingdom, with actual 1987:4 prices at 25.8 percent above the 1986 average, and 1992:4 prices at 39.2 percent above 1986, versus unweighted average increases of 19.2 percent and 24.6 percent, respectively, for France, Italy, and the Other Industrial countries. A widening divergence in 1988 reflects the lagged price increase expected for the United Kingdom, as discussed above.

Current Account Projections

A more accurate view of the payments positions of individual countries by 1992 requires examination of the current account balances corresponding to the detailed trade projections. Table 5.3 reports the baseline current account balance projections. For the trade and current account balances, the

1987 actual (A) and model (M) estimates are both reported, to provide a sense of the direction and size of bias in the projections.[13] (Note that the trade balance in table 5.3 is on the balance of payments basis, and thus differs slightly from the EAG-DOTS basis of table 5.2.)

For the United States, the current account deficit at first declines, but by 1992 rebounds to a new high of $168 billion. A rising factor services deficit offsets the modest decline in the trade deficit. This pattern is consistent with the current account projections in Chapter 3 (see table 3.2).

There is some improvement in relative terms, as the deficit falls from 48 percent of exports of goods and services in 1987 to 26 percent by 1992. Inflation of approximately 25 percent over the period, and real growth of almost 60 percent in the US export base, permit this relative reduction despite the rise in the nominal current account deficit. Even so, a current account deficit of over one-fourth of exports of goods and services remains extremely high, especially in view of the large net external debt that will have been accumulated. It is highly doubtful that persistent deficits of approximately $170 billion could be financed even though they were lower relative to the export base than the $154 billion current account deficit in 1987.

From table 5.3 it may be seen that there are several tiers of countries by prospective current account strength. In the top tier stand Germany, Japan, and, ironically in view of its debt problem, Brazil. By 1992 the current account surplus remains unchanged at 16 percent of exports of goods and services for Germany, and rises from 31 percent (model basis) to 34 percent for Japan. As for Brazil, the low income elasticity of imports (0.3) probably understates trend import growth (even after moderation by averaging with the uniform elasticity), and the country is likely to use up potential current account surpluses in increased growth rates.

There is an intermediate tier of other industrial countries whose external account trends are weaker. Thus, by 1992 the current account is −2 percent of exports of goods and services for France, −9 percent for Italy, and −2 percent for the Other Industrial countries. For Canada, the balance stands at −6 percent in that year, and the projection could be biased optimistically by some 6 percentage points of exports of goods and services (the difference between model and actual in 1987).

The weakest trend is for the United Kingdom. Its baseline current account

---

13. A detailed comparison of actual versus model-predicted trade balances for 1987 (applying the DOTS concept for trade in both cases, and using the base-year-averaged constant term) indicates that all errors in the predicted trade balance are less than 3 percent of exports of goods and services except for the following cases: US (5.4), CA (6.0), JA (−7.1), AR (4.0), ME (−9.0), TA (−9.6), KS (−5.1), OL (12.3), AN (−7.5), RO (11.5).

Table 5.3 Current account projections, base case, 1987–92

Country	Export trade balance[a] (billions of dollars)				Factor services (billions of dollars)				Transfers (billions of dollars)			
	1987A	1987M	1990M	1992M	1987A	1987M	1990M	1992M	1987A	1987M	1990M	1992M
US	−160.30	−142.02	−115.40	−132.57	20.40	20.40	−28.75	−51.73	−13.50	−13.45	−14.70	−15.59
UK	−16.40	−18.64	−58.38	−70.75	9.27	9.27	6.62	−0.64	−5.60	−5.62	−6.41	−7.00
FR	−7.50	−8.15	−12.66	−16.36	−0.40	−0.36	−0.48	−1.22	−4.30	−4.32	−4.93	−5.38
GE	70.2	66.12	71.50	89.80	3.60	3.58	13.45	23.92	−15.90	−15.89	−18.13	−19.80
IT	−0.50	−2.09	−14.29	−14.21	−5.30	−5.28	−8.53	−12.29	−1.60	−1.63	−1.86	−2.03
CA	8.70	14.29	10.92	13.72	−12.60	−12.57	−16.49	−20.10	1.60	1.56	1.78	1.94
JA	96.40	84.12	98.57	129.27	16.60	16.59	37.85	56.89	−3.70	−3.69	−4.39	−4.94
AR	1.00	1.36	3.60	3.82	−4.30	−4.32	−5.78	−6.90	0.00	0.00	0.00	0.00
BR	11.20	11.63	20.85	26.71	−7.80	−7.80	−8.67	−8.36	0.10	0.07	0.08	0.09
ME	9.70	7.62	9.86	11.89	−6.70	−6.64	−7.42	−8.02	0.70	0.67	0.76	0.83
TA	20.70	16.75	9.71	6.25	5.00	5.00	8.55	10.25	−0.70	−0.71	−0.81	−0.88
OP	36.00	36.00	21.05	25.65	2.00	2.00	−0.90	−4.85	−11.00	−11.00	−12.55	−13.71
OI	−8.90	−10.83	−24.04	−22.66	−13.20	−13.15	−19.25	−25.16	−3.20	−3.24	−3.70	−4.04
KS	6.50	8.36	2.54	−18.42	−3.40	−3.42	−0.91	0.10	1.00	1.02	1.16	1.27
OL	−1.70	0.68	5.31	4.11	−7.40	−7.39	−10.12	−12.14	3.20	3.21	3.66	4.00
AN	4.70	1.40	2.42	1.44	−11.00	−11.00	−15.14	−19.23	7.10	7.13	8.14	8.89
RO	−37.50	−34.94	1.58	4.54	−23.00	−23.00	−24.55	−21.14	34.00	34.00	37.70	40.38
SD	32.30	31.64	33.15	42.22	−38.10	−38.10	−80.51	−100.60	−11.90	−11.90	−14.20	−16.00

A = actual; M = predicted by EAG model. Country abbreviations are as in table 5.1.
SD = statistical discrepancy.
a. Balance of payments basis.

Table 5.3 (Continued)

Country	Current account balance (billions of dollars)				Current account/XGS			
	1987A	1987M	1990M	1992M	1987A	1987M	1990M	1992M
US	−154.00	−152.60	−134.74	−167.99	−0.48	−0.47	−0.26	−0.26
UK	−3.40	−6.53	−56.29	−76.06	−0.02	−0.04	−0.26	−0.29
FR	−1.50	−2.65	−4.46	−6.66	−0.01	−0.01	−0.02	−0.02
GE	45.20	51.18	58.76	84.84	0.13	0.16	0.14	0.16
IT	−0.70	−2.86	−19.09	−20.90	0.00	−0.02	−0.10	−0.09
CA	−6.30	0.17	−9.97	−11.80	−0.06	0.00	−0.06	−0.06
JA	86.60	73.19	94.83	136.44	0.34	0.31	0.30	0.34
AR	−3.80	−3.35	−2.38	−3.51	−0.51	−0.41	−0.19	−0.22
BR	1.20	1.54	9.72	15.47	0.04	0.05	0.22	0.28
ME	3.90	1.44	2.66	3.87	0.14	0.06	0.07	0.09
TA	18.00	14.41	5.48	−1.58	0.32	0.29	0.09	−0.02
OP	−5.00	−5.03	−26.74	−34.75	−0.04	−0.04	−0.22	−0.24
OI	−6.20	−8.99	−24.94	−22.93	−0.01	−0.02	−0.03	−0.02
KS	11.00	12.76	12.28	−6.86	0.08	0.09	0.06	−0.03
OL	−9.10	−6.31	−4.10	−8.29	−0.30	−0.19	−0.08	−0.14
AN	−4.70	−9.30	−13.85	−20.53	−0.08	−0.16	−0.17	−0.21
RO	−8.00	−5.65	46.11	63.45	−0.03	−0.02	0.12	0.13
SD	−36.90	−48.60	−66.70	−77.80	−0.01	−0.02	−0.02	−0.02

XGS = exports of goods and nonfactor services.

stands at -29 percent of exports of goods and services in 1992. The UK surplus on factor services disappears over time as the country accumulates current account deficits and makes interest payments on them, so that the seriously adverse trend in the trade balance as outlined above yields a similar trend for the current account.[14] Although it seems unlikely that the actual outcome would be this unfavorable, the projections serve both as a warning for UK policy formation and as a strong indication that the United Kingdom cannot be expected to absorb much if any of the counterpart of the US external correction.

Taiwan and Korea–Singapore–Hong Kong constitute another intermediate tier. Both areas show a pronounced decline in their current account balances as a percentage of exports of goods and services, from strong surpluses in 1987 to deficits of 2 and 3 percent, respectively, in 1992. However, the averaging of the uniform and specific elasticities probably causes an unduly negative trend in these estimates. With the projected growth rates for these two areas (8 percent) far above the averages for other countries, uniform elasticities violate the empirical rule of inverse correlation between income elasticity of imports and country growth rate (Chapter 4, note 39). In practice, the two areas thus comprise a somewhat stronger intermediate tier than the grouping of industrial countries just discussed.

The Rest of World group shows surprising strength, as its current account improves from a deficit of 2 percent of goods and services to a surplus of 13 percent. As this group includes several Asian countries that have experienced favorable trade growth in recent years (including China, India, and others such as Thailand), as well as European countries with favorable trends (such as Turkey and Portugal), this finding is not implausible. The favorable trend also results from the fact that Rest of World has not experienced significant real exchange rate appreciation against the dollar, so that it has trade gains in the pipeline from the dollar's decline in 1986–87 through its resulting real depreciation against Europe and Japan (a pattern that may also be seen in countries such as Brazil and, to a lesser extent, Mexico). Nonetheless, the trend is so strong for this area that its direction of bias, if any, would appear to be upward.[15]

---

14. A bias toward pessimism in the base year (predicted current account deficit of -4 percent of exports of goods and services, versus -2 percent actual) plays only a minor role in this outcome.

15. Note that the gains for Rest of World are concentrated (in absolute size) in trade with Italy, Taiwan, Other Industrial, and Korea–Singapore–Hong Kong (table 4.1 versus table 5A.4). This distribution is influenced by the unusually high cross-price elasticities of these suppliers in the Rest of World market (table 5A.1), combined with lagged effects of relative price improvement for the United States and other dollar-area countries from the dollar decline in 1986–87. The gains against Taiwan

The final and weakest tier of countries includes OPEC and all the other developing areas (AR, ME, OL, AN). Current account estimates for 1992 are weak for Argentina (− 22 percent of exports of goods and services), OPEC (− 24 percent), Other Latin America (− 14 percent), and Other Africa (− 21 percent). Although Mexico has a current account surplus (9 percent of exports of goods and services), its debt difficulties suggest that it too is more appropriately placed in a group unable to absorb much if any of the counterpart of US external adjustment.

The baseline projections of current account balances show a rising global statistical discrepancy, from − $49 billion in 1987 (model) to − $78 billion by 1992. It would be possible to impose constraints on the model that adjust estimates of the various components of the current account balance such that the statistical discrepancy does not rise above its value in the base year. However, such constraints could obscure the unadjusted trends, and it would be less clear whether the outcome for a given country derived from the underlying projections or from the discrepancy adjustment mechanism. In any event, real trade growth and inflation mean that the 1992 discrepancy is no higher relative to the trade base than in the base year. Thus, the statistical discrepancy declines slightly from 1.7 percent of world exports of goods and services in 1987 (model) to 1.6 percent by 1992.

US Trends: 1988–92

Table 5.4 and figures 5.1 through 5.4 report the path of the trade and current accounts over the period 1987–92. The table shows model-simulated exports, imports, trade balance, and current account (in current nominal dollars) for each year in this period. For comparison, the table also reports the corresponding projections in the base case from the HHC model in Chapter 3, as well as the actual outcome in 1987 and 1988. The trade and current account balances projected by the two models are close, although the absolute levels for both imports and exports tend to be higher in the HHC model.

---

and Korea–Singapore–Hong Kong may be exaggerated, as part of a possible overall understatement of their trends (and Rest of World is one of the largest markets for Korea–Singapore–Hong Kong). Otherwise, however, the large current account surplus for Rest of World in 1992 (both baseline and in the international adjustment program examined below) would appear to be valid, and reflects high inward transfers and relatively low nonfactor service imports (tables 5A.2 and 5A.3). Note also, however, that suppression of the emerging Rest of World surplus would not change the qualitative findings of the projections and policy simulations. See Chapter 1, note 26.

Table 5.4 US trade projections, base case, 1987–92
(billions of current dollars except as noted)[a]

	1987	1988	1989	1990	1991	1992
Exports						
EAG	252.6	304.7	359.1	402.8	449.1	500.9
EAG-BOP	251.7	303.7	357.9	401.5	447.6	499.3
HHC	249.6	339.0	404.2	445.8	496.1	553.6
Average	250.6	321.4	381.0	423.6	471.8	526.4
Actual	249.6	319.9				
Imports						
EAG	389.3	423.3	461.4	511.0	565.0	624.7
EAG-BOP	393.7	428.1	466.7	516.9	571.5	631.8
HHC	409.8	466.9	505.1	553.2	611.7	670.1
Average	401.8	447.5	485.9	535.0	591.6	651.0
Actual	409.8	446.4				
Trade balance						
EAG	−136.7	−118.5	−102.4	−108.2	−115.9	−123.7
EAG-BOP	−142.0	−124.4	−108.8	−115.4	−123.9	−132.6
HHC	−160.2	−127.9	−100.9	−107.4	−115.7	−116.4
Average	−151.1	−126.2	−104.8	−111.4	−119.8	−124.5
Actual	−160.2	−126.5				
Current account balance						
EAG	−152.6	−136.6	−122.2	−134.7	−150.7	−168.0
HHC	−153.9	−138.2	−114.9	−124.4	−135.6	−138.4
Average	−153.2	−137.4	−118.6	−129.6	−143.2	−153.2
Actual	−153.9	−135.3				
Current account balance as % of XGS						
EAG	−47	−35	−27	−26	−26	−26
HHC	−48	−33	−23	−23	−23	−21
Average	−48	−34	−25	−25	−24	−24

EAG-BOP = on balance of payments basis using the EAG model; XGS = exports of goods and nonfactor services. EAG and HHC are alternative projection models (see text).

a. Projections are at real exchange rates of 1987:4.

Source: (actual 1987 and 1988 data) US Department of Commerce, *Summary of US International Transactions: Fourth Quarter and Year 1988*, BEA-89-09 (Washington: US Department of Commerce, 14 March 1989).

Figure 5.1 US exports: alternative projections, 1987–92

billions of dollars

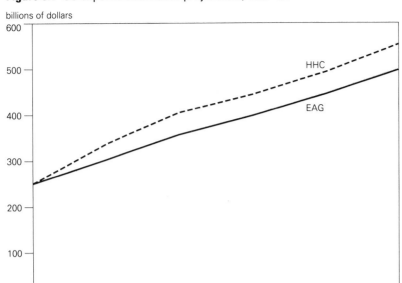

Figure 5.2 US imports: alternative projections, 1987–92

billions of dollars

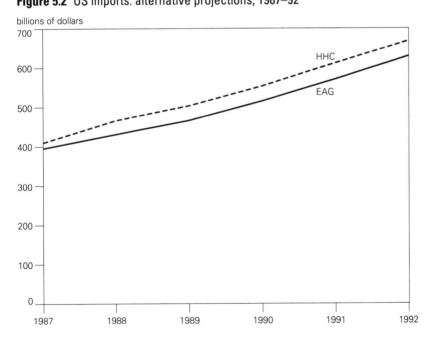

Figure 5.3 US trade balance: alternative projections, 1987–92

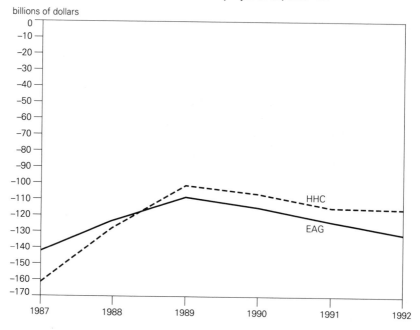

billions of dollars

As may be seen in the table and the figures, both the EAG and HHC models concur that the US trade imbalance shows an initial improvement through 1989 but then begins to deteriorate again. The trade deficit falls to no lower than $109 billion in the EAG model (balance of payments basis), or $101 billion in the HHC model. It then widens to $133 billion (EAG-BOP) or $116 billion (HHC) by 1992. The current account deficit similarly falls to a trough in 1989 in both models. It goes no lower than $122 billion in the EAG model, and $115 billion in the HHC model. The current account deficit then expands to a range of $138 billion (HHC) to $168 billion (EAG) by 1992. Relative to exports of goods and services, the current account deficit declines through 1988–89 but then stalls at a plateau of 26 percent (EAG) or 24 percent (HHC) in 1990–92.

Actual trade developments in 1987 and 1988 provide an initial test of the accuracy of the two projection models. Note that the HHC estimates for 1987 are also "actual" outcomes, as that model's projections begin only in 1988 (see Chapter 3). As may be seen, in 1987 the EAG model understates imports (BOP basis) by approximately $16 billion in 1987, and overstates exports by about $3 billion.

For 1988, there is a sizable difference between the predicted trade levels of the two models, but little difference in their trade and current account

Figure 5.4 US current account balance: alternative projections, 1987–92

billions of dollars

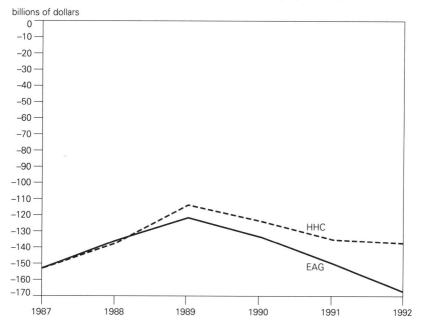

deficits. The HHC model shows a sharp increase in both imports and exports from the 1987 actual level. As discussed in Chapter 3, this rise occurs in considerable part because the original model had overstated both import and export prices and values by 1987, and the 1988 projections represent a phasing in of half of the difference between those model-predicted trade prices and the actual 1987 prices. Considering that the EAG model understated import values in 1987, the divergence between the two models for 1988 is substantial. For that year, exports are projected at $339 billion in the HHC model and only $304 billion in the EAG model, whereas imports are projected at $467 billion and $428 billion, respectively. There is thus an absolute gap of $35 billion to $40 billion between the absolute trade levels for both imports and exports, resulting in trade deficit estimates that are only slightly divergent.

Actual trade data for 1988 showed that exports rose by 28.2 percent, to $320 billion, and imports rose by 8.9 percent to $446 billion (table 5.4). As it turns out, these actual estimates for 1988 are virtually halfway between the EAG and HHC model estimates, on both the export and import sides.[16]

---

16. The divergence of $39 billion between the two models for imports is composed

The actual trade results for 1988 thus imply that the best estimates for this study may be obtained from a simple average of the HHC and EAG models. Table 5.4 reports these averages for the projections.[17]

The short-term projections of this study thus place the 1989 trade deficit at $105 billion (BOP basis), and the current account deficit at $119 billion. The deficits begin to widen once again thereafter, rising to an average estimate of $153 billion for the current account deficit by 1992, and $124 billion for the trade deficit in that year.

The central thrust of the aggregate projections of both the EAG and HHC models for the United States is that far more needs to be done to correct the external imbalance. Current account deficits that never fall below $100 billion and stand above $150 billion by 1992 are almost certainly unsustainable, and even if they could be financed they would mean constant short-term risk and long-term damage for the US economy (as discussed in Chapter 1).

Policy Scenarios

The broad policy lines required to achieve US external sector adjustment involve reduction of the US fiscal deficit, further depreciation of the dollar in real terms, and faster growth abroad. An additional but unattractive option is a slowdown or recession in US growth. As in the case of the HHC model of Chapter 3, the EAG model here does not explicitly calculate the impact of US fiscal adjustment. Instead, it applies changes in the real exchange rate, and the linkage is essentially that US fiscal correction must be taking place in the background on a basis compatible with real exchange rate depreciation; otherwise, attempted depreciation is likely to end up in nominal price increases without a corresponding reduction in the real exchange rate.

---

of a $20.5 billion excess over actual in the HHC model and an $18.3 billion shortfall in the EAG model; the divergence of $35 billion between the two models for exports is composed of an HHC excess of $19.1 billion and an EAG shortfall of $16.2 billion.

17. Note, however, that it is less clear that the nontrade elements of the current account should similarly be considered best estimated by the simple average. The HHC model is much more detailed for services, and in principle should provide a better estimate of that component of the current account. Nonetheless, as noted in Chapter 3, the capital earnings account in the HHC projections may be overstated, and adjustments on this component would move the HHC estimates closer to those of the EAG model.

Dollar Depreciation

To construct a policy package capable of correcting the US external deficit, it is first helpful to calibrate the parameters relating the amount of correction to policy changes. The first change is a 10 percent real depreciation of the dollar, phased in equally over four quarters in 1989. This depreciation is stated in real terms from the level of 1987:4.

Annex table 5A.5 shows the simulated trade matrix for 1992 under the 10 percent real depreciation just described. This depreciation is applied only against the currencies of the "strong" countries: Japan, Germany, the United Kingdom, France, Italy, the Other Industrial countries, Taiwan, and Korea–Singapore–Hong Kong. This set of countries with strong payments positions is the same as that so defined in Chapter 3. Its most notable exclusion is Canada, which bulks large in US trade. At the same time, it includes some industrial countries with much weaker payments positions than those of Germany, Japan, and the East Asian NICs.

As indicated in table 5A.5 as compared with table 5A.4, with 10 percent real depreciation against the strong countries the US trade deficit by 1992 declines from $123.7 billion in the base case (EAG-DOTS basis) to $80.5 billion, as the result of an increase in exports by $37.5 billion and a decrease in imports by $5.7 billion. The export increase amounts to 7.5 percent above baseline, a relatively brisk response considering that the strong countries against which the depreciation occurs account for only 58.5 percent of total US exports in 1992. That dollar import values decline at all is also a relatively favorable outcome, in view of the increasingly dominant perception that the price elasticity of US import demand is unity (which, if true, would mean dollar import values remain unchanged by depreciation because rising price fully offsets declining volume). The import reduction amounts to 0.9 percent of total imports, or 1.6 percent of imports from the strong-payments countries.

An examination of table 5A.5 shows important patterns of the impact of US real depreciation on other individual nations. Among those included in the strong-country group that appreciate, most have reductions in 1992 trade balances as expected. The largest absolute adjustment occurs in the Other Industrial countries, whose trade balance (already in deficit) declines by $21 billion. The United Kingdom experiences a relatively large trade balance reduction of $13 billion; France, a reduction of $7 billion; Italy, $6 billion; Korea–Singapore–Hong Kong, $20 billion; and Taiwan, $7 billion.

For the two largest surplus countries, the adjustments are disappointingly small. Japan's surplus changes only from approximately $128 billion to $122 billion. Germany's trade surplus remains unchanged at $107 billion; one reason is that even after averaging upward with the uniform elasticities, its trade elasticities are extremely low, and that a large portion of its trade is with countries that participate in the exchange rate appreciation.[18]

Beyond the price elasticities for trade (which are not particularly low for Japan; table 4.3), the failure of the German and Japanese surpluses to decline substantially under uniform appreciation of strong-country currencies is driven by a "balloon" effect stemming from the two countries' initial trade surpluses against other appreciating countries. Thus, when the German mark appreciates against the dollar by the same amount as the French franc, trade between Germany and France remains largely unaffected in terms of the two countries' own currencies but balloons in nominal dollar values because of the dollar valuation change. As the initial position is one in which German exports to France exceed German imports from France, a proportionate rise in the nominal dollar value of each causes a widening in the dollar value of the German bilateral trade surplus. This pattern is repeated in most trade combinations between Germany and Japan, on the one hand, and other countries in the appreciating group, on the other. The result is that the rising German and Japanese dollar trade surpluses against the other appreciating countries largely or fully offset the declining surpluses of the two countries in trade with the United States (and other dollar-area countries).

Overall, these results indicate a pattern of insufficient adjustment by the largest surplus countries (with the exception of Korea–Singapore–Hong Kong) and too much concentration of the adjustment on countries whose trade balances are already sufficiently weak that their inclusion in the "strong" group is problematic.

For countries in the nondepreciating "weak" group, there tends to be a favorable spillover effect of the depreciation of the dollar (and thus of their own currencies) against the currencies of the strong group. Canada's trade balance rises by $6 billion, or 3½ percent of exports. The Latin American countries (AR, BR, ME, OL) experience gains reaching 5 percent of exports in Brazil and 4 percent in Other Latin America. Other Africa also experiences a rise in its trade balance of approximately 4 percent, as does the Rest of World group (amounting to $20 billion given its large export base).

Comparison of tables 5A.4 and 5A.5 also provides illustrations of the workings of the EAG model. Consider first US trade with a strong-payments

---

18. Thus, in table 4.3 the country-specific estimates show a trade-weighted direct price elasticity of Germany's exports of only -0.51; that of its imports is -0.49. As the country begins in surplus, and considering that the sum of elasticities barely meets the Marshall–Lerner condition even after including the cross-price elasticity (Chapter 4), nominal values of exports rise by enough to offset the increase in nominal imports (in dollar terms).

country, Japan. US exports to Japan rise by $5.4 billion or 9.2 percent as the result of the dollar depreciation, while US imports from Japan decline by $4.2 billion (3.5 percent). (Imports from Japan decline much more in volume terms, and that they decline at all in nominal dollar terms reflects a relatively favorable specific/uniform averaged price elasticity.)

Less obviously, US exports to nonappreciating countries in the weak group also rise, while its imports from these countries rise as well, as the result of cross-price competition against strong-country sources. Thus, US exports to Canada rise by $2.7 billion (2.4 percent) even though the Canadian currency remains unchanged against the dollar, while US imports from Canada rise by $3.0 billion (2.5 percent), as the result of each country's improved ability to compete against third parties in each other's markets.

Faster Growth Abroad

A second basic means of adjustment is for the market for US exports to grow more rapidly as the result of faster foreign growth. The existence of high unemployment in Europe makes faster growth a natural policy option there. Several of the European countries in relatively weak payments positions would find it easier to adopt expansionary macroeconomic policies if the German economy were expected to grow faster, but encounter difficulties doing so otherwise because of the constraint of further erosion in trade balances already in sizable deficit against Germany. Japanese policy has sought recently to replace export demand by increased domestic demand to attain higher growth despite the rise in the yen; thus, policy has already moved in this direction in Tokyo.

Annex table 5A.6 shows the consequences of the adoption of policies leading to foreign growth higher than the baseline by 1 percentage point annually for the full period 1989–92. As there is no time lag for the influence of the income variable in the trade equations, this simulation amounts to a full 4 year-percentage points of additional growth impact. Once again the higher growth is specified for the strong-country group (excluding Canada).

The simulations indicate that higher growth abroad can contribute to US external adjustment, but is no panacea. Faster growth by 1 percentage point over a four-year period for the strong countries increases US exports and the US trade surplus by $17.9 billion, or 3.6 percent of exports, reducing the US trade deficit from the baseline value by only about one-seventh. Although still higher growth increments abroad would increase the size of this adjustment, the feasible scope for far larger growth increases is doubtful. (Note, however, that faster growth abroad also makes an important contribution to correction of the US current account deficit through improving the balance on services, particularly capital services after taking capital gains into account; see Chapter 3.)

The results of faster growth are once again more complex than would be anticipated on the intuitive expectation that the strong countries would have a generalized rise in imports and a corresponding decline in trade surpluses. Once again there is less adjustment in the key countries of Germany and Japan, and rather more forced upon such countries as France, the United Kingdom, and the Other Industrial countries, than might be desired.

As indicated by comparison of tables 5A.4 and 5A.6, 4 year-percentage points of higher growth in the strong countries does increase US exports, and reduce the US trade deficit, by $17.9 billion. It also increases Rest of World exports by $22.6 billion (4.5 percent of the baseline value). Otherwise the trade gains are modest (although in some cases significant in proportionate terms, as in the case of Brazil's gain, which amounts to 3.2 percent of baseline exports). In particular, Canada experiences only a small export increase (less than 1 percent). The explanation for Canada lies in the large share of the United States in its export market, as the growth increment does not apply to the United States.

The effects on countries in the strong group are more surprising. The trade surpluses of Germany and Japan remain virtually unchanged despite their faster growth. In contrast, there are major trade balance reductions for the Other Industrial countries (by $16 billion or 2.1 percent of baseline exports); France ($9.7 billion or 4.0 percent of baseline exports); and the United Kingdom ($11.9 billion or 6.1 percent of baseline exports).

The explanation for this skewed distribution of trade effects among the growth-accelerating countries is that, for each of them, not only are imports rising but so are exports. The reason is that they export not only to the weak countries but also to each other. Among the strong-country set, those countries that begin with a large trade surplus tend to have a base of exports to other strong countries that is higher than their base of imports from them. As a result, relatively similar proportionate increases in the volume of imports for all members of this stronger set imply within-group export gains for the strongest members (Japan, Germany) that are sufficient to offset the rise in imports from the United States and other nonexpanding countries. There is thus a balloon effect for the real volume of trade similar to the nominal balloon effect pertaining to coordinated exchange rate appreciation, that causes persistence of high German and Japanese trade surpluses. Correspondingly, the within-group disparity leaves the full burden of adjustment concentrated on the weaker members of the growth-accelerating group.

Slower US Growth

A third policy option is for US growth to slow below rates otherwise attainable. Slower growth would reduce US imports and the US trade deficit. Reduced growth is sometimes criticized as a solution to the trade problem on grounds that it would be only "temporary." This critique is not quite correct. Although imports would indeed rebound once normal growth was reestablished, the new trendline of income and therefore imports would be lower than the original baseline for the same future period. Only if the postslowdown rebound in growth were to rates well above average, by enough to permit a catching up to the baseline, would the trade deficit reduction from slower growth be wholly transitory.

The real reason for concern about slower growth is that if this policy approach leads to a GNP well below the potential level, there is a sacrifice in output that could be unnecessary under more appropriate policies. Only if the economy is overheating and inflation is a primary risk could the option of growth slowdown become relatively more attractive, and in this case its trade effects would be a side benefit but not the principal objective of the approach.

Table 5A.7 reports the simulated trade matrix for 1992 under conditions of US growth that is lower by 1 percentage point annually than in the base case, for the full period 1989–92. As indicated in the table, slower US growth is relatively powerful in reducing the US external deficit. Under slower growth, the US trade deficit in 1992 stands at only $78 billion (EAG basis), for a reduction by over one-third from the baseline level.

The distribution of foreign adjustment holds few surprises in the case of slower US growth: it broadly follows the importance of the United States in the exports of each trading partner. The largest absolute adjustments are reductions in trade balances by $10.4 billion for Japan, $8 billion for Canada, and $5.9 billion for Korea–Singapore–Hong Kong, respectively, compared with the baseline outcome. These three areas are also the largest single suppliers to the United States, accounting for 21 percent, 18 percent, and 10 percent of US imports in 1987, respectively (table 4.1). In contrast, the reduction in trade balance for Germany is a more modest $3.9 billion, reflecting Germany's smaller share in the US market (7 percent in 1987).

An important feature of adjustment through slower US growth is its adverse impact on Latin America, Africa, and other developing areas excluding the East Asian NICs. With slower US growth, the trade balance of Latin America (AR, BR, ME, and OL) declines by $4.5 billion from its baseline value in 1992. In contrast, under 10 percent dollar depreciation against strong-country currencies the Latin American trade balance rises by $7.2 billion, and in the scenario of faster foreign growth the region's trade balance rises by $5.6 billion. As expected, it is important to the debtor countries whether the United States adjusts through slower growth or through exchange rate correction and higher growth in the strong-payments countries.

Policy Parameters

As a basis for determining a policy package capable of achieving a targeted, sustainable level for the US external deficit, it is useful to identify rules of thumb indicating the change in the trade and current accounts for a unit change in each of the three broad policy areas: exchange rate, foreign growth, and US growth. Table 5.5 reports such parameters for the United States. The table indicates the results from both of the models of this study: the multicountry EAG model of this chapter and the HHC model of the US current account in Chapter 3.

The parameters reported in table 5.5 are derived by comparing the results of the policy scenarios in tables 5A.5 and 5A.6 against the base case projections in table 5A.4, for strong-country policy action, and from corresponding estimates not reported in the tables for appreciation or extra growth by the strong countries plus Canada, and by all foreign countries. Table 5A.7 provides the basis for the parameters for changes in US growth.

A reassuring feature of these estimates is that the HHC and EAG models give results that are relatively close, even though they adopt substantially different approaches. Thus, the HHC model operates at the aggregate level for the United States with no partner-country detail, whereas the EAG model is calculated for individual trade flows with the world divided into 17 areas, and its aggregate US results are from summation over the relevant US–partner combinations. Even the model structure is different, as the HHC model contains no explicit term for cross-price competition against third parties (and cannot do so as its exports are to a single, comprehensive market).

Both models show that 1 percent real depreciation of the dollar against the currencies of the strong-payments areas increases US exports and the trade balance by 1992 by approximately $4 billion, and the current account position by approximately $6 billion. Stated in relative terms, the EAG results indicate that the 1 percent real depreciation against the strong currencies provides a current account balance improvement equal to 1.2 percent of exports (with the corresponding HHC estimate at 1.0 percent, lower primarily because of its larger estimate for baseline exports).

The EAG and HHC models show greater divergence in the estimated impact of a 1 percent dollar decline against the strong countries plus Canada,

Table 5.5 Policy parameters for the United States
(billions of current dollars except as noted)

| | Change in 1992 trade | | | | | | | | | | | |
| | EAG model | | | | | | HHC model | | | | | |
Instrument	X	M	TB	TB/X%	CA	CA/X%	X	M	TB	TB/X%	CA	CA/X%
Exchange rate depreciation (1% real)												
Against all countries	7.2	−0.3	7.5	1.5	10.2	2.0	4.4	−0.8	5.2	0.9	7.8	1.4
Against strong countries	3.7	−0.6	4.3	0.9	5.8	1.2	3.5	−0.5	4.0	0.7	5.6	1.0
Against strong countries + Canada	6.0	−0.5	6.5	1.3	8.9	1.8	3.7	−0.7	4.4	0.8	6.4	1.2
Increased foreign growth (1% for 1 year)												
In all countries	8.3	0.0	8.3	1.9	11.5	2.3	10.5	0.0	10.5	1.9	19.8	3.6
In strong countries	4.5	0.0	4.5	1.1	6.2	1.2	4.5	0.0	4.5	0.8	9.2	1.7
In strong countries + Canada	6.5	0.0	6.5	1.5	9.1	1.8	6.9	0.0	6.9	1.3	13.3	2.4
Decreased US growth (1% for 1 year)	0.0	−11.5	11.5	2.3	14.8	3.0	0.0	−11.0	11.0	2.0	15.0	2.7

X = change in exports; M = change in imports; TB = change in trade balance; CA = change in current account balance; TB/X% = change in trade balance as a percentage of 1992 exports; CA/X% = change in current account balance as a percentage of 1992 exports.

and against all foreign countries. For these broader groupings, the EAG model shows a considerably larger response ($7.5 billion trade balance and $10.2 billion current account impact per percentage point, when all other countries appreciate, versus only $5.2 billion and $7.8 billion, respectively, in the HHC model; the impact is $6.5 billion and $8.9 billion, versus $4.4 billion and $6.4 billion, when only Canada is added to the strong countries). In the EAG model, the ratio of trade balance adjustment from strong-country appreciation to total potential adjustment when all foreign countries appreciate (57 percent, table 5.5) is approximately the same as the share of these countries in US trade (58.5 percent of imports and 50.0 percent of exports in 1987). In contrast, in the HHC model of Chapter 3, strong-country appreciation achieves 77 percent of total potential adjustment from appreciation by all foreign countries. The divergence stems from the fact that, by operating directly on US–partner trade flows, the EAG model implicitly attaches greater weight to bilateral trade shares than to multilateral trade shares (the HHC weights for the exchange rate effect on exports), thereby increasing the importance of Canada in particular; and from the fact that the specific countries in the strong group have a larger weight in the HHC exchange rate index, which refers to only 18 countries, than is represented by these countries in total trade.

Both models place the impact of 1 percent higher growth in the strong-payments countries for a period of one year at an improvement of approximately $4½ billion in the US trade balance by 1992. The two models also give closely similar trade balance results for a higher rate of growth in the strong countries plus Canada. However, the HHC parameter is somewhat higher for increased growth in all foreign countries, again because of different weighting procedures.

With respect to the current account, the larger effect of foreign growth in the HHC model is magnified. Thus, even in the case of faster growth in the strong countries excluding Canada, in which the two models show the same trade impact ($4.5 billion per year-percentage point), the HHC model indicates a current account impact considerably larger than the EAG estimate ($9.2 billion versus $6.2 billion). As discussed in Chapter 3, the HHC model incorporates the effect of higher foreign growth on profitability of US direct investment abroad, an influence not captured in the EAG model. For slower US growth, the two models both show a reduction of approximately $11 billion in the 1992 trade deficit as the result of a 1-percentage-point cutback annually over four years. The two models are also in agreement on the current account impact, at $15 billion per year-percentage point growth cutback.

Table 5.6 reports policy parameters for policy action by individual foreign countries. For each country, the table shows the change from the 1992

Table 5.6 Individual country unilateral policy parameters, results for 1992

Country	Change in trade balance[a]				Current account parameters[d]		Change in current account balance (% of exports of goods and services)[e]	
	Value (billions of dollars)		As % of exports of goods and services					
	Appreciation[b]	Growth[c]	Appreciation	Growth	Intercept	Slope	Appreciation	Growth
US	7.46	11.51	1.16	1.79	12.50	1.36	1.58	2.44
UK	−2.65	−5.17	−1.01	−1.98	22.20	1.35	−1.37	−2.67
FR	−1.76	−5.47	−0.55	−1.69	13.10	1.15	−0.63	−1.95
GE	−2.24	−6.88	−0.43	−1.31	−39.20	1.37	−0.58	−1.80
IT	−1.88	−3.79	−0.82	−1.65	−2.10	1.25	−1.02	−2.06
CA	−3.04	−2.77	−1.56	−1.42	−29.30	1.30	−2.03	−1.85
JA	−2.35	−3.18	−0.59	−0.80	−48.30	1.45	−0.85	−1.15
AR	−0.07	−0.23	−0.44	−1.48	−8.10	1.18	−0.52	−1.75
BR	−0.31	−0.27	−0.55	−0.48	−15.10	1.14	−0.63	−0.55
ME	−0.40	−0.64	−0.88	−1.41	−11.40	1.27	−1.12	−1.78
TA	−1.03	−1.13	−1.26	−1.38	−10.30	1.47	−1.85	−2.03
OI	−4.45	−11.65	−0.46	−1.20	1.40	1.21	−0.55	−1.45
KS	−3.02	−3.35	−1.14	−1.27	15.00	1.16	−1.32	−1.47
OL	−0.42	−1.11	−0.70	−1.88	−13.50	1.23	−0.86	−2.31
AN	−0.76	−0.99	−0.77	−1.00	−22.50	1.11	−0.85	−1.11
RO	−2.82	−5.43	−0.58	−1.12	57.20	1.26	−0.73	−1.42

For an explanation of country abbreviations see table 5.1.

a. From baseline.

b. Resulting from a 1% real appreciation of the currency against the US dollar (1% depreciation for US).

c. Resulting from a 1% increase in the country's growth rate for 1 year (1% decrease for US).

d. Obtained by estimating the equation CA = a + bTB, where CA is the current account and TB the trade balance (billions of dollars).

e. Using the estimated coefficients in the previous two columns.

baseline projections that would result from an appreciation of the country's currency (in isolation) by 1 percentage point, or an increase in the country's growth rate (also in isolation) by 1 percentage point for one year. The table presents these changes in terms of billions of current dollars, and as percentages of each country's 1992 baseline exports.

The median values in the table indicate that a unilateral 1-percentage-point appreciation of a country's real exchange rate against the dollar (in 1989) causes a decline of 0.70 percent in the country's 1992 trade balance as a percentage of exports of goods and nonfactor services, with a range from 0.43 percent for Germany to 1.56 percent for Canada. A unilateral increase of growth by 1 year-percentage point reduces a country's 1992 trade balance by 1.38 percentage points of exports of goods and services (median), with a range from 0.48 percent for Brazil to 1.98 percent for the United Kingdom.

The third pair of columns in the table reports a simple equation for translating the 1992 trade balance of each country into its current account balance. These equations are merely approximations, and are based on multiple simulations of the alternative cases for growth and exchange rates. Thus, the UK current account balance in 1992 may be approximated as $22 billion plus the coefficient 1.35 times the UK trade balance for that year. The intercept term tells whether the country has a surplus or a deficit on capital services and transfers (or asymmetrical relationships of nonfactor services to merchandise trade). The coefficient on trade tends to be greater than unity because trade in goods and nonfactor services is a multiple of merchandise trade.

As may be seen, Rest of World has a large positive intercept ($57 billion), indicating that it receives large inward transfers and achieves a large surplus on nonfactor services, both of which overshadow its deficit on factor services (table 5A.2). In contrast, Germany and Japan have large negative intercepts, reflecting in the German case large outward transfers and in the case of Japan a large difference between nonfactor service imports and exports.

On the basis of the coefficients in these current account equations, the final pair of columns in table 5.6 translates the trade change in response to unilateral appreciation or growth acceleration into changes in the current account as percentages of exports of goods and services. These changes parallel the trade changes, but at a higher level. The median impact of 1 percent unilateral appreciation is a current account reduction equal to 0.85 percent of exports of goods and services, while a unilateral growth acceleration of 1 year-percentage point causes a median current account reduction of 1.78 percent of exports of goods and nonfactor services.

A Feasible Adjustment Package

The policy parameters identified above and the baseline projections of current account balances provide the basis for designing a policy package capable of reducing the US external deficit to a target level while avoiding undue pressure on the payments of certain other countries and areas already likely to experience some external sector weakness even in the absence of US adjustment.

Program Design

The following principles are applied in this package. First, the group of countries participating in the measures that form the counterpart to US depreciation (and, implicitly, US fiscal adjustment) needs to be as broad as possible given the magnitude of the correction needed. Second, however, it is clear that there are separate tiers of foreign scope for bearing external sector balance reductions, and thus that the degree of foreign adjustment measures should be differentiated by tier. Third, the overall exchange rate changes and acceleration of foreign growth need to be substantial.

The policy target for the US current account deficit in 1992 is $50 billion or less. The reasons for choosing this target are discussed in Chapter 1. Essentially, a deficit of this magnitude would be consistent with stabilizing or modestly reducing over time the ratio of net external debt to GNP; the external finance required to cover this deficit as well as gross US capital outflows would be available if foreigners merely reinvested their earnings on assets in the United States; and a more ambitious target of zero deficit would imply such sharp exchange rate changes, especially for the high-surplus countries, that political opposition abroad could be expected. In contrast, the prospective deficit of over $150 billion annually in 1992 in the absence of policy action is far too large for safety, and even if financed would be corrosive to longer-term US growth.

The principal constraint from the standpoint of other countries is that no country should be forced into extreme external deficit as the consequence of US external adjustment. Another constraint is that increases in foreign growth rates should be within the realm of the feasible, and should not be so ambitious as to exceed potential output growth and provoke inflation.

The general target for current account balances of countries other than the United States is that any deficits by 1992 not exceed 10 percent of exports of goods and nonfactor services. As the US current account deficit target is well below this level relative to exports of goods and services,[19] it would

---

19. In the base case, the EAG model places 1992 exports of goods and nonfactor

be inappropriate to push other countries into greater relative deficit in a package designed to achieve US external adjustment. In addition, the policy package seeks to reduce sharply the current account surpluses of the high-surplus countries, as a percentage of exports of goods and services.

In the special cases of Taiwan and Korea–Singapore–Hong Kong, the permitted current account deficit is set at a higher level of up to 12 percent of exports of goods and services. As discussed above (and developed further below), in these countries the averaging of country-specific and uniform elasticities does appear to introduce a bias toward understatement of future trade and current account balances, and a modestly higher ceiling for permissible current account deficits is thus appropriate.

It is clear from the results of tables 5.2, 5.3, and 5A.4 to 5A.6 that a comprehensive package must concentrate adjustment heavily in a few high-surplus countries, most notably Japan and Germany. Otherwise these countries will maintain extremely high surpluses while an excessive adjustment burden will be placed on other countries.

It is also clear from the analysis above that the intensity of adjustment measures should be differentiated by tiers of countries. The most intensive adjustment must occur in Germany and Japan. Major adjustment is also called for in Taiwan and Korea–Singapore–Hong Kong. Intermediate measures are appropriate for France, Italy, and the Other Industrial countries. In view of their strong current account trends, Brazil and the Rest of World countries can also absorb an intermediate level of adjustment (and, correspondingly, can benefit from the higher growth and anti-inflationary exchange rate appreciation involved). To a still lesser extent, Canada and Mexico can adopt some adjustment measures in the direction of higher growth and appreciation. In contrast, the payments outlook is too weak for Other Latin America, Argentina, Africa, and OPEC to participate in adjustment. And in the case of the United Kingdom, the current account trendline is so negative that the country must adjust in the opposite direction, depreciating rather than appreciating in real terms against the dollar.

Table 5.7 presents the Feasible Adjustment Package (FAP) designed to meet these criteria (after numerous experiments and with the aid of the policy parameters in tables 5.5 and 5.6). The package imposes a large appreciation against the dollar for the German mark (23 percent against the 1987:4 real level) and Japanese yen (28 percent). These appreciations would be phased in steadily over the course of 1989.[20] In addition, during 1989–

---

services at $747 billion. A current account deficit of $50 billion would be only 6.7 percent of exports of goods and services, or less in view of the rise in the exports base in an adjustment program.

20. As noted in Chapter 1, if the phase-in stretched through 1990 there would be

92 both countries should accelerate their annual growth rates by 1 percentage point above baseline levels. In practice, this growth performance would mean maintaining the relatively high growth rates of 1988 rather than allowing them to decline as expected.

For Taiwan and Korea–Singapore–Hong Kong, the package also calls for sizable real appreciation (12 percent and 14 percent, respectively). Because the two areas are already assumed to grow at extremely high rates (8 percent), however, they would not be in a position to accelerate growth further.[21]

The intermediate tier of industrial countries (France, Italy) plus Brazil and Rest of World should appreciate by a modest 5 percent in real terms against the 1987:4 dollar. They should also accelerate growth by an intermediate amount of 0.5 percentage point above baseline rates, through the full period 1989–92.

The Other Industrial countries are a special case in the intermediate group. Almost half of their total trade is accounted for by three countries in strong payments positions: the Netherlands, Belgium, and Switzerland.[22] These countries may be expected to maintain exchange rate parity with Germany within what amounts to a strong deutsche mark bloc within the European Monetary System, followed by Switzerland as well. Accordingly, the FAP assigns a weighted-average exchange rate appreciation for the Other Industrial countries that treats approximately half of this group like Germany, and the other half like France and Italy. The resulting weighted

---

little sacrifice in US external adjustment, but if delayed longer—even if phased in at a steady pace through the end of 1991—correction of the US external imbalance would be seriously undermined. The two-year pipeline from exchange rate change to trade change means further delay is costly to adjustment by 1992.

21. The aggregation of Korea, Hong Kong, and Singapore in the EAG model requires uniform treatment of these three countries. However, considering that Singapore has had current account balances averaging near zero in recent years, there is little basis for real appreciation in that country. Hong Kong does not collect current account statistics, but in 1987 Balassa and Williamson concluded that the Hong Kong dollar (fixed at 7.80 to the US dollar since 1983) could appropriately be revalued by 10 to 15 percent. The currency remains unchanged against the US dollar, and inclusion of Hong Kong in the FAP appreciation is probably more appropriate than of Singapore. IMF, *International Financial Statistics*, March 1989; Bela Balassa and John Williamson, *Adjusting to Success: Balance of Payments Policy in the East Asian NICs*, POLICY ANALYSES IN INTERNATIONAL ECONOMICS 17 (Washington: Institute for International Economics, June 1987), 38.

22. Thus, in 1987 these three countries had total trade turnover (exports plus imports) of $447.5 billion, or 47.1 percent of the total for Other Industrial. Table 4.1 and IMF, *Direction of Trade Statistics 1988*. In 1987, Belgium had a current account surplus of $2.9 billion; the Netherlands, $3.1 billion; and Switzerland, $5.9 billion. IMF, *International Financial Statistics*, March 1989.

Table 5.7 A Feasible Adjustment Package

Group	1989 real exchange rate appreciation against dollar[a] (%)	1989–92 annual growth increment above baseline (%)
Strong A		
Japan	28	1.0
Germany	23	1.0
Strong B		
Korea–Singapore–Hong Kong	14	0.0
Taiwan	12	0.0
Intermediate A		
Other Industrial	13.5	0.75
Intermediate B		
France	5	0.5
Italy	5	0.5
Brazil	5	0.5
Rest of World	5	0.5
Intermediate C		
Canada	3.5	0.25
Mexico	2.5	0.25
Weak A		
Argentina	0	0
OPEC	0	0
Other Africa	0	0
Other Latin America	0	0
Weak B		
United Kingdom	−3	0
United States	−10.7[b]	0

a. From 1987:4 base.
b. Real trade-weighted depreciation.

real appreciation is 13.5 percent (0.47 × 23 + 0.53 × 5), while the growth acceleration is 0.75 percentage point annually (halfway between that for Germany, on one hand, and for Italy and France, on the other).

Canada and Mexico can also afford to contribute to international adjustment, and enjoy its benefits, but in lesser degree (2½ to 3½ percent real appreciation, and growth acceleration by ¼ percentage point annually). In contrast, the United Kingdom needs to depreciate the pound sterling in real terms against the 1987:4 dollar by 3 percent, and is not in a position to accelerate growth above the baseline rates.

Impact on the United States

Table 5A.8 reports the 1992 trade matrix that results from application of the FAP. The package reduces the EAG-estimated trade deficit for the United States to $35.3 billion. On a balance of payments basis, the trade deficit amounts to $44.3 billion. The corresponding current account deficit is $48.4 billion (table 5.8), or 6 percent of exports of goods and nonfactor services. This outcome is within the target range of less than $50 billion for the US external deficit by 1992.[23]

An important feature of this projection is that the current account deficit is surprisingly close to the trade deficit (balance of payments basis); they differ by only $4 billion. In contrast, in the baseline projection the current account deficit exceeds the trade deficit by $35 billion. The baseline result is more in keeping with the common expectation that a large divergence between the two balances will emerge in the future, because of the growing deficit on capital services associated with the rising net debtor position of the United States.

The explanation for this important favorable aspect of the adjustment scenario is that, in the current account bloc of the EAG model, the United States enjoys a large surplus on nonfactor services when merchandise trade is in balance. As indicated in table 5A.3, exports of nonfactor services are set at 29 percent of merchandise exports, whereas imports of nonfactor services amount to only 18 percent of merchandise imports. Essentially, the United States has comparative advantage in nonfactor services (as might be inferred from the strong US push for service sector liberalization in the Uruguay Round of trade liberalization). In the baseline projection, even

---

23. The interim time path of the correction is as follows. Under the FAP, the US current account deficit declines to $137 billion in 1988, $142 billion in 1989, $103 billion in 1990, and $57 billion in 1991. There is thus a J-curve effect of deterioration from baseline in 1989 but improvement thereafter.

though goods imports are large relative to exports, this differential permits a surplus on nonfactor services of $32 billion. When adjustment raises exports relative to imports, the nonfactor service surplus balloons to $56 billion by 1992, enough to largely offset the deficit of $45 billion on capital services and $16 billion on transfers. The result of a surprisingly narrow excess of the current account deficit over the trade deficit by 1992 under successful adjustment is also evident in the HHC current account model of Chapter 3 (table 3.7).

US Impact: HHC Model Estimates

Application of the FAP to the model of Chapter 3 (HHC) yields the results for 1992 shown in table 5A.9. The current account deficit falls by that year to $18 billion. US exports stand at $624 billion and imports at $661 billion.[24] The corresponding estimates using the multicountry EAG model are a current account deficit of $48 billion, exports of $580 billion, and imports of $625 billion (tables 5.8 and 5A.8), on a balance of payments basis. Both the HHC and EAG models thus place the trade deficit in 1992 at approximately $40 billion, under an adjustment program designed to bring the current account deficit below $50 billion. The principal reason for a lower current account imbalance in the HHC model is that the balance on factor services is actually in surplus (at $13.8 billion; table 5A.9), whereas in the EAG model it is in deficit (at − $45 billion in 1992). In contrast, the EAG model shows a more favorable balance on nonfactor services.

As noted in Chapter 3, there is reason to believe that the factor services component of the HHC model understates the deficit by 1992 by some $17 billion, as the result of strong asymmetry in rates of return on even the incremental capital stocks accumulated as the result of US current account deficits through 1992. If this figure is applied as an adjustment, the HHC current account deficit for 1992 under the FAP program amounts to $35 billion, closer to the $48 billion of the EAG model.

---

24. Note that reduction of the deficit from $138 billion to $18 billion, or by $120 billion, is consistent with application of the policy parameters of table 5.5 to the weighted exchange rate and growth changes for the FAP. Thus, real dollar depreciation by 10.7 percent contributes 10.7 × 7.8 = $83 billion to the reduction in the 1992 current account deficit, while foreign growth acceleration by 0.4 percentage point annually over four years further reduces the deficit by 0.4 × 4 × 19.8 = $32 billion. Using the EAG model parameters, the corresponding effects are 10.7 × 10.2 = $109 billion from exchange rate change and 0.4 × 4 × 11.5 = $18.4 billion from foreign demand acceleration. Both sets of parameters yield changes in the range of $120 billion, although in the HHC model the relative contribution of exchange rate change is smaller.

Moreover, in the HHC model there is an especially favorable impact of lower current account deficits on the factor service balance, because the model (both in its original HH form and in the HHC adaptation) applies all of the residual adjustment in capital stock holdings resulting from changes in the current account to accumulation of US holdings of foreign assets, where the rate of return is particularly high (as discussed in Chapter 3).[25] In view of this consideration, the HHC model probably magnifies the upward bias in the factor services balance in scenarios that achieve major reductions in the US current account deficit.

The economic forces for an improved factor services balance under adjustment do include influences captured by the HHC model but omitted in the EAG model. Thus, higher foreign growth in the adjustment package boosts the rate of return on foreign assets, and depreciation of the dollar revalues the dollar equivalent of earnings on foreign direct investment, both included in the HHC model but not in the EAG model. In short, although the current account outcome for 1992 under the FAP adjustment scenario would seem likely to involve a deficit higher than the $18 billion predicted by the HHC model, the deficit could be lower than the $48 billion projected using the EAG model.

Effects on Other Countries

Table 5.8 indicates the current account balances of the 16 other world areas in 1992 under the FAP. Table 5.9 reports these balances as percentages of exports of goods and services, along with the corresponding current account outcomes under the baseline assumptions. Comparison of tables 5.3 and 5.8 shows the major corrections in global payments imbalances achieved by the adjustment package. The current account deficit of the United States declines from $168 billion to $48 billion (EAG model). The surplus of Germany declines from $85 billion to $16 billion, while the Japanese surplus is somewhat more resilient, but nonetheless declines from $136 billion to $63 billion. Thus, the three massive and extreme imbalances are sharply reduced. In relative terms, the US current account deficit falls from the baseline outcome of 26 percent of exports of goods and services to only 6 percent, while the German surplus declines from the baseline 16 percent to just 3 percent. The 1992 current account surplus for Japan falls from 34 percent of exports of goods and services to 16 percent.

---

25. Thus, under FAP adjustment US foreign assets by 1992 rise from $1.07 trillion to $1.33 trillion, while foreign holdings in the United States remain unchanged at $2.2 trillion (tables 3.2 and 5A.9). As a result, 1992 US factor earnings rise from $126 billion to $159 billion, while factor payments remain unchanged at $146 billion.

Table 5.8 Current account projections under the Feasible Adjustment Package[a]

(billions of dollars except as noted)

Country	Trade balance	Factor services balance	Net transfers	Current account	Current account/XGS
US	− 44.33	− 44.91	− 15.59	− 48.43	− 0.06
UK	− 32.68	2.05	− 7.00	− 22.53	− 0.07
FR	− 13.01	− 1.43	− 5.38	0.43	0.00
GE	41.04	21.54	− 19.80	15.69	0.03
IT	− 4.17	− 11.66	− 2.03	− 6.27	− 0.02
CA	12.52	− 20.25	1.94	− 14.15	− 0.07
JA	80.84	54.19	− 4.94	63.44	0.16
AR	4.84	− 6.84	0.00	− 2.33	− 0.13
BR	30.10	− 8.01	0.09	19.07	0.31
ME	12.88	− 7.92	0.83	5.01	0.10
TA	1.91	9.54	− 0.88	− 9.30	− 0.11
OP	25.86	− 4.86	− 13.71	− 34.89	− 0.24
OI	− 69.12	− 29.47	− 4.04	− 83.08	− 0.08
KS	− 36.80	− 1.35	1.27	− 27.47	− 0.10
OL	9.24	− 11.77	4.00	− 2.03	− 0.03
AN	10.53	− 18.73	8.89	− 10.16	− 0.09
RO	21.85	− 19.72	40.38	89.16	0.16
SD	51.50	− 99.61	− 15.98	− 67.84	− 0.01

SD = statistical discrepancy; XGS = exports of goods and nonfactor services. Country abbreviations are as in table 5.1.
a. BOP basis.

This reduction of imbalances among the three largest trading nations is accomplished while avoiding undue adjustment burdens for other countries. As indicated in table 5.9, the trendlines for France and Italy actually improve as the result of the sharp differentiation of their appreciation from that of Germany and the Other Industrial countries, their key trading partners. Thus, the baseline projection places the French current account deficit at 2 percent of exports of goods and services; in the FAP it stands at zero. For Italy, the corresponding deficits are 9 percent and 2 percent of exports of goods and services. In particular, the adjustment program provides major improvement for the United Kingdom. Its 1992 deficit declines from 29 percent of exports of goods and services to 7 percent.

The outcome under the adjustment program also meets the constraints discussed above for other countries. The 1992 current account deficit is held

Table 5.9 Distribution of adjustment under the Feasible Adjustment Package

Country/group	Trade balance as % of exports, 1992[a]		Current account balance as % of exports of goods and services, 1992[b]		US bilateral balance (billions of dollars)[a]			
							Change	
	Baseline	FAP	Baseline	FAP	1987A[c]	FAP:1992	Magnitude	As % of 1987 trade[d]
United States	-24.70	-6.06	-26	-6				
United Kingdom	-31.99	-10.63	-29	-7	-4.1	3.9	8.0	24.8
France	-5.19	-3.10	-2	0	-2.5	-0.5	2.0	10.9
Germany	23.52	11.80	16	3	-16.1	-17.1	-1.0	-2.9
Italy	-3.71	1.93	-9	-2	-5.6	-6.2	-0.6	-3.7
Canada	11.18	10.00	-6	-7	-13.4	-1.9	11.5	9.0
Japan	35.17	20.66	34	16	-56.8	-30.0	26.8	23.6
Argentina	18.41	22.67	-22	-13	0.1	0.6	0.5	29.3
Brazil	48.59	49.72	28	31	-3.6	-7.8	-4.2	-36.7
Mexico	14.38	15.27	9	10	-4.1	0.3	4.4	13.4
Taiwan	1.80	-4.36	-2	-11	-17.2	-3.2	14.0	43.7
OPEC	23.00	23.00	-24	-24	-11.4	-16.4	-5.0	-15.1
Other Industrial	-8.24	-13.89	-2	-8	2.2	39.7	37.5	57.7
Korea–Singapore–Hong Kong	-4.70	-11.33	-3	-10	-22.8	-14.5	8.3	15.0
Other Latin America	1.27	9.94	-14	-3	0.0	2.2	2.2	9.0
Other Africa	-1.68	7.56	-21	-9	-1.3	1.2	2.5	32.1
Rest of World	-8.57	-4.81	13	16	1.6	14.4	12.8	20.9

a. EAG basis.
b. BOP basis.
c. Actual 1987, EAG/DOTS database.
d. Exports plus imports.

at or below 10 percent of exports of goods and services for almost all countries, and this result is a major improvement for some (Other Africa, Other Latin America). Although the Argentine deficit slightly exceeds this ceiling, it is still much lower in relative terms than in the base case. And the 1992 deficits for Taiwan and Korea–Singapore–Hong Kong lie within the special ceiling of 12 percent of exports of goods and services set forth above, in view of the possible adverse bias for these areas from averaging specific and uniform income elasticities.[26]

The absolute magnitudes of the (nominal dollar) current account balances in table 5.8 are generally in ranges that represent acceptable adjustment. Although the Japanese surplus remains above $60 billion, it falls by more than half relative to the export base. Similarly, the seemingly large deficit of the Other Industrial countries is manageable when compared to the export base (table 5.9). Although the deficit for Korea–Singapore–Hong Kong appears large, its estimation is probably exaggerated (see box 5.2).

For its part, the large surplus of the Rest of World countries reflects primarily the baseline outcome. As discussed above, there may be some upward bias in the projected balances for the area. It should be noted, however, that the adjustment program does not obtain US external balance correction through reduction of Rest of World balances (on the contrary, the Rest of World surplus rises as the region depreciates modestly in real terms), so that the FAP results for the United States are not subject to overstatement of adjustment because of correction at the expense of possibly nonexistent Rest of World surpluses.

Allocation of Adjustment

Table 5.9 reports the nominal dollar bilateral trade balances of the United States against the other countries in 1987 (actual) and 1992 with adjustment. The two final columns state the change in this balance, in absolute terms and as a percentage of two-way trade between the United States and the partner country in 1987. These columns thus indicate the partner source of the improvement in the nominal US trade balance. The largest absolute gains come in US trade with the Other Industrial countries and with Japan. Gains are also large in trade with Taiwan, Canada, Korea–Singapore–Hong Kong, and Rest of World. In proportionate terms, gains are also large in trade with Argentina and Other Africa. The trade balance with Brazil

---

26. The OPEC deficit remains unchanged. By the structure of the model, OPEC automatically respends a fixed proportion of its export revenue, so that the current account outcome is unaffected by alternative policy scenarios.

deteriorates, but by less than in the base case. The absence of exchange rate effects on oil trade means the trade balance with OPEC deteriorates as well.

The most disappointing bilateral pattern is that the US deficit with Germany widens further. As noted above, this outcome reflects the low price elasticities of US–German trade, combined with the large initial bilateral imbalance. Nonetheless, the sharp reduction in Germany's overall current account surplus indicates a broadly successful participation of Germany in international adjustment under the FAP package, despite failure of the bilateral trade surplus with the United States to decline.

The intuitive policy objective is that the imbalances in international payments should be corrected through a large reduction or elimination of the US current account deficit, combined with a similar reduction or elimination of the surpluses of the high-surplus countries: Germany, Japan, Taiwan, and Korea, and (to a lesser extent) the strong countries within the Other Industrial grouping (Belgium, the Netherlands, and Switzerland). Thus, in late 1987 a group of 33 economists from 13 countries set as broad targets that the US current account deficit should be reduced from $150 billion to a range of zero to $50 billion. They proposed that this correction be achieved through a cut in the Japanese current account surplus from $85 billion to a range of $10 billion to $30 billion; that of Germany, from $40 billion to a range of − $10 to + $10 billion; that of Taiwan, from $18 billion to a range of zero to $10 billion; and that of Korea, from $7 billion to a range of zero to $5 billion. Implicitly, the current account balances of other countries were not expected to change much in this adjustment pattern.[27]

The EAG model simulations (as reported in tables 5A.4 and 5A.8) suggest that although the changes in foreign surpluses can be relatively similar in profile to those proposed by the group of 33 economists, the remaining surpluses are higher than that group expected (especially for Japan), because the baseline 1992 surpluses are much larger than the 1987 levels that group considered as a point of departure.[28] The FAP does eliminate the surpluses of Taiwan and Korea–Singapore–Hong Kong, and sharply cuts that of Germany. However, the Japanese surplus remains high despite an extremely large appreciation of the Japanese yen. Even in the German case, the trade

27. Institute for International Economics, *Resolving the Global Economic Crisis: After Wall Street*, SPECIAL REPORT 6 (Washington: Institute for International Economics, December 1987), 17.

28. Moreover, adjustment by Belgium, the Netherlands, and Switzerland means that the Other Industrial countries make an important contribution to the reduction in foreign surplus not anticipated by the group of 33 economists. In addition, the absolute surplus reduction is larger than the group expected, so that although the Japanese contribution is similar in dollar magnitude, it is a smaller proportionate share. See Chapter 1, note 45.

surplus in 1992 remains high ($59 billion, table 5A.8); only the large German deficits on transfers and nonfactor services bring the current account surplus to a much lower level ($16 billion).

Under external adjustment several industrial countries have smaller deficits than in the baseline scenario. The reason is that there are at least three adjustments taking place: reduction of the US external deficit, moderation of a massive emerging UK deficit, and avoidance of a large deficit position that would otherwise arise for Europe with respect to Germany. The design of the FAP takes all three goals into account (as well as trends for other countries) by setting a ceiling on the current account deficit relative to exports.

In this regard, the sharp appreciation of the German mark contributes much more to avoidance of intra-European imbalances than to correction of the US deficit. Thus, in the baseline projection the combined trade deficit of France, Italy, and the United Kingdom with Germany amounts to $46 billion in 1992. FAP adjustment cuts this deficit in half (tables 5A.4 and 5A.8). In contrast, as noted above, the bilateral balance with the United States does not improve at all as a result of the adjustment package.

Developing Countries

A general concern about the foreign country distribution of international adjustment is whether the United States can adjust without causing adverse effects for developing countries. The bilateral changes reported in table 5.9 do indeed indicate that, except for Brazil, the developing countries do not escape a reduction in their trade balances with the United States despite the absence of their participation in the policy package of exchange rate appreciation and growth acceleration. Compared against baseline projections (rather than 1987 results as in table 5.9), the United States increases its trade balance in 1992 as the result of FAP adjustment by approximately $900 million against Mexico, $200 million against Argentina, $300 million against Brazil, $400 million against the rest of Latin America, $800 million against Africa, and $3.6 billion against Rest of World (from tables 5A.4 and 5A.8).

Table 5.9 also shows, however, that as compared with the baseline projections for 1992, the adjustment package generally causes an improvement rather than a deterioration in the trade and current account balances of the developing countries. As a result of FAP international adjustment, the current account balance as a percentage of exports of goods and nonfactor services rises by 9 percentage points for Argentina, 3 for Brazil, 1 for Mexico, 11 for Other Latin America, 12 for Other Africa, and 3 for Rest of World (which includes Asia excluding the NICs, developing countries in Europe, and non-OPEC countries in the Middle East). The developing countries thus gain more in trade balances against other countries in the adjustment package than they lose in their trade balances against the United States. This result holds even for Brazil, Mexico, and Rest of World, despite their participation in the package through moderate appreciation.

The overall trade of these countries benefits from the fact that (with few exceptions) they do not appreciate against the dollar in real terms, so that their exports become more competitive in third-country markets as the dollar declines internationally. Moreover, the reduction in their bilateral trade balances with the United States stems from displacement of third-country supply by US products in their import markets, rather than from an overall increase in their imports or reduction in their exports to the United States. Indeed, because of improved competitiveness against third countries, their exports to the US market increase (through the cross-price effect). Even the three appreciating developing countries gain, because the size of their appreciations is sufficiently small that they depreciate on a trade-weighted basis (in view of the much larger appreciations by Japan and Germany; table 5.10).

The largest trade gains in the FAP package, as compared with the baseline outcome, are for Other Latin America, Other Africa, and Rest of World. For Other Latin America, there are major export gains in the large Other Industrial country market (table 5A.8 versus table 5A.4). Other Africa experiences relatively large export gains in the markets of Europe and Japan. Rest of World obtains large export gains in the markets of Japan, Korea–Singapore–Hong Kong, and the Other Industrial countries. In short, the calculations in the FAP package confirm the results of the initial policy scenarios above in finding that US external adjustment should actually benefit the developing country trade positions, as long as the United States does not resort to domestic recession to accomplish this adjustment.

A more profound question concerning unfavorable side effects on developing countries arises from a wholly different issue. The analysis here indicates that the adjustment will involve a widespread counterpart affecting many industrial countries, especially if exchange rate changes are less differentiated between intermediate and high-surplus countries than in the FAP. Under these circumstances, it will be a key policy challenge for the intermediate countries to avoid pressures for new protection. The model makes no allowance for induced increases in protective barriers in countries experiencing reductions in trade balances. If the intermediate industrial countries already trending toward deficit impose new trade restrictions against the developing countries as the result of additional pressures on their external accounts from US adjustment, the adverse spillover could be large indeed.

On the favorable side, the EAG simulations do not make a special allowance for the impact of lower international interest rates that could be expected from US fiscal adjustment. With a decline by perhaps 2 percentage points to more normal real levels, interest rate savings on variable-rate external debt could amount to some $10 billion for Third World debtor countries. On the basis of the feedback to US exports examined in Chapter 7, the result would be an increase in the US trade balance by approximately $4 billion, further contributing to US external adjustment.

Exchange Rate Implications

The exchange rate adjustments in the FAP represent one basis for judging the appropriate level of fundamental equilibrium exchange rates (FEERs). These changes provide a current account deficit for the United States that is at a sustainable level, while taking into account plausible limits on foreign growth acceleration and on the current account positions of other countries.

Table 5.10 reports the trade-weighted real exchange rate changes for the FAP using both bilateral and multilateral trade weights. For the United States, the program involves a real exchange rate depreciation of 10.7 percent below the 1987:4 level. The real appreciation amounts to approximately 21 percent for Japan and 15 percent for Germany. These appreciations are smaller than the 28 percent and 23 percent real movements against the 1987:4 dollar. This fact is of paramount importance. It means that the exchange rate movements proposed here are less traumatic than they might seem based on real changes against the dollar. Because much of the trade of Japan and especially Germany is with countries whose currencies would also be appreciating against the dollar, their trade-weighted appreciations are considerably more moderate than suggested by the movements against the dollar.

The table shows that the real appreciation on a trade-weighted basis is quite modest for Taiwan, Korea–Singapore–Hong Kong, and the Other Industrial countries (in the range of 3 to 5 percent). For the other intermediate countries (France, Italy, Brazil, and Rest of World), there is actually a real trade-weighted depreciation of 4 to 5 percent, because their 5 percent real appreciations against the dollar (1987:4) are swamped by their depreciations in the range of 18 to 25 percent against the German mark and the Japanese yen. The trade-weighted real depreciation of the weak countries that keep a constant real exchange rate against the dollar is even more pronounced (at 7 to 10 percent). The United Kingdom depreciates the most, by about 13 percent on a trade-weighted real basis.

Table 5.10 also reports nominal exchange rates for 1987:4; December 31,

1987; August 15, 1987; and March 24, 1989. The dollar declined by about 5 percentage points from the 1987:4 average to December 31, 1987 (Chapter 2). Unfortunately, it then proceeded to rise in the first eight months of 1988, buoyed by official intervention at the turn of the year and by the market's seeming surprise at the trade deficit reductions that economists had long been predicting but that only began to arrive in early 1988. As this reversal proceeded, it undoubtedly picked up some self-reinforcing dynamics from trend-following speculators (the bandwagon effect). Nonetheless, the failure of monthly trade data to show continued improvement later in the year, and the postelection recognition that massive efforts remained to be taken on the fiscal deficit, brought a renewed decline of the dollar in the fourth quarter.

As shown in table 5.10, the dollar rose by nearly 20 percent against the German mark, the French franc, and the Italian lira from December 31, 1987, to August 15, 1988. Against the Japanese yen it rose by 7 percent over the same period. Only the Canadian dollar moved in the proper direction in the first three quarters of 1988, as it appreciated by approximately 6 percent. By March 24, 1989, the rise in the dollar against the yen had been only slightly reduced, and the dollar stood 18 percent above its December 31, 1987, level against the mark.

The table reports the nominal exchange rates for the end of 1989 that correspond to the real changes called for in the FAP program. Thus, after taking account of differential inflation between the United States and the country in question (from table 5.1), the nominal exchange rate proposed for the dollar by the end of 1989 stands at 1.327 German marks, 102.3 Japanese yen, and so forth. Note that these rates do not incorporate feedback effects from appreciation. To the extent that the changes accelerate US inflation and decelerate inflation in Germany, Japan, and other appreciating countries, the nominal rates would have to move correspondingly further.

The table also states the percentage appreciation of the nominal exchange rate for each currency in question against four benchmark levels: 1987:4; December 31, 1987; August 15, 1988; and March 24, 1989. As shown in the table, the amount of additional nominal appreciation required to reach the FAP rates for 1989 was increased by the 1988 strengthening of the dollar against the European currencies particularly. Thus, at the end of 1987 only 19 percent additional nominal appreciation of the German mark was required. By August 15, 1988, the gap had reached 41.6 percent for the mark, and despite the decline in the fourth quarter of 1988, renewed dollar strength in the first quarter of 1989 meant that by March 24 the mark needed to appreciate by 40.4 percent against the dollar (or, equivalently, the dollar to decline by 28.8 percent against the mark) to achieve the target of 23 percent real appreciation against the 1987:4 dollar. For the yen, also, by

Table 5.10 Exchange rate changes implied by the Feasible Adjustment Package

Country/group	Change (real) against 1987.4 (%)	Nominal rate (currency units/dollar) 1987:4	12/31/87	8/15/88	3/24/89
United States					
Strong A					
Japan (yen/$)	28	135.8	123.5	132.2	130.8
Germany (DM/$)	23	1.706	1.582	1.879	1.863
Strong B					
Korea (won/$)	14	799.2	792.3	723.3	673.2
Taiwan (New Taiwan dollars/$)	12	29.5	28.5	28.6	27.3
Intermediate A					
Other Industrial	13.5				
France (FF/$)	5	5.755	5.34	6.38	6.32
Italy (lire/$)	5	1,248	1,169	1,394	1,371
Brazil (cruzados/$)	5	60.06	72.25	267.41	997.50
Rest of World	5				
Intermediate B					
Canada (Canadian dollars/$)	3.5	1.311	1.300	1.224	1.188
Mexico (pesos/$)	2.5	1,784.6	2,209.7	2,281.0	2,349.5
Weak A					
Argentina (australs/$)	0	3.42	3.75	11.96	15.51
OPEC	0				
Other Africa	0				
Other Latin America	0				
Weak B					
United Kingdom (pounds/$)	−3	0.570	0.534	0.583	0.579

a. Figures for the US represent depreciation of the dollar in trade-weighted terms.
b. Not calculated because of the high degree of uncertainty about domestic inflation rates.

Sources: EAG model; New York Times, 1 January 1988 and 16 August 1988; Wall Street Journal, 27 March 1989.

FAP:1989	% nominal appreciation required by end-1989, from:				Trade-weighted real appreciation vs. dollar (%)[a]	
	1987:4	12/31/87	8/15/88	3/24/89	Bilateral weights	Multilateral weights
					−10.68	−10.63
102.3	32.8	20.7	29.2	27.9	22.36	20.32
1.327	28.6	19.2	41.6	40.4	14.93	15.39
680.6	17.4	16.4	6.3	−1.1	4.61	5.04
24.6	19.9	15.9	16.3	11.0	2.82	2.84
					2.82	5.33
5.32	8.2	0.4	19.9	18.8	−5.22	−4.48
1,171	6.6	−0.2	19.0	17.1	−4.62	−4.42
b	b	b	b	b	−1.08	−4.24
					−4.42	−4.80
1.268	3.4	2.5	−3.6	−6.3	0.01	−5.93
b	b	b	b	b	−1.01	−6.77
b	b	b	b	b	−7.92	−7.12
					−10.18	−9.62
					−8.39	−9.39
					−7.38	−9.36
0.578	−1.4	−7.6	1.0	0.2	−13.74	−12.93

March 1989 the required appreciation was considerably larger (27.9 percent) than would have been the case if the exchange rate had stayed at its December 31, 1987, low (20.7 percent), and almost as large as from the August 15 dollar peak during 1988.

The movement of the French franc and the Italian lira in tandem with the German mark meant that by late March 1989 they too required substantially more appreciation against the dollar than might be suspected from the 5 percent real appreciation against the 1987:4 level. By March 24, 1989, the needed appreciation stood at 18.8 percent for the French franc against the dollar, and 17.1 percent for the Italian lira. In contrast, the two currencies would have required almost no further movement if they had remained at their December 31, 1987, rates against the dollar. In sum, rebound of the dollar against the Japanese and major European currencies after the end of 1987 and through early 1989 seriously complicated the task of reaching exchange rates appropriate for US external adjustments.

Exchange rate developments in 1988 and early 1989 were more appropriate for the currencies of the East Asian NICs, Canada, and the United Kingdom. Thus, by March 24, 1989, the Korean won had fully achieved (and slightly surpassed) the target appreciation, the British pound sterling was at almost exactly the target exchange rate against the dollar, and the Canadian dollar had actually moved beyond the rate called for in the FAP by some 6 percent. The path of the Canadian dollar meant that the trade-weighted rebound of the US dollar in 1988–89 was less than might be suspected from its rise against the yen and, especially, the major European currencies. Substantial appreciation was still called for in the case of the New Taiwan dollar, however.

As discussed in Chapter 1, an important policy implication of these exchange rate findings is that a realignment of exchange rates within the European Monetary System (EMS) is urgent. Table 5.10 suggests that the German mark should rise by some 18 to 20 percent relative to the French franc and the Italian lira, and presumably against the Danish krone (but not the Belgian franc or the Dutch guilder) within the EMS. (Denmark, Belgium, and the Netherlands do not appear individually in the EAG model but are included in the Other Industrial countries.)[29]

The broader implications for exchange rates include the need for a regime that avoids counterproductive trends such as that which developed in the first several months of 1988, and the importance of close coordination. In

---

29. The bloc of strong currencies within the EMS would also appropriately rise against currencies of other members of the European Community that have not pursued tight parities within the EMS, namely, the United Kingdom, Spain, Portugal, and Greece.

particular, it will take considerable shared recognition of the risks of the underlying trends for the major industrial countries to pursue the type of joint adjustment program proposed here. Such changes as sharply differentiated exchange rate changes among the industrial countries (including realignment within the EMS) have not been part of the exchange rate strategy that has been evolving since the Plaza Agreement of September 1985.[30]

Alternative Adjustment Packages

Bergsten has argued that the target for the US current account should be a zero balance by 1992, rather than a deficit of $50 billion.[31] Complete elimination of the deficit would further reduce the risks associated with the external imbalance. However, this goal would also require more ambitious policy measures. On the basis of the policy parameters of tables 5.5 and 5.6, a package capable of eliminating the US current account deficit by 1992 could be constructed by adding to the FAP an additional ¼ percentage point annual growth acceleration in the strong countries (except Korea–Singapore–Hong Kong and Taiwan) plus Canada (worth about $6 billion) and increasing the size of currency appreciations by 4 percentage points for all countries appreciating in the FAP package (except Mexico). Overall the resulting real depreciation of the dollar against its 1987:4 level would amount to approximately 15 percent. The Zero Balance Program (ZBP) applied to the EAG model achieves a current account balance of − $1.8 billion in 1992.

In broad terms it would require nearly a 50 percent increase in the adjustment effort to cut the US current account deficit to zero by 1992, rather than to $50 billion.[32] It seems unlikely, however, that Germany and Japan

---

30. On the contrary, at the Plaza the Europeans were concerned to ensure that the choice of intervention currency did not place pressure on the cross rates within the EMS. Later, the Louvre Accord in February 1987 compounded the error by concluding not only that there was no need for major differential movements among individual rates, but that exchange rates overall were "within ranges broadly consistent with underlying economic fundamentals." The events of 1987 and the projections of this study suggest otherwise, on both counts. See Yoichi Funabashi, *Managing the Dollar: From the Plaza to the Louvre* (Washington: Institute for International Economics, 1988), 18–21, 177–78.

31. C. Fred Bergsten, *America in the World Economy: A Strategy for the 1990s* (Washington: Institute for International Economics, 1988).

32. An outcome of zero on the current account would be a reduction of the deficit by $150 billion instead of $100 billion. A ¼-percentage-point higher growth rate would be a 50 percent (or more) increase in growth acceleration for all intermediate countries, including the weaker members of the Other Industrial grouping. A trade-weighted dollar decline of 15 percent instead of 10.7 percent would be nearly a 50 percent rise in exchange rate adjustment.

would be prepared to accept a proportionate increase of their adjustment over the FAP case. To do so would imply real exchange rate appreciation of 42 percent for Japan and 35 percent for Germany. Instead, the ZBP package examined here adds 4 percentage points to the appreciation by all adjusting countries, thereby causing much less concentration of the marginal adjustment beyond the FAP in Germany and Japan (but even so, raising appreciation of the yen to 32 percent, and of the mark to 27 percent). In contrast, for the intermediate countries that would have appreciated by 5 percent in the FAP, an appreciation of 9 percent in the ZBP is nearly a doubling of the policy adjustment.

The resulting current account balances as percentages of exports of goods and nonfactor services by 1992 are as follows: United Kingdom, −3; France, −2; Germany, 2; Italy, −4; Canada, −15; Japan, 14; Argentina, −10; Brazil, 31; Mexico, 12; Taiwan, −13; OPEC, −23; the Other Industrial countries, −9; Korea–Singapore–Hong Kong, −11; Other Latin America, 0; Other Africa, −5; and Rest of World, 15. The most serious deterioration resulting from escalation of the goal for US adjustment is in the case of Canada. Otherwise, changes in the 1992 current account balances relative to exports from the outcomes under the FAP (table 5.9) are moderate. The deterioration for France, Italy, and the Other Industrial countries is modest, considering the narrowing of the gap between their share of adjustment and that of Germany and Japan from the FAP configuration. The obstacle to the ZBP adjustment package might thus not be so much excessive burden on intermediate countries (aside from the Canada problem) as the larger overall real appreciation against the dollar compared with the FAP.

Many policymakers in Germany and Japan may be expected to oppose even the FAP, however, on grounds that it would involve excessive strain on their economies. In particular, they could resist real appreciations against the 1987:4 dollar by the 23 percent and 28 percent estimates calculated as necessary just to cut the US external deficit to $50 billion, let alone larger appreciations to achieve a US current account balance of zero.

A less ambitious adjustment package might have approximately the following features. The Japanese might insist that real appreciation of the yen against the dollar be held to no more than 20 percent; the Germans, that the mark rise by only 18 percent against the dollar. The Germans might further insist that any realignment of the EMS limit appreciation of the mark against the French franc and the Italian lira to no more than 10 percentage points. These currencies might thus rise by 8 percent in real terms against the dollar, whereas the implied average rise for the Other Industrial country currencies would be 12.7 percent against the dollar. With lesser adjustment by Germany and Japan, it might be possible to make up some of the loss for US adjustment through increasing the real appreciation by Canada, Mexico, Rest of World, and Brazil by 1 percentage point above their appreciations prescribed in the FAP (although the United Kingdom would retain its 3 percent real depreciation against the dollar).

In this Second-Best Adjustment Package (SBAP), which would still retain the FAP acceleration in growth rates, the consequences would be as follows. The US current account deficit would fall to $54 billion by 1992, only modestly above the target level. However, the reduced concentration of adjustment upon Germany and Japan would leave the strain of larger imbalances among other countries. The Japanese current account surplus in 1992 would stand at $87 billion (21 percent of exports of goods and services) versus $63 billion (16 percent) in the FAP, and the German current account surplus would be at $32 billion versus $16 billion (or 6 percent of exports of goods and services versus 3 percent). In contrast, France would develop a current account deficit of $9 billion, Italy a deficit of $18 billion, and the Other Industrial countries a deficit of $77 billion, all higher than in the FAP because of the greater currency appreciation imposed by greater rigidity on intra-EMS realignment. By implication, the European countries would need greater financing from higher-surplus Germany in this scenario.

Policy Implications

The simulations of this chapter have several major implications for policy. First, the projections confirm the central finding with the HHC model in Chapter 3 that far more must be done if the US external deficit is to be brought under control. Although the EAG model is constructed on a basis of much greater country disaggregation, and applies a much less detailed bloc for services and other nontrade components in the current account, it arrives at a time path for the US external deficit that is uncannily close to that of the HHC model in Chapter 3. Both show that the trade and current account deficits will reach their troughs in 1989, and that the deficits will then begin to widen again. Both find that the current account deficit will not fall below $100 billion, and that by 1992 it will once again be in a range of $150 billion. In short, the analysis of this study casts serious doubt on any policy of benign neglect that would simply hope the external deficits will take care of themselves.

Second, both the EAG and HHC models find that an additional trade-weighted real depreciation of the dollar by about 10 percent from its level in 1987:4 is required, together with some acceleration of demand growth by key trading partners, if the US current account deficit is to be brought down to a sustainable level of $50 billion by 1992.

Third, the EAG model tends to confirm the HHC model results showing

Box 5.2 The Impact of Alternative Elasticity Assumptions

As developed in Appendix A, the baseline and policy scenario projections reported above employ an average between the empirically estimated trade elasticities for each country combination of trade (Chapter 4) and a set of "uniform" elasticities obtained from averaging over all countries. Table 5A.10 examines the sensitivity of the projections to the choice among country-specific, uniform, and specific/uniform average elasticities.

As shown in the table, for the United States the baseline trade deficit for 1992 is somewhat lower under uniform elasticities than with specific or averaged elasticities. The reason is that the specific elasticities incorporate an adverse asymmetry between the income elasticity for imports and that for exports (as discussed in Chapter 4). Nonetheless, the differences are not large.

The US results for alternative policy scenarios are also relatively stable with respect to choice of elasticity set. The largest difference occurs for the FAP. Here, the sharp appreciation of the yen combined with a high specific elasticity for Japanese exports to the United States (as well as other price elasticity differences) makes the trade response to the adjustment package almost $30 billion greater than in the central, averaged (uniform/specific) elasticity case. Thus, the central projections above may tend to understate the external sector correction in response to the policy package, which may provide partial reassurance to those who consider a more ambitious goal (such as complete elimination of the US external deficit) imperative.

For the United Kingdom there is little difference among alternative elasticity sets for any of the scenario results. This finding is important, because it indicates that the dramatic prospective deterioration of the UK external balance is not a curiosity caused by aberrant estimates for trade elasticities. The three alternative elasticity sets also yield relatively unchanging results for Italy, Brazil, and Rest of World.

For France, the uniform elasticities show a much more favorable baseline trend than the specific elasticities, as the result of the strong adverse asymmetry of income elasticities (table 4.3).

Otherwise the results are parallel across policy scenarios. In the case of Germany, the three elasticity sets show similar results in all scenarios except the FAP. This scenario, which involves sharp appreciation of the mark, shows a wide divergence between the specific and uniform elasticity cases, reflecting the unusually low price elasticities estimated specifically for Germany.

Canada shows the most extreme sensitivity to the elasticity set. In the base case, the uniform elasticities show a large 1992 trade surplus, whereas the specific elasticities show a small deficit. Once again the reason is the unfavorable income elasticity asymmetry (table 4.3). Moreover, the specific price elasticities cause a much greater response to exchange rate change than the uniform elasticities. As noted above, the specific price elasticity for US exports to Canada is especially high (at the upper bound). Thus, in the FAP, the uniform elasticities predict a 1992 trade surplus of $46.7 billion, whereas the specific elasticities project a trade deficit of $20 billion. The average specific/uniform elasticity approach is thus a crucial methodological decision in the Canadian case, and the projections for Canada may advisedly be seen as less stable than those for most other countries.

Korea–Singapore–Hong Kong is the other major trading area with high sensitivity to the elasticity set. In this case the uniform elasticities show a large baseline trade deficit for 1992, whereas the specific elasticities show a large surplus. This divergence is from the extremely favorable asymmetry of income elasticities between exports and imports (table 4.3). As discussed above, the decision to average the two sets permits perhaps the best central estimate. Nonetheless, because the baseline projections impose much higher growth for Korea–Singapore–Hong Kong income than for that of its trading partners (8 percent versus 2½ to 3 percent for the industrial countries), the loss of the historical favorable asymmetry on income elasticities means that the area is suddenly under long-term trade pressure. As noted above, the tendency for high-growth countries to have relatively lower import income elasticities and higher observed export income elasticities (so that their high growth rates do not become as incompatible) suggests that the elasticity averaging technique leaves a downward bias for the trendline in the Korea–Singapore–Hong Kong trade accounts. (The same phenomenon applies

Box 5.2 (continued)

in a much milder degree in the projections for Taiwan.)

The results for Japan also warrant comment. There the choice of elasticities has limited influence on the baseline trends, or on the results of across-the-board policy scenarios (with the partial exception of higher strong-country growth, as the uniform elasticities have a higher income elasticity of imports than the specific Japanese estimate). A much more substantial difference arises, however, in the FAP, which calls for a sharp exchange rate appreciation for Japan. There is a $50 billion difference in the 1992 trade balance between the specific and uniform elasticities under FAP adjustment. As Japan's price elasticities tend to be below average, it has a higher 1992 trade surplus despite FAP appreciation if the specific elasticities are used instead of the uniform set. Nonetheless, the swing between the outcome under the averaged elasticity set and that from either the specific or the uniform elasticity is moderate when viewed as a percentage of exports of goods and services (less than 7 percent for 1992).

Overall, table 5A.10 suggests that the choice of elasticity set does not fundamentally alter the policy findings. However, the cases of Canada and Korea–Singapore–Hong Kong are particularly sensitive to specific versus uniform elasticities, and more generally the most reliable course is to apply the average between these two elasticity sets.

the importance of faster growth abroad for the US external balance. In both models, 1-percentage-point additional growth for one year in Europe, Japan, Canada, Taiwan, and Korea increases the 1992 US trade balance by almost $7 billion, and the current account by $9 billion to $13 billion.

Fourth, a key new dimension of policy findings is provided by the country detail in the EAG model. In particular, the simulations indicate that it will be necessary to concentrate the exchange rate appreciation heavily on Germany and Japan, and to a lesser extent on Taiwan and Korea, if undue payments burdens on other countries are to be avoided as the US makes its external sector correction.

Fifth, the simulations show that even with sharp real appreciation of the yen, the Japanese current account surplus will remain large (at over $60 billion in 1992). In the absence of any correction, the current account surpluses would soar far higher (to $84 billion for Germany and $136 billion for Japan). Although the heavy outward transfers and deficit on nonfactor services mean that after exchange rate adjustment the German current account surplus is moderate although its trade surplus is high, in the Japanese case the current account surplus is a more persistent feature of the international trading and payments system.[33] The concept of persistent surplus countries is of course not new, as it is a normal element of international allocation of capital from older and richer countries to newer economies scarce in capital and with higher rates of return. The direction of this surplus will have to shift, however, from its financing of the US external deficit to more appropriate destinations.

In the face of continued high surpluses, it is important for Japan in particular to move toward an effort in international transfers that is more compatible with its stronger position. Thus, table 5A.2 shows that in 1987 Japan's net outward transfers (unrequited) amounted to only $3.7 billion, or just 1.5 percent of exports of goods and nonfactor services. If instead Japan had been providing transfers equal to the US rate of 4.2 percent of exports of goods and services, its net outward transfers would have tripled, to $10.7 billion. Although Japanese authorities have frequently announced ambitious plans to expand external economic assistance, it is important that these intentions translate into a reality consistent with the country's chronic surplus status.

Sixth, the analysis here strongly implies that a realignment of currencies within the EMS will be required. Germany and a core group of other strong-currency European countries (Belgium, the Netherlands, and Switzerland) should ideally appreciate their currencies by as much as 18 to 20 percent against the currencies of other European countries such as France and Italy. Otherwise, serious pressures on the external accounts of these other countries may be expected to emerge as the United States carries out its adjustment. At the political level, there could be the risk of increased protectionist pressures within Europe as the response to such erosion. Alternative simulations suggest that a realignment by only 10 percent between the German mark and weaker European currencies might not be incompatible with US adjustment, but that it would result in larger German surpluses

---

33. Although additional reductions in the Japanese surplus could be obtained through still further real appreciation of the yen unmatched by additional appreciation by other currencies against the dollar, the FAP appreciation of 28 percent for the yen would already appear to be at the outer limits of what is politically feasible. Similarly, it is unclear that Japanese authorities would be prepared to seek sustained growth levels either for the economy or for domestic demand at higher than the 5 percent rate assumed in the FAP, for fear of inflationary consequences.

and larger deficits elsewhere in Europe that would presumably require greater ongoing financing from Germany.

Seventh, the projections here identify special external-sector difficulties for the United Kingdom. It is the only major country that is likely to have to depreciate in real terms against the dollar to avoid dangerously high external deficits. Thus, the United Kingdom is not in a position to contribute to the counterpart of the US external adjustment.

Eighth, the policy simulations indicate that, despite these various challenges, it should be possible to achieve US external adjustment while at the same time avoiding US recession or intolerable pressures on the payments of other countries. A tailored package of exchange rate adjustments and growth acceleration permits the United States to reduce its current account deficit to $50 billion by 1992 while ensuring that no foreign country is forced by that adjustment into a precarious payments position involving a current account deficit of greater than 10 percent of exports of goods and services. The program to accomplish this outcome really involves addressing at least three imbalances: that of the United States, that between Germany and other European countries, and that of the United Kingdom.

Ninth, for the United States, an important feature of the projections is that, after adjustment, the current account deficit should not be greatly larger than the trade deficit. A large surplus on nonfactor services should cover the bulk of the deficit on capital services and transfers.

Tenth, the simulations indicate that the developing countries should be able to weather, and actually benefit from, US external adjustment. They can maintain their real exchange rates fixed against the dollar, and in doing so improve their competitive positions in the European and Japanese markets. The calculations for the FAP indicate in particular that there are substantial trade gains for Other Latin America, Other Africa, and Rest of World, which includes Asia except for the NICs, the European developing countries, and the nonoil Middle East. The more important Europe and Japan are in the markets of these developing countries, the greater the potential benefits from the faster growth and appreciated exchange rates in these industrial areas, which comprise the bulk of the adjustment package. For other developing countries more dependent on the US market, the effects of US adjustment tend to be positive but modest.

Only if the United States found it could not adjust without undergoing a major recession would the spillover effects for developing countries turn decidedly negative. Another important caveat is that any new trade protection erected in Europe and Japan because of new trade pressures associated with US adjustment would indeed carry negative consequences for the developing countries.

The findings of this chapter also confirm the broader, macroeconomic implications of Chapters 2 and 3. Foremost, an indirect implication of these findings is that forceful fiscal correction in the United States is imperative. The large prospective depreciation of the dollar still in store against the German and Japanese currencies could easily dissipate into largely nominal rather than real exchange rate correction as the consequence of accelerated inflation in the United States if the fiscal correction that needs to go hand in hand with exchange rate correction is absent.

With regard to exchange rate policy, the successive recent attempts by the G-7 industrial countries to stabilize the dollar, from the Louvre Accord in February 1987 to the Toronto summit in June 1988, were premature at best and misguided at worst. The decision of the G-7 authorities at the end of 1987 to intervene strongly in support of the dollar turned out to be ill-advised and caused an undue and counterproductive rise in the dollar. The dollar was at its closest level to a sustainable real rate at the very end of 1987, although even then it was about 5 percent overvalued. Thereafter it rose considerably in the first half of 1988, and, after a lull in late 1988, rose again in early 1989. Yet at the Toronto summit the G-7 authorities reportedly "rebased" their exchange rate targets and set limits of plus or minus 5 percent around the then-current exchange rates as their goals, according to then-US Secretary of Commerce C. William Verity Jr.[34] They did so even though at that time the dollar had already rebounded from its end-1987 level of 121 yen and 1.58 marks to 126 yen and 1.75 marks.[35] By early 1989 the Federal Reserve appeared willing to risk an even stronger dollar as the consequence of rising interest rates to damp inflationary forces.

An arguable defense for the successive attempts to set a floor to the dollar beginning in early 1987, after the coordinated effort to bring it down that began with the Plaza meeting in September 1985, is that an optimal speed of dollar decline might have been more gradual than markets might otherwise have imposed. It takes time for exporters to respond, and for firms in appreciating countries to shift toward domestic sales. But by mid-1988 it should have been clear that the upward reversal of the dollar was perverse from the policy standpoint, and that a gradual further decline should have been achieved instead.

Another important implication of the results here is that international monetary coordination must go beyond a simple accord that all rates should stabilize about where they are, or even that they should all move down in tandem by some agreed percentage. Instead, it will be necessary to be much more candid about divergence among individual rates. As the FAP policy

---

34. Reuters, 15 August 1988.

35. *Wall Street Journal*, 4 January and 20 June 1988.

simulation shows, a wide wedge will be required between the further appreciation of the yen and the mark, on one hand, and most other industrial country currencies, on the other. A corollary of this finding is that the EMS will have to face up sooner rather than later to a realignment that permits currencies such as the French franc and the Italian lira to depreciate against the German mark.[36]

These are the principal implications of the analysis of this chapter for policy at the international level. There are other country-specific implications that warrant attention as well (such as the strong trend toward improvement in the Brazilian case).

All of the results presented here concentrate on the nominal trade and current account prospects of international adjustment. Chapter 6 integrates the results of the US model in Chapter 3 and the international model of Chapters 4 and 5 to explore the corresponding implications for adjustment in real terms. Because changes in trade prices tend to moderate the extent of nominal trade and current account balance correction (for example, as higher import prices offset lower import volumes), the real (constant price) trade changes that must be carried out can be considerably larger than suggested by the nominal changes. These real changes are what matter for real economic growth and employment. The need for large real trade changes raises questions concerning the productive capacity of the United States to provide the increased exports and import substitutes, and regarding the potential lack of demand in Europe and Japan as foreign economies lose the real stimulus formerly coming from the surplus corresponding to the US external deficit.

Similarly, the prospects for international adjustment as it affects the developing countries raise issues that go beyond this chapter's focus on nominal balances. Chapter 7 examines the outlook for developing countries in a period of US external sector adjustment, and the potential contribution that the developing countries might make to that adjustment under more favorable conditions for their access to external finance.

---

36. Thus, a special simulation was performed in which there is no change at all in the exchange rates among the currencies in the EMS, but the same trade-weighted change of all of them against the dollar as in the FAP (placing appreciation of the German mark, French franc, and Italian lira against the 1987:4 dollar at 15.8 percent, and of the OI currencies on average at 12.2 percent), and in which all other FAP assumptions are maintained. In this simulation the 1992 German current account surplus rises to $46 billion, the French deficit to $27 billion, and the Italian deficit to $38 billion.

Statistical Annex to Chapter 5

Table 5A.1 Matrix of adjusted cross-price elasticities

Exporter	US	UK	FR	GE	IT	CA	JA	AR
				Importer				
US	0.000	0.548	0.430	0.495	0.516	0.282	0.482	1.12
UK	0.444	0.000	0.552	0.471	0.537	0.624	0.413	2.42
FR	0.590	0.442	0.000	0.453	0.495	0.630	0.413	0.63
GE	0.434	0.412	0.484	0.000	0.464	0.624	0.403	0.58
IT	0.488	0.547	0.532	0.480	0.000	0.631	0.414	0.86
CA	0.397	0.781	0.581	0.491	1.374	0.000	0.405	2.41
JA	0.385	0.452	0.572	0.472	0.552	0.608	0.000	0.62
AR	0.550	1.972	0.425	0.514	0.447	0.370	0.589	0.00
BR	0.543	0.534	0.664	0.512	0.601	0.678	1.395	0.49
ME	0.536	0.536	0.425	0.514	0.448	0.512	0.589	0.91
TA	0.437	0.469	0.748	0.490	0.558	1.672	0.401	0.65
OI	0.431	0.439	0.471	0.373	0.461	0.617	0.721	0.59
KS	0.938	0.462	2.140	0.484	0.555	1.775	0.795	2.41
OL	0.539	0.533	0.423	0.511	0.446	0.369	0.584	0.41
AN	0.546	0.530	0.548	1.003	0.555	0.370	0.577	0.34
RO	0.529	0.510	0.900	0.479	0.593	0.365	0.509	0.34
WTDE	0.491	0.468	0.546	0.443	0.504	0.435	0.562	0.73

US, United States; UK, United Kingdom; FR, France; GE, Germany; IT, Italy; CA, Canada
JA, Japan; AR, Argentina; BR, Brazil; ME, Mexico; TA, Taiwan; OP, OPEC; UP, Unite
Kingdom-oil; MP, Mexico-oil; OI, Other Industrial; KS, Korea–Singapore–Hong Kong; O
Other Latin America; AN, Other Africa; RO, Rest of World.

WTDE = Trade-weighted average elasticity.

			Importer					
BR	ME	TA	OI	KS	OL	AN	RO	WTDE
.695	0.236	0.634	0.781	0.684	0.639	1.423	0.484	0.510
.571	0.843	0.647	0.363	0.570	0.425	1.111	0.752	0.512
.635	0.842	0.647	0.356	0.574	0.412	0.442	0.519	0.452
.613	0.828	0.633	0.384	0.568	0.417	0.464	0.503	0.463
.651	0.847	0.648	0.370	0.576	0.427	1.094	1.330	0.556
.828	0.841	0.646	0.495	1.447	0.786	0.501	0.533	0.456
.635	0.822	0.491	0.432	0.474	1.000	1.637	0.508	0.478
.332	0.156	0.353	0.608	0.426	0.567	0.502	0.467	0.522
.000	0.155	0.354	0.605	0.424	0.557	0.653	0.610	0.627
.338	0.000	0.354	0.608	0.425	0.565	0.504	0.467	0.535
.666	3.134	0.000	0.411	0.758	1.591	1.847	1.570	0.633
.621	0.815	0.616	0.909	0.551	0.410	0.450	0.781	0.526
.662	0.847	1.286	0.852	1.926	1.585	0.490	1.166	1.040
.325	0.155	0.352	0.600	0.425	0.546	0.504	0.465	0.533
.338	0.156	0.348	0.600	0.424	0.569	0.479	0.454	0.554
.652	0.155	0.777	0.602	0.682	1.023	0.472	0.728	0.637
.656	0.381	0.618	0.535	0.709	0.685	0.748	0.709	0.555

Table 5A.2 Estimated current account balances, 1987
(billions of dollars)

Country	Merchandise Exports	Merchandise Imports	Nonfactor services Exports	Nonfactor services Imports	Transfers	Factor services	Current account balance
US	249.6	409.9	71.5	72.1	−13.5	20.4	−154.0
UK	130.1	146.5	45.7	36.4	−5.6	9.3	−3.4
FR	140.3	147.7	55.4	44.8	−4.3	−0.4	−1.5
GE	278.8	208.6	52.8	65.5	−15.9	3.6	45.2
IT	116.7	117.2	31.2	24.5	−1.6	−5.3	−0.7
CA	97.6	88.8	13.7	17.7	1.6	−12.6	−6.2
JA	224.6	128.2	30.1	52.8	−3.7	16.6	86.6
AR	6.4	5.4	1.0	1.4	0.0	−4.3	−3.7
BR	26.2	15.0	2.2	4.4	0.1	−7.8	1.3
ME	23.5	13.8	4.5	4.3	0.7	−6.6	4.0
TA	53.2	32.6	2.9	9.8	−0.7	5.0	18.0
OP	129.1	93.1	0.0	32.0	−11.0	2.0	−5.0
OI	439.6	448.6	152.6	133.5	−3.2	−13.2	−6.3
KS	122	115.4	17.3	10.5	1.0	−3.4	11.0
OL	25.7	27.4	4.7	7.9	3.2	−7.4	−9.1
AN	49.5	44.8	7.4	13.0	7.1	−11.0	−4.8
RO	220.2	257.7	33.0	14.5	34.0	−23.0	−8.0
Total	2,333.1	2,300.7	526.0	545.1	−11.8	−38.1	−36.6
Statistical discrepancy	32.4			19.1	−11.8	−38.1	−36.6

For an explanation of country abbreviations see table 5A.1.

Sources: International Monetary Fund, *International Financial Statistics*, August 1988; *Balance of Payments Statistics*, various issues; *Direction of Trade Statistics*, Yearbook 1988; IMF, *World Economic Outlook*, April 1988, 143–159; Bank for International Settlements, *Statistics on External Indebtedness*, July 1988; Central Bank of Brazil; Banco de Mexico; US Department of Commerce.

Table 5A.3 Parameters of the current account model

Country	γ_x	γ_m	T_0	F_0	η_x	η_m	C	g_T
US	0.9967	1.0115	−13.45	0.00	0.2865	0.1759	−153.96	0.030
UK	0.9915	1.0261	−5.62	9.27	0.3511	0.2482	−3.330	0.045
FR	0.9443	0.9612	−4.32	−0.36	0.3950	0.3031	3.000	0.045
GE	0.9476	0.9813	−15.89	3.58	0.2150	0.2980	45.230	0.045
IT	0.9887	1.0279	−1.63	−5.28	0.2671	0.2087	2.850	0.045
CA	1.0060	1.0415	1.56	−12.57	0.1405	0.1997	−7.240	0.045
JA	0.9709	0.9486	−3.69	16.59	0.1341	0.4122	86.960	0.060
AR	0.9930	0.8752	0.00	−4.32	0.1600	0.2660	−3.720	0.045
BR	0.9850	0.9132	0.07	−7.80	0.0820	0.2940	−0.790	0.045
ME	0.8757	0.7037	0.67	−6.64	0.1900	0.3080	3.880	0.045
TA	1.0000	0.9362	−0.71	5.00	0.0540	0.3000	18.060	0.045
OP	1.0261	1.1005	−11.00	2.00	0.0000	0.3440	−5.000	0.045
OI	0.9580	0.9129	−3.24	−13.15	0.3472	0.2977	−6.240	0.045
KS	0.9809	1.0113	1.02	−3.42	0.1421	0.0909	10.390	0.045
OL	0.6855	0.6375	3.21	−7.39	0.1815	0.2900	−10.300	0.045
AN	1.0162	0.9827	7.13	−11.00	0.1500	0.2900	−4.740	0.045
RO	0.8385	0.7640	34.00	−23.00	0.1500	0.0563	−8.000	0.035

γ = ratio of balance of payments (BOP) trade to IMF *Direction of Trade Statistics* (DOTS) data; x = exports; m = imports; T = transfers (billions of dollars); 0 = base year; F = factor services (billions of dollars); η = ratio of nonfactor trade to merchandise trade; C = current account balance (billions of dollars); g_T = assumed growth rate for nominal transfers (annual percentage).

Sources: Calculated from *International Financial Statistics*, August 1988; IMF, *Balance of Payments Statistics*, Vol. 38, Yearbook 1987, Part I and May–July 1988; IMF, *World Economic Outlook*, April 1988, 150–51; *OECD Economic Outlook*, 43, June 1988; US Department of Commerce.

Table 5A.4 Baseline trade projections, 1992
(billions of dollars)

Exporter	Importer							
	US	UK	FR	GE	IT	CA	JA	AR
US	0.00	31.89	16.05	21.27	9.86	110.27	58.85	2.3?
UK	24.04	0.00	17.63	21.96	10.14	3.68	3.59	0.0‹
FR	17.75	23.76	0.00	37.26	29.29	2.03	4.10	0.5⁑
GE	43.30	43.76	56.76	0.00	40.91	3.59	9.54	1.5?
IT	16.71	15.29	30.76	34.61	0.00	1.83	3.34	0.6‹
CA	121.06	4.16	1.60	2.16	1.18	0.00	9.20	0.1⁑
JA	119.36	14.58	6.22	19.40	3.32	8.28	0.00	0.8?
AR	1.96	0.15	0.25	0.82	0.56	0.14	0.50	0.0(
BR	14.91	1.78	2.20	3.20	2.65	1.05	3.37	1.2⁑
ME	21.59	0.71	0.45	0.64	0.08	0.89	0.40	0.1⁑
TA	29.41	2.38	1.21	3.09	0.91	1.98	12.53	0.02
OP	30.83	2.58	6.04	5.80	9.92	1.14	28.08	0.0€
UP	3.94	0.00	1.63	1.95	0.63	0.66	0.08	0.0(
MP	8.30	0.13	0.35	0.00	0.09	0.15	1.47	0.0(
OI	43.10	81.31	81.60	138.59	44.80	5.27	22.35	1.4⁑
KS	67.71	10.06	3.94	10.17	2.81	4.50	27.82	0.1⁑
OL	20.13	2.24	1.77	4.01	1.75	1.15	2.96	1.1?
AN	9.04	4.66	8.39	6.25	6.67	0.51	5.81	0.12
RO	31.50	17.94	20.86	37.34	24.91	3.58	41.46	0.6⁑
Totals								
Exports	500.92	195.00	244.99	455.68	183.64	169.67	363.18	13.6⁑
Imports	624.65	257.37	257.70	348.53	190.46	150.71	235.44	11.1?
Trade balance	−123.73	−62.37	−12.71	107.16	−6.82	18.96	127.73	2.52

For an explanation of country abbreviations see table 5A.1.

				Importer				
BR	ME	TA	OP	OI	KS	OL	AN	RO
6.79	29.34	19.27	14.27	67.40	39.75	21.95	9.39	42.25
0.61	0.40	0.80	9.51	54.31	6.48	1.87	6.34	17.72
1.32	0.57	0.99	8.28	66.00	4.07	5.02	14.73	29.27
2.19	1.33	2.72	10.63	176.41	7.31	2.93	8.82	43.92
0.67	0.33	0.88	10.89	45.50	3.80	1.83	4.74	11.82
1.03	0.59	1.84	1.42	6.37	3.57	1.58	1.01	12.72
1.56	1.35	21.87	15.96	40.30	54.22	7.51	5.09	43.30
0.99	0.13	0.84	0.55	2.32	0.18	1.31	0.59	2.41
0.00	0.36	0.26	2.54	6.29	1.47	3.55	1.40	5.59
0.58	0.00	0.47	0.08	2.11	0.64	1.69	0.13	1.85
0.05	0.09	0.00	2.54	3.35	11.97	1.47	1.64	4.90
4.03	0.02	2.98	0.00	14.92	9.45	3.85	2.14	21.67
0.00	0.00	0.00	0.00	6.99	0.00	0.00	0.00	0.00
0.00	0.00	0.00	0.00	0.60	0.00	0.00	0.00	0.00
2.04	1.71	6.30	13.18	203.36	16.17	7.08	13.02	70.85
0.22	0.27	3.85	5.23	17.42	20.28	3.50	3.46	54.83
1.60	0.21	1.09	0.72	21.43	2.62	4.92	0.63	4.82
0.56	0.06	1.90	0.74	12.22	1.67	0.67	5.78	19.56
2.40	0.55	10.05	13.98	66.85	63.72	1.55	7.13	157.22
1.80	43.54	77.51	143.50	752.17	236.26	73.21	84.61	501.73
6.63	37.28	76.12	110.49	814.15	247.38	72.28	86.04	544.72
5.17	6.26	1.40	33.00	−61.98	−11.11	0.93	−1.42	−42.99

Table 5A.5 Scenario 1: 1992 trade with a 10 percent dollar depreciation against strong countries[a]

(billions of dollars)

Exporter	Importer							
	US	UK	FR	GE	IT	CA	JA	AR
US	0.00	36.16	17.82	23.60	10.92	112.97	64.26	2.52
UK	24.27	0.00	19.21	23.95	11.02	3.67	3.85	0.04
FR	17.97	25.85	0.00	40.61	31.80	1.97	4.39	0.56
GE	43.86	47.61	61.75	0.00	44.40	3.55	10.23	1.60
IT	16.31	16.60	33.51	37.71	0.00	1.74	3.58	0.65
CA	124.78	4.64	1.82	2.41	1.37	0.00	9.86	0.22
JA	115.13	15.87	6.78	21.16	3.61	7.82	0.00	0.84
AR	2.02	0.18	0.27	0.91	0.61	0.14	0.54	0.00
BR	15.41	1.96	2.44	3.51	2.91	1.07	3.74	1.24
ME	22.31	0.85	0.49	0.70	0.09	0.90	0.43	0.16
TA	26.59	2.59	1.31	3.37	0.99	1.76	13.44	0.02
OP	30.83	2.58	6.04	5.80	9.92	1.14	28.08	0.06
UP	3.94	0.00	1.63	1.95	0.63	0.66	0.08	0.00
MP	8.30	0.13	0.35	0.00	0.09	0.15	1.47	0.00
OI	42.43	88.01	88.75	150.68	48.64	5.16	23.34	1.47
KS	62.00	10.95	4.18	11.09	3.05	4.01	29.03	0.18
OL	20.83	2.45	1.95	4.41	1.91	1.16	3.19	1.19
AN	9.35	5.11	9.23	7.19	7.81	0.52	6.36	0.12
RO	32.56	19.62	23.65	40.90	27.50	3.61	44.57	0.69
Total exports	538.37	205.79	261.21	486.65	194.47	177.36	372.31	14.45
Total imports	618.92	281.15	281.18	379.93	207.27	151.97	250.43	11.54
Trade balance	−80.55	−75.37	−19.97	106.72	−12.80	25.39	121.87	2.91

For an explanation of country abbreviations see table 5A.1.
a. In 1989; excluding Canada.

				Importer				
BR	ME	TA	OP	OI	KS	OL	AN	RO
7.10	29.89	21.66	14.27	75.52	44.03	23.05	10.64	43.97
0.57	0.39	0.86	9.51	59.09	6.97	1.86	6.48	18.17
1.33	0.56	1.06	8.28	71.87	4.39	5.15	15.25	30.19
2.21	1.29	2.92	10.63	191.32	7.87	3.00	9.14	45.28
0.67	0.31	0.94	10.89	49.55	4.09	1.84	4.86	11.23
1.07	0.60	2.11	1.42	7.04	4.09	1.64	1.05	13.23
1.54	1.26	23.27	15.96	43.82	58.05	7.42	5.15	44.63
1.00	0.13	0.90	0.55	2.55	0.20	1.35	0.61	2.49
0.00	0.36	0.28	2.54	6.90	1.58	3.66	1.47	5.84
0.58	0.00	0.51	0.08	2.31	0.78	1.74	0.13	1.92
0.05	0.07	0.00	2.54	3.65	12.78	1.42	1.66	4.93
4.03	0.02	2.98	0.00	14.92	9.45	3.85	2.14	21.67
0.00	0.00	0.00	0.00	6.99	0.00	0.00	0.00	0.00
0.00	0.00	0.00	0.00	0.60	0.00	0.00	0.00	0.00
2.05	1.63	6.76	13.18	218.61	17.40	7.25	13.49	72.40
0.22	0.26	4.02	5.23	18.75	20.80	3.39	3.58	55.68
1.62	0.21	1.17	0.72	23.55	2.83	5.05	0.66	4.99
0.57	0.06	2.04	0.74	13.43	1.80	0.69	6.00	20.25
2.47	0.55	11.09	13.98	73.60	70.29	1.63	7.41	165.68
4.91	45.08	77.16	143.50	801.25	236.41	77.89	91.26	539.81
7.10	37.58	82.56	110.49	884.08	267.41	73.99	89.71	562.56
7.82	7.50	−5.40	33.00	−82.82	−31.00	3.90	1.55	−22.76

Table 5A.6 Scenario 2: 1992 trade with 1 percent higher growth in strong countries, 1989–92[a]
(billions of dollars)

Exporter	Importer							
	US	UK	FR	GE	IT	CA	JA	AR
US	0.00	34.58	17.46	22.61	10.38	110.27	62.32	2.32
UK	24.04	0.00	19.28	24.02	11.09	3.68	3.74	0.04
FR	17.75	25.98	0.00	39.55	31.56	2.03	4.41	0.55
GE	43.30	47.85	61.27	0.00	44.33	3.59	10.21	1.57
IT	16.71	16.72	33.64	37.42	0.00	1.83	3.55	0.64
CA	121.06	4.33	1.73	2.27	1.23	0.00	9.65	0.19
JA	119.36	15.94	6.81	21.22	3.64	8.28	0.00	0.83
AR	1.96	0.15	0.26	0.87	0.58	0.14	0.53	0.00
BR	14.91	1.91	2.40	3.42	2.89	1.05	3.52	1.21
ME	21.59	0.77	0.49	0.70	0.09	0.89	0.42	0.15
TA	29.41	2.60	1.32	3.38	0.99	1.98	13.49	0.02
OP	30.83	2.63	6.14	5.90	10.10	1.14	28.59	0.06
UP	3.94	0.00	1.66	1.98	0.64	0.66	0.08	0.00
MP	8.30	0.13	0.36	0.00	0.09	0.15	1.50	0.00
OI	43.10	86.66	89.22	149.53	48.83	5.27	23.50	1.45
KS	67.71	11.00	4.31	11.12	3.07	4.50	29.53	0.19
OL	20.13	2.34	1.91	4.24	1.87	1.15	3.11	1.17
AN	9.04	4.86	8.87	6.52	7.03	0.51	6.06	0.12
RO	31.50	19.62	22.43	40.83	27.23	3.58	43.89	0.68
Total exports	518.77	203.74	257.13	482.32	195.67	171.34	375.33	14.05
Total imports	624.65	278.06	279.57	375.59	205.64	150.71	248.09	11.17
Trade balance	−105.88	−74.32	−22.44	106.73	−9.97	20.63	127.25	2.89

For an explanation of country abbreviations see table 5A.1.
a. Excluding Canada.

				Importer				
BR	ME	TA	OP	OI	KS	OL	AN	RO
6.79	29.34	20.43	14.41	72.15	42.12	21.95	9.39	42.25
0.61	0.40	0.84	9.61	57.58	6.82	1.87	6.34	17.72
1.32	0.57	1.05	8.36	70.67	4.31	5.02	14.73	29.27
2.19	1.33	2.87	10.73	189.67	7.73	2.93	8.82	43.92
0.67	0.33	0.94	11.00	49.75	4.08	1.83	4.74	11.82
1.03	0.59	1.98	1.43	6.73	3.81	1.58	1.01	12.72
1.56	1.35	23.07	16.12	44.06	57.20	7.51	5.09	43.30
0.99	0.13	0.91	0.55	2.48	0.19	1.31	0.59	2.41
0.00	0.36	0.28	2.57	6.81	1.60	3.55	1.40	5.59
0.58	0.00	0.50	0.08	2.30	0.70	1.69	0.13	1.85
0.05	0.09	0.00	2.56	3.66	12.77	1.47	1.64	4.90
4.03	0.02	3.04	0.00	15.19	9.62	3.85	2.14	21.67
0.00	0.00	0.00	0.00	7.11	0.00	0.00	0.00	0.00
0.00	0.00	0.00	0.00	0.61	0.00	0.00	0.00	0.00
2.04	1.71	6.80	13.32	218.97	17.10	7.08	13.02	70.85
0.22	0.27	4.09	5.28	19.05	21.60	3.50	3.46	54.83
1.60	0.21	1.17	0.72	23.44	2.86	4.92	0.63	4.82
0.56	0.06	2.02	0.75	13.02	1.77	0.67	5.78	19.56
2.40	0.55	10.64	14.12	73.10	67.84	1.55	7.13	157.22
53.46	44.08	80.32	144.94	798.43	243.74	76.29	87.20	524.32
26.63	37.28	80.62	111.61	876.38	262.11	72.28	86.04	544.72
26.82	6.80	−0.30	33.34	−77.95	−18.37	4.01	1.17	−20.40

Table 5A.7   Scenario 3: 1992 trade with 1 percent lower US growth, 1989–92
(billions of dollars)

Exporter	US	UK	FR	GE	IT	CA	JA	AR
				Importer				
US	0.00	31.89	16.05	21.27	9.86	110.27	58.85	2.32
UK	22.20	0.00	17.63	21.96	10.14	3.68	3.59	0.04
FR	16.22	23.76	0.00	37.26	29.29	2.03	4.10	0.55
GE	39.57	43.76	56.76	0.00	40.91	3.59	9.54	1.57
IT	15.27	15.29	30.76	34.61	0.00	1.83	3.34	0.64
CA	113.11	4.16	1.60	2.16	1.18	0.00	9.20	0.19
JA	109.07	14.58	6.22	19.40	3.32	8.28	0.00	0.83
AR	1.79	0.15	0.25	0.82	0.56	0.14	0.50	0.00
BR	13.62	1.78	2.20	3.20	2.65	1.05	3.37	1.21
ME	19.73	0.71	0.45	0.64	0.08	0.89	0.40	0.15
TA	26.88	2.38	1.21	3.09	0.91	1.98	12.53	0.02
OP	29.63	2.58	6.04	5.80	9.92	1.14	28.08	0.06
UP	3.79	0.00	1.63	1.95	0.63	0.66	0.08	0.00
MP	7.97	0.13	0.35	0.00	0.09	0.15	1.47	0.00
OI	40.26	81.31	81.60	138.59	44.80	5.27	22.35	1.45
KS	61.88	10.06	3.94	10.17	2.81	4.50	27.82	0.19
OL	19.32	2.24	1.77	4.01	1.75	1.15	2.96	1.17
AN	8.50	4.66	8.39	6.25	6.67	0.51	5.81	0.12
RO	29.70	17.94	20.86	37.34	24.91	3.58	41.46	0.68
Total exports	500.80	192.93	243.39	451.86	182.11	161.71	352.75	13.52
Total imports	578.51	257.37	257.70	348.53	190.46	150.71	235.44	11.17
Trade balance	−77.71	−64.45	−14.31	103.33	−8.35	11.00	117.31	2.35

For an explanation of country abbreviations see table 5A.1.

				Importer				
BR	ME	TA	OP	OI	KS	OL	AN	RO
6.79	29.34	19.27	14.15	67.40	39.75	21.95	9.39	42.25
0.61	0.40	0.80	9.43	54.31	6.48	1.87	6.34	17.72
1.32	0.57	0.99	8.21	66.00	4.07	5.02	14.73	29.27
2.19	1.33	2.72	10.54	176.41	7.31	2.93	8.82	43.92
0.67	0.33	0.88	10.80	45.50	3.80	1.83	4.74	11.82
1.03	0.59	1.84	1.41	6.37	3.57	1.58	1.01	12.72
1.56	1.35	21.87	15.83	40.30	54.22	7.51	5.09	43.30
0.99	0.13	0.84	0.54	2.32	0.18	1.31	0.59	2.41
0.00	0.36	0.26	2.52	6.29	1.47	3.55	1.40	5.59
0.58	0.00	0.47	0.08	2.11	0.64	1.69	0.13	1.85
0.05	0.09	0.00	2.52	3.35	11.97	1.47	1.64	4.90
4.03	0.02	2.98	0.00	14.92	9.45	3.85	2.14	21.67
0.00	0.00	0.00	0.00	6.99	0.00	0.00	0.00	0.00
0.00	0.00	0.00	0.00	0.60	0.00	0.00	0.00	0.00
2.04	1.71	6.30	13.07	203.36	16.17	7.08	13.02	70.85
0.22	0.27	3.85	5.18	17.42	20.28	3.50	3.46	54.83
1.60	0.21	1.09	0.71	21.43	2.62	4.92	0.63	4.82
0.56	0.06	1.90	0.73	12.22	1.67	0.67	5.78	19.56
2.40	0.55	10.05	13.86	66.85	63.72	1.55	7.13	157.22
50.50	41.36	74.96	142.29	749.22	230.38	72.39	84.06	499.82
26.63	37.28	76.12	109.57	814.15	247.38	72.28	86.04	544.72
23.86	4.07	−1.16	32.73	−64.93	−16.99	0.11	−1.97	−44.90

Table 5A.8 Trade projections under the Feasible Adjustment Package, 1992
(billions of dollars)

Exporter	Importer							
	US	UK	FR	GE	IT	CA	JA	AR
US	0.00	33.32	18.28	27.08	11.05	124.27	76.34	2.66
UK	25.52	0.00	20.47	28.05	11.67	3.92	5.74	0.06
FR	18.81	24.42	0.00	47.85	33.00	2.12	5.16	0.58
GE	44.19	39.34	62.56	0.00	45.08	3.59	12.03	1.60
IT	17.22	15.05	35.13	46.38	0.00	1.91	5.04	0.68
CA	126.13	4.41	1.83	2.75	1.38	0.00	11.38	0.22
JA	106.39	12.36	6.93	24.53	3.69	7.44	0.00	0.83
AR	2.09	0.18	0.27	1.06	0.61	0.14	0.62	0.00
BR	15.52	1.83	2.52	3.99	3.00	1.10	4.17	1.26
ME	22.63	0.70	0.51	0.82	0.09	0.95	0.49	0.16
TA	26.62	2.17	1.32	4.00	1.00	1.84	17.21	0.02
OP	30.83	2.58	6.09	5.90	10.01	1.15	28.59	0.06
UP	3.94	0.00	1.64	1.98	0.63	0.66	0.08	0.00
MP	8.30	0.13	0.35	0.00	0.09	0.15	1.50	0.00
OI	42.93	79.59	89.71	172.44	49.52	5.34	26.75	1.50
KS	61.99	9.70	4.33	13.31	2.92	4.05	36.01	0.18
OL	21.50	2.33	2.00	4.99	1.95	1.21	3.70	1.21
AN	9.64	4.87	9.44	8.12	7.70	0.54	7.54	0.12
RO	33.43	18.64	24.16	47.56	28.33	3.75	51.42	0.70
Total exports	582.39	227.43	278.89	499.81	215.90	182.38	370.27	15.30
Total imports	617.69	251.61	287.53	440.83	211.73	164.14	293.76	11.83
Trade balance	−35.30	−24.18	−8.63	58.98	4.18	18.24	76.51	3.47

For an explanation of country abbreviations see table 5A.1.

				Importer				
BR	ME	TA	OP	OI	KS	OL	AN	RO
7.67	31.27	23.47	14.39	82.66	47.51	23.75	10.83	47.83
0.75	0.44	0.94	9.59	67.01	7.52	1.95	7.28	20.49
1.44	0.60	1.18	8.34	77.48	4.68	5.21	15.41	32.63
2.30	1.28	3.02	10.72	205.87	8.23	3.05	9.12	47.85
0.73	0.34	1.01	10.98	56.23	4.36	1.88	5.08	13.86
1.15	0.61	2.21	1.43	7.54	4.45	1.66	1.05	14.18
1.55	1.15	23.58	16.09	48.21	59.47	6.87	4.27	46.90
1.06	0.14	0.94	0.55	2.77	0.21	1.37	0.62	2.68
0.00	0.37	0.29	2.56	7.52	1.66	3.70	1.47	6.26
0.63	0.00	0.53	0.08	2.55	0.84	1.76	0.13	2.12
0.06	0.07	0.00	2.56	4.01	13.67	1.46	1.65	5.45
4.07	0.02	2.98	0.00	15.12	9.45	3.85	2.14	21.87
0.00	0.00	0.00	0.00	7.08	0.00	0.00	0.00	0.00
0.00	0.00	0.00	0.00	0.61	0.00	0.00	0.00	0.00
2.18	1.67	7.14	13.29	237.10	18.40	7.35	13.54	77.54
0.24	0.27	4.36	5.27	20.54	22.89	3.41	3.59	60.71
1.74	0.21	1.21	0.72	26.01	2.97	5.14	0.66	5.42
0.61	0.06	2.11	0.74	14.54	1.89	0.70	6.03	23.04
2.61	0.57	11.74	14.09	80.63	74.35	1.63	7.43	177.16
57.24	46.11	83.10	144.70	845.99	253.77	82.98	97.71	578.22
28.78	39.07	86.72	111.42	963.50	282.53	74.73	90.32	606.01
28.46	7.04	−3.62	33.28	−117.51	−28.76	8.24	7.39	−27.79

Table 5A.9 US balance of payments, projected (HHC, Feasible Adjustment Package), 1988–92

(billions of dollars)

	1988	1989	1990	1991	1992
Merchandise exports	339.15	410.08	477.01	553.24	624.17
Agricultural	29.11	31.21	33.46	35.88	38.46
Nonagricultural	310.04	378.87	443.55	517.36	585.70
Volume	315.91	357.19	394.36	437.80	472.16
Deflator	97.99	106.03	112.42	118.13	124.01
Merchandise imports	466.86	510.25	555.81	606.45	660.88
Oil	38.96	46.21	56.18	63.91	72.36
Nonoil	427.90	464.04	499.63	542.54	588.52
Volume	379.24	352.48	346.75	349.59	362.99
Deflator	112.99	131.70	144.09	155.18	162.11
Trade balance	−127.71	−100.17	−78.80	−53.22	−36.71
NONA	−117.86	−85.17	−56.08	−25.18	−2.82
Services exports	179.01	198.54	215.96	241.11	271.85
Factor	101.01	111.91	120.15	136.48	159.34
DI income	46.53	62.40	72.27	85.97	101.86
Other private	50.52	45.74	44.11	46.60	53.47
Gov't	3.96	3.77	3.78	3.91	4.01
Nonfactor	78.00	86.63	95.80	104.63	112.51
Services imports	176.22	190.37	204.41	219.77	237.12
Factor	104.37	114.44	123.78	134.05	145.55
DI income	18.55	21.16	23.46	25.93	28.72
Other private	61.58	68.80	74.71	81.38	88.89
Gov't	24.25	24.48	25.61	26.74	27.94
Nonfactor	71.84	75.93	80.63	85.72	91.57
Services balance	2.79	8.16	11.54	21.34	34.74
Factor services	−3.36	−2.53	−3.63	2.43	13.79
Unilateral transfers	−13.00	−13.59	−14.21	−14.86	−15.54
Current account	−137.92	−105.59	−81.47	−46.74	−17.52
As % of GNP	−2.83	−2.02	−1.45	−0.78	−0.27
Net external assets	−591.37	−696.97	−778.44	−825.18	−842.70
Claims on foreigners					
DI	303.98	354.46	403.23	451.84	500.79
Other private	582.96	544.82	546.00	604.77	713.44
Gov't	116.59	116.59	116.59	116.59	116.59
Foreign claims on US					
DI	272.91	297.99	326.91	360.32	398.58
Other private	1,019.50	1,105.40	1,202.19	1,311.27	1,434.19
Other on gov't	302.49	309.46	315.16	326.80	340.75

DI = direct investment; NONA = nonagricultural, nonoil.

Table 5A.10 Trade balances under alternative policy scenarios and elasticities, 1992
(billions of dollars)

Country	Baseline			10% appreciation against dollar in strong countries[a,b]			1% faster growth in strong countries[c]			1% slower growth in US[c]			Implementation of FAP		
	S	A	U	S	A	U	S	A	U	S	A	U	S	A	U
US	-128.4	-123.7	-107.5	-68.1	-80.5	-74.3	-112.9	-105.9	-86.7	-77.3	-77.7	-65.9	-7.0	-35.3	-36.5
UK	-67.9	-62.4	-56.4	-79.0	-75.4	-71.1	-82.4	-74.3	-66.1	-70.3	-64.4	-58.2	-25.8	-24.2	-20.3
FR	-29.3	-12.7	1.6	-36.7	-20.0	-8.1	-44.0	-22.4	-3.7	-31.4	-14.3	0.5	-36.4	-8.6	15.0
GE	111.3	107.2	102.7	116.9	106.7	95.0	111.0	106.7	101.9	106.3	103.3	99.9	83.8	59.0	28.9
IT	-6.3	-6.8	-8.4	-12.8	-12.8	-14.9	-9.1	-10.0	-12.0	-8.2	-8.3	-9.6	3.8	4.2	2.2
CA	-3.2	19.0	36.4	-2.0	25.4	45.9	-2.1	20.6	38.9	-10.5	11.0	27.8	-20.3	18.2	46.7
JA	141.5	127.7	117.0	138.7	121.9	109.7	145.3	127.2	112.2	128.9	117.3	108.8	103.8	76.5	52.7
AR	-0.9	2.5	5.1	-1.6	2.9	6.0	-0.6	2.9	5.5	-1.1	2.3	4.9	-2.0	3.5	7.2
BR	27.7	25.2	21.3	28.8	27.8	24.9	29.5	26.8	22.9	26.1	23.9	20.3	29.5	28.5	25.2
ME	3.9	6.3	3.3	1.3	7.5	4.8	4.5	6.8	3.7	1.2	4.1	1.5	-2.2	7.0	4.4
TA	5.3	1.4	-6.3	-4.6	-5.4	-11.8	4.9	-0.3	-9.8	2.5	-1.2	-8.6	-5.2	-3.6	-9.5
OP	33.0	33.0	33.0	33.0	33.0	33.0	33.3	33.3	33.3	32.7	32.7	32.7	33.3	33.3	33.3
OI	-64.0	-62.0	-48.9	-75.9	-82.8	-72.0	-80.6	-78.0	-63.4	-66.8	-64.9	-52.1	-124.7	-117.5	-89.1
KS	20.2	-11.1	-47.4	-5.9	-31.0	-65.1	17.0	-18.4	-59.5	12.8	-17.0	-51.9	-5.0	-28.8	-63.5
OL	-4.9	0.9	7.9	-4.0	3.9	13.6	-1.6	4.0	10.8	-5.1	0.1	6.3	-0.6	8.2	19.3
AN	-0.6	-1.4	-2.5	-0.5	1.6	4.0	1.0	1.2	1.3	-1.1	-2.0	-3.2	3.6	7.4	11.7
RO	-37.3	-43.0	-50.9	-27.6	-22.8	-19.5	-13.3	-20.4	-29.3	-38.8	-44.9	-53.3	-28.7	-27.8	-27.8

S = country-pair specific elasticities; A = average of specific and uniform elasticities; U = uniform elasticities. Country abbreviations are as in table 5A.1.

a. Strong countries include UK, FR, GE, IT, JA, TA, OI, and KS.

b. In 1989.

c. During 1989–92.

6

Real Effects of US External Adjustment and Macropolicy Implications

The analyses of Chapters 3 through 5 dealt primarily with adjustment of the US current account deficit in nominal dollar terms. Chapter 3 applied a current account forecasting model to determine the prospects for the US external deficit in the absence of concrete policy measures for adjustment, and examined the impact of alternative policies. Chapter 4 developed a multicountry model to examine the implications of US adjustment for other countries, and Chapter 5 simulated the model under alternative policy scenarios. This chapter translates these results for nominal external balances into estimates for real changes in the volumes of trade.

Real Trade Changes and Output

Although prospective nominal trade and current account balances are important for analyzing financing needs and progress toward adjustment, they do not tell the full story. The impact of external adjustment on US and foreign growth and employment will depend not on nominal changes, but on changes in real trade flows.

Important differences arise between the real, or volume, changes in imports and exports and the corresponding changes in nominal dollar values. An obvious difference stems from ongoing inflation. Thus, with inflation at 4½ percent annually and an initial trade deficit of $150 billion, the nominal trade deficit would rise by approximately $7 billion annually with no change in the physical volume of imports or exports, and thus no change in the production and employment related to them.

A more subtle but potentially more important divergence between real and nominal trade, in the other direction, arises from changes in the terms of trade, or the ratio of import prices to export prices. When a country depreciates its real exchange rate, its import prices tend to rise relative to

259

Figure 6.1 US manufacturing and total GNP, 1960–86

trillions of 1982 dollars (log scale)

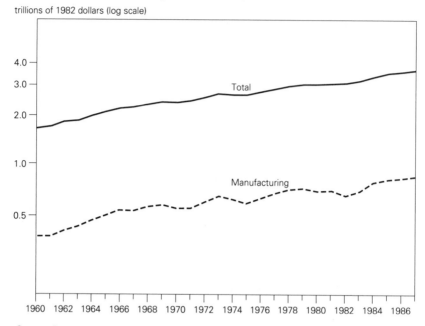

Source: Economic Report of the President, February 1988, 250, 261.

its export prices. Thus, if German suppliers continue to charge the same price in marks for a product and the dollar has depreciated by 10 percent against the mark, the dollar price of the imported product will rise by 10 percent. In contrast, US exporters who base their price on the domestic dollar value of the good will tend to keep their export price unchanged in dollars (although they may feel they can raise their prices somewhat to capture some of the gain otherwise passed along to German customers, who face mark prices for US goods that decline by as much as 10 percent).

Because the terms of trade tend to deteriorate for the depreciating country attempting to reduce its external deficit, the real volume of the trade balance change tends to exceed the nominal value of the change. Thus, if the objective is to reduce the US trade deficit by approximately $100 billion in nominal dollars, the real change is likely to have to be substantially larger (for example, an increase in the real volume of exports combined with a reduction in the real volume of imports amounting to a total of $150 billion to $200 billion at constant prices). The production and employment requirements necessary to accomplish the external adjustment can thus be considerably larger than implied by the size of the change in the nominal dollar trade deficit.

Figure 6.2 US manufacturing and total employment, 1960–86

millions of workers (log scale)

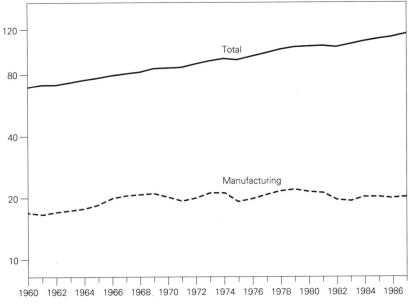

Source: *Economic Report of the President,* February 1988, 284, 296.

Appendix F develops a simple model relating the change in the real trade balance to the change in the nominal trade balance. This chapter applies this model as well as the models of Chapters 3 and 5 to examine the prospective impact of US external adjustment on production in the United States and abroad. The objective of this analysis is to identify the role that external adjustment will play in the evolution of real economic growth in the United States and abroad over the medium term. In broad terms, correction of the US external deficit can be expected to boost the demand for US production and dampen the demand for foreign production over the next several years. For the United States, the rise in external demand may be expected to fulfill the function of offsetting the reduction in domestic demand associated with elimination of the fiscal deficit.

The adverse effect of the external sector on US manufacturing in the 1980s may be seen by reviewing the longer-term growth of the sector. Figure 6.1 shows the level of real GNP for the US economy as a whole and for the manufacturing sector alone from 1960 to 1987; figure 6.2 presents the corresponding levels of total and manufacturing employment. The diagrams are presented on a logarithmic scale, so that constant percentage growth rates appear as straight, upward-sloping lines.

It is clear from figure 6.2 that growth in US manufacturing employment ended in 1979. By contrast, total US employment in the 1980s broadly continued its trendline of growth of the previous two decades. The corresponding divergence between total-economy growth and manufacturing growth when stated in terms of GNP (figure 6.1) is less dramatic. Nonetheless, even for production it is apparent that there was a break in the trendline of manufacturing growth in the period 1981–86, when the sector's output expanded more slowly relative to total GNP than in the past.

In broad terms, the poor relative performance of manufacturing output and, especially, employment in the 1980s reflected the discrimination against tradeable goods imposed by overvaluation of the dollar.[1] A dollar too strong by some 40 percent or more caused a sharp disincentive to produce for export or for import substitution, and an incentive to shift production to nontradeable areas such as services and housing. Total employment in the economy continued to rise as millions of jobs were created in the services sector, but the share of manufacturing in output and employment suffered. The share of manufacturing in employment lagged even more than that in output, in part because the overly strong dollar imposed intense pressure to cut costs and therefore to boost productivity of labor and other inputs.

Trade Balance Drag on US Growth in the 1980s

As indicated in Chapter 2, the external deficits of the United States in the early 1980s acted as a major source of demand for the rest of the world economy. Correspondingly, these deficits exerted a contractionary influence on the US economy. Although the expansionary force of fiscal deficits largely offset the influence of declining real trade balances, because the economy was at less than full capacity the drag from the external sector was still a relevant obstacle to growth. Thus, in 1984 through 1987, US manufacturing capacity utilization was at an average of 80.6 percent, and in the year of the largest real trade deficit (1986), utilization was somewhat lower (79.8 percent). Although capacity utilization in 1984–87 was well above the level in the recession year 1982 (71.1 percent), it remained below the monthly peaks of the two previous cycles (87.7 percent in 1973 and 86.5 percent in 1978–80).[2]

---

1. Branson and Love estimate that the strong dollar caused a loss of 1.1 million manufacturing jobs in the United States from 1980 through 1985, or 5.7 percent of 1985 manufacturing employment. William H. Branson and James P. Love, "The Real Exchange Rate and Employment in US Manufacturing: State and Regional Results," *NBER Working Paper* 2435 (Cambridge, Mass.: National Bureau of Economic Research, 1987).

2. *Federal Reserve Bulletin*, June 1988, June 1985, June 1983, A46.

Table 6.1 shows the relationship of US external deficits in the 1980s to production. At constant 1982 prices, the balance on goods and services systematically declined from a surplus of $57 billion in 1980 to a peak deficit of $138 billion in 1986. The corresponding trend for merchandise trade alone was from a deficit of $12 billion in 1980 to a peak deficit of $169 billion in 1986. Note that the real deficits declined in 1987 (and again in 1988), even though the nominal deficits rose (Chapter 3), reflecting the divergence between the real and nominal measures just discussed.

The contribution of the external sector to demand for domestic US production may be seen in the final portion of table 6.1. For each year, the change in the real external balance from the previous year is expressed as a percentage of real GNP. Thus, in 1984 net exports of goods and services fell by $64 billion at 1982 prices, amounting to −1.95 percent of GNP. As may be seen, for every year during the period 1981–86 the contribution of the external sector to demand for US production was negative. That is, in each of these years there was a further increase in the size of the real external deficit. The influence of the foreign sector on demand for production only turned positive in 1987 and 1988, as the real external deficit began to decline.

These estimates provide a measure of the negative impact of the rising external deficit on US growth during this period. For example, at the extreme it might be said that US GNP growth in 1984 would have been higher by 1.95 percentage points if there had been no rise in the real deficit on goods and services in that year. In practice, higher demand for domestic production from the absence of a rising trade deficit would have translated in part into higher inflation and rising interest rates, and so growth might not have been higher by this full amount (especially considering that US growth in 1984 was already at a high recovery rate of 6.8 percent). At the same time, the direct effects calculated in the table make no allowance for the demand multiplier, which tends to make the ultimate growth impact larger than the initial change in net demand from the external sector. From this standpoint, the growth impact estimates are understated. The simple cumulative change in real net external demand over the period 1981–86 amounted to approximately −6 percent of GNP (table 6.1).

The downward pressure exerted on production from the external deficit is more vivid when attention is concentrated on the manufacturing sector. Table 6.1 reports the change in the real nonoil, nonagricultural (NONA) trade balance in each year, expressed as a percentage of value added in manufacturing. As indicated, the drag on manufacturing production from each year's deterioration in the manufacturing trade balance was substantial, and reached as high as 7.2 percent in 1984.

The relatively large negative real effect of trade on demand for manufacturing output in the period 1981–86 (a simple average of −3.8 percent

Table 6.1 Real impact of trade on US production, 1980–88
(billions of 1982 dollars except as noted)

Year	Exports Goods and services	Goods	Non-agricul-tural	Imports Goods and services	Goods	Nonoil
1980	388.9	241.8	202.7	332.0	253.6	170.8
1981	392.7	238.5	199.5	343.4	258.7	186.3
1982	361.9	214.0	176.8	335.6	249.5	188.2
1983	348.1	207.6	171.9	368.1	282.2	221.7
1984	371.8	223.8	188.5	455.8	351.1	287.1
1985	367.2	231.6	201.2	471.4	367.9	307.6
1986	378.4	243.7	213.0	515.9	412.3	337.0
1987	427.8	280.1	245.2	556.7	439.0	361.1
1988	504.8	341.5	303.3	605.0	469.8	383.4

NONA = nonoil, nonagricultural goods; NXGS = net exports of goods and services; TBNONA = trade balance in nonoil, nonagricultural goods.

Sources: *Economic Report of the President,* February 1988, 250, 261, 271; *Survey of Current Business,* July 1986, 56; July 1988, 40, 70; September 1988, 3, 9; US Department of Commerce, *The National Income and Product Accounts of the United States, 1929–82, Statistical Tables,* 213; US Department of Commerce, "Gross National Product: Fourth Quarter 1988 (Final)," BEA-89-10, 23 March 1989.

annually) is consistent with the severe pressure that much of the sector (especially nondefense) was under during this period, and with the resulting trend toward protectionism. The cumulative effect of deterioration on the real NONA trade balance amounted to $156 billion (at 1982 prices) from 1980 through 1986. This erosion amounted to a direct reduction in demand by 23.4 percent of 1980 manufacturing output, and by 19.4 percent of 1986 manufacturing production.

These comparisons show the massive adverse effect that US external disequilibrium in the 1980s has had on the manufacturing sector. Correspondingly, they indicate the buoyant prospects for manufacturing in coming years from the standpoint of rising demand from the external sector. Thus, already in 1987 and 1988 the reduction in the real NONA trade deficit amounted to a cumulative impact of more than 5 percent of manufacturing GNP (table 6.1).

The comparisons also pose sobering questions, however, about US industrial capacity for external adjustment. Suppose an objective were to restore the real NONA trade surplus of $32 billion (1982 prices) attained in

Trade balance			Relative change in trade balance (%)		
Goods and services	Goods	NONA	NXGS/ GNP	TB/ GNP	TBNONA/ Mfg. GNP
56.9	−11.8	31.9	1.67	1.50	3.26
49.3	−20.2	13.2	−0.24	−0.26	−2.81
26.3	−35.5	−11.4	−0.71	−0.47	−3.64
−20.0	−74.6	−49.8	−1.46	−1.23	−6.05
−84.0	−127.3	−98.6	−1.95	−1.61	−7.22
−104.3	−136.3	−106.4	−0.58	−0.26	−1.03
−137.5	−168.6	−124.0	−0.92	−0.89	−2.24
−128.9	−158.9	−115.9	0.23	0.26	1.01
−100.2	−128.3	−80.1	0.75	0.80	4.26

1980. This target would require approximately $112 billion in additional net NONA exports (1982 prices), representing 13 percent of estimated 1988 manufacturing GNP. If 85 percent capacity utilization is taken as a practical limit beyond which inflationary pressures become dangerous, this increase in manufactured output cannot be obtained by increased capacity utilization alone. Thus, in the third quarter of 1988, manufacturing capacity utilization stood at 82.7 percent.[3] An increase in output by 13 percent without capacity expansion would push the utilization rate to 93.5 percent, well above the effective full-utilization ceiling. However, capacity can be expected to grow over the adjustment period, especially if improved trade projects stimulate manufacturing investment. Estimates of the required increase in real net exports, and corresponding implications for manufacturing capacity, are examined further below.

---

3. *Federal Reserve Bulletin*, December 1988, A46.

Table 6.2 Changes in real trade balances with the United States relative to trade and GNP, 1980–86

(billions of 1980 dollars except as noted)

Country	Total exports (1980)	GNP (1980)	Exports to US 1980	Exports to US 1986
United Kingdom	115.3	460.5	10.6	17.6
France	116.0	664.6	4.9	9.2
Germany	192.9	817.1	11.8	26.0
Italy	77.7	396.1	4.1	10.7
Canada	67.5	258.3	41.1	73.0
Japan	130.5	1,058.9	31.9	70.7
Argentina	8.0	66.2	0.7	1.0
Brazil	20.1	243.3	3.5	8.3
Mexico	15.5	145.9	10.1	13.8
Taiwan	19.8	40.8	6.8	19.4
OPEC	301.3	575.8	54.2	25.4
Other Industrial	335.5	1,126.3	15.3	29.6
Korea–Singapore–Hong Kong	54.5	90.3	12.1	32.4
Other Latin America	46.6	128.9	15.3	17.2
Other Africa	53.1	206.8	5.8	8.3
Rest of World	191.0	2,521.9	11.3	28.0
Total	1,745.3	8,801.7	239.5	390.6

Sources: IMF, *International Financial Statistics;* World Bank, *World Development Report 1982;* EAG data base (see Chapter 4).

US Trade Stimulus to Foreign Growth, 1980–86

It is possible to apply the EAG trade data base developed in Chapter 4 to examine the impact of US trade trends in the 1980s on economic growth in other countries and regions. Real trade at constant 1980 prices may be obtained from the EAG trade data matrices (such as table 4.1) by dividing nominal dollar values by export unit values for each supplying country.[4]

The real US trade balance showed persistent declines during 1981–86, and then began to reverse (table 6.1). The maximum extent of the favorable

---

4. Export unit values of the oil-exporting countries are applied to obtain the real volume of exports from OPEC and from the Mexico and United Kingdom oil sectors (MP and UP, respectively; see Chapter 4).

		Change in trade balance with US				
Imports from US		Trade balance with US			As % of 1980 exports	As % of 1980 GNP
1980	1986	1980	1986	Value		
12.7	10.1	−2.1	7.5	9.6	8.33	2.08
7.5	6.4	−2.6	2.8	5.4	4.66	0.81
11.0	9.3	0.8	16.7	15.9	8.24	1.95
5.5	4.3	−1.4	6.4	7.8	10.04	1.97
35.4	40.1	5.7	32.9	27.2	40.30	10.53
20.8	23.8	11.1	46.9	35.8	27.43	3.38
2.6	0.8	−1.9	0.2	2.1	26.25	3.17
4.4	3.4	−0.9	4.9	5.8	28.86	2.38
15.1	10.9	−5.0	2.9	7.9	50.97	5.41
4.7	4.9	2.1	14.5	12.4	62.63	30.39
17.0	9.2	37.2	16.2	−21.0	−6.97	−3.65
32.5	27.5	−17.2	2.1	19.3	5.75	1.71
10.4	11.3	1.7	21.1	19.4	35.60	21.48
12.0	9.5	3.3	7.7	4.4	9.44	3.41
4.8	2.7	1.0	5.6	4.6	8.66	2.22
24.4	17.8	−13.1	10.2	23.3	12.20	0.92
220.8	192.0	18.7	198.6	179.9	10.31	2.04

impact of US trade on growth in foreign countries may thus be detected by comparing the base year of 1980 against 1986 as the terminal year. Table 6.2 makes this comparison, and reports the corresponding trade effects in terms relative to each country's total exports and GNP for 1980.

It is clear from table 6.2 that the rise in the US trade deficit in the 1980s played a wide-spread role of stimulus to growth in other countries. With the sole exception of OPEC, all of the 16 foreign countries and country groupings examined in Chapters 4 and 5 experienced increases in their bilateral real trade balances with the United States from 1980 to 1986. (The reduction for OPEC reflected declining volume of OPEC oil exports to the United States as its member nations sought to support the price of oil.) The trade balance increases against the United States were large. Overall, foreign trade balances with the United States rose by $180 billion from 1980 to

1986.[5] This increase amounted to approximately 10 percent of the total real export value of foreign countries in the base year 1980, and about 2 percent of total foreign GNP.

The most extreme impact on trade and growth in foreign countries occurred in the East Asian NICs. The increased real trade balance against the United States amounted to nearly two-thirds of base year total exports for Taiwan, and one-third for Korea–Singapore–Hong Kong. Because of the high share of trade in these economies, these trade changes were high percentages of base year GNP: 30 percent and 21 percent, respectively.

The other two countries with especially large impacts were the two countries bordering the United States. For Canada, the rise in the real trade balance with the United States from 1980 to 1986 amounted to 40 percent of 1980 total exports and 11 percent of 1980 GNP. For Mexico, the corresponding effects were 51 percent of exports but only 5 percent of GNP, reflecting a relatively low share of exports in the Mexican economy in 1980.

Japan is the other industrial country for which the impact from US trade trends was especially large. Its bilateral real trade surplus with the United States rose from 1980 to 1986 by an amount equivalent to 27 percent of its total 1980 exports, and 3.4 percent of 1980 Japanese GNP. For the other major industrial countries, the impact tended to be in the range of 8 to 10 percent of 1980 exports and some 2 percent of GNP. Among the developing countries, the impact of rising trade balances with the United States was pronounced in Argentina and Brazil, where the proportionate changes were almost identical to those for Japan.

As noted in Chapter 2, from 1980 to 1986 slightly more than one-half of total growth in Germany stemmed from the rise in that country's overall trade balance, and the corresponding figure for Japan was approximately one-fourth. Considering that real GNP growth amounted to a cumulative 9.0 percent in Germany and 24.6 percent in Japan over this period,[6] the rise in GNP attributable to the direct effect of the increase in the total trade balance amounted to 4.7 percentage points in Germany and 6.5 percentage points in Japan. Thus, the increase in the real bilateral trade balance with the United States accounted for 51 percent of total increased output attributable to the external sector for Germany, and for 52 percent of that increase for Japan.[7] In both of the major surplus countries, then, rising real trade

---

5. Note that this estimate is almost exactly the same as that indicated in table 6.1 (change in trade balance on goods), although the two estimates are obtained from different approaches (US balance of payments data for table 6.1 and individual country trade and export unit value data reported to the IMF for table 6.2).

6. *OECD Economic Outlook*, June 1988, 170.

7. Considering that third countries might have been unable to run deficits with

balances against the rest of the world almost exactly matched the increase in trade balances against the United States. This pattern is consistent with the finding in Chapter 5 that future adjustment of international payments balances will involve not only correction of the US deficit but also adjustment of emerging deficits of other areas against these two high-surplus countries.

Overall, the pattern that emerges from table 6.2 is that of a relatively large and generalized favorable impact of the rising US trade deficit during the early 1980s on the trade and growth of other countries. The implication for the future is that there will be correspondingly important and widespread contractionary pressures on other countries as the United States reduces its trade deficits, as examined below.

The Scope of Real Adjustment: United States

Chapters 3 and 5 projected the US trade and current accounts under two alternative scenarios: a baseline case of existing policy and growth prospects, and a case implementing a Feasible Adjustment Package (FAP) of further real depreciation of the dollar combined with modest increases in growth rates abroad from baseline trends. The real trade estimates corresponding to those nominal projections may be used to examine the growth implications for the United States and other countries.

First, however, it is useful to establish a broad range for prospective real US adjustment on the basis of the summary model developed in Appendix F relating real to nominal trade adjustment. In that formulation, the ratio of real to nominal external adjustment rises as the pass-through ratios for exchange rate change rise, declines as the price elasticities for trade rise, and declines as the base period ratio of exports to imports increases. Application of the equation for the ratio of real to nominal trade balance change to the specific elasticities and pass-through ratios used in the HHC model of Chapter 3 yields a ratio of 1.88; application of the corresponding parameters used in the EAG model of Chapters 4 and 5 results in a real-to-nominal adjustment ratio of 2.00.[8] For purposes of summary calculation, an

Germany and Japan as large as they did if they had not enjoyed rising trade positions relative to the United States, these estimates may understate the share of the external demand expansion in the two high-surplus countries attributable to the US external deficit.

8. Applying equation 17 of Appendix F to the following parameters. For HHC: export price elasticity $(d) = -0.822$; import price elasticity $(e) = -1.147$; export price pass-through $(a) = 0.8$; import price pass-through $(b) = 0.9$; ratio of exports to imports for 1987 $(H) = 0.62$. For the EAG model: $d = -1.43$; $e = -0.929$; $a = 1$; $b = 1$.

estimate of 1.9 is thus appropriate for the ratio of real to nominal trade balance adjustment.

How large must the US real adjustment be to achieve the target correction in the external accounts? The objective set forth in Chapters 3 and 5 is to reduce the US current account deficit from approximately $150 billion in 1987 to $50 billion by 1992. An initial question is, how much of the $100 billion reduction must take place in goods and nonfactor services, and how much will occur in factor services?

The projections for the FAP provide a basis for identifying trends in factor services. In the HHC model (Chapter 3), under the FAP scenario the factor services balance declines by only $6.6 billion from 1987 (actual) to 1992 (table 5A.9). In the EAG model (Chapter 5), under the FAP the factor services balance by 1992 stands at $65.3 billion below its actual 1987 level (although $20 billion of this deterioration is attributable to that model's treatment of the 1987 $20 billion factor services surplus as a nonrecurrent gain from exchange rate revaluation of direct investment abroad). Although in principle the HHC model is much more fully elaborated in the factor services bloc, it appears to have an optimistic bias (as discussed in Chapter 3). Therefore a simple average of the two model results may be the most appropriate basis for calculating the change in the factor services balance, placing it at a decline by $36 billion from 1987 to 1992 even under the favorable FAP scenario.

On this basis, to obtain a reduction by $100 billion in the current account deficit from 1987 to 1992, it will be necessary for the balance on goods and nonfactor services to rise by $136 billion, in nominal 1992 dollars. After adjusting for 4½ percent annual inflation over this period, the rise in the external balance on goods and nonfactor services must amount to $109 billion by 1992, at 1987 prices. This amount must be multiplied by 1.9 to estimate the full real adjustment after taking into account the loss in terms of trade, as discussed above. Thus, the rise in the real trade balance for goods and nonfactor services from 1987 to 1992 should be $207 billion at 1987 prices.

The distribution of this increase would be approximately as follows. Real exports would rise by $118 billion (at 1987 prices), and nonfactor service exports by $34 billion; real imports would decline by $46 billion, and nonfactor service imports by $8 billion (with constant ratios of nonfactor to

---

Note that the elasticities are for the averaged specific and uniform estimates, and that the export elasticity adds in the (adjusted) cross-price elasticity. Note also that, despite the higher elasticities in the EAG model, the ratio of real to nominal adjustment is slightly higher than when the HHC parameters are used, because the EAG model assumes complete pass-through of exchange rate changes to prices.

merchandise trade).[9] To accomplish this outcome, real exports would need to grow at an average rate of 8 percent annually over the five-year period, while real imports would need to decline at a rate of 2.6 percent annually. The $207 billion rise in net exports of goods and nonfactor services amounts to 4.6 percent of 1987 GNP. To accomplish this adjustment over the four years 1989–92, it will be necessary for domestic demand (consumption, government spending, investment) to grow more slowly than domestic production by approximately 1.1 percentage points of GNP annually. With real GNP growing in the range of 2½ percent annually, domestic demand should therefore grow by only about 1.4 percent each year. Because relatively brisk expansion of investment will be required to permit the required expansion of output in the tradeable goods sector, the rate of growth of consumption and real government spending should be somewhat lower, leaving little scope for increases in per capita terms. The need to freeze real consumption and government spending per capita over the medium term is perhaps the most tangible expression for the US population of the real burden of adjustment in the external sector.[10]

The real adjustment bulks large when compared to the base for manufacturing production. Of the $207 billion real increase in the external balance, $164 billion would occur in merchandise trade. The great bulk of this change will have to occur in the manufacturing sector. If the entire amount were in manufactures, it would amount to 16½ percent of manufacturing GNP in 1987. The implication is that external adjustment should exert a strong demand stimulus to the manufacturing sector over the medium term, sharply reversing the drag on the sector from external demand over the period 1981–86 (as analyzed above). Specifically, over the four years 1989–92 there could be some 4 percent annual expansion in manufacturing to meet the needs of the external sector, and another 1.1 percent annual growth to accommodate rising domestic demand (as just examined). Growth of over 5 percent annually would more than double the average annual growth of 2.5 percent from 1980 to 1986 (using three-year averages for the two respective endpoints).[11]

---

9. The distribution is estimated on the basis of equal proportionate increases in exports and reductions in imports from a 1992 hypothetical base that allows for income growth.

10. Technically, however, the terms of trade loss is a better measure of the real burden of adjustment. Compression of consumption in itself does not represent a welfare loss because in the absence of terms of trade loss there is a fully offsetting increase in savings and thus portfolio assets, which at the margin have a value equal to incremental consumption.

11. Calculated from Council of Economic Advisers, *Economic Report of the President 1988*, 261.

Table 6.3   Changes in real trade in the projection models
(billions of 1987 dollars except as noted)

	1987	1992 Base case			1992 FAP		
		P%	Q%	Real change	P%	Q%	Real change
Exports							
HHC/NA	220.0	31.9	77.5	170.5	33.8	98.9	218.6
EAG	252.6ª	23.3	60.8	153.6	23.3	87.0	219.7
Imports							
HHC/NO	367.0	44.8	12.5	45.9	61.4	−0.7	−2.6
EAG/NO	360.7ª	29.5	25.8	92.9	40.2	14.7	53.1
Trade balance							
HHC/NONA	−146.9			124.6			221.2
EAG/NO	−108.1ª			60.8			166.6

NA = nonagricultural; NO = nonoil (in the EAG model, oil imports from OPEC, the United Kingdom, and Mexico only are excluded); NONA = nonoil, nonagricultural; P% = percentage change in price; Q% = percentage change in quantity.
a. Model.

Source: Tables 3.2 and 4.1, and EAG projections.

More specific estimates of the real impact of external adjustment on the US economy may be obtained from the model projections of Chapters 3 and 5. In addition, those projections permit an examination of the real changes in store even under baseline conditions, as well as those under more successful adjustment.

Table 6.3 presents the real trade changes for the United States indicated in the HHC and EAG projection models (Chapters 3 and 5, respectively). The estimates in the table refer to nonoil imports (approximated in the case of EAG by exclusion of imports from OPEC and of oil imports from the United Kingdom and Mexico) and, in the case of HHC, to nonagricultural exports. The calculations thus refer approximately to the manufacturing sector.

As indicated in the table, the two specific model projections give approximately the same magnitude of real adjustment as calculated on the basis of the aggregative approach just discussed: in the broad range of $200 billion at 1987 prices by 1992 under the FAP. In contrast, the prospective adjustment is much smaller (especially in the EAG model) under the base case with no further exchange rate or growth changes.

The principal difference between the two models in their real forecasts lies in the greater price increase and smaller quantity increase for imports under the HHC model.[12] Thus, nonoil import prices in the base case rise by 44.8 percent in HHC and only 29.5 percent in EAG, and in the FAP the divergence is greater (61.4 percent versus 40.2 percent). As a result, the volume of real imports grows more slowly in the HHC model than in the EAG under both scenarios.

The greater price rises in the HHC model (which may also be seen but to a lesser degree on the export side) do not arise from exchange rate scenarios or domestic inflation, which are the same for the two models in the projection analyses. Instead, the divergence originates in a much larger pipeline effect of price increases attributable to developments already in place through the base year. As discussed in Chapter 3, the HHC model arbitrarily boosts import prices by 8.7 percent in 1988 and export prices by 3.9 percent, to close half of the gap between actual and predicted prices in 1987. Moreover, the HHC model contains a distributed lag relationship of price increases to past exchange rate change, whereas the EAG forecasting model assumes instantaneous impact of the exchange rate change (with the exceptions of supply from Japan and the United Kingdom). Essentially, the economic issue between the two models is whether the United States stands to experience a greater or lesser terms of trade deterioration from inherited import price increases already in the pipeline before 1988.

The HHC estimate for real trade balance adjustment by 1992 under the FAP gives a considerably larger value ($221 billion at 1987 prices) than the summary approach examined above ($164 billion for merchandise trade). The difference is attributable in part to the lower ratio of nonfactor service exports to merchandise exports in the HHC projection (18 percent; table 3.7), and in part to the fact that the HHC model shows a somewhat larger reduction in the trade and (especially) current account deficits under the FAP than does the EAG model. For its part, the EAG model's projections in table 6.3 are extremely close to the real trade adjustment calculated in the summary approach above ($167 billion versus $164 billion). In sum, the two model projections may be seen as confirming the real adjustment summary estimates for the United States set forth above.

Real Impact of US External Adjustment on Foreign Countries

The simulations of the EAG model in Chapter 5 may be applied to examine the impact of real trade changes in other major countries to be expected as

---

12. Thus, although the two models show closely parallel paths for the nominal values of trade (figures 5.1 and 5.2), there is greater divergence between them on the question of the decomposition of import growth into volume and price changes.

the United States reduces its external imbalance. For this purpose, the projections of real 1992 trade flows at 1980 prices are compared to the model's estimated trade base for 1987 (also at 1980 prices) to determine the percentage change in real trade for each country. The analysis is most usefully conducted excluding the exports of OPEC (as well as UP and MP, the "countries" constituting oil exports from the United Kingdom and Mexico, respectively), as oil trade in the model is unaffected by exchange rate changes (although growth acceleration does affect demand for oil), and because aggregate price deflators including oil are probably less meaningful than those excluding it (although the disturbance from oil should be less in the future than during the period 1980–86 as oil prices collapsed). Moreover, with oil excluded it is possible to interpret the changes in real trade balances as essentially changes in trade in manufactures, for most of the industrial countries.

Table 6.4 reports the percentage changes in real nonoil exports and imports for each of the 16 trading partners of the United States disaggregated in the EAG model of Chapter 5. It is apparent from the table that there is already some international adjustment contained in real trade flows under baseline conditions. Thus, from 1987 to 1992, in the absence of policy changes Japan's exports grow by 24.1 percent in real terms whereas its real imports rise by 53.7 percent. There is a similar, but much less substantial, real adjustment in Germany (where baseline exports rise by 24.5 percent in real terms and imports by 33.7 percent). The trends in real trade conform to the main patterns identified in Chapter 5. Thus, in the base case the United Kingdom experiences a sharp disparity between real growth of its exports (10.3 percent) and that of its imports (43 percent); Brazil experiences a major differential in the opposite direction (51.8 percent growth in exports, 33.7 percent in imports).

The baseline projections for real trade vividly reveal a trend toward declining real trade balances for Taiwan and Korea–Singapore–Hong Kong. In both cases, real exports rise by much smaller percentages than real imports (especially in Taiwan, at 27.2 percent and 92.2 percent, respectively).

As examined at length in Chapters 3 and 5, however, the adjustment of the US external deficit in the base case is inadequate. If countries instead adopt the exchange rate and growth changes suggested in the FAP (table 5.7), the real trade balance changes will be considerably larger for several key countries. For Germany, the FAP cuts real export growth over the five-year period to a total of 11.1 percent, and boosts real import growth to 57 percent. For Japan, the corresponding real trade growth under the FAP turns negative for exports (− 1.1 percent) and reaches 85 percent for imports. Real adjustment goes in the other direction for the United Kingdom, where the FAP permits real export growth to reach 34.2 percent and suppresses import growth to 27.7 percent.

Table 6.4 Changes in real nonoil[a] trade, 1987–92
(billions of 1987 dollars, except where noted)

Country	1987 (Model) Exports	1987 (Model) Imports	% Real increase in: Exports Baseline	Exports FAP	Imports Baseline	Imports FAP	Change in real trade Baseline Exports	Baseline Imports	Baseline Balance	FAP Exports	FAP Imports	FAP Balance
United States	252.6	360.7	60.8	87.0	25.8	14.7	153.6	92.9	60.8	219.7	53.1	166.6
United Kingdom	115.2	139.6	10.3	34.2	43.0	27.7	11.9	60.0	−48.1	39.4	38.7	0.7
France	145.8	144.2	30.4	41.3	35.6	38.0	43.3	51.3	−7.0	60.3	54.8	5.4
Germany	284.0	199.6	24.5	11.1	33.7	57.0	69.7	67.3	2.4	31.4	113.8	−82.4
Italy	114.0	101.7	26.6	41.8	39.5	42.8	30.4	40.1	−9.8	47.6	43.6	−4.0
Canada	100.1	81.1	34.2	39.4	45.8	55.2	34.2	37.1	−3.0	39.4	44.8	−5.4
Japan	216.6	106.5	24.1	−1.1	53.7	85.1	52.3	57.2	−4.9	−2.5	90.6	−93.0
Argentina	7.1	6.5	55.2	73.5	34.0	32.7	3.9	2.2	1.7	5.2	2.1	3.1
Brazil	27.7	13.5	51.8	59.8	33.7	39.3	14.4	4.6	9.8	7.3	5.3	11.3
Mexico	17.4	19.9	30.7	37.5	49.9	54.0	5.3	9.9	−4.6	16.6	10.7	−4.2
Taiwan	47.4	30.2	27.2	21.7	92.2	102.9	12.9	27.8	−15.0	6.5	31.1	−20.8
OPEC	0.0	82.5	0.0	0.0	4.6	−2.8	0.0	3.8	−3.8	10.3	−2.3	2.3
Other Industrial	452.4	465.4	28.6	27.5	33.5	44.7	129.5	155.9	−26.4	0.0	−207.8	−83.6
Korea–Singapore–Hong Kong	120.1	100.4	54.2	45.4	89.8	101.1	65.2	90.2	−25.0	124.2	101.5	−47.1
Other Latin America	40.4	38.9	46.7	66.3	38.9	36.7	18.9	15.1	3.7	54.5	14.3	12.5
Other Africa	50.9	49.3	33.8	54.5	33.7	31.5	17.2	16.6	0.6	26.8	15.6	12.2
Rest of World	257.9	309.3	56.6	72.0	35.2	40.3	146.1	108.8	37.3	185.6	124.5	61.1

a. Excludes all OPEC exports and oil exports from the United Kingdom and Mexico.

Source: EAG projections.

The FAP pushes the asymmetrical real trade growth effects even further for Taiwan and Korea–Singapore–Hong Kong. Thus, in Taiwan real exports rise only 21.7 percent, and real imports by 103.1 percent.

Although 1980 prices are used in the real trade estimates, the proportionate changes of real exports and real imports may be applied to the nominal values of trade in 1987 to obtain estimates of the real trade changes at 1987 prices. These estimates are reported in table 6.4. The most notable absolute changes are for Germany and Japan. In both cases, the real trade balance declines from 1987 to 1992 by some $80 billion to $90 billion at 1987 prices under the FAP. In contrast, in the base case there is almost no change in the real trade balance of either country over the period, indicating that there is sufficient adjustment in the pipeline to prevent existing trade surpluses from widening in real terms but not enough to reduce these surpluses.

To place the real trade changes into the context of potential impact on domestic economic growth, table 6.5 expresses them as percentages of 1987 GNP and manufacturing output. Under the FAP, the decline in the real trade balance of Germany amounts to a relatively large 7.3 percent of base year GNP. The corresponding decline in Japan stands at 4.1 percent of GNP, almost the same relative magnitude as the change in the opposite direction for the United States (table 6.5 and the discussion above). The changes are more dramatic if it is assumed that all of the real trade change will come in the manufacturing sector. The reduction in the real trade balance would amount to 22.9 percent of 1987 manufacturing output in Germany and 13.5 percent in Japan; the real trade balance increase in the United States would amount to 17.0 percent (using the EAG model, or 16 percent using the summary model).

The calculations for Japan and especially Germany strongly suggest that these countries will need to pursue domestically oriented programs of growth maintenance. Otherwise the international adjustment process could push their economies into low growth or even recession, in view of the large relative magnitude of the real trade changes identified here.

For the other industrial countries, the impact is more moderate. Under the FAP, the United Kingdom would experience a small rise in real trade balances, and there would be larger increases for France and Italy (at some 2½ to 3 percent of their 1987 manufacturing output). The results for Canada show negative demand pressure from the external sector, amounting to 1.3 percent of GNP under the FAP. In the Canadian case, comparison of the real trade decline against manufacturing output alone overstates the contractionary effect, as a major share of Canadian exports is in primary products.

The FAP involves a large contractionary effect from the real trade balance change for Germany, but a significant expansionary effect for France and

Table 6.5 Changes in real nonoil trade balances, 1987–92, relative to 1987 production
(billions of 1987 dollars except as noted)

Country/group	1987 Production		Real trade balance change		Trade balance change as % of 1987			
					GNP		Mfg.	
	GNP	Mfg.	Baseline	FAP	Baseline	FAP	Baseline	FAP
United States	4,526.7	997.4	60.8	166.6	1.3	3.7	6.1	16.7
United Kingdom	669.6	174.1	−48.1	0.7	−7.2	0.0	−27.6	0.0
France	878.3	193.2	−7.0	5.4	−0.8	0.6	−3.6	2.8
Germany	1,125.6	360.2	2.4	−82.4	0.2	−7.3	0.7	−22.9
Italy	751.5	165.3	−9.8	4.0	−1.3	0.5	−5.9	2.4
Canada	402.0	68.3	−3.0	−5.4	−0.8	−1.3	−4.4	−7.9
Japan	2,290.8	687.2	−4.9	−93.0	−0.2	−4.1	−0.7	−13.5
Argentina	72.8	22.6	1.7	3.1	2.3	4.3	a	a
Brazil	250.5	70.1	9.8	11.3	3.9	4.5	a	a
Mexico	149.2	38.8	−4.6	−4.2	−3.1	−2.8	a	a
Taiwan	99.4	38.8	−15.0	−20.8	−15.1	−20.9	−38.7	−53.6
Other Industrial[b]	1,149.3	n.a.	−26.4	−83.6	−2.3	−7.3	n.a.	n.a.
Korea–Singapore– Hong Kong	179.7	49.6	−25.0	−47.1	−13.9	−26.2	−50.4	−95.0
Other Latin America[b]	133.3	n.a.	3.7	12.5	2.8	9.4	n.a.	n.a.
Other Africa[b]	211.5	n.a.	0.6	12.2	0.3	5.8	n.a.	n.a.
Rest of World[b]	2,685.3	n.a.	37.3	61.1	1.4	2.3	n.a.	n.a.

a. Not applicable; exports not primarily manufactured goods.   n.a. = not available.
b. 1986 production data.

Sources: Table 6.4; World Bank, *World Development Report 1988*; IMF, *International Financial Statistics*, October 1988; OECD, *National Accounts; 1974–1986, Vol. II Detailed Tables*; Taiwan District, Republic of China, *Financial Statistics*, October 1988; Republic of China, *Taiwan Statistical Data Book 1987*.

Italy. If instead the Second-Best Adjustment Package (SBAP) of Chapter 5 is adopted, in which the differential appreciation between Germany and the intermediate European countries is limited to 10 percent, the real trade balance effect for Germany is considerably moderated. Real exports rise by 15.9 percent instead of 11.1 percent, and real imports by 49.8 percent instead of 57 percent. The real trade balance declines by $54.2 billion at 1987 prices, or by 4.8 percent of 1987 GNP (rather than 7.3 percent in the FAP). However, in this case the outcome places contractionary pressure on France and Italy that is absent in the FAP. Thus, the real trade balance for France declines by $18 billion at 1987 prices, or by 2.1 percent of 1987 GNP, and Italy's real trade balance declines by $26.1 billion (1987 prices), or by 3.5 percent of 1987 GNP. The swing in real demand effects between the FAP and the SBAP thus amounts to +2.5 percent of 1987 GNP for Germany, but −4.9 percent of 1987 GNP for France and −5.9 percent for Italy.

The most extreme cases of demand contraction from external adjustment under the FAP are those of Taiwan and Korea–Singapore–Hong Kong. The reductions in real trade balances under the FAP amount to 20.9 percent of 1987 GNP in Taiwan and 26.2 percent in Korea–Singapore–Hong Kong. The effects are even more extreme when compared with the manufacturing base: a reduction of 53.6 percent of 1987 manufacturing output in the case of Taiwan, and 95 percent in the case of Korea–Singapore–Hong Kong.

The extreme estimates relative to manufacturing output are exaggerated by the tendency of the East Asian NICs to import intermediate inputs and export finished products. The ratio of their manufactured exports to manufacturing GNP is thus high. Indeed, if manufacturing activity were limited to trivial finishing of imported semi-manufactures, manufactured exports could be many times larger than value added in the manufacturing sector. Thus, in 1987 total US exports (which included substantial amounts of agricultural and other nonmanufactured goods) amounted to only 25 percent of value added in manufacturing (tables 6.3 and 6.5). In contrast, in Taiwan this ratio stood at 122 percent, while in Korea–Singapore–Hong Kong it was 242 percent (tables 6.4 and 6.5); in both cases exports were almost exclusively manufactured goods.

Ideally the change in the real trade balance for manufactures should be compared not to value added (GNP) in manufacturing, but to value added plus the value of intermediate inputs from nonmanufacturing sectors plus imported inputs. The trade figure is a total product value concept, and is most appropriately compared to the total value rather than value added of domestic production. For large economies with relatively little reliance on imported intermediate inputs, and when examining the manufacturing sector as a whole so that the bulk of intermediate inputs already come from within the "sector" itself, the divergence between total production value and value added is limited. As the estimates for Taiwan and Korea–Singapore–Hong Kong illustrate, however, the same cannot be said for smaller economies relying on imported inputs.

Even after adjustment incorporating imported intermediate inputs and inputs from nonmanufacturing sectors, however, the estimates for the East Asian NICs would still show potentially very large contractionary effects from international adjustment over the medium term. To some extent the size of this adjustment is biased upward because of the use of blended country-specific and international ("uniform") trade elasticities, combined with the assumption that the East Asian NICs will continue to grow much faster than the rest of the world (as discussed in Chapter 5). Even so, the strong suggestion from the projections here is that these economies will need to look to internal demand over the medium term to offset a negative demand effect from declining real trade balances. The alternative of persistent high real and nominal surpluses would raise the question of political tolerance abroad and possible pressures for new protection against their products.

Tables 6.6 and 6.7 provide additional detail on the real trade changes under the baseline and FAP scenarios. The tables indicate the percentage changes of real trade flows between each pair of the 17 individual countries examined in Chapter 5, from 1987 to 1992. (The 1987 base applies the model estimate rather than actual 1987 trade, to provide a clearer picture of changes attributable to exchange rate changes and growth trends rather than to base year model error.) [13]

In the base case (table 6.6), US real exports tend to rise faster than real imports for most trading partners. Real exports rise especially rapidly to Taiwan and Korea–Singapore–Hong Kong, as the result of high growth in these areas.

The impact of external adjustment is shown in table 6.7, which shows the same percentage increases under the FAP. The table shows much higher US real export increases to Germany (86 percent versus 46 percent in the base case) and Japan (116 percent versus 66 percent). It also shows much lower real import increases from the countries adopting the greatest adjustment under the FAP: 4 percent instead of 26 percent for imports from Germany; − 20 percent instead of + 15 percent from Japan; 0 instead of 14 percent from the Other Industrial countries; − 14 percent instead of + 7 percent from Taiwan; and 11 percent instead of 38 percent from Korea–Singapore–Hong Kong.

---

13. In addition, as the model does not attempt to backcast oil trade, the base period for oil exports (from OP, UP, and MP) in tables 6.6 and 6.7 is the first year of the forecasting period, 1988.

Table 6.6 Changes in real trade flows, base case, 1987–92
(percentages)

Exporter	US	UK	FR	GE	IT	CA	JA	AR
					Importer			
US	n.a.	72.43	58.15	46.26	44.27	60.44	66.23	66.05
UK	9.99	n.a.	19.36	21.03	22.20	6.17	9.02	−13.58
FR	33.19	46.22	n.a.	25.94	33.13	16.31	54.88	33.50
GE	25.50	39.11	24.46	n.a.	28.73	11.58	43.35	25.72
IT	23.19	46.13	34.71	31.16	n.a.	17.48	50.57	28.42
CA	31.08	32.32	49.86	34.50	35.91	n.a.	43.78	52.31
JA	14.55	38.30	29.67	29.83	32.55	12.82	n.a.	24.89
AR	58.90	69.42	34.92	53.92	37.01	56.34	51.52	n.a.
BR	50.85	53.75	56.33	42.74	58.44	42.70	48.26	31.98
ME	26.21	55.07	32.85	32.93	35.98	27.09	29.20	−1.16
TA	7.04	43.75	32.10	33.02	36.34	8.00	54.39	12.84
OP	45.27	5.27	5.00	4.75	5.00	5.66	8.54	9.07
UP	45.27	n.a.	5.00	4.75	5.00	5.66	8.54	n.a.
MP	45.27	5.27	5.00	n.a.	5.00	5.66	8.54	n.a.
OI	13.55	29.20	34.65	27.83	36.17	9.04	27.12	30.06
KS	37.83	61.83	62.12	51.60	64.82	27.05	61.85	39.12
OL	30.19	42.22	55.74	44.41	54.14	41.52	57.50	17.41
AN	29.63	29.53	33.08	32.61	44.24	18.27	43.02	43.94
RO	35.52	65.32	56.44	55.64	62.20	23.89	59.64	50.60

US, United States; UK, United Kingdom; FR, France; GE, Germany; IT, Italy; CA, Canada; JA, Japan; AR, Argentina; BR, Brazil; ME, Mexico; TA, Taiwan; OP, OPEC; UP, United Kingdom-oil; MP, Mexico-oil; OI, Other Industrial; KS, Korea–Singapore–Hong Kong; OL, Other Latin America; AN, Other Africa, RO, Rest of World.

n.a. = not applicable

The specific trade flow matrices also reveal important patterns for other major countries. Under the adjustment scenario, real exports from Japan not only decline by 20 percent to the United States; they also decline by 20 percent or more to Canada, Mexico, Other Latin America, and Other Africa— essentially, other areas tied to the dollar or almost so. There are similar but smaller real export declines for Germany. However, real German exports to Japan, Taiwan, and Korea–Singapore–Hong Kong all rise substantially, as the result of lesser appreciation by Germany than Japan and the high growth in the East Asian NICs.

			Importer					
BR	ME	TA	OP	OI	KS	OL	AN	RO
44.63	62.46	117.21	9.55	54.85	105.88	53.21	65.57	48.23
−13.77	−6.78	29.80	−14.01	9.24	41.05	1.33	2.96	1.97
23.95	13.80	85.90	11.07	28.87	70.06	42.19	24.91	24.90
13.13	11.20	55.88	3.23	23.84	60.14	10.56	18.57	12.25
16.39	14.16	80.58	−30.23	38.54	91.41	43.10	30.88	9.50
46.78	29.92	140.69	−3.13	36.27	113.29	40.69	45.08	35.96
10.02	8.52	55.94	2.71	30.70	53.91	11.66	10.95	14.10
43.32	34.92	159.68	48.22	51.52	101.44	45.66	61.39	51.48
n.a.	40.38	139.83	35.92	51.33	148.38	63.37	87.13	41.90
31.16	n.a.	101.25	−4.20	34.15	127.94	46.32	62.19	34.41
47.16	2.91	n.a.	−5.06	33.57	76.71	33.32	46.03	33.41
9.14	8.93	16.63	n.a.	4.78	16.63	9.14	9.14	9.14
n.a.	n.a.	n.a.	n.a.	4.78	n.a.	n.a.	n.a.	n.a.
n.a.	n.a.	n.a.	n.a.	4.78	n.a.	n.a.	n.a.	n.a.
17.13	16.20	105.95	82.94	27.11	64.16	30.18	38.59	17.42
41.34	47.41	97.79	−1.15	49.06	102.71	61.79	55.89	68.89
49.12	34.77	139.55	14.02	63.33	171.42	31.49	45.91	35.48
30.21	30.71	100.09	3.51	37.51	84.66	30.16	34.11	24.62
54.62	31.94	105.84	5.47	58.94	112.29	47.82	45.46	48.23

Early Evidence of Real Adjustment

As indicated above, the watershed change from the early 1980s, when rising US external deficits exerted a demand stimulus on the rest of the world economy, to the next few years when the reverse must occur, requires US domestic demand to grow more slowly than output over the medium term, and foreign domestic demand to outstrip domestic output. Figure 6.3 indicates that this process has already begun. The diagram shows real growth of domestic demand and GNP for the seven largest industrial

Table 6.7 Changes in real trade flows, Feasible Adjustment Package, 1987–92
(percentages)

				Importer				
Exporter	US	UK	FR	GE	IT	CA	JA	AR
US	n.a.	80.13	80.10	86.22	61.79	80.82	115.64	90.34
UK	20.38	n.a.	42.77	59.32	44.90	16.59	79.89	19.24
FR	34.36	43.08	n.a.	54.02	42.77	15.63	85.63	33.69
GE	4.13	1.69	11.53	n.a.	15.35	−9.28	46.98	3.91
IT	20.89	36.94	46.49	67.37	n.a.	16.77	116.88	29.99
CA	31.99	35.69	65.43	66.06	53.75	n.a.	71.77	71.69
JA	−20.25	−8.41	12.75	28.20	14.92	−20.78	n.a.	−2.29
AR	69.35	106.55	48.32	99.21	50.32	64.87	86.45	n.a.
BR	49.59	50.94	70.76	69.73	71.23	42.77	75.00	31.51
ME	29.05	49.09	46.16	65.38	49.19	32.96	55.50	3.57
TA	−13.50	17.23	28.68	53.54	33.91	−10.37	89.30	1.42
OP	45.27	5.27	5.96	6.65	5.98	6.15	10.51	9.07
UP	45.27	n.a.	5.96	6.65	5.98	6.15	10.51	n.a.
MP	45.27	5.27	5.96	n.a.	5.98	6.15	10.51	n.a.
OI	−0.33	11.43	30.44	40.13	32.62	−2.80	34.03	18.57
KS	10.70	36.82	56.31	74.05	50.38	0.23	83.78	14.47
OL	39.06	48.36	75.49	79.36	72.22	49.33	96.88	22.22
AN	38.28	35.20	49.82	72.41	66.48	23.25	85.63	48.65
RO	37.01	63.57	72.58	88.84	75.75	23.55	88.61	48.88

For an explanation of country abbreviations see table 6.6; n.a. = not applicable.

economies and for the rest of the OECD (ROECD).[14]

As may be seen in the figure, US domestic demand grew considerably faster than output in the years 1983–86, but in 1987 and 1988 grew more slowly than GNP (with 1988 results forecasted by the IMF in October 1988). In contrast, for Japan and Germany domestic demand grew substantially more slowly than GNP in the period 1981–85, but for 1986–88 grew more rapidly than production. The same reversal is evident for France and ROECD, with 1983–85 as the period of export-led growth and 1986–88 as a period of shift toward domestic demand. The United Kingdom also experienced more rapid growth of domestic demand than output in 1986 and especially 1988, although in this case the divergence was a sign of disequilibrium

---

14. The data are from *OECD Economic Outlook*, 43, June 1988, 170–71; and International Monetary Fund, *World Economic Outlook*, October 1988, 23.

Importer								
BR	ME	TA	OP	OI	KS	OL	AN	RO
63.36	73.19	164.59	10.47	89.91	146.05	65.74	91.00	67.81
10.22	4.64	56.26	− 10.62	38.93	68.85	9.11	21.94	21.52
28.94	13.02	112.11	6.64	44.04	85.85	40.33	24.41	32.58
− 3.42	− 13.05	40.43	− 15.37	17.51	46.54	− 6.48	− 0.33	− 0.57
20.80	12.58	97.66	− 33.01	63.05	109.21	39.98	33.68	22.28
57.62	31.32	178.75	− 5.60	55.88	156.96	42.37	46.48	46.51
− 14.69	− 27.87	31.31	− 19.10	22.14	31.85	− 20.16	− 27.20	− 3.46
54.34	39.02	189.35	49.44	80.58	128.03	52.46	68.80	68.54
n.a.	40.36	157.14	30.55	72.48	168.25	61.75	87.14	51.25
39.13	n.a.	121.11	− 5.71	58.15	190.90	48.95	62.53	49.93
44.14	− 23.04	n.a.	− 14.52	42.78	80.19	18.63	31.33	32.65
10.12	9.63	16.63	n.a.	6.21	16.63	9.14	9.14	10.12
n.a.	n.a.	n.a.	n.a.	6.21	n.a.	n.a.	n.a.	n.a.
n.a.	n.a.	n.a.	n.a.	6.21	n.a.	n.a.	n.a.	n.a.
10.60	0.46	105.50	62.53	30.58	64.54	19.03	26.99	13.23
32.13	27.61	96.81	− 12.55	54.17	100.76	38.55	42.00	64.08
62.51	38.96	166.91	14.98	98.22	207.25	37.29	52.64	52.34
40.01	38.62	122.95	4.38	63.60	109.06	36.24	39.98	46.77
60.54	31.52	129.09	1.31	82.62	135.96	48.62	44.34	59.11

rather than adjustment in view of the need for reduced external deficits (Chapter 5).

Japan achieved an especially impressive transition to domestic-led growth. Whereas its GNP growth exceeded that of real domestic demand by 0.9 percentage point in 1985, domestic demand grew more rapidly than GNP by 1.6 percentage points in 1986, by 0.9 percent in 1987, and by 1.6 percent in 1988. The shift was also large in Germany, from − 1.1 percentage points (domestic demand less GNP growth) in 1985 to 1.3 percent in 1986–87, although by 1988 the differential had narrowed to only 0.3 percent.

The challenge is to sustain and widen these differentials between the growth of domestic demand and that of output, to accomplish the real trade balance shifts identified above. The baseline projections of this study indicate that the initial adjustment process evident in 1987–88 is likely to stall well before the US external deficit is reduced to sustainable levels. Moreover, a considerable portion of the shift away from export-led growth in Japan and

Europe appears to have occurred to the benefit of real trade balances of countries (including the NICs) other than the United States. Thus, it is evident in figure 6.3 that the opening of a sizable positive gap between domestic demand growth and output growth began in 1986 for Germany and Japan, whereas in the United States the shift to an excess of output growth over domestic demand growth did not occur until 1987, and it was smaller on average in 1987–88 (at an average of 0.7 percentage point) than the gaps of opposite sign in Germany and Japan (which averaged 1 percentage point).

Policy Implications

Successful maintenance of the positive wedge between output growth and domestic demand expansion in the United States, and of a corresponding negative wedge in other major industrial countries, will depend importantly on the policy stance. In the United States, the clear need is for greater fiscal restraint, as discussed in Chapter 2. The OECD estimates that there has been only a modest move toward fiscal restraint in the United States since 1986. In 1987, the cyclically adjusted general government financial balance moved in a restrictive direction by 0.8 percent of GNP. However, in 1988 there was no change at all, and the OECD projects fiscal tightening amounting to only 0.3 percent of GNP for 1989.[15]

The pattern also shows less-than-decisive fiscal movements in the opposite direction in key trading partner countries. Thus, in Japan the fiscal stance actually tightened by 0.7 percent of GNP (cyclically adjusted) in 1987, loosened by 0.5 percent in 1988, and was expected to tighten again by 0.2 percent of GNP in 1989. The buoyant growth of domestic demand in Japan in 1988 thus does not appear to have been driven so much by fiscal expansion as by other factors, including real wealth effects from the exchange rate appreciation and from increasing values in the stock market and in land prices. Similarly, in Germany there has been no consistent move in the direction of fiscal stimulus as part of an international adjustment pattern. Whereas the cyclically adjusted government balance moved in an expansionary direction by 0.3 percent of GNP in 1987 and 1 percent in 1988, it was projected to tighten by 0.6 percent of GNP in 1989. The six largest industrial countries other than the United States showed fiscal tightening by 0.4 percent of GNP in 1987, loosening by 0.3 percent in 1988, and projected tightening again by 0.2 percent in 1989.[16]

---

15. *OECD Economic Outlook*, 43, June 1988, 24.

16. *Ibid.*

Figure 6.3 Growth in real domestic demand and GNP, major industrial countries, 1980–88. ——— , GNP; ----- , domestic demand

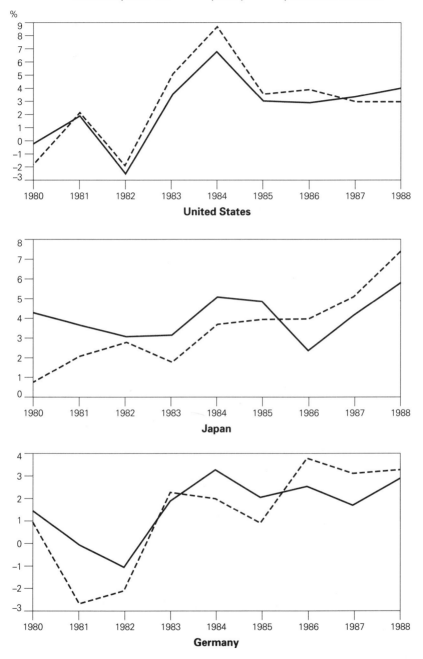

Figure 6.3 (continued)

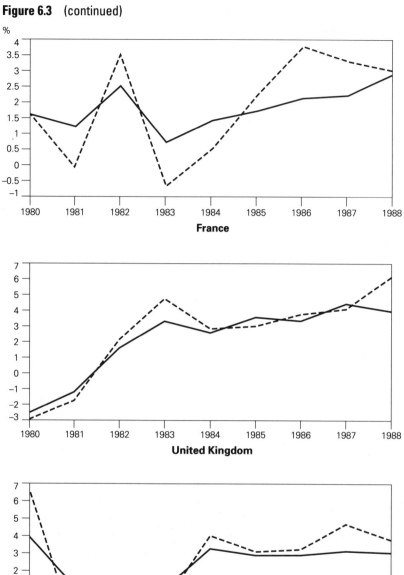

France

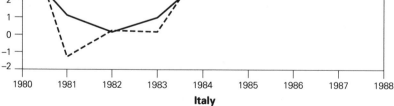

United Kingdom

Italy

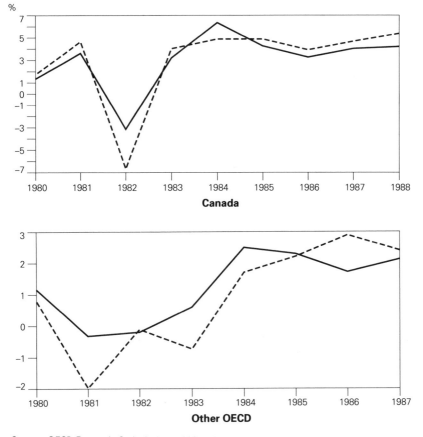

Canada

Other OECD

Source: OECD Economic Outlook, June 1988, 170, 177.

It may be asked whether other countries should be expected to engage in fiscal stimulus to contribute to the process of international adjustment. It may be argued that the United States should reduce its fiscal deficit, but that other countries should not increase theirs, in part because of the need to reduce real interest rates internationally and thus remove pressure from credit markets originating in fiscal deficits.

The calculations of this chapter suggest that it will be difficult for Germany and Japan in particular to maintain the high growth assumed in the FAP (3½ percent annually for Germany, and 5 percent annually for Japan) without a more decisive move toward fiscal expansion. The contractionary effects of external adjustment on these economies, at 7½ percent of 1987

GNP for Germany and 4 percent for Japan (table 6.5) are so large that maintenance of high growth is likely to require substantial domestic expansion.

Monetary stimulus can provide part of this expansion. There is a tendency for domestic money supplies to expand as Germany, Japan, and other countries intervene in exchange markets to prevent an excessive rise in their currencies against the dollar (thereby accumulating foreign reserves and increasing the money base if fully offsetting sterilization measures are not taken). Thus, in 1987 central bank money stock in Germany expanded by 8.1 percent, above the target range of 3 to 6 percent, while M2 plus certificates of deposit in Japan grew at 11.8 percent (against a target of 11 percent).[17] This expansion appears to have played an important role in the strong growth performances of both countries in 1988. In addition, there should be a natural spillover of lower interest rates from US fiscal adjustment to foreign country interest rates.

To the extent that monetary authorities become concerned about possible inflationary pressures, however, and in view of the tendency to link monetary policy with price stability targets, further scope for monetary stimulus could be limited. In this case, it would be necessary to shift the emphasis from monetary to fiscal policy.

The central point is that in the face of contractionary demand effects from the external sector, domestic fiscal and monetary policy in Germany and Japan in particular, but also in other industrial countries (except the United States and the United Kingdom), will need to be poised to provide support for continued economic growth over the medium term. It is unclear that the buoyant growth results of 1988 can be sustained without specific policy action, especially if the United States successfully adopts fiscal contraction and moves toward external adjustment. In particular, domestic stimulus is likely to be needed merely to offset the reversal of the external demand associated with previous US trade deficits. The extent of stimulus would need to be even greater to achieve acceleration of growth beyond baseline tendencies, as the foreign contribution to an international adjustment program.

For the United States, recent work by Bryant, Helliwell, and Hooper facilitates a more concrete delineation of the type of macroeconomic policies that are likely to be required for US external adjustment.[18] The three authors

---

17. *OECD Economic Outlook*, 43 June 1988, 14.

18. Ralph C. Bryant, John F. Helliwell, and Peter Hooper, "Domestic and Cross-Border Consequences of US Macroeconomic Policies" (Washington: Brookings Institution, conference on Macroeconomic Policies in an Interdependent World, 12–13 December 1988).

conducted simulations with 16 leading macroeconomic models prepared by researchers in the public and private sectors to obtain central tendencies of macroeconomic response to policy measures. Their results may be integrated with the policy package developed in this study to identify the likely magnitude of policy changes required to achieve US external adjustment.

Bryant, Helliwell, and Hooper (BHH) find that reduction of the US fiscal deficit by 1 percentage point of GNP causes a 2 percent decline in the nominal (and, approximately, the real) value of the dollar. They note that, theoretically, fiscal restraint can cause either an appreciation or a depreciation of the exchange rate. By reducing income and thus demand for imports, fiscal contraction can lead to an appreciation of the exchange rate (as the result of an improvement in the trade balance). However, in the capital market, the impact is in the opposite direction. Fiscal restraint tends to reduce the interest rate, reducing the attraction of the home market to capital inflow and thus bidding down the price of the home currency. Arguing that the asset market has dominated in currency determination, the authors find that fiscal restraint results in depreciation of the dollar.

For monetary policy, the authors find that a 1 percent rise in the stock of money causes a depreciation of the dollar by 1.5 percent in the first year, moderating to 1 percent in subsequent years. Because prices are relatively sticky in the models they survey, this nominal depreciation is in large part a real depreciation as well.

BHH find that fiscal contraction by 1 percent of GNP cuts real GNP by approximately 1½ percent in the first year (by Keynesian demand multiplier effects), but by the third year the output impact is cut to −1 percent as the positive effects of lower interest rates on investment ("crowding in") and external sector response to the lower exchange rate begin to be felt, and by the fifth year the effect has moderated to −0.6 percent. Their simulations indicate that a 1 percent rise in the money supply generates an increase in real GNP by ¼ percentage point during the first three years.

The fiscal and monetary package that would correspond to the FAP for external adjustment set forth in this study would thus appropriately have the following shape. The broad strategy would be to combine fiscal contraction with monetary expansion. This approach would roll back the policy mismatch of the Reagan years, in which tight money was combined with loose fiscal policy. Monetary expansion would be designed to offset the contractionary effects of fiscal restraint, given that in the external adjustment package of this study it is found that there is no need for reduction in US growth, and the judgment that recession is an unnecessarily costly way to achieve external balance.

The FAP calls for a reduction in the real dollar by approximately 11 percent. The Gramm–Rudman–Hollings timetable for US fiscal adjustment projects a cut of $150 billion in the US fiscal deficit over four years, or approximately 3 percent of GNP. This fiscal target may be adopted as appropriate to implement the fiscal component of the FAP program. If the BHH parameter is applied, fiscal restraint amounting to 3 percent of GNP would induce a real decline in the dollar of 6 percent. It would thus be necessary to obtain an additional dollar decline of 5 percentage points from monetary policy to obtain the real depreciation of approximately 11 percent in the FAP. Again the BHH parameters suggest that this effect could be obtained by an expansion of the money supply by 5 percent (using the ratio of 1 to 1 subsequent to the first year impact). For example, this increase could be accomplished by setting annual money growth targets at 6¼ to 7¼ percent instead of 5 to 6 percent over the four-year period.

The output effects of this fiscal–monetary package would be as follows. GNP would stand 3 percent lower after the 3 percent of GNP fiscal tightening (with the third-year parameter of 1 percentage point GNP per percentage point fiscal cutback). This negative effect would be partly offset by the 5 percent increase in the money supply, which would raise GNP by 1¼ percent. The BHH parameters thus imply a net contractionary effect on the economy from this macroeconomic package (− 3 percent from the fiscal side + 1¼ percent from monetary expansion = − 1.75 percent). However, the analysis of this chapter indicates that the real impact of the external adjustment package would be an expansion in net external demand by approximately $200 billion at 1987 prices, or by considerably more than the cutback of the fiscal deficit. It is ambiguous, then, whether the package would be on balance contractionary or expansionary.[19]

In practice, the appropriate strategy would be to monitor the paths of inflation and output and further adjust the macro package as necessary. If inflation (which was a growing problem by early 1989) became more severe, it would be appropriate to moderate the package toward less monetary growth. If output began to show signs of faltering (confirming the BHH parameter implications of contractionary impact), and at the same time inflation were receding as a risk, it would be appropriate to increase monetary expansion in the program.

One key aspect of this mapping of the FAP external adjustment measures (including the 11 percent real exchange rate decline) to fiscal and monetary policy requires further comment. There is considerable ambiguity about the exchange rate impact of fiscal adjustment. It is quite possible that a firm program to correct the US fiscal deficit could have, at least initially, a positive

---

19. Under the assumption that the Keynesian multiplier is the same for external demand as for net government demand.

effect on foreign confidence in the US economy, and that the impact could thus be to strengthen rather than weaken the dollar. At the same time, the risks of a hard landing for the dollar reviewed in Chapter 2 suggest that the problem might be quite the opposite: a plunge in the dollar, overshooting the 11 percent required for adjustment. At the theoretical level, a decline in the dollar well beyond any amount justified by fiscal adjustment would certainly not be unheard of in the light of actual experience in 1986–87, when the dollar fell by some 30 percent (without a fiscal contraction of 15 percent of GNP as would have been required if the HHB parameters were ironclad). In that episode, a "bubble" in the dollar's value (which peaked in 1985:1) was essentially being reversed, so that the dollar decline far exceeded the normal relationship to fiscal adjustment.

If the market did bid the dollar up after fiscal adjustment, it would be appropriate to seek other instruments to push the dollar down to the target level compatible with external adjustment. One instrument that would be worth considering is reinstatement of the withholding tax on foreign earnings on assets held in the United States. Initial experimentation with low rates for such a tax could define the likely exchange market effect, and could probably be implemented without provoking sharp collapse. Higher rates could then be imposed if the dollar proved stubbornly strong. More simply, jawboning by high officials could probably go a long way to moderate the dollar's strength.

If instead the tendency was toward downward overshooting of the dollar, firm statement of policymaker commitment to a particular target zone for the dollar could conceivably help stabilize the rate. The resort to monetary tightening to stem overshooting would be unfortunate, because of the need for monetary expansion to offset fiscal contraction. However, the likelihood is that improved confidence associated with a firm calendar for US fiscal correction would not yield an excessive decline in the dollar.

Comparable fiscal–monetary parameters are not available for analysis of macroeconomic policies abroad that could implement the FAP measures for US external adjustment. However, if the US parameters are taken as a broad guide, fiscal stimulus equivalent to some 1 percent of GNP could be required to offset each 1 percent contraction in demand from the external sector. In view of the estimates here that real external balance reduction in Germany would amount to some 7 percent of 1987 GNP by 1992 under the FAP, the implication is that fiscal stimulus of a comparable amount could be required to offset the drag from the external sector. Fiscal expansion of this size seems highly unlikely, however, and a loosening of the fiscal stance by some 1 percent of GNP annually over four years would seem the maximum that might be contemplated. Stimulus to investment from some further monetary expansion could help fill the gap. More generally, supply-side measures are widely considered important in the German case, suggesting that fiscal relaxation should come on the side of lower taxes, and that regulatory reform could help provide a stimulus to investment. It is perhaps felicitous that the European Community's move toward complete integration of the internal market by 1992 comes when it does, because there could be a considerable further boost to domestic investment from this source.

For Japan, offsets to the negative impact of the external sector amounting to 4 percent of GNP (table 6.5) would seem more manageable using the traditional monetary and fiscal instruments. As suggested above, there should be considerable further room for fiscal action, as to date fiscal expansion has been limited. Widely recognized needs for public infrastructure investment are compatible with a greater move toward fiscal expansion.

At the microeconomic level, the question arises as to whether special policies will be required to achieve US external adjustment. The principal question is whether manufacturing capacity can expand sufficiently rapidly to meet the real increases in net exports outlined above. As indicated in table 6.3 and in the discussion above, the real US trade balance under external adjustment would need to increase by an amount equal to 16 to 18 percent of 1987 manufacturing GNP, if the full increase occurred in the manufacturing sector.

From 1980 to 1988, US manufacturing capacity rose by 21.3 percent, or at an annual rate of 2.5 percent.[20] Over a four-year period capacity should thus rise by 10 percent. As noted above, in 1988:3 capacity utilization stood at 82.7 percent, leaving a 2.8 percent potential rise in manufacturing output before exhausting an operational full-utilization rate of 85 percent. Combined fuller use of capacity and addition of new capacity at past rates would thus permit an increase in manufacturing output of 13 percent above the 1988 level, or 20.6 percent above the 1987 level (as 1988:3 output stood 6.7 percent higher than in 1987).

The potential for manufacturing output almost 21 percent above the 1987 level even at normal capacity expansion rates thus suggests that capacity should be adequate to meet the rise in demand from a real trade balance increase calculated here (16½ to 18⅓ percent of 1987 manufacturing output), but only with extremely limited growth in manufacturing output destined to domestic consumption and investment. The room for meeting rising foreign demand is somewhat more comfortable, considering that the comparison between real trade change and manufacturing GNP somewhat overstates the former relative to the latter by comparing total product value

---

20. Calculated from *Federal Reserve Bulletin*, April 1983, June 1985, May 1986, and December 1988, A44 and A46.

to value added, rather than value added plus inputs from nonmanufacturing and from imports.

Lawrence has examined this issue and concluded that manufacturing capacity constraints should not be an obstacle to successful correction of the US external deficit.[21] He specifies a longer adjustment period (through 1995), but with more complete elimination of the external deficit. Lawrence notes that some sectoral bottlenecks could develop in areas such as rubber, chemicals, aerospace, and paper; but he finds that capacity should be adequate more generally, particularly in important export sectors such as electric and nonelectric machinery.[22]

In sum, for the United States there are plausible macroeconomic policies that should make possible the type of external sector correction outlined in Chapter 5. Moreover, this adjustment should be feasible at the sectoral level.

---

21. Robert Z. Lawrence, "The International Dimension," in Robert E. Litan, Robert Z. Lawrence, and Charles L. Schultze, eds., *American Living Standards* (Washington: Brookings Institution, 1988), 23–65.

22. *Ibid.*, 46.

7

US External Adjustment and the Developing Countries

The analysis of Chapter 5 found that a program for reduction of the US current account deficit to $50 billion by 1992 would have generally neutral or positive effects on the trade balances of the developing countries. This chapter extends the developing country analysis to ask the question in reverse: to what extent would special policies in support of the developing countries, and in particular, financial policies to alleviate the debt crisis, contribute to US external adjustment?

The Debt Crisis and US Trade

As a first step in this analysis, it is useful to examine the past impact of the debt crisis on US external accounts. The data base of the External Adjustment with Growth model developed in Chapter 4 provides a basis for examining this question. The trade pattern that would have been expected to result from the debt crisis was one in which US exports to troubled debtors rose by less than otherwise might have been anticipated, as those nations were forced to curtail imports; US imports from these countries would have been expected to rise faster than otherwise anticipated, as the countries adopted real exchange rate devaluation and other measures to stimulate exports in an attempt to deal with their balance of payments crisis.

Table 7.1 presents data on US trade with the developing countries in 1981 (before the debt crisis) and in 1987. The table distinguishes between troubled debtor nations (including Argentina, Brazil, Mexico, Other Latin America, and Other Africa) and other developing countries (Taiwan, Korea–Singapore–Hong Kong, and the Rest of World nations: the non-OPEC and non-NIC developing nations of Asia, the Middle East, Europe, and the eastern bloc; the inclusion of the Soviet Union as a developing country is an anomaly of the aggregations available). For purposes of comparison, the table also reports US trade with the industrial countries and with OPEC.

Table 7.1 Trends in US nonoil trade with troubled debtor countries and other areas, 1981–87
(billions of dollars except as noted)

Partner	US exports				
	1981	1987	% Change	HYPA	HYPB
Troubled debtors					
AR	2.19	1.09	−50.2	2.49	2.68
BR	3.80	4.04	6.3	4.32	4.64
ME	17.79	14.58	−18.0	20.25	21.74
OL	12.88	11.67	−9.4	14.66	15.74
AN	5.72	3.34	−41.6	6.51	6.99
Total	42.38	34.72	−18.1	48.23	51.79
Other LDCs					
TA	4.77	7.41	55.3		
KS	10.75	16.14	50.1		
RO	25.39	23.02	−11.2		
Total	40.91	46.57	13.8		
Industrial countries	129.72	158.54	22.2		
OPEC	20.73	10.56	−49.1		
Total	233.74	250.39	7.1		

AR, Argentina; BR, Brazil; ME, Mexico; OL, Other Latin America; AN, Other Africa; TA, Taiwan; KS, Korea–Singapore–Hong Kong; RO, Rest of World.
HYPA = Applying percentage change of other less developed countries (LDCs);
HYPB = Applying percentage change of industrial countries.

The table refers to nonoil trade only, to avoid distortions from the sharp gyrations in oil prices during this period (with nonoil estimates obtained by omitting all imports from OPEC and oil imports from Mexico and the United Kingdom).

As table 7.1 indicates, the nominal dollar value of US exports to troubled debtor countries declined by 18 percent from 1981 to 1987, with reductions in all markets except that of Brazil. In contrast, US imports from these countries rose by 69 percent. The nominal US trade balance with Latin America and Africa thus declined by $24 billion over this period.

Because the US trade balance deteriorated sharply with most countries during this period, it is inappropriate to conclude that the observed $24 billion decline in the balance with troubled debtor nations was solely

US imports					Change in US trade balance with area		
1981	1987	% Change	HYPA	HYPB	Actual	HYPA	HYPB
0.86	0.96	11.6	2.09	1.65	−1.20	−0.93	−0.30
4.11	7.67	86.6	10.01	7.89	−3.32	−5.38	−2.94
5.01	13.96	178.6	12.20	9.62	−12.16	−4.73	−0.66
8.21[a]	13.08[a]	59.3	20.00	15.76	−6.08	−10.01	−4.69
5.62	4.61	−18.0	13.69	10.79	−1.37	−7.28	−3.90
23.81	40.28	69.2	57.99	45.71	−24.13	−28.33	−12.49
8.16	24.62	201.7			−13.82		
14.21	38.89	173.7			−19.29		
12.48	21.37	71.2			−11.26		
34.85	84.88	143.6			−44.37		
131.63	252.89	92.0			−92.44		
0	0						
199.23[b]	376.64[b]	89.1			−160.76		

a. Applying US c.i.f. import figures for US imports, rather than OL export data as in Chapter 4.
b. EAG data base.

attributable to the debt crisis. Table 7.1 includes two standards for comparison. The first is that of all other developing nations: the East Asian NICs (Taiwan and Korea–Singapore–Hong Kong) and those in Asia, the Middle East, and Europe (Rest of World). US exports to this bloc of developing countries rose by 13.8 percent from 1981 to 1987, in contrast to the 18 percent decline in US exports to the troubled debtors. This contrast indicates that the nations of Latin America and Africa had to resort to severe import compression to deal with the debt crisis, and these cutbacks had a negative effect on US exports.

On the other side of trade, US imports, the East Asian NICs and Rest of World achieved much higher growth in exports to the United States than did the troubled debtors (144 percent versus 69 percent). Thus, adjustment to the debt crisis does not appear to have occurred primarily, if at all, as an exceptional expansion of exports, at least not to the United States.

As the "other" developing country group includes the extremely strong cases of Taiwan and Korea–Singapore–Hong Kong, another norm for comparison may be obtained from US trade with the industrial countries. From 1981 to 1987, US nominal dollar exports to the industrial countries rose by 22 percent, again indicating that the troubled debtors were forced to adopt sharp curtailments in their imports relative to international norms. But again on the other side of the ledger, the industrial country norm indicates that there was no special export adjustment, as troubled debtor exports to the United States rose by only 69 percent as against the 92 percent increase in exports of industrial countries to the United States.

Table 7.1 reports estimates of hypothetical 1987 US trade with the troubled debtor nations under two alternative assumptions: that their trade would have grown by the same proportions as that of the "other" developing countries (Taiwan, Korea–Singapore–Hong Kong, Rest of World), indicated as HYPA; and that it instead could have grown proportionately with that of the non-US industrial countries (HYPB). For example, HYPB exports for the troubled debtors in 1987 are calculated by applying the 92 percent increase observed for industrial country exports to the United States.

The final columns of the table report what would have happened to the US trade balance with the troubled debtor countries if their trade with the US had grown according to the "other" developing countries norm (HYPA) or the industrial country norm (HYPB). As indicated, whereas the US trade balance with the debtor countries declined by $24 billion from 1981 to 1987 in actuality, it would have declined even more (by $28 billion) if these countries had achieved the same trade growth as the "other" developing country group. Thus, although the troubled debtor countries did cut their imports from the United States relative to levels that would have occurred based on the pattern for other developing countries, they did not increase their exports to the United States by as much as the other countries did (whereas the hypothesis of special impact from the debt problem suggests that the debtor countries would have increased their exports by more than the control group). Indeed, their shortfall on the export side exceeded that on the import side.

The industrial countries provide a more modest standard for comparison. In this case (HYPB), the US trade balance with the debtor nations would have declined by $12 billion, or only half the actual decline of $24 billion. Again the hypothetical comparison would show a sharper US trade balance deterioration if the debtor countries had been able to achieve the same export growth as the industrial countries, in view of the severe import cutbacks of the debtors, but they did not do so.

In sum, if actual nominal trade data are used, it would appear that the US trade balance with troubled debtor nations declined by at most $12 billion as the result of the debt crisis, and that the full extent of the decline was accounted for by abnormally compressed debtor country imports rather than unusually high exports from these countries to the United States. (As indicated in the table, the sharp rise in US nonoil imports from Mexico represents an exception to this general finding on the debtor country export side.) Even an estimate of $12 billion as the amount of US trade deterioration resulting from the debt crisis makes the assumption that the appropriate standard for comparison is trends with industrial countries; if trends in trade with the East Asian NICs and developing countries in Asia, the Middle East, and Europe are adopted as the basis for comparison, there is no evidence that the debt crisis affected the US trade balance at all. However, this alternative basis for comparison is probably extreme, not only because it includes the dynamic export economies of Taiwan, Korea, Singapore, and Hong Kong, but also because there are some countries within this group (such as Yugoslavia) that themselves were reacting to debt problems.

Even comparison with industrial country trade patterns may be subject to a downward bias in calibrating the magnitude of the impact of the debt crisis on US trade, however. The reason is that the period 1981–87 was not only one of debt crisis but also a phase of declining commodity prices. As a result, the nominal value of debtor country exports tends to understate their real export growth.

The analysis of table 7.1 may be repeated using real trade flows at 1980 prices. This exercise yields the following results. From 1981 to 1987, real exports of troubled debtor countries to the United States rose by 109 percent (versus 69 percent nominal), whereas real imports of these countries from the United States declined by 22 percent (versus 18 percent nominal). For the comparison group of "other" developing countries, real exports to the United States rose by 162 percent (versus 144 percent nominal), and real imports from the United States rose by 7.8 percent (versus 13.8 percent nominal). The alternative comparison group, the industrial countries, experienced a rise of 70 percent in their real exports to the United States (versus 92 percent nominal), and a rise of 15.7 percent in their imports from the United States (versus 22 percent nominal).

Recalculation of the hypothetical trade for debtor countries in 1987, applying the "other" developing country and industrial country norms, yields the following results. With the "other" developing country standards, the real nonoil trade balance of the United States with the troubled debtor countries would have deteriorated by $39 billion at 1980 prices. With the industrial country norm, this balance would have declined by only $12 billion (the same outcome as when using nominal data). In actuality, the real US trade balance with the troubled debtor group declined by $37 billion from 1981 to 1987. On the basis of real trade flows, then, the impact of the debt crisis on the US trade balance amounted to virtually nil once again if the "other" developing countries comparison is applied, but to $25 billion (at 1980 prices) if the industrial country comparison is used.

In summary, the debt crisis probably caused a deterioration in the US trade balance of some $12 billion in current dollar terms, up to a maximum of $25 billion at constant 1980 prices. The actually observed US trade balance with Latin America (excluding Venezuela) and Africa (excluding Nigeria and Algeria) declined by $24 billion from 1981 to 1987, but a substantial portion of this decline could have been expected even without the debt crisis because of the worldwide trend of a declining US trade balance in this period. Application of proportionate trends of industrial country trade with the United States would estimate this "normalized" deterioration at $12 billion, leaving the other $12 billion of the observed decline as the probable impact of the debt crisis. However, because commodity prices were falling in this period, real exports from the debtor countries to the United States rose more rapidly than nominal exports, and in real terms the debt crisis impact could have been as high as $25 billion.[1]

Impact of Improved Credit Access

The 1982 debt crisis brought a seizing up of normal private financial flows to most of Latin America. New lending since that year has been primarily in the form of coordinated "new money packages" that are essentially involuntary (or, in the more felicitous official adjective, not "spontaneous").

The cutback in external finance may be seen in the sharp decline in current account deficits of the debtor countries. External finance is the counterpart in the capital account of the deficit on goods and services in the current account. As indicated in figure 7.1, under alternative groupings of debtor countries there was a systematic pattern of sharp reductions in nominal dollar current account deficits from 1982 to 1984–85, and only a slight rebound since then. Sub-Saharan Africa was an exception to this pattern, as its current account deficit declined but proportionately by considerably less than in Latin America.

---

1. Note, however, that because the exports with falling prices were generally noncompetitive commodities rather than manufactures for which the United States has import substitutes, the larger "real" effect does not necessarily mean that the production and employment implications for the United States were correspondingly larger than implied by the nominal estimates.

Figure 7.1 Current account deficits of debtor countries, 1980–88. - - - - , Countries with recent debt-servicing problems; .... , 15 heavily indebted countries; ———— , Latin America; ...... , sub-Saharan Africa.

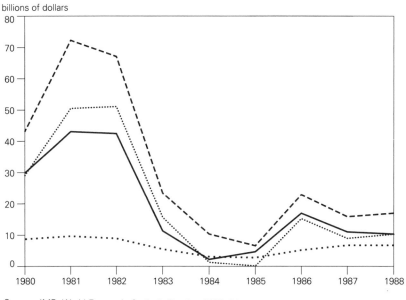

Source: IMF, *World Economic Outlook,* October 1988, 94.

Figure 7.2 shows the net interest payments by these same country groupings from 1980 to 1988. Comparison of the two figures shows that in broad terms the debtor countries shifted from refinancing the entirety of their interest payments (or even more than interest) in 1980–82 to refinancing only a modest proportion of interest obligations by the late 1980s. Thus, Latin America owed net interest of $38.6 billion in 1981 and received $42.9 billion in capital inflows.[2] In contrast, in 1984 the region had a net interest bill of $44.1 billion and obtained net finance of only $2.5 billion. By 1988, interest amounted to $38.8 billion, whereas net capital inflows had returned to only $10.4 billion.[3]

In short, by 1988 there was a gap between net interest payments and capital inflows amounting to approximately $30 billion in Latin America. The impact of possible solutions to the debt problem on US external

---

2. The amount of the current account deficit. Technically, capital inflows can differ from the size of the current account deficit by the amount of change in reserves.

3. International Monetary Fund, *World Economic Outlook,* October 1988, 97–105.

Figure 7.2 Net interest payments of debtor countries, 1980–88.
- - - - , Countries with recent debt-servicing problems;
·········· , 15 heavily indebted countries; ——— , Latin America;
······ , sub-Saharan Africa.

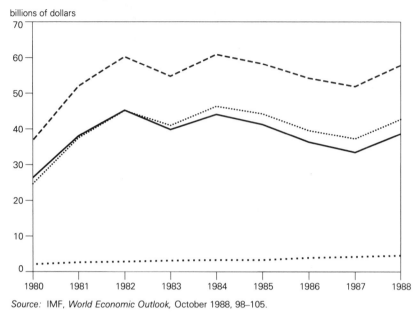

billions of dollars

Source: IMF, *World Economic Outlook,* October 1988, 98–105.

adjustment may be examined by considering what would happen to US accounts if a major portion of this gap were closed. The pessimists argue that it should be closed through forgiveness of a considerable portion of debt and interest. The optimists hold that the gap can at least be narrowed as countries make progress in reducing debt-to-export ratios and gradually return to the capital markets, and through increased public-sector capital flows. Intermediate strategies involve some mixture of voluntary debt reduction (for example, through World Bank guarantees of "exit bonds" that convert a bank's claim to, say, 50 cents on the dollar in exchange for a full guarantee of that remaining amount) and increased lending through new money packages.

Trade Shares Analysis

The 1987 EAG trade matrix developed in Chapter 4 may be used to calculate the impact of improved credit access for the debtor countries by applying country trade shares to the implied trade changes for each debtor area. An increase in external finance (or reduction in interest payments) by $15 billion annually for Latin America may be postulated as an example of such improvement. As sub-Saharan Africa is also experiencing severe difficulties, this exercise may also usefully include $5 billion in additional credit (or lower interest payments) for Africa as well.

Allocation of additional credit by country would tend to be in proportion to interest payments, especially if a program involved such measures as interest capitalization. The shares of the four Latin American country groupings in the EAG data base in net payments of interest and profits in 1987 were as follows: Argentina, 16 percent; Brazil, 35 percent; Mexico, 24 percent; and Other Latin America, 25 percent.[4] On this basis, the EAG trade shares may be applied to determine what would happen to the US trade balance if the trade balance declined by the following amounts of additional external finance: Argentina, $2.4 billion; Brazil, $5.2 billion; Mexico, $3.7 billion; Other Latin America, $3.8 billion; and Other Africa, $5 billion.

In view of the sharp concentration of adjustment to the debt crisis on the side of import reduction (as examined above), it is likely that the bulk of these changes would occur in the form of higher imports rather than reduced exports from the debtor countries. The experiment here assumes that one-fifth of the trade balance change would occur in the form of lower exports and four-fifths as higher imports. These changes are then multiplied by each area's trade shares in 1987 with each of the other 16 countries and groupings in the EAG data base to obtain the distribution of trade changes across trading partners reported in table 7.2. For simplicity, the calculations assume that none of the trade change occurs in oil (in view of its relative short-term insensitivity to price and thus to the exchange rate changes likely to be associated with the trade and current account balance changes), so that imports from OPEC and oil imports from Mexico and the United Kingdom remain unchanged.

As may be seen in the table, a program of $20 billion in increased credit to Latin America and Africa could be expected to raise US exports by over $5 billion and reduce imports by more than $1 billion annually. The total effect would be somewhat greater, because the table reports only the first-round effect. There would be a second round, because part of the increased imports would come from the debtor nations themselves. Thus, Other Latin America has an export share of 13 percent in the Argentine market, so that

---

4. Excluding Venezuelan interest payments, as Venezuela is in the OPEC country grouping. Economic Commission for Latin America and the Caribbean, *Preliminary Balance of the Latin American Economy, 1987* (Santiago: CEPAL, December 1987), table 14. Note that the Mexican share of interest paid tends to be understated, because net payments deduct over $1 billion in accrued interest on private holdings abroad that in fact do not enter the country.

Table 7.2 Trade impact of $20 billion in increased credit to debtor nations, constant shares analysis
(millions of dollars)ᵃ

Exporter	US	UK	FR	GE	IT	CA	JA	AR
				Importer				
US								34
UK								
FR								9
GE								29
IT								11
CA								2.
JA								14
AR	−71.9	−5.7	−10.8	−30.7	−18.9	−5.5	−17.4	
BR	−299.6	−37.1	−44.4	−79.0	−51.5	−25.1	−72.9	18
ME	−528.9	−9.1	−10.8	−13.9	−1.4	−28.3	−6.6	4
TA								
OP								
OI								25.
KS								3.
OL	−236.6	−25.1	−18.5	−43.3	−17.9	−13.9	−29.9	23
AN	−94.7	−49.9	−103.0	−76.8	−75.0	−7.2	−67.8	1
RO								
Total change								
Exports	5,056.3	673.0	1,358.8	1,529.7	608.8	354.0	1,289.6	−21
Imports	−1,231.7	−127.0	−187.5	−243.8	−164.6	−80.1	−194.6	1,80
Trade balance	6,288.0	799.9	1,546.3	1,773.5	773.5	434.1	1,484.2	−2,02

US, United States; UK, United Kingdom; FR, France; GE, Germany; IT, Italy; CA, Cana
JA, Japan; AR, Argentina; BR, Brazil; ME, Mexico; TA, Taiwan; OP, OPEC; UP, Uni
Kingdom-oil; MP, Mexico-oil; OI, Other Industrial; KS, Korea–Singapore–Hong Kong; (
Other Latin America; AN, Other Africa; RO, Rest of World.

a. Each entry shows the change in the bilateral trade flow in question.

the rise in Argentine imports causes higher Other Latin American exports that partially offset the initial rise in that region's imports and the decline in its exports specified in the experiment. Overall, the trade balance of the five debtor regions (AR, BR, ME, OL, AN) declines by $17.5 billion rather than the full $20 billion in the first round. If it is assumed for simplicity that after all subsequent rounds the full $20 billion change would be distributed in the same pattern as the $17.5 billion in the first round, the

	Importer							
BR	ME	TA	OP	OI	KS	OL	AN	RO
1,305.9	2,202.9					898.4	304.3	
184.9	49.5					100.3	333.2	
284.1	53.5					226.1	703.3	
481.3	125.1					173.1	453.1	
136.1	27.1					76.5	249.4	
156.1	60.1					68.6	45.4	
287.0	151.4					399.3	310.1	
130.0	4.4	−19.3	−22.4	−80.5	−5.8	1.4	4.9	−71.4
0.0	15.8	−3.4	−59.3	−110.0	−21.8	63.2	23.7	−121.0
62.5	0.0	−6.4	−2.2	−50.8	−8.9	32.7	3.4	−24.7
9.0	11.1					74.1	76.1	
0.0	0.0					0.0	0.0	
401.1	187.1					330.2	617.5	
39.4	28.2					141.8	163.4	
276.1	13.3	−7.8	−10.3	−216.5	−7.9	152.7	11.2	−37.7
67.5	4.7	−17.1	−11.8	−133.0	−11.4	23.5	219.1	−273.5
268.3	13.3					64.9	372.1	
−636.2	−553.2	174.3	0.0	1,788.6	407.7	25.4	−590.9	725.7
4,089.4	2,947.4	−53.9	−106.1	−590.8	−55.9	2,826.7	3,890.0	−528.2
4,725.6	−3,500.6	228.3	106.1	2,379.4	463.6	−2,801.3	−4,480.9	1,253.9

final effect would be to increase US exports by $5.8 billion, reduce US imports by $1.4 billion, and raise the US trade balance by $7.2 billion, or 36 percent of the $20 billion total.

Table 7.2 also shows that surplus countries Japan and Germany would participate in the increased trade balances. France has a relatively high share in the increased trade balance resulting from the program, primarily because of its high share in increased imports by Africa.

In sum, a program that would close half of the gap between interest payments and capital inflows for Latin America, as well as provide complementary funding one-third as large for Africa, would amount to some $20 billion annually. Such a program would increase the US trade balance by approximately $7 billion annually, and thus contribute modestly to the necessary reduction of some $100 billion or more in the US external deficit.

Model Simulation

A more complete analysis of the impact of increased financing may be obtained by simulating the EAG model of Chapter 5 under conditions in which increased credit is made available to the debtor countries. Two scenarios are considered: DEBT1 assumes increased annual financing amounting to $20 billion at 1987 prices, and DEBT2 $40 billion. Allowing for world inflation, these amounts correspond to approximately $25 billion and $50 billion by 1992, respectively.

This increased finance (and/or reduced interest obligations) is allocated among the five debtor areas in the EAG model in the same proportions as in the experiment just examined. Latin America receives three-fourths of the additional financing, apportioned in relation to net interest payments, and Africa receives one-fourth.

Implementation of the EAG model requires translation of these financing (and thus current account) targets into real exchange rate and growth rate changes. As the baseline projections assume that these countries are all growing at 4½ percent annually, the maximum feasible acceleration of growth is probably only 1½ percent. Growth faster than 6 percent for most Latin American and African countries would encounter other constraints not circumvented by additional external finance (including speed of increase in capital equipment and likely domestic inflationary pressures in nontradeable sectors).

The policy parameters of table 5.6 may be applied to estimate the changes in real exchange rate and growth acceleration from baseline for each country that would generate the target rise in the current account deficit that could be financed with a program of additional external credit. In addition to the ceiling of 1½ percent for growth rate acceleration, the experiments limit real appreciation of the exchange rate to 35 percent or less, on grounds of plausibility. Table 7.3 shows the changes in the policy variables (exchange rate and domestic growth) estimated on the basis of the current account targets and these policy parameters. The table also reports the simulation results for the current account balances of these debtor areas. It may be seen that the simulation outcomes come close to the target current account

Table 7.3 Alternative scenarios for debtor country finance

	DEBT1 ($25 billion)[a]					DEBT2 ($50 billion)[a]				
	AR	BR	ME	OL	AN	AR	BR	ME	OL	AN
Target current account change, 1992 (billions of dollars)	−3.0	−6.6	−4.5	−4.7	−6.2	−6.0	−13.1	−9.0	−9.8	−12.4
Real exchange rate change in 1989 (%)	17.5	14.0	2.0	0	0	35.0	34.0	12.5	8.0	3.5
Acceleration in annual growth (%)	1.5	1.5	1.5	1.1	1.1	1.5	1.5	1.5	1.5	1.5
Simulated current account change, 1992 (billions of dollars)	−3.0	−6.5	−4.5	−4.2	−5.8	−4.3	−12.9	−8.7	−9.1	−11.6

a. Increase in annual financing, nominal 1992 values.

Table 7.4　Changes in trade from baseline under DEBT1 scenario, 1992 (millions of dollars)

Exporter	US	UK	FR	GE	IT	CA	JA	AR
				Importer				
US	0	17.9	8.2	15.1	12.3	77.6	109.2	6⌐
UK	34.1	0	11.6	14.6	12.9	1.5	3.9	12
FR	32.5	10.1	0	25.5	39.9	0.8	4.3	139
GE	61.3	18.6	41.4	0	55.9	1.4	10.1	400
IT	25.3	7.8	20.4	24.6	0	0.7	3.5	165
CA	185.4	2.9	1	1.4	3.6	0	10	52
JA	182.3	6.1	4	12.7	4.2	3.4	0	2⌐
AR	−24.3	−31.5	1.6	−28.5	1.8	2.1	−9.4	
BR	−887.3	−39.8	−56.4	−26.2	−45.9	−34.8	−402.9	240⌐
ME	−243.3	−14.4	0.5	−0.2	0.1	−23.7	−0.4	23⌐
TA	40.4	1	1	2.1	1.1	2.1	13.2	4
OP	0	0	0	0	0	0	0	1
UP	0	0	0	0	0	0	0	
MP	0	0	0	0	0	0	0	
OI	61.6	50.6	60.9	119.7	60	2.1	47.8	368
KS	204.4	4.2	9.4	6.6	3.5	5.1	60.3	61
OL	34.8	1.1	0.8	2.7	1.8	0.3	4.5	191
AN	15.3	2.3	5.2	8.5	8.4	0.1	8.7	2
RO	52.5	8.3	21.6	25.3	36.2	0.8	65.7	169
Total exports	8,010.2	783.6	1,774.6	1,865.6	991	711.2	1,853.4	125⌐
Total imports	−225	45.2	131.2	204	195.8	39.8	−71.6	2,701⌐
Trade balance	8,235.4	738.4	1,643.3	1,661.7	795.2	671.4	1,925.1	−2,576

For an explanation of country abbreviations see table 7.2.

changes (except for Argentina in the high-finance case, where the limit on acceptable real exchange rate appreciation is reached).

Table 7.4 reports the matrix of trade changes for the year 1992 under the intermediate financing scenario (DEBT1). These changes are stated in nominal dollar values from the baseline 1992 projections. As may be seen, there are small changes in cells in the trade matrix that do not directly involve the debtor countries as suppliers or purchasers (in contrast to the absence of any entries in such cells in the constant trade-shares analysis of

	Importer								
BR	ME	TA	OP	OI	KS	OL	AN	RO
,002.7	3,704.3	10.5	23	104.2	9.5	1,753.3	462.2	69.2
106.4	32.5	0.3	15.3	40.1	1	123.2	331.7	41.9
202.4	43.9	0.4	13.3	45.5	0.7	476.4	690.1	49.3
318	125.5	1.1	17.1	168.5	1.2	157.2	412.9	75
111.9	33.3	0.3	17.6	30.8	0.6	196.1	303	49.2
181.3	51.8	0.8	2.3	5.5	1.5	129.3	61.7	20.6
280.7	153.4	11.2	25.7	31.9	11	587	252.8	76
169.5	16.9	15.3	0.8	−51.8	1.2	64.3	−3.6	0.7
0	49.5	1.3	4.1	−113.2	7.7	288.1	103.2	−244.7
101	0	0.3	0.1	−3.8	−16.3	179.6	11.3	−22.5
11.1	14.8	0	4.1	2.4	2.6	175.2	159.2	22.9
109.7	0.5	0	0	0	0	76.8	42.7	0
0	0	0	0	0	0	0	0	0
0	0	0	0	0	0	0	0	0
295.1	177.7	2.4	21.2	317.9	2.7	576.8	947.2	198.7
44	36	3.1	8.4	26	10.7	417.5	276	197.5
301.2	15.4	0.2	1.1	22.8	0.3	250.3	29.6	6.7
80.4	5.7	0.4	1.2	12.8	0.2	42.7	269.9	27.7
880.4	40.6	5.1	22.5	74	14	115.8	365.8	336.6
,156.6	−7.8	457.5	231.2	3,310.7	1,373.7	864.7	518.6	2,234.7
,195.9	4,501.8	52.7	178.1	713.7	48.4	5,609.6	4,715.6	904.8
,352.5	−4,509.7	404.8	53.2	2,597.0	1,325.3	−4,744.9	−4,197.0	1,329.8

table 7.2). These changes arise because of the cross-price elasticities, which cause changes in US exports to Germany (for example) when Brazilian supply becomes less competitive in that market.

Table 7.5 shows the current account changes for each area resulting from the two debt financing scenarios. For the United States, the intermediate program results in an improvement by $11 billion in the 1992 current account balance from the baseline outcome (− $168 billion; Chapter 5). The high-financing scenario improves the US 1992 current account by $19

Table 7.5   Changes in 1992 current account balances from baseline under alternative financing scenarios
(billions of dollars)

Country	DEBT1	DEBT2
United States	11.2	18.9
United Kingdom	1.1	2.2
France	2.3	4.3
Germany	2.0	4.3
Italy	1.1	2.2
Canada	0.8	2.2
Japan	2.3	4.8
Argentina	−3.0	−4.3
Brazil	−6.5	−12.8
Mexico	−4.5	−8.7
Taiwan	0.5	0.9
OPEC	0.0	0.0
Other Industrial	3.6	6.6
Korea–Singapore–Hong Kong	1.6	4.1
Other Latin America	−4.2	−9.1
Other Africa	−5.8	−11.6
Rest of World	1.5	3.8
Five debtors[a]	−23.9	−46.5

a. AR, BR, ME, OL, AN.

billion. Note, however, that if the increases in current account balances for all nondebtor countries are constrained to equal the reductions in the debtor country current account balances, the former must be reduced by approximately 15 percent, so that the adjusted US current account gains stand at $9.6 billion in the DEBT1 scenario and $16.2 billion in the DEBT2 scenario.[5]

---

5. Placing the US share of nondebtor current account increase at approximately the

Conclusion

The broad thrust of these analyses is that the debt crisis contributed moderately to the external imbalance of the United States, and that measures to resolve the crisis could contribute modestly to the needed US external adjustment. However, the debt crisis is by no means the dominant cause, or the key to the solution, of the US external sector problem. A nominal trade balance erosion on the order of $12 billion as the consequence of the debt crisis accounts for less than one-tenth of the total US external sector deterioration, and the upper bound of the estimate (based on real rather than nominal trade changes) is $25 billion, still only one-sixth of the US external sector erosion in the 1980s.

As for future prospects, it is far more feasible that the intermediate financing program (DEBT1) could be mobilized than that the more ambitious scenario (DEBT2) might be realized. Extra financing of $40 billion at 1987 prices seems unlikely, and could raise questions of excessive debt buildup for many debtor countries. Additional credit of $20 billion annually (DEBT1 in 1987 prices) would appear more feasible. This program would essentially require doubling the original Baker Plan targets, however, and even those goals were not attained in the first three years after then-US Treasury Secretary James A. Baker III launched his debt program.[6]

The plausible prospects for the contribution of additional finance to developing countries to US external adjustment are thus limited. The improvement of approximately $10 billion in the 1992 current account under the DEBT1 scenario would be the equivalent of approximately 1 percentage point smaller required real appreciation of the dollar in the Feasible Adjustment Package outlined in Chapter 5, or a reduction by one-tenth in the required exchange rate change. Resolution of the debt problem remains of crucial importance for the economic growth of the debtor nations, and to a lesser degree for the safety of the international banking system, but its role in facilitating correction of the US external deficit is likely to be secondary even under optimistic assumptions.

---

same 36 percent (average) as found in the constant-shares trade analysis. Note that the current account model treats each country's parameters individually, and there is no assurance in experiments such as the two presented here that changes in current accounts sum to zero.

6. Moreover, one important instrument for dealing with the debt problem, the exit bond, might not provide near-term cash flow benefits of the type assumed in the scenarios. Thus, Williamson formulates his exit bond proposal in a form that involves relatively rapid payout of the reduced obligation, such that the annual flow of debt servicing is unchanged in the initial years. John Williamson, *Voluntary Approaches to Debt Relief*, POLICY ANALYSES IN INTERNATIONAL ECONOMICS 25 (Washington: Institute for International Economics, September 1988).

Appendices

Appendix A   Recalibration of the EAG Model for Projection Purposes

The EAG model of Chapter 4 achieves generally good explanation of trade flows in the past. Experimentation with the model reveals, nonetheless, three areas in which modifications are desirable to obtain the most reliable projections possible.

Base Year Averaging

The most obvious area for improvement concerns the discrepancy between actual and predicted trade for 1987. For the backcasts from 1978 to 1987, and in the parameter estimation process, 1987 has no special weight. However, for forecasting purposes it becomes the base year, the point of departure for projections through 1992. The unusually large gaps between model prediction and actual trade results for 1987 (as discussed in Chapter 4) are thus of special concern.

The strategy adopted in the projections below takes account of the 1987 error terms in the following way. The EAG model remains unchanged except that the constant terms in all trade equations are adjusted such that the revised predicted trade flow for 1987 lies halfway between the actual trade flow and the original predicted trade flow.[1] This approach is based on the judgment that there is informational content in the divergences between actual and predicted values for the ''base'' year of the future year forecasts, 1987, but that there is also longer-term information in the unadjusted model that warrants equal weight in the calibration of the revised model for forecasting purposes. For example, insofar as underprediction of Japanese exports in 1987 contains the information that a curtailment of these exports may be expected but did not arrive in 1987 as soon or fully as predicted, the approach here should provide a more accurate forecast than the alternative of simply discarding the entire discrepancy between actual and predicted in 1987 and recalibrating the model to force exact adherence to the 1987 actual base.

---

1. In particular, in terms of equation 1 in Chapter 4, the constant term becomes: $\alpha' = \alpha_e + \ln (1 + 0.5[\{q_a / q_e\} - 1])$ where the prime refers to the revised constant, subscript e refers to the estimate and subscript a to the actual value.

This recalibration approach using "base year averaging" does not change the predicted responses of the model to policy changes at the margin. All of the elasticities remain unchanged, so that the impact of a change in growth or exchange rates has the same proportionate effect as in the initially estimated model, although these changes operate on a 1987 base that is closer to the actual than in the original model.

Specific and Uniform Elasticities

As in any empirical analysis, it is reasonable to ask whether the EAG model has strong biases and quirks for individual countries that result from idiosyncrasies in specific parameter estimates, or whether the central results hold up even under plausible alternative parameters. For example, the discussion in Chapter 5 identifies a serious adverse trend for the United Kingdom, and points out the role of the high income elasticity of imports in leading to this result (and notes a parallel tendency in the opposite direction for Brazil).

The principal trends in the baseline projections, and the response of the system to exchange rate and growth changes, are comprised of two forces. The first is the underlying structure and levels of trade. For example, what happens to Canadian policy inevitably has a major impact on the United States, because Canada is the largest single US trading partner. The second set of influences is the particular trade elasticities estimated in the model. The trade structure is given, but any statistical estimates are subject to error.

To examine the sensitivity of the model results to the particular elasticity estimates, it is possible to rerun the projections applying uniform elasticities. Thus, instead of accepting the empirical estimates that the United Kingdom has a trade-weighted income elasticity of imports of 2.35 whereas Brazil has an elasticity of only 0.42 (table 4A.2), it may be imposed that these two countries and all others have identical income elasticities for imports. Similarly, a uniform direct price elasticity may be imposed for all trade flows. Divergences of model results between the original estimates and those imposing standard elasticities may then be attributed to differences of specific countries' elasticities from the general averages.

To ensure comparability between the basic estimates and those in a uniform elasticity test, it is necessary to apply the trade-weighted averages of the initial elasticities as the standard estimates. These values appear in tables 4A.2 and 4A.3, as discussed above. Thus, for the uniform elasticity case, it is assumed that every country has an income elasticity of demand for imports equal to 1.97, and that the direct price elasticity for each country's exports to each partner is -0.768 (the trade-weighted averages).

The standard elasticity for cross-price effects is more complicated. Here the appropriate concept is a uniform elasticity of substitution. The corresponding cross-price elasticity must inevitably vary with the share of the exporting country in the imports of the importing country, as shown in Appendix B. Thus, the "uniform elasticity case" first identifies the trade-weighted elasticity of substitution implied by the full set of initial cross-price elasticity estimates.[2] It then applies the relevant trade shares in each trading partner combination to calculate the specific cross-price elasticity that corresponds to the uniform (aggregate trade-weighted) elasticity of substitution.

A separate question is whether the uniform elasticities should be different from those derived on an aggregate, trade-weighted basis from the original elasticities. In particular, there is a certain tradition in the empirical literature that trade elasticities tend to be underestimated, in part because of poor data.[3] However, the enforcement of minimum values (of 0.3) on the elasticities in the original, constrained estimates tends to lessen any overall downward bias in the estimates.

Moreover, the trade-weighted values appear consistent with the results of most contemporary models. Thus, the trade-weighted income elasticity of approximately 2 is virtually identical to the US income elasticity estimated in the HHC model of Chapter 3. The direct price elasticity of -0.768 is somewhat lower than the stylized price elasticity of approximately unity that is applied in many models.[4] However, these models typically do not decompose the price elasticity into the two components distinguished in the EAG model: direct and cross-price. When a country reduces its price (for example, through real depreciation) in isolation, the impact on its exports is shown by the addition of these two elasticities. As the trade-weighted cross-price elasticity is 0.55 in the EAG model (table 4A.4), the

---

2. From Appendix B, $\sigma = -S/[1 + (s_i/s_{Ni})] = -Ss_{Ni}$, where σ is the cross-price elasticity, S is the elasticity of substitution, s_i is the share of exporter i in the imports of the country in question, and s_{ni} is the share of all other exporting countries in these imports. Accordingly, from the trade shares in the 1987 actual trade data (table 4.1) and the cross-price elasticities estimated in table 4A.4, it is possible to calculate the implicit elasticity of substitution for each country trading pair. This value turns out to be -0.709. This estimate may be biased downward (in absolute value), in view of the more typical value in the range of -2.5 (as discussed in Chapter 4).

3. The classic statement is in Guy H. Orcutt, "Measurement of Price Elasticities in International Trade," *Review of Economics and Statistics*, vol. 32 (May 1950), 117–32.

4. Thus, in the Brookings Institution survey of major international macroeconomic models, the average price elasticity for nonoil imports among the six models considered is 1.0; the maximum is 1.1, and the minimum 0.7. Ralph C. Bryant, Gerald Holtham, and Peter Hooper, eds., *External Deficits and the Dollar: The Pit and the Pendulum* (Washington: Brookings Institution, 1988, 133).

sum of the two elasticities (absolute value) is 1.318, consistent with and moderately higher than the stylized-fact parameter of 1 for the trade price elasticity. Thus, there is little basis for examining a second uniform-elasticity case that imposes a higher (or for that matter, lower) general level for all of the elasticities than the averages initially estimated.

With the imposition of uniform elasticities, it becomes necessary to recalibrate the constant terms. This recalibration is set to force the new predicted results for 1987 equal to the 1987 values predicted by the original forecasting model (which itself has recalculated constant terms, using the base year averaging between model and actual values described above).[5] In this way, the only differences between the main projections and those using the uniform elasticities derive from the changes in the elasticities as applied to the underlying variables (such as income) over time, with no change in the base year.

Experimentation with the forecasting model using both the country-specific and the uniform elasticities shows that in some key countries and some policy scenarios the results can diverge sharply. The most extreme case is for Canada. The high price elasticity for US exports to Canada (table 4A.3) causes important differences between the country-specific elasticity projections and those using uniform elasticities. In the case of a proposed adjustment package involving dollar depreciation, the specific elasticity model forecasts a trade deficit for Canada in 1992, whereas the uniform elasticity model projects a large trade surplus. Largely because of the Canada phenomenon, US trade is also much more responsive to the exchange rate using specific rather than uniform elasticities. These and other important differences (including for France, Korea–Singapore–Hong Kong, and Rest of World) are noted in the discussion in Chapter 5 of alternative projection results.

In view of important cases of sensitivity to the choice between country-specific and uniform elasticities, it appears to be the safest course to apply a simple average of the two alternative elasticity sets as the basis for the central projections of this study. Thus, for any given elasticity, the parameter value applied in the principal projections in Chapter 5 is an average of the specific estimate for the country pair in question (tables 4A.2 through 4A.4) and the overall uniform elasticity (for example, 1.97 for the income elasticity). Note that this hybrid set of elasticities once again requires recalibration of the constant term, so that the base year (1987) trade estimate is identical to

---

5. The reestimation of the constant applies the same approach as set forth in footnote 1 above, except that in this case the ratio of the recalculated to the original estimate is forced to unity, and the coefficient 0.5 in the final term of the equation for α' becomes unity.

that obtained in the base year averaging procedure for the original, specific elasticities, as discussed above.

Consistency Constraints for Cross-Price Elasticities

A third refinement of the model deals with a problem that arises in calculation of the trade effects of competition among alternative suppliers in a given market, working through the cross-price elasticity. Experimentation with the model shows that in some "instances important inconsistencies arise in these cross-price effects. For example, in dollar depreciation scenarios, the increase in US exports to Mexico exceeds the decline in exports from appreciating countries (such as Japan and Germany). With Mexico's real exchange rate held unchanged against the dollar, the only source of increased US exports to Mexico is from improved competitiveness against alternative suppliers, working through the cross-price term. The problem is that the independent estimate of the US cross-price elasticities in the Mexican market (1.346, table 4A.4) is inconsistent with the cross-price elasticities estimated for other suppliers (typically at the lower bound of 0.3). As a consequence, the cross-price term generates net increases in Mexican imports, whereas it should merely reallocate among suppliers an unchanged total of imports.

Appendix B develops a method of enforcing consistency across the cross-price elasticities of the alternative suppliers to a given market. This constraint is specified for the principal exchange rate scenarios examined in Chapter 5, and imposes the requirement that reduced exports by the group of "strong," appreciating countries exactly offset the increased exports to the market in question from the "weak," nonappreciating countries. Table 5A.1 reports the constrained cross-price elasticities for the averaged specific/uniform elasticity set used in the central projections.[6]

---

6. As may be seen for the US–Mexico example, the cross-price elasticity for the United States is now much lower (0.236), whereas the elasticity is much higher for other, appreciating suppliers such as Japan (0.822), permitting zero net change in Mexican imports from the cross-price effect (considering the large volume of US–Mexico exports and the smaller base of exports of appreciating countries to Mexico).

Appendix B   The Cross-Price Elasticity

An important feature of the multicountry model of Chapter 4 is its inclusion of a specific term to capture the competition of a particular supplier against other foreign suppliers in a specific market. The income-compensated cross-price elasticity σ_{ij} tells the percentage change in the quantity exported from country i to country j when the prices of goods from all other foreign suppliers in the market of country j rise by 1 percent, and when the size of the market remains constant in volume.

Relationship to the Elasticity of Substitution

The cross-price elasticity may be derived from an elasticity of substitution between the supplier in question and all other suppliers of imports into the market in question. By definition, the (quantity) elasticity of substitution S equals the percentage change in the ratio of the quantity imported from the supplier in question to that imported from all other sources, for a given percentage change in the corresponding ratio of their respective prices. Thus:

(1) $S = [\%\delta(q_i/q_{Ni})]/[\%\delta(P_i/P_{Ni})]$

where, for sales in the market of country j (and omitting the j for simplicity) q_i is the export volume of country i, q_{Ni} is the export volume of all other suppliers ("non-i"), P_i is the price of country i, and P_{Ni} is the average price for all other foreign suppliers. The term $\%\delta$ refers to proportionate change. Because the percentage change in a ratio equals the percentage change of the numerator less that of the denominator, equation 1 may be written as:

(2) $S = [\%\delta q_i - \%\delta q_{Ni}]/[\%\delta P_i - \%\delta P_{Ni}]$.

In the case of a 1 percent rise in the price of the supplying country i with other prices held constant, the denominator of equation 2 becomes unity, and

(2a) $S = \%\delta q_i - \%\delta q_{Ni}$.

For the substitution effect, the focus is on the reallocation of a fixed quantity of imported supply among the alternative suppliers, rather than on any change in the total quantity imported. Thus, because total import quantity remains unchanged,

(3) $\%\delta q_i(s_i) + \%\delta q_{Ni}(s_{Ni}) = 0$

where s refers to initial market share, and subscripts i and Ni to the supplier country i in question and all other supplier countries, respectively. From equation 3:

(3a) $\%\delta q_{Ni} = -\%\delta q_i(s_i/s_{Ni})$.

Substituting into equation 2a:

(4) $S = \%\delta q_i - [-\%\delta q_i(s_i/s_{Ni})]$
$= \%\delta q_i[1 + s_i/s_{Ni}]$

so that:

(4a) $\%\delta q_i = S/[1 + (s_i/s_{Ni})]$.

The cross-price elasticity of demand for exports from country i to market j with respect to the price of supply from all other sources, in turn, is the percentage change in the former (quantity) for a given percentage change in the latter, or

(5) $\sigma_i = (\%\delta q_i)/(\%\delta P_{Ni})$

where the variables are as before and, again, the notation j for market j is omitted. When the average price of all other suppliers rises by 1 percent, and the price of supplier i remains unchanged, the quantity demanded from supplier i changes as:

(5a) $\%\delta q_i = \sigma_i(\%\delta P_{Ni})$.

A 1 percent rise in the price of competing suppliers, P_{Ni}, will thus generate a change of σ_i percent in exports of country i to the market in question.

Considering that a 1 percent change in the relative price of supplier i and all other suppliers may be obtained either by a 1 percent change in the price of supplier i or by a 1 percent change of opposite sign in the price of all other suppliers, equation 4a—the percentage change in q_i resulting from a 1 percent rise in the price of country i's supply (P_i), working through the substitution elasticity—must equal equation 5a—the percentage change in q_i resulting from a 1 percent rise in the price of all competing countries' prices, but working through the cross-price elasticity—except that the sign on equation 4a must be reversed. Thus, the cross-price elasticity needed for the term σ_{ij} in Chapter 4 may be estimated from equations 4a and 5a (and treating the proportionate price change of non-i supply in the latter equation as unitary) as:

(6) $\sigma_i = -S/[1 + (s_i/s_{Ni})] = -Ss_{Ni}$.

The final expression in equation 6 indicates that the income-compensated cross-price elasticity of demand for country i's exports to country j equals the quantity elasticity of substitution among all foreign suppliers in this market, multiplied by the share of all supplier countries other than i in this market. In intuitive terms, the impact of competitors' prices on a country's exports to a third-country market depends on the inherent substitutability of the products from the competing source (S) and the size of the other suppliers' existing sales (s_{Ni}), with a larger existing competitor presence offering greater opportunity for competitive inroads.

Consistency Constraint

The cross-price term in the multicountry trade model is designed to reallocate the supplier composition of imports into a given market when relative prices of alternative suppliers change, but not to change total imports into the market. The direct price terms (foreign suppliers versus the domestic price in the importing country) determine the total level of imports. Nonetheless, the empirical estimates of the cross-price elasticities are conducted individually rather than jointly for all suppliers. It is therefore possible for inconsistencies to arise. Thus, as noted in Appendix A, in the initial estimates for US exports to Mexico, the cross-price elasticity is relatively high, but both the volumes of exports of most other countries to Mexico and the magnitudes of their cross-price elasticities are low. The result is that when the model is simulated for a decline in the dollar against the German mark and the Japanese yen (for example), the rise in US exports caused by the cross-price term exceeds the decline in other countries' supply to Mexico, and total Mexican imports spuriously rise from what should be a simple reallocation among suppliers of an unchanged import volume.

It is possible to adjust the cross-price elasticity terms so that the elasticities are forced to be consistent across the various suppliers to a given market. As the policy simulations typically involve appreciation of a group of strong countries against the dollar but absence of appreciation by a second group of weak countries (including by definition the United States), the consistency constraint may be formulated to ensure that when such a change in relative exchange rates occurs, the increased exports from the weak countries to the market in question in response to the relative price term are equal to the decreased exports of the strong countries from this same substitution effect.

Consider the impact of a 1 percent appreciation of all strong-currency countries against the dollar. In the market of a specific country, j, and for a specific supplier, i, the change in the cross-price term P_{Ni}'/P_i will depend on the weight of strong countries in the basket of alternative suppliers competing with country i in market j. If country i is a weak-currency country (or the

United States), and all its competitors in market j are strong-currency countries, the cross-price term will merely rise by the 1 percent appreciation of the strong countries. If all the competitors are weak-currency countries, the cross-price term will not change at all (rise by zero). More generally, the cross-price variable will rise by a trade-weighted average of the appreciations by the strong countries (1 percent) and the weak countries (zero) in the market in question. Thus, the cross-price variable will rise by $[a]\Phi^s_{Ni}$, where a is the percentage appreciation of the exchange rate of the strong countries, and Φ^s_{Ni} is the share of strong-country suppliers in the imports of the country j in question, excluding imports from the supplier i of direct interest. When the supplier i in question is itself a strong country, the change in prices of competitors will once again be given by the weight of strong countries among them in the market in question, but this time the change in the relative price term must subtract the appreciation by the supplier i itself (that is, the percentage change in the price ratio equals the percentage change in the numerator, or the weighted-average price of competitors, minus the percentage change in the denominator, or the price of country i itself). Thus:

(7) $\quad \% \, [P_{Ni}/P_i] = a\Phi^s_{Ni}, \, i \in w; \qquad = a[\Phi^s_{Ni} - 1], \, i \in s$

where the left hand side is the proportionate change in the cross-price variable, w indicates weak countries, s strong countries, and ϵ indicates membership in the weak or the strong group, respectively.

From equation 1 in Chapter 4, the change in trade from the standpoint of cross-price competition is merely the proportionate change in the cross-price term (given by equation 7 here) multiplied by the base value of the trade flow in question and by the cross-price elasticity. The consistency constraint seeks to ensure that the trade changes for supply from the appreciating, strong countries just offset the opposite changes from non-appreciating, weak countries.

For sales to a given market j, let:

(8) $\quad z = - \left[\sum_{i \epsilon s} \sigma_{ij} X_{ij} \, a(\Phi^s_{Ni} - 1) \right] \Big/ \left[\sum_{i \epsilon w} \sigma_{ij} X_{ij} \, a\Phi^s_{Ni} \right].$

The denominator of the right hand side of equation 8 is the increase in exports from weak countries to market j caused by the cross-price effect, whereas the numerator is the negative of the corresponding decrease in exports from strong countries to this market. The consistency constraint seeks to ensure that their ratio, z, is unity. As it is unlikely to be so from the initial, statistically estimated cross-price elasticities, the ratio is forced to unity by increasing the cross-price elasticities for all strong countries by the multiple $[1 + k]$ and decreasing those for all of the weak countries by the multiple $[1 - k]$, where k can be either positive or negative, so that when equation 8 is applied to the adjusted cross-price elasticities, $z = 1$. This procedure imposes symmetrical adjustment on the cross-price elasticities of the strong group and the weak group of countries.

As all the adjusted cross-price elasticities for the strong suppliers will be multiplied by $[1 + k]$ and all those for the weak suppliers by $[1 - k]$, we seek:

(9) $[1 + k]/[1 - k] = 1/z$.

That is, when the numerator of the right hand side of equation 8 is multiplied by $[1 + k]$ and the denominator by $[1 - k]$, the resulting expression will be $1/z$ times as large as the original value, shrinking (expanding) it from greater than unity (less than unity) to unity.

Rearranging equation 9:

(10) $k = [1 - z]/[1 + z]$

and:

(11) $\sigma'_{ij} = \sigma_{ij}[1 + k], \qquad i \in s;$
$\qquad = \sigma_{ij}[1 - k], \qquad i \in w$

where σ'_{ij} is the cross-price elasticity after adjustment for the consistency constraint.

Table 5A.1 reports these adjusted cross-price elasticities for the multi-country model. They are calculated under the assumption that the strong-country grouping includes Japan, Germany, France, Italy, the United Kingdom, Canada, Korea–Singapore–Hong Kong, Taiwan, and the Other Industrial countries. All other countries (including the United States) are in the weak category.

Appendix C   Trade Prices During the Dollar's Decline

A stylized fact that has emerged since the beginning of the dollar's decline in early 1985 is that trade prices have failed to reflect the change in the exchange rate by a wide margin. The general argument is that foreign firms have been reluctant to give up market share, and thus have raised their dollar prices in the US market by less than implied by full pass-through of the exchange rate change.[1] More recent research has suggested, however, that the seeming paradox of modest US import price increases tends to vanish when two considerations are taken into account: the use of foreign wholesale prices rather than consumer prices as the base for expected prices, and the peculiarities in the treatment of computer prices in the US import price deflator.[2]

The central economic fact is that foreign wholesale prices abruptly halted their upward climb as the dollar began to decline. In part this pattern reflected the coincidental decline in the price of oil in 1986; in part, it represented a feedback effect of a lower dollar to goods prices abroad.

In addition, US statistics estimate computer prices on the basis of dollar values divided by "quantity." Because the physical productivity of computers (for example, in millions of instructions per second) has risen dramatically, a given dollar value of computer sales is treated as a declining price multiplied by a rising "quantity." Whatever the merits of this approach (which would appear to overstate the effective economic quantity), its effect is to introduce a large downward trend in computer prices, which have a large and growing weight in US trade. These same estimated prices are applied to computers in US imports, contributing to a relatively slow growth in US import prices.

The hypothesis of low pass-through of exchange rate change may be examined informally by comparing the actual dollar export prices of major foreign countries against the levels that would be expected on the basis of

1. See, for example, Richard Baldwin, "Some Empirical Evidence on Hysteresis in Aggregate US Import Prices," *NBER Working Paper* 2483 (Cambridge, Mass.: National Bureau of Economic Research, January 1988); and, for Japanese trade prices, Bonnie E. Loopesko and Robert A. Johnson, "Realignment of the Yen-Dollar Exchange Rate: Aspects of the Adjustment Process in Japan," *International Finance Discussion Papers* 311 (Washington: Federal Reserve Board, August 1987).

2. Ellen Meade and Lucia Foster, "Import Prices and Foreign Production Costs" (Washington: Federal Reserve System, mimeographed, December 1987).

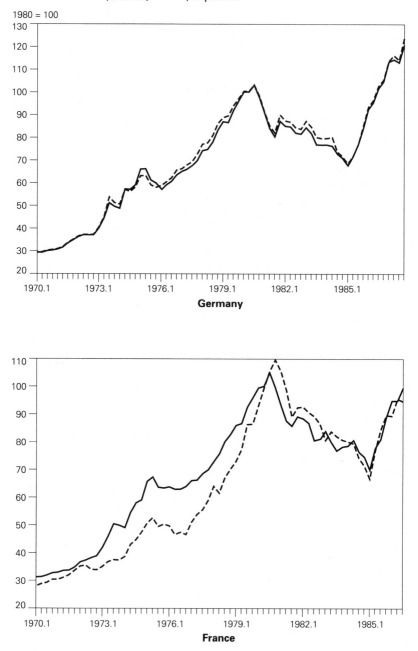

Figure C.1 Actual and expected export prices in six countries, 1970–85.
———, Actual; ----, expected.

Germany

France

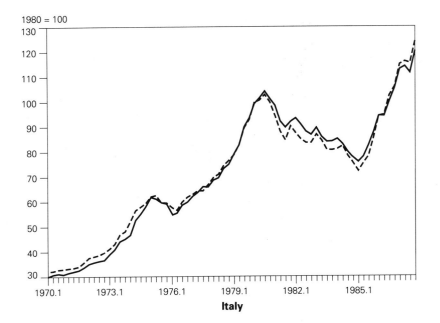

1980 = 100

Italy

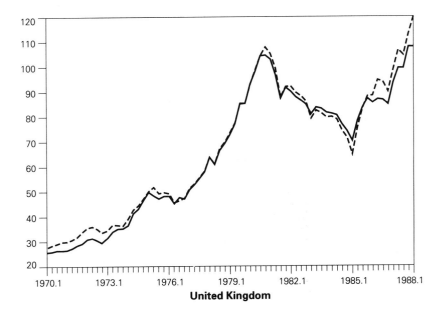

United Kingdom

Figure C.1 (continued)

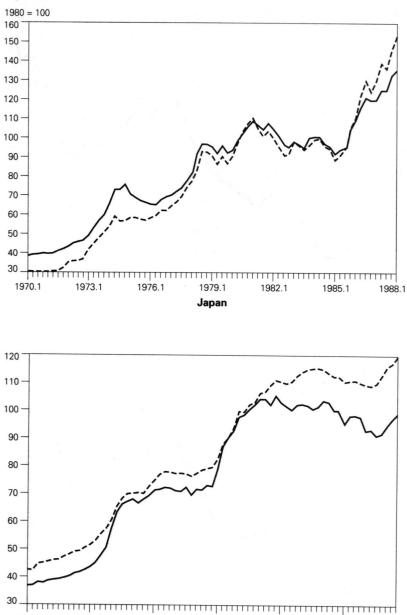

1980 = 100

Japan

Canada

Source: IMF.

these countries' wholesale price indexes divided by the exchange rate against the dollar. Figure C.1 presents these comparisons for the six large industrial countries.

For Germany and Italy there is a nearly perfect overlay between the graph for the actual dollar export price index and that for the wholesale price index divided by the exchange rate.[3] The adherence is relatively close for France as well, especially beginning in 1984. For Japan and the United Kingdom, the two series also move closely together, but there is greater evidence of a lag in the actual export price behind the expected value in 1986–87. Thus, from 1985:1 to 1988:1, the actual dollar export price index for Japan did rise sharply, by 43.4 percent; but the expected Japanese export price (the wholesale price divided by the yen/$ rate) rose by even more, 71.5 percent. Thus, it seems likely that some further catch-up in export prices from Japan and the United Kingdom remains in the pipeline, and/or that their pass-through ratios may be less complete than for the continental European countries.

The only major industrial country with a large divergence between the trends of the actual and expected export prices is Canada. As figure C.1 shows, by 1983 a sizable wedge had opened between Canada's actual and expected US dollar export prices, although the two series did move in parallel in the period 1984:1–1987:3. The decline in energy prices probably played a role in this divergence.

These simple tests suggest that actual trade prices have moved more closely in tandem with expected prices than the stylized facts might imply. Yet some models of US import prices find large shortfalls from predicted levels after the dollar's decline. One reason may be that firms discriminatorily hold down prices in the US market, but for a given observed value of average foreign export prices this thesis would imply the anomaly of compensating price increases above expected levels in non-US markets.

An important part of the paradox is merely that those models that apply foreign consumer prices as the basis for expected prices (as in the case of the HH model of Chapter 3) were confronted with a historic divergence between consumer and wholesale prices. Figure C.2 presents the trends of wholesale and consumer prices in the six large industrial country trading partners of the United States. In most cases, the two series moved closely together over most of the past two decades. However, there is a general pattern of interruption of this trend and much slower growth of wholesale

---

3. Data are from the International Monetary Fund, *International Financial Statistics*, quarterly series for dollar export price index (74D), wholesale price index (63), and average exchange rate (RF).

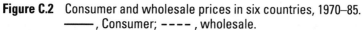

Figure C.2 Consumer and wholesale prices in six countries, 1970–85.
———, Consumer; – – – –, wholesale.

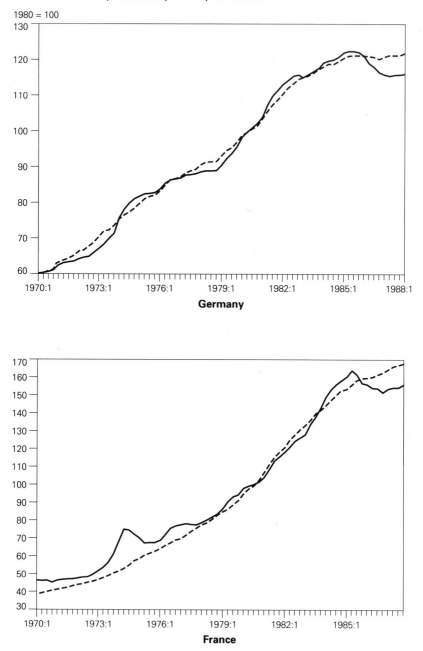

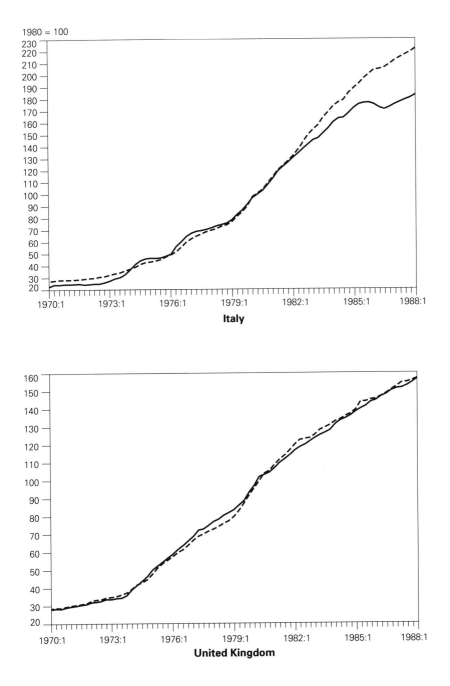

1980 = 100

Italy

United Kingdom

Figure C.2 (continued)

1980 = 100

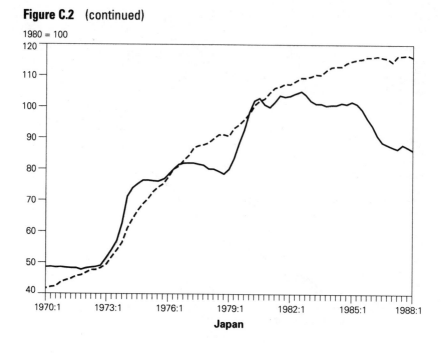

Japan

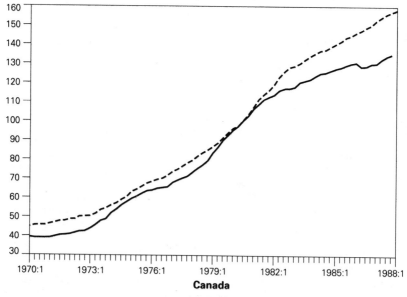

Canada

Source: IMF.

prices than of consumer prices in recent years. The only exception is in the United Kingdom. The presence of a sharp divergence between wholesale and consumer prices in Japan beginning in 1986 and the absence of a divergence in the United Kingdom suggests an important role for oil imports (in view of the collapse of oil prices in 1986), as Japan is a large importer of oil while the United Kingdom is a net exporter.

The case of Japan is the most extreme. Although the slowdown in wholesale prices relative to consumer prices had already begun in 1980–84, the dramatic shift occurred in 1985:1–1988:1. In this period, Japanese consumer prices rose by 1.4 percent, while wholesale prices fell by 14.8 percent. Wholesale prices also fell in this period in Germany and France.

In sum, the paths of dollar export prices of major foreign trading partners show that the dollar's decline has generally been passed on into higher dollar prices, with the most complete and prompt pass-through in the continental European countries. In part the high and early pass-through in Europe reflects the importance of intra-European trade and its denomination in European currencies (such that dollar depreciation changes little but the dollar price after translation from German marks, for example). The unusual slowdown or actual decline in domestic wholesale prices in these countries in this same period has meant, however, that the resulting increase in dollar export prices has been lower than might otherwise have been expected. Those models that rely on consumer prices, in particular, tend to overpredict foreign export prices, because the close relationship between consumer and wholesale prices that had existed in the past broke down in the 1986–87 period.

Appendix D   Trends in US and International Oil Trade

Increases in the price of oil caused major macroeconomic disturbances in the 1970s. In the 1980s the price of oil has eroded substantially, with less noticed but extremely large effects on international trade patterns. This appendix reviews past trends and estimates a central forecast for oil trade through 1992.

Boom and Bust in Oil Trade

Figure D.1 shows the nominal dollar trade of the oil-exporting countries[1] since 1971. Their exports surged from some $20 billion in 1971 to $125 billion in 1974 with the first OPEC price rise. From 1978 to 1980 the second price rise brought exports to $302 billion, but by 1982 there had been substantial erosion, to $224 billion, and declining export volumes (and, in 1986 especially, prices) cut earnings to only $118 billion in 1986. Earnings recovered only modestly in 1987, to $130 billion. The imports of the oil-exporting countries responded, with a lag and in moderated magnitudes. They rose from $11 billion in 1971 to a peak of $163 billion in 1982 before falling to $83 billion in 1987. The oil exporters' trade surplus peaked at $170 billion in 1980, and by 1987 was back down to only $46 billion. This reversal by $124 billion in the 1980s was of approximately the same size as the more widely recognized deterioration in the US trade balance over this period.

Figure D.2 presents the trade data in real terms, deflated by unit values of exports from the industrial countries (1980 = 100). In real terms, the second oil shock only increased exports at their 1980 peak to about one-third above the level they had reached in 1974. More dramatically, the subsequent erosion meant that by 1987 real export earnings of the oil-exporting countries stood at only about half (53 percent) of the level they had achieved in 1974 with the first oil shock. The price the oil-exporting countries have had to pay as a result has been a decline in real imports by 57 percent from their peak level in 1982.

There has been a corresponding boom and bust in US oil imports. Figure D.3 depicts the value and volume of oil imports into the United States since

---

1. Defined by the International Monetary Fund as countries earning at least two-thirds of their export receipts from oil in 1976–78. This group is primarily OPEC, and excludes such subsequently important exporting countries as Mexico.

Figure D.1 Trade and reserves of oil-exporting countries, 1971–87

billions of dollars

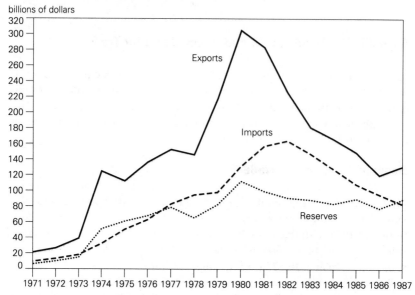

Source: IMF, *International Financial Statistics,* various issues.

Figure D.2 Real trade of oil-exporting countries, 1971–87

billions of 1980 dollars

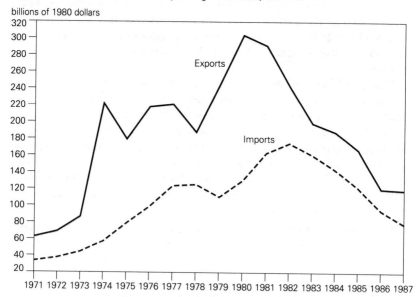

Source: Calculated from *International Financial Statistics,* various issues.

Figure D.3 US oil imports and prices, 1971–87. ---, billions of dollars (left scale); ········, dollars/bbl (left scale); ——, mmbd (right scale).

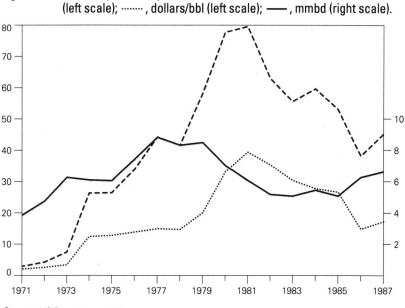

Source: US Department of Commerce.

1971. The first oil shock caused imports (c.i.f.) to surge from $4.3 billion in 1972 to $26 billion in 1974. In 1981, after the second shock, US oil imports peaked at $80 billion. By 1986 the value of imports had fallen to $38 billion. Oil imports recovered only modestly to $45 billion in 1987.

US oil trade has been affected importantly by trends in volume as well as price. The first OPEC price shock followed closely a large rise in the volume of US imports related to adverse US production trends. Thus, US imports rose from 3.9 million barrels per day (mmbd) in 1971 to 6.3 mmbd in 1973. Despite the price shock (and in part because gasoline price controls insulated consumers from the new price signals), this trend continued through 1977, when oil import volume peaked at 8.8 mmbd. Conservation and rising domestic production then cut imports to a low of 5 mmbd in 1985, although with the attraction of lower prices after the 1986 price collapse, by 1987 US imports had revived to 6.5 mmbd. As for the price itself, the average import price per barrel rose from $2.48 in 1972 to about $12.00 in 1974–75, surged again to a peak of $36.42 in the second oil shock, and then eroded to $28.44 in 1985 and broke to $16.58 in 1986.[2]

---

2. Calculated as the unit value of total oil imports divided by total barrels per day, crude and refined.

Prospects for US Oil Imports

In early 1987 the National Petroleum Council (NPC) issued a report stressing the prospective rise in US dependence on oil imports.[3] Just as the two oil shocks had provided the incentives that led to the development of Alaskan North Slope and other new oil production, the erosion and then collapse of oil prices in the 1980s (and the prospective depletion of North Slope fields) meant that for the latter half of the 1980s the outlook was for new drilling to be insufficient to replace reserves, even at a relatively high price range.

The NPC study considered two price ranges, expressed in terms of 1986 constant dollars. The upper range assumed a price of $18 per barrel in 1986, $22 by 1990, and $28 by 1995. The lower range assumed prices of $12, $14, and $17, respectively. Under the high-price scenario, the NPC study expected domestic production to decline from 8.97 mmbd in 1985 to 7.96 mmbd in 1990 and 6.99 mmbd by 1995; in the low-price scenario, it placed domestic production at 8.42 mmbd in 1985, 7.14 mmbd in 1990, and 5.65 mmbd by 1995.

The study projected that domestic consumption would rise from 15.7 mmbd in 1985 to 16.3 mmbd in 1990 and 17.0 mmbd in 1995 under the high-price scenario, and to 17.6 mmbd in 1990 and 19.0 mmbd in 1995 in the low-price case. Correspondingly, it projected that oil imports would have to rise from 5.0 mmbd in 1985 to 7.0 mmbd in 1990 and 8.7 mmbd in 1995 under the high-price scenario, and to 9.2 mmbd in 1990 and 12.2 mmbd in 1995 under low prices.[4]

By mid-1988 it appeared that the oil market was extremely close to the low-price scenario of the NPC. Thus, adjusting for wholesale price inflation, and staging the real price increases assumed by the NPC in equal increments, by 1988 the current price corresponding to the NPC low price was $13.95 per barrel. Although the actual average unit price of oil imports in the first four months of 1988 was $16.71 per barrel,[5] that price reflected the spot market price of late 1987 (which had averaged $17.12 per barrel in the final four months). In contrast, for the first four months of 1988 the spot price averaged only $14.80, and at mid-June the price was only $13.85 per barrel.[6]

---

3. "NPC Scores US Import Vulnerability," *Oil and Gas Journal*, 23 March 1987, 20–24.

4. These figures add 0.8 mmbd oil exports to the net import figures calculated by the NPC.

5. US Department of Commerce, *Advance Report on US Merchandise Trade: April 1988*, FT900 ADV (Washington: US Department of Commerce, 14 June 1988), 15.

6. "Arabian Light," *Wall Street Journal*, 17 June 1988.

Table D.1 US oil imports, actual and projected, 1985–95

Year	Volume (mmbd)	Price (dollars/bbl)	Import value (billions of dollars)
1985	5.0	28.44	52.4
1986	6.2	16.58	37.6
1987	6.5	18.73	44.7
1988	7.2	14.77	38.6
1989	8.2	15.14	45.3
1990	9.2	16.41	55.1
1991	9.8	17.62	63.0
1992	10.4	18.89	71.7
1993	11.0	20.24	81.3
1994	11.6	21.63	91.6
1995	12.2	23.09	102.8

mmbd = millions of barrels per day.

Sources: Survey of Current Business, and IMF, *International Financial Statistics* (for 1985–87); based on US Department of Commerce, *Advance Report on US Merchandise Trade: April 1988,* FT900 Adv (for 1988).

The June price almost exactly coincided with the level in the NPC low-price scenario.

Table D.1 presents projections of US oil imports through 1995, and reports actual imports for 1985–87. The estimates for 1988 are based on actual volume averages for the first four months, actual import value for the first four months, and an assumed average price of $14.00 per barrel for the last eight months of the year. For 1989 through 1995, the import volumes are based on the NPC low-price scenario, with interpolation by equal annual increments for the years between the 1990 and 1995 NPC estimate years. The average price per barrel is similarly interpolated, and converted from 1986 dollars to current-year dollars on the basis of assumed US wholesale price inflation of 4½ percent annually in 1988–90 and 3 percent thereafter.

As indicated, the value of US oil imports in 1988 was estimated to decline by about 14 percent, as the result of a reduction of some 21 percent in average price.[7] However, in 1989 import value returns to slightly above the 1987 level, and by the early 1990s it grows at approximately 14 percent

---

7. The actual outcome for 1988, available only subsequent to the preparation of these estimates in mid-1988, was a decline from $44.8 billion in 1987 to $41.8 billion (c.i.f.), or by 6.6 percent. US Department of Commerce, *US Merchandise Trade: December 1988,* FT 900.

annually (or almost 10 percent in constant dollars). Even so, the nominal dollar value of US oil imports does not return to its 1981 peak of $80 billion until 1993, and its real value at that time is well below the 1981 level.

Income Elasticity of Demand

For purposes of simulation, it is useful to know the elasticity of oil imports with respect to income. The NPC estimates imply that, evaluated at 1990, the elasticity of oil consumption with respect to income is approximately 0.6, whereas the elasticity of oil imports with respect to consumption is 1.9. As a result, the elasticity of oil imports with respect to income is approximately 1.1.[8]

Conoco has estimated that, from 1985 through 2000, oil demand in non-Communist countries will rise at about 1 percent annually and GNP at 3 percent annually, with an implied long-term income elasticity of demand of one-third.[9] However, global oil consumption rose by 3 percent in 1988, giving a higher ratio to world output growth than the average (for all energy) of 0.5 over recent years.[10] The EAG multicountry model of this study applies an income elasticity of 0.5 to project the oil imports of Europe, Japan, and other non-oil-exporting countries other than the United States, and for simulating the effects of changes in their income growth.

---

8. From 1990 to 1995, oil consumption rises by 1.6 percent annually. Assuming GNP rises by 2.7 percent annually over the period, the income elasticity of oil consumption is 1.6/2.7 = 0.59. In 1990, imports provide 52 percent of consumption, and since at the margin all additional consumption must come from imports, the elasticity of imports with respect to consumption is 1.0/0.52 = 1.92. The product of the two elasticities gives the elasticity of imports with respect to income: 0.59 × 1.92 = 1.13.

9. "NPC Scores US Import Vulnerability," 22.

10. *Wall Street Journal*, 6 March 1989.

Appendix E   Current Accounts for Major Countries: Trends and Adjustments

This appendix examines the trends in current account balances for 17 major trading nations and groups from 1979 through 1986. It first depicts the country allocation of the counterpart of the large decline in the US external balance in this period. It then calculates estimates for adjusted current accounts by allocating the large "statistical discrepancy" that exists in the global accounts.

Trends Since 1979

Figure E.1 shows the reported current account balances for the major trading nations and other country groupings for 1979 through 1986.[1] As figure E.1 indicates, the decline of approximately $150 billion in the US current account balance from 1980 until 1987 was mirrored by a $150 billion rise in the combined current account balances of Germany and Japan (from deficits of $15.7 billion and $10.7 billion, respectively, in 1980 to surpluses of $32.5 billion and $83.2 billion, respectively, estimated for 1987).

Trends in other major areas thus tended to net out to zero over this period. OPEC experienced a current account decline comparable to the United States' $150 billion from 1980 to 1986. In contrast, there were major reductions in current account deficits in Latin America, a move to large surplus by Taiwan, and a sizable swing from deficit to surplus for Korea. Italy, France, Canada, and the United Kingdom had generally offsetting fluctuations, although the Other Industrial countries as a group experienced a major reduction in external deficits. Africa excluding Nigeria remained in modest deficit over the period.

Specifically, from 1980 to 1986 the United States joined OPEC in losing a combined $283 billion on current account. More than half of the corresponding gain was taken up by Germany and Japan alone ($149 billion). The remaining improvement on current account was divided relatively

---

1. As reported in International Monetary Fund (IMF), *World Economic Outlook*, October 1987; *International Financial Statistics*, Yearbook 1986; Central Bank of China, *Financial Statistics: Taiwan District, Republic of China*, August 1987; and "The Asian NICs and U.S. Trade," *World Financial Markets*, January 1987.

Figure E.1 Current account trends in 18 countries and regions

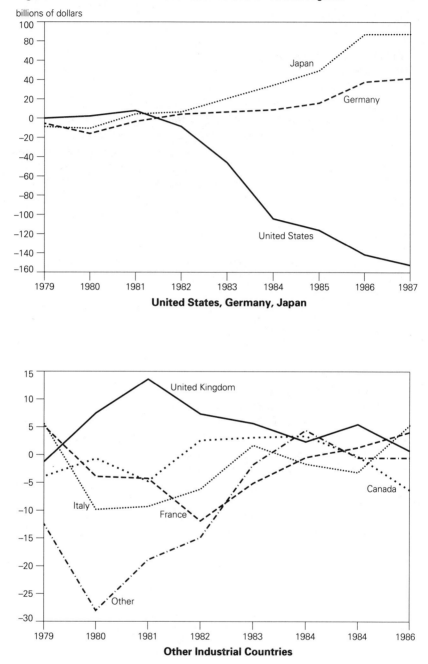

United States, Germany, Japan

Other Industrial Countries

billions of dollars

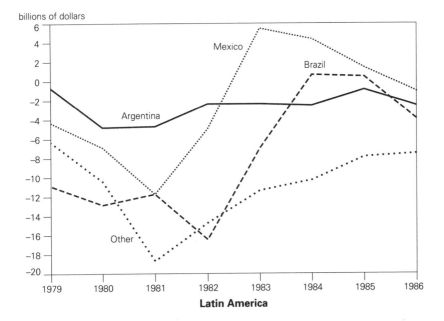

Latin America

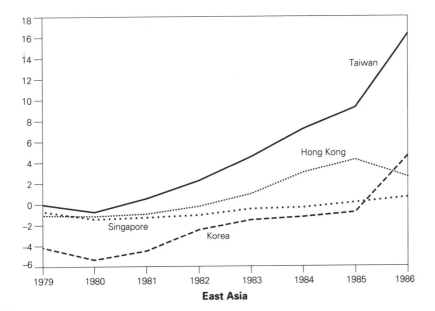

East Asia

Figure E.1 (continued)

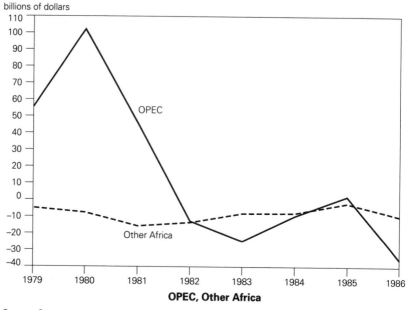

OPEC, Other Africa

Source: See note 1.

evenly among four major country groupings: Latin America excluding Venezuela (nearly $20 billion), Korea–Singapore–Hong Kong ($15 billion), four of the large industrial countries (Italy, Canada, France, and the United Kingdom, $13 billion), and the Other Industrial countries ($26 billion). In addition, Taiwan experienced a comparable gain on its own ($17 billion).

These trends confirm the broad stylized facts of this period: rising external deficits in the United States in association with the overvalued dollar; a corresponding rise in current account balances in most of the rest of the world; serious erosion for OPEC from the time of the peak real price of oil in 1980 to its recent trough in 1986; and increases in current account balances in Latin America because of the cutoff of external credit, and in East Asia as the result of impressive export performance.

Adjusting for the Statistical Discrepancy

The analysis of global current accounts has been clouded by the presence of a large discrepancy between the sum of individual country current account balances and the zero global total that should result. The sum of current account balances for industrial and developing countries was measured at

−$17 billion in 1979, and this discrepancy rose to −$109 billion at its peak in 1982. The world as a whole cannot be in deficit, and the discrepancy means that some countries are either overstating their current account deficits or understating their current account surpluses. The error stayed in the range of nearly $100 billion in 1983–84 before declining to $57 billion in 1986. Adding other countries (including Eastern Europe) provides little explanation (only about a $3 billion surplus annually in 1982–85).[2] An important policy question is thus whether the seemingly extreme US external deficit might be overstated because there has been some $100 billion missing in the global accounts annually, and conceivably a substantial part of this missing surplus could represent an exaggeration of the seriousness of the US situation.

The International Monetary Fund (IMF) has prepared a special analysis of the global discrepancy that provides a basis for examining this question. The IMF analysis finds that some $3 billion to $5 billion annually of the discrepancy arises from the omission from global balance of payments statistics of official transfers flowing through international organizations. The largest source of the discrepancy, however, is from incomplete reporting of income on foreign portfolio investment. Thus, the difference between reported payments of such income and reported receipts by creditor countries rose from $10 billion in 1979 to $51 billion in 1985, and accounted for three-fourths of the increase in the global discrepancy over this period.[3]

The IMF study is able to allocate a portion of the statistical discrepancy by area. Figure E.2 indicates the recorded current account and the correction that may be attributed to the industrial countries for 1979 through 1986, and the same series for the developing countries (including OPEC). The attributable adjustments fall considerably short of capturing the full statistical discrepancy. Thus, for the year of the largest discrepancy, 1982, the IMF identifies an allocable adjustment of $22 billion that should be added to the reported current account of the industrial countries, and $17 billion for developing countries, for a total adjustment of only $39 billion—less than half of the entire statistical discrepancy of $109 billion.

An important pattern evident in figure E.2 is that the attributable correction bears virtually no relationship to the magnitude of the current account balance for the area. The combined deficit recorded for the industrial countries widens sharply in 1980, contracts in 1981–83, and increases again in 1984–85; yet the attributable correction is on a plateau with gently sloped edges. The same profile for the attributable correction may be seen for developing countries, even though they show a dramatic deterioration in the current

---

2. IMF, *World Economic Outlook*, April 1987, 104–05.

3. *Ibid.*

Figure E.2 Statistical discrepancy on current account, 1979–86

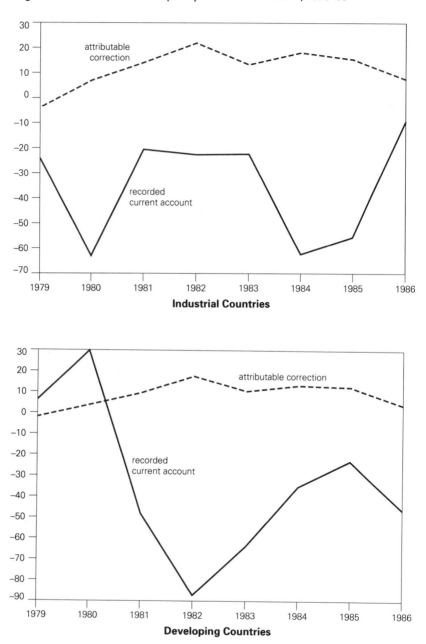

Industrial Countries

Developing Countries

Source: IMF, World Economic Outlook, April 1987, 105.

account from 1980 to 1982 and then a large recovery (with oil playing a major role in the initial years).

The lack of relationship of the attributable correction to the size of the current account balance for each grouping suggests that it would be inappropriate to estimate the adjusted current account by applying a proportionate correction to the recorded current account deficit of each country. Instead, the attributable correction seems to be more of a simple additive adjustment that swells in the early 1980s and then subsides, and is related more to the passage of time than to the particular recorded current account balance.

More detailed IMF estimates for 1983 provide a basis for allocation of the statistical discrepancy by region. The global statistical discrepancy for the categories of services and transfers (the main problem areas) in that year amounted to an estimated $58.1 billion. Of this amount, the IMF attributed $14 billion to the industrial countries, $31.2 billion to developing countries, $-$2.9 billion to Eastern Europe, and $3.1 billion to international organizations. The remaining $12.6 billion discrepancy in these two broad categories could not be allocated. The study disaggregated the figure for developing countries into $2.9 billion for offshore financial centers, $11.5 billion for Middle Eastern oil-exporting countries, and $16.8 billion for other developing countries.[4]

The estimates for services and transfers provide the best available basis for allocation of the full statistical discrepancy. On this basis, in 1983 the industrial countries accounted for 31 percent of the total discrepancy, Middle Eastern oil exporters for 28 percent, and other developing countries for 41 percent. (This distribution ignores the adjustments allocated to the offshore financial centers, Eastern Europe, and the international organizations. The last two groups are addressed by deducting the relevant amounts from the global statistical discrepancy.)

These percentages may be applied to the total statistical discrepancy in each year from 1979 through 1986 to obtain the estimated adjustment required for each of the three regions: industrial, oil-exporting, and other developing countries. The total discrepancy must first be reduced by the amount attributable to "other countries" (Eastern Europe) and international organizations.

To obtain adjusted current account estimates at the country level, a scaling principle is required for the intragroup allocation of the adjustments. As indicated above, scaling in proportion to the current account balance appears

---

4. IMF, *Final Report of the Working Party on the Statistical Discrepancy in World Current Account Balances*, SM/87/13 (Washington: IMF, 12 January 1987), 203.

inappropriate. The basis adopted here is total trade turnover (imports plus exports), as an indication of size in international economic activity.[5]

In sum, the calculations here obtain the adjusted current account as follows. For the three large country groupings (industrial, OPEC,[6] and other developing countries), the total world statistical discrepancy reduced by amounts allocable to "other countries" and international organizations is multiplied by respective grouping shares. The discrepancy attributable to an individual country in a grouping is then obtained based on that country's share in total trade turnover for all countries in the group.

The adjusted current account for the United States is of special interest and illustrates the procedure. Thus, in 1982, the global discrepancy of $109 billion may be pared to $103 billion by deducting the amount allocable to "other countries" (Eastern Europe) and international organizations (table E.1). Industrial countries accounted for 31 percent, or $31.9 billion. The United States represented 18.3 percent of trade turnover of the industrial countries in the base year chosen (1980). So the amount of the adjustment allocated to the United States for 1982 is $5.8 billion (0.183 × $31.9 billion). Table E.2 reports the full set of recorded and adjusted current account balances for 17 major trading countries and areas, for 1979 through 1986.

An important implication of these estimates is that, as the IMF analysis concluded, adjustment to account for the global statistical discrepancy makes little difference to the policy interpretation of trends in current account performance. For the important case of the United States, the 1986 current account deficit recorded at $141.4 billion is reduced to $138.5 billion by the adjustment procedure followed here. The reduction by only $3 billion is inconsequential in terms of policy interpretation; the US deficit remains massive and unsustainable.

This finding is all the more plausible when three factors are recognized. First, the global statistical discrepancy has fallen by half since 1982, so that there is a lesser adjustment to be made. Second, the US share in international

---

5. An alternative would be to allocate in proportion to each country's reported receipts in services and transfers, as it is understatement in these categories (particularly capital services) that accounts for the bulk of the statistical discrepancy. However, because countries seriously underreporting these receipts would have a low measured base for the allocation, this alternative would tend to allocate the missing receipts disproportionately to those countries already fully reporting. Instead, trade turnover as a proxy for international economic size provides a guideline for the expected size of service and transfer receipts.

6. The analysis allocates the adjustment for Middle Eastern oil-exporting countries to the OPEC grouping for which current account data are readily available.

Table E.1 Global statistical discrepancy, 1979–86
(billions of dollars)

Year	Total current account, industrial and developing countries	Other countries	International organizations	Discrepancy to be allocated
1979	− 17	− 3	2	− 18
1980	− 32	− 2	3	− 31
1981	− 69	− 3	3	− 69
1982	− 109	3	3	− 80
1983	− 86	3	3	− 103
1984	− 96	4	4	− 88
1985	− 79	3	5	− 71
1986	− 57	1	5	− 51

Source: IMF, *World Economic Outlook,* April 1987, 105.

trade is smaller than might be suspected, at only 18 percent of trade by the industrial countries, reflecting the well-established inverse correlation between the size and openness of economies. Third, because they keep better statistics, the industrial countries (including the United States) have a lower share in the global statistical discrepancy (about one-third) than in world trade (over two-thirds). For these reasons, even though the United States has the lion's share of national current account deficits, its share of the global statistical discrepancy is small.

As in the case of the United States, the other industrial countries show relatively minor adjustments to reported current account balances in the estimates allocating the global statistical discrepancy. The adjustments are largest in relative terms for OPEC. In 1986, its adjusted current account deficit stands at $22.3 billion instead of $36.6 billion. The other sizable adjustment is for Korea–Singapore–Hong Kong. For this group, the 1986 current account surplus rises from $7.5 billion to $11.1 billion after adjustment. The relatively large adjustment for the three countries reflects their high share in developing country trade turnover (17.2 percent), and thus in the portion of the global statistical discrepancy allocated to that group. Otherwise, the developing countries show only minor adjustments to their current accounts. For example, Brazil's reported $4.1 billion deficit in 1986 moderates to a deficit of $2.9 billion, not a sufficient change to indicate a

Table E.2 Current account balance: reported and adjusted, 1979–86
(billions of dollars)

Country		1979	1980	1981	1982	1983	1984	1985	1986
United States	R	−1.0	1.9	6.9	−8.7	−46.3	−107.0	−116.4	−141.4
	A	0.0	3.7	10.8	−2.9	−41.8	−102.0	−112.4	−138.5
United Kingdom	R	−1.4	7.0	13.0	6.9	5.0	1.9	4.9	−0.2
	A	−0.9	7.8	14.8	9.6	7.1	4.2	6.8	1.2
France	R	5.1	−4.2	−4.8	−12.1	−5.2	−0.9	−0.9	3.4
	A	5.6	−3.3	−2.7	−9.0	−2.8	1.7	3.0	4.9
Germany	R	−6.0	−15.7	−5.2	4.1	4.2	8.4	15.2	37.2
	A	−5.2	−14.3	−2.1	8.8	7.8	12.4	18.4	39.5
Italy	R	5.4	−10.0	−9.5	−6.4	1.4	−2.3	−3.5	4.8
	A	5.8	−9.3	−8.0	−4.2	3.1	−0.4	−2.0	5.9
Canada	R	−4.1	−1.0	−5.1	2.2	2.5	2.6	−0.9	−6.7
	A	−3.8	−0.5	−4.0	3.8	3.7	4.0	0.2	−5.9
Japan	R	−8.8	−10.7	4.8	6.9	20.8	35.0	49.3	85.8
	A	−8.2	−9.7	7.0	10.2	23.4	37.8	51.6	87.4
Argentina	R	−0.6	−4.8	−4.7	−2.4	−2.4	−2.5	−1.0	−2.6
	A	−0.5	−4.5	−4.1	−1.6	−1.7	−1.8	−0.4	−2.2

Table E.2 (Continued)

Country		1979	1980	1981	1982	1983	1984	1985	1986
Brazil	R	−10.7	−12.8	−11.7	−16.3	−6.8	0.5	0.3	−4.1
	A	−10.3	−12.1	−10.1	−14.0	−5.0	2.5	1.9	−2.9
Mexico	R	−4.2	−6.8	−11.7	−4.9	5.3	4.2	1.2	−1.3
	A	−3.8	−6.2	−10.3	−2.9	6.9	5.9	2.6	−0.3
Other Latin America	R	−6.0	−10.5	−18.6	−14.7	−11.4	−10.2	−7.9	−7.5
	A	−5.0	−8.8	−14.8	−9.1	−7.0	−5.4	−4.0	−4.7
Korea–Singapore– Hong Kong	R	−6.0	−8.1	−7.1	−4.1	−1.4	1.1	3.3	7.5
	A	−4.7	−5.9	−2.2	3.2	4.2	7.3	8.3	11.1
OPEC	R	55.6	102.7	46.5	−13.3	−24.8	9.6	1.8	−36.6
	A	60.6	111.4	65.8	15.5	−2.4	15.0	21.7	−22.3
Other Industrial	R	−12.3	−27.8	−18.8	−15.2	−2.0	3.8	−1.0	−1.0
	A	−10.8	−25.2	−13.1	−6.7	4.6	11.1	4.9	3.2
Other Africa	R	−5.1	−7.0	−16.2	−14.3	−8.0	−8.1	−1.4	−9.8
	A	−4.0	−5.1	−11.9	−7.8	−3.0	−2.6	3.1	−6.6
Taiwan	R	0.0	−0.9	0.5	2.2	4.4	7.0	9.2	16.2
	A	0.4	−0.2	2.0	4.5	6.2	8.9	10.8	17.3

R = reported; A = adjusted.

Source: See note 1 and text.

reversal in policy interpretation.[7]

In sum, the best available estimates of how the world statistical discrepancy should be allocated among countries indicate that there is little qualitative change in the pattern of international payments after adjustment, especially in the case of major industrial countries including the United States. The limited evidence available suggests that substantial increases in estimated surpluses (or reductions in deficits) would primarily be focused on OPEC and, perhaps, the East Asian NICs. As these adjustments are far from firm, and because the official estimates do not appear to be far wrong for the industrial countries (and several important developing countries), the data strategy adopted in this study is to work with the existing current account estimates rather than attempt to adjust them. The analysis of Chapter 5 does, however, pay close attention to the behavior of the global statistical discrepancy over time in the projections and simulations.

7. It may be added that even if the "true" current account of Brazil is $1 billion higher than the recorded figure, because the discrepancy would largely reflect private capital earnings not captured in the balance of payments—primarily income on flight capital—the extra earnings would not be available to the government's foreign exchange receipts, and thus would not reduce the country's requirements for new borrowing. Moreover, in the specific case of Brazil, this adjustment may be overstated, because the country has had relatively less capital flight over recent years than some other major Latin American countries.

Appendix F Real Versus Nominal External Adjustment

The United States needs to reduce its external current account deficit by some $100 billion to $150 billion in nominal terms. To the extent that it accomplishes this objective through depreciation of the dollar against other currencies, the price of imports expressed in dollars will rise. The rising price of imports works against the declining quantity of imports in determining the net outcome for the dollar value of imports, so that the volume (or real) import reduction substantially exceeds the nominal import reduction. On the export side, dollar depreciation tends to boost dollar prices of US exports. Although this higher price provides a benefit in nominal export earnings at a fixed volume of exports, it tends to moderate the quantity increase in exports that would occur if there were no induced dollar export price rise, because the rise partially offsets the new attraction to foreign purchasers that would otherwise occur in the price reduction they face in buying US goods. Usually the rise in the import price will exceed that of the export price, causing the terms of trade (ratio of export price to import price) to decline (although for the small country exporting standardized commodities, the terms of trade may remain unchanged).

In general, the real or volume reduction in the trade deficit must exceed the nominal dollar reduction, because terms of trade changes are working against the latter. It is important for policy purposes to know how large the real change must be relative to the nominal change. Thus, a nominal reduction of $150 billion in the US trade deficit would amount to about 3 percent of GDP. However, if the ratio of real to nominal adjustment were as high as 2 to 1 (as examined below), this nominal correction would require the reduction in domestic US absorption of real goods and services by an amount on the order of 6 percent of GDP. The greater the ratio of real to nominal adjustment, the more adverse the impact on potential consumption and on domestic inflationary pressures. Viewed in another, traditional way, the issue concerns the extent to which the United States must incur a loss in the external terms of trade (price of exports relative to price of imports) to carry out its external adjustment. This appendix sets forth a simple formulation of trade adjustment to examine the likely range for the ratio of real to nominal adjustment.

I am indebted to Anne McGuirk for helpful comments.

355

Let R be the exchange rate, in dollars per unit of foreign currency. Let X^q be the volume of exports, and X^v their dollar value. Let M^q be the volume of imports, and M^v their dollar value. Let H equal the ratio of exports to imports in the base period. Define the initial value of exports as equal to the initial volume of exports, and the initial value of imports equal to the initial volume of imports (so that quantities differ from values only in the postdepreciation period). Let the subscript x refer to exports and m to imports, and the superscript f to foreign currency and $\$$ to dollars.

For US exports, the price faced by foreign purchasers in their own currency equals:

(1) $\quad P_x^f = P_x^\$/R.$

The proportionate change in foreign purchases of US exports (volume) will equal the proportionate change in the foreign currency price of US exports resulting from dollar depreciation, multiplied by the foreign price elasticity of demand for US exports, or:

(2) $\quad x^q = dp_x^f$

where d is the price elasticity of foreign demand for US exports and other notations are before (except that the lowercase version of a variable indicates proportionate change).

To determine the proportionate change in the foreign currency price of the US export following a depreciation of the dollar, it is necessary to know the pass-through ratio, or the fraction of the depreciation that is translated into a change in the price in the target market as opposed to absorbed in changed profit margins by the supplying firm. Thus, if the pass-through ratio is 0.7 for US exporters, when the dollar declines by 10 percent against the German mark they will reduce the mark price of their products by 7 percent and raise the dollar price by 3 percent. Thus, the change in the foreign price is determined by the pass-through ratio and the dollar depreciation as:

(3) $\quad p_x^f = -ar$

where a is the pass-through ratio, r is the proportionate change in the dollar/foreign currency exchange rate, and the negative sign reflects the fact that the foreign currency price declines as the dollar depreciates.

From equations 2 and 3,

(4) $\quad x^q = -dar.$

Equation 4 gives the proportionate change in export quantity resulting from dollar depreciation by proportion r. The corresponding change in the dollar value of exports may be derived from the fact that value equals price times quantity.[1] Specifically, the proportionate change in export dollar value equals the proportionate change in quantity plus the proportionate change in the export price plus the product of these two proportionate changes (an interaction term):

(5) $\quad x^v = x^q + p_x{}^s + x^q p_x{}^s.$

The proportionate change in the dollar export price is the amount of the depreciation multiplied by the fraction not passed on to foreign purchasers but absorbed instead in higher profit ratios by US exporters, or:

(6) $\quad p_x{}^s = (1 - a)r.$

From equations 4, 5, and 6:

(7) $\quad x^v = -dar + (1 - a)r - da(1 - a)r^2.$

On the import side, the dollar price of imports equals the foreign exchange price charged by suppliers as translated through the exchange rate, or:

(8) $\quad P_m{}^s = P_m{}^f / R.$

When the dollar depreciates by the proportion r, foreign firms pass through the fraction b of the change and absorb the remainder in lower profit margins. Thus,

(9) $\quad p_m{}^s = br$

and

(10) $\quad p_m{}^f = -(1 - b)r$

where again the negative sign enters because foreign currency prices fall if the pass-through is incomplete.

Import quantity responds to the change in import price according to the price elasticity of US demand for imports, e, as applied to the proportionate change in the dollar price of imports, or:

(11) $\quad m^q = e p_m{}^s = ebr.$

The proportionate change in import value equals the proportionate change in quantity, plus the proportionate change in the import price, plus the interaction term, or:

(12) $\quad m^v = m^q + p_m{}^s + m^q p_m{}^s.$

---

1. With $V = PQ$, or value equals price times quantity, in proportionate change terms $v = q + p + pq$. That is, $V_1 = P_1 Q_1$ where the subscript indicates the period. But $P_1 = P_0(1 + p)$, and $Q_1 = Q_0(1 + q)$, so $[(P_1 Q_1)/(P_0 Q_0)] - 1$, which is the proportionate change in value (v), equals $(1 + p)(1 + q) - 1 = q + p + pq$.

From equations 9, 11, and 12,

(13) $m^v = ebr + br + eb^2r^2$.

These proportionate changes may now be applied to absolute levels to obtain absolute changes in nominal and real trade balances. In the base period, US imports are M, and US exports are HM. After depreciation, the quantity of US exports rises by the base period quantity (HM) multiplied by the proportionate change in export quantity (x^q). The quantity of US imports declines by the base period quantity (M) multiplied by the proportionate change in import quantity (m^q). From equations 4 and 11, the quantity change in the trade balance is thus:

(14) $\Delta T^q = HM(-dar) - M(ebr)$.

Similarly, the absolute change in nominal exports equals the base value (HM) times the proportionate change in export value (x^v), and the absolute change in import value equals their base value (M) times their proportionate value change (m^v). From equations 7 and 13, the absolute change in the value of the trade balance is:

(15) $\Delta T^v = HM[-dar + (1 - a)r - da(1 - a)r^2] - M(ebr + br + eb^2r^2)$.

If equation 14 is divided by equation 15, the result is the ratio of the real trade balance adjustment to the nominal trade balance adjustment, Z. Note that all exchange rate change terms (r) cancel except for two terms in the denominator, and the initial absolute value of imports also cancels. The result of dividing equation 14 by 15 is:

(16) $Z = \dfrac{-Hda - eb}{-Hda + H(1 - a) - Hda(1 - a)r - eb - b - eb^2r}$.

The denominator of equation 16 may be rearranged into two expressions, the first equal to the numerator and thus representing the component of volume change in the total trade balance value change, and the second being the remainder of that total change and thus the valuation impact of the price change and the interaction effects. Thus,

(17) $Z = \dfrac{-Hda - eb}{[-Hda - eb] + [H(1 - a)(1 - dar) - b(1 + ebr)]}$

and, from equations 4 and 11,

$$Z = \dfrac{-Hda - eb}{[-Hda - eb] + [(1 - a)H(1 + x^q) - b(1 + m^q)]}.$$

From the denominator of the final formulation of equation 17, it may be seen that the valuation effect includes a positive component that rises as the pass-through for export prices (a) declines, and that is applied to a base magnitude reflecting base period volume (unit import volume multiplied by the base period ratio of exports to imports, H) plus the quantity change in exports (x^q) to represent the new level of export volume. Similarly, the denominator includes a negative valuation effect that becomes more negative as the import price pass-through (b) rises, and that is applied to an import quantity base equal to unity plus the proportionate change in quantity (m^q).

The ratio of real to nominal adjustment declines as the ratio of exports to imports (H) rises. The larger exports are relative to imports, the easier adjustment becomes and the less is the need for deterioration in the terms of trade.[2]

Otherwise, the ratio of real to nominal adjustment tends to decline as the pass-through ratios decline, as the absolute values of the trade elasticities rise, and as the absolute value of the import elasticity rises relative to that of the export elasticity. The role of the pass-through may be seen as follows. The more US exporters raise their dollar prices when the dollar depreciates (lower export price pass-through), the smaller will be the rise in export quantity relative to export dollar value. The more foreign suppliers reduce their foreign currency prices in response to dollar depreciation (lower import price pass-through), the smaller will be the decline in import quantity relative to the decline in import value.

As for trade elasticities, in the extreme small-country case of infinite foreign elasticity of demand for exports, there is no deterioration in the terms of trade at all; it is thus plausible that, as export demand elasticity rises, the ratio of real to nominal adjustment should decline. On the import side, a higher price elasticity of demand for imports means that a small price increase generates a relatively large adjustment, so that the terms of trade need not deteriorate as much to accomplish a given adjustment. Finally, the differential impact of the import and export price elasticities stems from the fact that exports begin at a smaller base than imports.

These tendencies may be seen in table F.1, which shows the value of Z under alternative values of the pass-through ratios and trade elasticities, for the 1987 ratio of exports to imports (0.62) and assuming a depreciation of 10 percent ($r = 0.1$). The table examines combinations of export and import

---

2. If $A = -da$, $B = -eb$, $G = (1 - a)(1 - dar)$, and $D = -b - eb^2r$, then the derivative of Z with respect to H is:

$$\partial Z/\partial H = \frac{[H(A + G) + B + D]A - [HA + B][A + D]}{[H(A + G) + B + D]^2}.$$

This derivative is negative when evaluated at reasonable central values (such as $a = b = 0.8$; $d = e = -1$; $r = 0.1$; and the 1987 figure for H, 0.62).

Table F.1 Ratio of trade balance volume change to trade balance value change[a]

Import price pass-through	Export price pass-through					
	0.5	0.6	0.7	0.8	0.9	1.0
	$E_x = -1, E_m = -1$					
0.5	1.23	1.32	1.42	1.52	1.63	1.74
0.6	1.36	1.45	1.55	1.65	1.75	1.86
0.7	1.48	1.57	1.66	1.76	1.86	1.97
0.8	1.59	1.68	1.77	1.87	1.97	2.08
0.9	1.69	1.78	1.87	1.96	2.06	2.17
1.0	1.78	1.87	1.96	2.05	2.15	2.25
	$E_x = -1.5, E_m = -1.5$					
0.5	1.12	1.17	1.22	1.28	1.33	1.38
0.6	1.18	1.23	1.28	1.33	1.38	1.43
0.7	1.24	1.28	1.33	1.37	1.42	1.46
0.8	1.29	1.33	1.37	1.41	1.45	1.49
0.9	1.33	1.36	1.40	1.44	1.48	1.52
1.0	1.36	1.39	1.43	1.46	1.50	1.54
	$E_x = -0.5, E_m = -0.5$					
0.5	1.72	2.14	2.71	3.57	4.98	7.72
0.6	2.39	3.05	4.05	5.77	9.37	21.79
0.7	3.43	4.62	6.75	11.62	34.39	−42.58
0.8	5.30	7.98	14.86	72.32	−28.05	−12.24
0.9	9.57	19.91	66858.28	−21.45	−11.09	−7.64
1.0	28.79	−80.14	−17.71	−10.24	−7.33	−5.79
	$E_x = -1.5, E_m = -0.5$					
0.5	1.28	1.37	1.46	1.54	1.62	1.70
0.6	1.48	1.57	1.66	1.74	1.82	1.90
0.7	1.72	1.81	1.89	1.96	2.04	2.12
0.8	2.01	2.08	2.15	2.22	2.29	2.37
0.9	2.35	2.41	2.46	2.52	2.59	2.65
1.0	2.77	2.80	2.83	2.87	2.92	2.98
	$E_x = -0.5, E_m = -1.5$					
0.5	1.19	1.28	1.39	1.50	1.63	1.77
0.6	1.28	1.37	1.46	1.57	1.69	1.82
0.7	1.34	1.43	1.52	1.62	1.73	1.85
0.8	1.40	1.48	1.56	1.66	1.76	1.87
0.9	1.44	1.52	1.60	1.68	1.78	1.88
1.0	1.47	1.54	1.62	1.70	1.79	1.89

a. Ratio of base period exports to imports = 0.62 (US 1987 ratio). Calculations are based on a depreciation of 10 percent.

E_x = export price elasticity; E_m = import price elasticity.

price pass-through ratios of 0.5 to 1.0. Most estimates would place these ratios at relatively high levels. Thus, in the Helkie–Hooper model, the import pass-through ratio (b) is 0.9, whereas a feedback effect of depreciation to dollar prices of 0.2 means that the export price pass-through (a) is 0.8 (Chapter 3).

The table explores the ratio Z under alternative assumptions about export and import price elasticities (d and e, respectively). In the unfavorable case of price elasticities of only 0.5 for each, the ratio is highly unstable, as the denominator can approximate zero and the ratio can change sign. This instability is suggestive of the collapse of adjustment feasibility, as the Marshall-Lerner condition (sum of trade elasticities exceeding unity) verges on being violated.

In the more stable cases of unitary trade elasticities, higher trade elasticities (1.5 each), or combinations of high elasticities for one direction of trade flow and low for the other, the ratio of real to nominal adjustment shows rather systematic patterns. As suggested above, it is lowest for low pass-through and high trade elasticities (first case, second section of table F.1), and highest for complete pass-through combined with relatively low import price elasticity (final case, fourth section).

The central expected values for the parameters would probably be in the following range: pass-through ratios of about 0.8, and elasticities of about −1.0. For this case, the ratio of real to nominal adjustment for the United States is 1.87 (first section of the table, fourth row and fourth column). The simple average for all cases, excluding the perverse cases of low trade elasticities (section 3 of the table) is $Z = 1.70$.

In economic terms, the finding that the real trade balance adjustment is nearly twice as large as the nominal adjustment has important implications. It suggests that there will be considerable pressure on resource availability in the United States in the coming years as the country seeks to correct a nominal deficit of some 3 percent of GNP at a cost of potentially nearly twice that amount. In one regard this effect is positive: it means an inherent source of strong demand in the economy for years to come. However, if the economy's tendency is not toward recession but instead toward inflation, the relatively large real adjustment could mean increased difficulties because of inflationary pressures. Both considerations highlight the role of fiscal correction: strong demand for US net exports means that the fiscal deficit may be reduced with little risk of recession. At the same time, this resource pressure means that fiscal correction will be necessary to moderate inflationary tendencies as the external adjustment takes place.

The large real adjustment also means that capacity for production of tradeable goods could be a problem. Policy will have to provide carefully for noninflationary growth and capacity expansion while meeting the real external adjustment requirements. Policy in Europe and Japan could help by ensuring growth abroad, because the more US external adjustment can be based on expansion of foreign markets, the less it will have to rely on dollar depreciation, the smaller will be the loss of terms of trade, and the more manageable the real adjustment will be.

Index

Absorption approach
    to external deficit correction, 103,
        116
Adjustment policy, international
    alternative programs for, 36
    comparison of forecasting models
        for, 122–28
    EAG model as basis for designing,
        28–40
    requirements for, 29–30
    role of other countries in, 48–50
    See also Feasible Adjustment Pack-
        age (FAP); Second-Best Adjust-
        ment Package (SBAP); Zero
        Balance Package (ZBP)
Aggregate demand. See Economic
    growth
Alexander, Sidney, 103
Argentina
    current account projections for, 197
    effect of US trade patterns on, 268
    growth of trade in, 141
    individual treatment in EAG model,
        132

Backcasts
    accuracy of EAG model, 157–68
Baker, James A., III, 66, 311
Baker Plan targets, 311
Balance of payments
    projections for 1992: all countries,
        188–92
Balance of payments, US

adjustment with Japan under FAP,
    34
HHC base case projections for, 97
in HH model, 81
projections for, 197–202
quarterly estimates in HH model for,
    79
Balassa, Bela, 152n, 215n
Baldwin, Richard E., 86n, 327n
Balloon effect, 26–27, 204, 206
Barro, Robert J., 53n
Baseline projection
    for US agricultural exports, 93
    for US external deficits by various
        forecasters, 10–13
    for principal variables in forecasting
        model, 88, 186–88
Belgium, 30, 48, 73
Bergsten, C. Fred, 4n, 28, 34n, 43n,
    66n, 75n, 98, 116n, 153n, 231
BHH. See Bryant, Helliwell, Hooper
    (BHH)
Bosworth, Barry, 102n
Brady, Nicholas, 71
Branson, William H., 262n
Brazil
    adjustment of trade surplus under
        FAP, 214, 215
    EAG projected trade surplus for,
        191
    effect of adjustment for statistical
        discrepancy, 351
    effect of US trade patterns on, 268
    individual treatment in EAG model,
        132

Brooke, Anthony, 147n
Brookings Institution
  synthesis of models: medium-term
    projection for US current ac-
    count, 100, 122–27
Bryant, Helliwell, Hooper (BHH)
  policy simulations, 46–47, 288–90
Bryant, Ralph C., 47n, 79n, 84, 100,
    122, 124, 126n, 127, 128n, 288–
    90, 317n
Bryant–Hoitham analysis, 84
Bush, George, 71, 72
Bussman, W. V., 13n

Camdessus, Michel, 71
Canada, 25, 26, 115
  adjustment measures under FAP,
    214, 216
  current account projections for, 195
  EAG projected trade surplus for,
    191
  effect of US trade patterns on, 268
  individual treatment in EAG model,
    132
  as oil exporter, 134
Capacity utilization, 92
Capital market
  dollar exchange rate and, 62, 64
  returns on US assets abroad, 98
  See also Foreign direct investment
Capital services
  analysis in EAG model of, 9, 184
  in HHC model, 99
Capital stock
  base case projection for, 90–92
  variable in HH model, 80
China
  current account projections for, 196
  as oil exporter, 134
Cline, William R., 34n, 116n, 148n,
    153n
Congressional Budget Office, 10n
Council of Economic Advisers, 42n,
    43n, 54n, 63n, 92n, 271n
Credit availability
  impact on debtor countries of, 300–
    11
Current account
  adjustment for statistical discrep-

ancy, 346–54
  calculation using EAG model, 183–
    86
  HHC base case projection for, 96
  policy target in 1992 for other coun-
    tries, 213–14
  projections from 1987 to 1992, 192–
    97
  projections using EAG model for
    world, 8
  trends in major countries, 343–46
Current account, US
  deficit in, 1
  effect of dollar depreciation on,
    109–15
  in HH model, 81
  medium-term projections for, 100–2
  policy target in 1992 for, 29, 213
  projections for, 197–202
  reduction of deficit in, 22
  target for deficit in simulation of,
    28–29
  See also Trade deficit, US

Data Resources, Inc. (DRI), analysis,
    100–1, 122–26
Data sources for EAG model, 138–46
Debtor countries
  creditworthiness constraints on, 74
  effect of international adjustment
    on, 50
  effect of US current account deficit
    on, 73
  effects of US trade adjustment on,
    295–300, 311
  simulation of impact of credit avail-
    ability for, 306–11
Distortions
  rising in international payments
    balance, 13–15
Dollar
  appreciation in 1988, 128–29
  attempt to stabilize, 65
  decline in value of, 62–70
  effect of overvaluation of, 2, 61–62
  effect on trade prices of decline in,
    327–35
  reasons for need for real decline,
    69–70

See also Exchange rates; Hard landing
Dollar depreciation
    effect of, 104–15, 355–62
    effect on US external deficit of 10 percent, 203–5, 207–8
    pass-through ratios and, 359
    as policy implication, 233
Domestic adjustment, US, 42–44
Domestic demand. *See* Economic growth
Dooley, Michael, 131n

EAG model. *See* External Adjustment with Growth (EAG) model
Economic growth
    balloon effect on trade volume with foreign, 27
    changes for industrial economies and US in, 281–83
    distinctions between domestic demand and, 116–19
    effect of US trade deficit on foreign, 266–69
    effect on external account of, 115–22
    HHC base case projections for, 88–97
    Keynesian equilibrium analysis of, 76–77
    as policy to adjust US trade balance, 233, 236
    See also GNP, US and foreign
Economic growth, US
    avoidance of reduction in, 30
    effect of policies to decrease, 27, 207–8
    effect of trade deficit on, 262–65
Economic policy coordination, need for international, 75
Economic Recovery Tax Act of 1981, 51
Elasticities, cross-price, 153
    consistency constraint for, 323–25
    derivation from elasticity of substitution, 321–23
    standardization in EAG model for, 316–19
Elasticities, income
    country comparisons for, 9
    estimates for constrained and un-

constrained, 148–50
    recalibration for EAG model, 316–19
    for US oil imports, 137, 340–42
    for world oil imports, 342
Elasticities, price
    estimates for constrained and unconstrained, 150–51, 153
    in HH model, 83–84
    recalibration in EAG model for, 316–19
Elasticities, trade, 359–60
    analysis in EAG model of, 9
    approach to external deficit reduction, 103
    effect of alternative assumptions for, 234–36
    empirical results, 148–68
    estimated, 149–57
    estimation technique for, 146–48
    recalibration of estimates for forecasting, 316–19
    See also Marshall–Lerner condition
Elasticity of substitution, 83, 147–48, 321–23
EMS. *See* European Monetary System (EMS)
Estimation technique, EAG model, 146–48
European countries, intermediate, 29–30
European countries, surplus. *See* Belgium; Netherlands; Switzerland
European Monetary System (EMS)
    exchange rates under, 49
    realignment of currencies as policy implication, 237, 240
    realignment of currencies in FAP, 31
    role in international adjustment of, 39–40
Exchange rates
    effect of rise in foreign, 26–27
    HHC base case projection for, 89–90
    impact of US fiscal policy changes on, 102, 290–91
    lagged response of trade volumes to changes in, 4–5, 84
    pass-through in HH model of changes in, 83
    pass-through of changes in, 327–35

Exchange rates, real
comparison of changes in HHC and EAG models of, 67
effect of 1988 changes in US trade balance, 128–29
as variable in HHC and EAG model projections, 24–25
Expenditure reduction, 116
Expenditure switching, 116
Exports, US
response to foreign income growth, 205–6
External account. See Trade accounts; External adjustment, US
External adjustment, international. See Adjustment policy, international
External adjustment, US
distribution among other countries, 26–28
effect of foreign economic growth on, 115–22
effect on manufacturing of, 292–93
estimates of impact of, 44–45
and global aggregate demand, 76–77
lack of effectiveness of policy for, 70–73
policy recommendations for, 202–12
ratio of real to nominal, 269–73
real compared to nominal effects of, 40–45
See also Balloon effect; Economic growth; Elasticities, trade; Exchange rates
External Adjustment with Growth (EAG) model, 67
backcasts using, 157–68
baseline projections of, 10–13
base year and projections for, 19–20
calculation of country current account balance in, 183–86
description and components of, 8–9
geographical detail of, 132–33
projections of, 19–20
refinements of, 315–19
treatment of lags and pass-throughs in, 181–82
External deficit, US. See Trade deficit, US

Factor services account
deficit in, 97–100
effect of dollar depreciation on, 108–9
effect of foreign economic growth on, 119–20
HH model definition of, 81
trends under FAP in HHC and EAG models for, 270
Feasible Adjustment Package (FAP)
currency changes under, 30–32
derived from EAG model simulations, 30–32
effect on trade and current accounts of, 32–35
as instrument to reduce current account surpluses, 214–17
policy recommendations for US external adjustment, 213–31
with proposed US fiscal and monetary policy, 290–91
simulations of, 42–44
trends in factor services in HHC and EAG models, 270
Feedback effect, HH model, 83, 361
Feldstein, Martin, 72, 114, 121n
Fiscal deficit, US
as cause of external deficit, 1, 20
effect of high, 53–54, 57
effect of reduction or elimination of, 21–22
mandate of Gramm–Rudman–Hollings to eliminate, 46
Fiscal policy, US
in baseline projections, 10
effect of adjustment on exchange rate, 22–23
as stimulus, 2, 52
theories of effect on external deficit, 102–4
Foreign direct investment
actual HHC projection for US rate of return on, 97–100
effect of foreign economic growth on, 119–20
Foster, Lucia, 327n
France
adjustment of trade surplus under FAP, 214, 215
currency appreciation under FAP, 31

current account projections for, 195
external deficits of, 74
individual treatment in EAG model,
132
predicted future economic weakness
of, 15, 26, 191
Francis, Jonathan, 147n
Funabashi, Yoichi, 231n

Gap factor
in effect of exchange rate change on
export and import values, 111–
12
Gault, Nigel, 100–1, 122, 125, 126,
128n
Gephardt amendment, 66
Germany
adjustment of trade surplus under
FAP, 214
changes in real trade balance under
US external adjustment scenarios, 274–80
currency appreciation under FAP,
30
effect of US trade patterns on, 268
fiscal policy in, 287
increasing trade surplus of, 13, 16,
20, 26, 74
individual treatment in EAG model,
132
policy implications for, 48
present trade surplus in, 1, 73
GNP, US and foreign
as variable in HHC and EAG model
projections, 23–24
Gramm–Rudman–Hollings (GRH)
deficit reduction timetable of, 289
implementation to eliminate fiscal
deficit, 21, 46, 47
mandate of, 53
Group of Seven (G-7), 5, 24
effect of exchange rate policy of, 239
intervention after Louvre Accord, 39

Haas, Richard, 131n
Hard landing
risk for dollar of, 3, 46, 64–66, 290

Haynes, Stephen E., 80n, 152n
Helkie, William L., 6, 79, 80, 83
Helkie–Hooper–Cline (HHC) model
adaptations of original HH model,
6–8, 85–88
base case projections for, 10–13, 88–
97
simulation of effect of dollar depreciation on US current account,
104–15
Helkie–Hooper (HH) model
description, 79–84
modifications to, 85–88
prediction errors in, 84–86
Helliwell, John F., 47n, 288–90
Holtham, Gerald, 79n, 84, 126n, 317n
Hong Kong, 16–17, 49
See also Korea–Singapore–Hong
Kong
Hooper, Peter, 6, 13n, 47n, 79, 80, 83,
116n, 126n, 164n, 288–90, 317n
Houthakker, Hendrik S., 9n, 80n, 151
Houthakker–Magee phenomenon, 9n,
83, 151, 154

IMF. See International Monetary Fund
(IMF)
Imports
estimated price elasticities for, 154
impact of economic growth on, 116
India, 196
Industrial countries, intermediate
current account balances in, 17–18
external deficit projections for, 13,
15
policy implications for, 49
Inflation
HHC base case projection for, 89
tailoring of FAP to rise in, 290
Institute for International Economics,
35n, 223n
Interest rates, US
effect of high, 2, 51–52, 61
effect of lowering, 21–22
HHC base case projection for, 92–93
Internal deficit, US. See Fiscal deficit,
US
International Monetary Fund (IMF),
88, 347, 349, 185–86

medium-term projections for US
current account, 100
Intervention
by Group of Seven (G-7) after
Louvre Accord, 39
Investment, US, 60–63
Islam, Shafiqul, 98
Italy
adjustment of trade surplus under
FAP, 214, 215
currency appreciation under FAP,
31
current account projections for, 195
individual treatment in EAG model,
132
predicted trade deficit of, 15, 26,
191

Japan
adjustment of trade surplus under
FAP, 214
changes in domestic demand in,
282–83
changes in real trade balance under
US external adjustment scenarios, 274–80
currency appreciation under FAP,
30
current account projections, 195
current account trends and adjustment, 343, 346, 350–51
effect of rise in real trade balance,
42
effect of US trade patterns on, 268
export growth of, 141
fiscal and monetary policy in, 287,
292
increasing trade surplus of, 13, 16,
20, 73–74
individual treatment in EAG model,
132
policy implications for, 48
present trade surplus in, 1, 73
role in reduction of US balance of
payments deficit under FAP, 34
trade surplus correction as policy
implication, 236–37
J-curve, 5, 70, 93
Johnson, Robert A., 327n

Kendrick, David, 147n
Keynes, J. M., 76–77
Korea, 1, 49, 73
present trade surplus in, 1, 73
Korea–Singapore–Hong Kong, 16–17,
25, 30
adjustment of trade surplus under
FAP, 214, 215
changes in real trade balance under
US external adjustment, 274,
276
currency appreciation under FAP,
30
current account projections for, 196
current account trends and adjustment, 346, 351–52
effect of adjustment for statistical
discrepancy, 351
export and import growth of, 141
group treatment in EAG model of,
132
import and export elasticities for,
17, 235
Krugman, Paul, 17n, 22n, 86n, 103–4,
120n, 156n

Laffer curve, 51
Latin American countries
as debtor nations, 73
effect of international adjustment
on, 50, 204, 207
Lawrence, Robert Z., 44n, 292–93
Litan, Robert E., 44n, 292n
Loopesko, Bonnie E., 327n
Louvre Accord of 1987, 24, 65
Love, James P., 262n

McKinnon, Ronald, 103
Macroeconomic policy, US, 53–57
See also Fiscal policy, US; Monetary
policy, US
Magee, Stephen P., 9n, 80n, 151
Mann, Catherine L., 83n, 116n, 164n
Manufacturing, US
output and growth in 1980s, 261–65
Marquez, Jaime, 131n
Marris, Stephen N., 3n, 28, 64n, 110,
111n, 114

Marshall–Lerner condition, 9, 83, 155–56, 361
Masson, Paul, 131n
Meade, Ellen, 327n
Meeraus, Alexander, 147n
Merchandise trade
determinants in HH model, 79–81
Mexico
adjustment measures under FAP, 214, 216
effect of US trade patterns on, 268
export growth of, 141
individual treatment in EAG model, 132
Monetary coordination, international, 239–40
Monetary policy, US
as stimulus for fiscal expansion, 2, 52, 287–88
Mundell, Robert, 103
Mundell–Fleming model, 22, 103, 104n

National Petroleum Council (NPC), 7, 137, 188, 340–42
Net external assets, US
HHC base case projection for, 96–97
Netherlands, 30, 48, 73
Newly industrializing countries (NICs)
adjustment policy implications for, 49
current account surpluses in, 16–17
effect of US trade patterns on, 268
estimated effect of adjusted US trade deficit, 278–80
NICs. See Newly industrializing countries (NICs)
Nonfactor services
analysis in EAG model of, 9
in HH model, 81
Nonoil trade, 80

OECD. See Organization for Economic Cooperation and Development (OECD)
Oil-exporting countries, 132

Oil trade
analysis in EAG model of, 8–9, 133–34, 136–37
artificial exporting "countries," 133
HHC base case projection for US imports, 93
trends and forecast for, 337–42
OPEC
current account trend and adjustment for, 343, 346, 347
identification in EAG model of, 8–9
trade growth of, 141
treatment of imports in EAG model, 138
Orcutt, Guy H., 317n
Organization for Economic Cooperation and Development (OECD), 134nn
medium-term projections for US current account, 100
Other African countries
current account projections for, 197
as debtor nations, 73
group treatment in EAG model, 132
Other Industrial countries
adjustment of trade surplus under FAP, 214, 215
currency appreciation under FAP, 30–31
current account projections for, 195
fiscal policy in, 287
group treatment in EAG model of, 132
Other Latin American countries
group treatment in EAG model of, 132
trade and current account projections for, 191, 197

Pass-through ratio, 359–61
Petroleum trade. See Oil trade
Plaza Agreement of 1985, 3, 24, 42, 66, 75
Policy
actions estimating impact of HHC and EAG model outputs, 25–26
actions to achieve real adjustment of external trade imbalance, 40–45
EAG model base case projections for, 186–202

implications for international adjustment, 37–40
implications for other countries, 48–50
implications for United States, 45–48
implications resulting from simulations for US external adjustment, 233–40
simulation using HHC and EAG models for adjustment to, 23–28
in US to reduce external imbalances, 20–23
Policy parameters
for other countries, 210–12
for United States, 122–26, 208–10
Prices
of exports and imports in HH model, 81
gap between wholesale and consumer, in HH model, 86–88
Protectionism, US
as outcome of continued high trade deficits, 3–4, 66
See also Gephardt amendment

Reagan–Bush administration, 51, 52, 53–57, 75
Real trade effects
external adjustment scenarios for real changes in other countries, 273–80
Recession, US
and subsequent recovery: 1982 to present, 52
Resource availability, US, 2, 58–63
Rest of World countries
adjustment of trade surplus using FAP, 214, 215
baseline trends for, 19
currency appreciation in FAP, 31
current account projections for, 196
residual grouping in EAG model, 132–33

Saving, private
decline as cause of external deficits, 2, 20
effect of US fiscal deficit on, 54

SBAP. See Second-Best Adjustment Package (SBAP)
Schultze, Charles L., 44n, 292n
Schumacher, Bruce, 147n
Second-Best Adjustment Package (SBAP)
effect of, 36
scenario for, 232–33
Singapore, 16–17, 49
as oil exporter, 134
See also Korea–Singapore–Hong Kong
Soviet Union, 134, 295
Statistical discrepancy
adjustment of world current accounts for, 346–54
Stern, Robert M., 147n
Stone, Joe A., 80n, 152n
Switzerland
as trade surplus country, 30, 48, 73
Symansky, Steven, 131n

Taiwan, 25, 30, 49
adjustment of trade surplus under FAP, 214
changes in real trade balances under US external adjustment scenarios, 274–80
currency appreciation in FAP, 30
current account projections for, 196
export and import growth of, 141
growth assumption under base case, 187
import and export elasticities for, 17
individual treatment in EAG model, 132
present trade surplus in, 1, 16, 73
Thailand
current account projections for, 196
Time lags
for direct and cross-price terms, 135, 136, 148, 164, 168
Toronto summit, 239
Trade accounts
effect of economic growth on, 115–22
projections using EAG model for world, 8
real effects in 1980s of world, 41–42
Trade adjustment, US real

difference from nominal adjustment
of, 40–41
effect on other countries of, 44–45
effect on US economy of, 42–44
Trade balance. *See* Balance of payments
Trade deficit
base case projection for, 93, 96
EAG projections for 1992, 191
in other industrial countries, 1
Trade deficit, US
effect of reduction or elimination of,
1, 22
effect on domestic economic growth
of, 262
estimated adjustment applying EAG
and HHC with FAP, 269–73
estimated real adjustment effect on
foreign countries, 273–80
estimate of correction with 10 percent dollar depreciation, 203–5
origins of, 2
proposed policy to correct, 46–48
recent trends in, 4–5
reduction as component in international adjustment program, 29
relation to fiscal deficit, 57–58
risks of continuation of, 3–4, 63–66
See also Current account, US
Trade equations
in EAG model, 8, 135
in HH model, 80, 82–83
prediction errors in HH model, 85–
86
Trade patterns, US
effect on economic growth in other
countries, 266
effects of debt crisis in developing
countries, 295–300
Trade surplus
concentration in certain countries,
73–75
in Germany, Japan, Korea, and Taiwan, 1
increase in Germany and Japan of,
13, 16

United Kingdom
adjustment measures under FAP,
214

changes in trade balance under US
external adjustment scenarios,
274–80
current account projections for, 195–
96
individual treatment in EAG model,
132
moderation of external deficit as
component of adjustment, 29
predicted future trade deficit, 13,
18–19, 20, 191, 192
trade deficit in, 1
United States
balance of payments and current account projections for, 195, 197–
202
causes of external imbalance, 2, 20
changes in domestic demand in, 282
currency depreciation under FAP,
32
current account trends and adjustment, 343–46
effect of adjustment for statistical
discrepancy, 350, 351
effect of trade deficit on domestic
economic growth in, 262–65
estimated income, price, and cross-
price elasticities for, 149–54,
156
export and import growth in, 141
fiscal and monetary policy in, 286–
93
fiscal and trade deficits in, 2
individual treatment in EAG model,
132
international adjustment program
for, 29
level for external balance of payments, 28
macroeconomic policy for external
adjustment for, 288
policy implications for external adjustment of, 233–40
policy target for 1992 current account deficit, 213
real and hypothetical effects on
trade with debtor countries,
295–300, 311
trends and forecast for oil trade of,
337–42

US Department of Commerce, 1n, 4n, 44n, 86n, 93nn, 168n
US Department of Treasury, 12

Verity, C. William, Jr., 239

Wharton Economic Forecasting Associates (WEFA)
medium-term projections for US current account, 100, 126

Williamson, John, 22n, 28, 29n, 103n, 215n, 311n
World Bank, 187n
World trade
growth rate for period 1973-87, 140–41

Zero Balance Package (ZBP)
applied to EAG model, 231–32
effect of, 36

Other Publications from the Institute

POLICY ANALYSES IN INTERNATIONAL ECONOMICS SERIES

1 **The Lending Policies of the International Monetary Fund**
John Williamson/August 1982

2 **"Reciprocity": A New Approach to World Trade Policy?**
William R. Cline/September 1982

3 **Trade Policy in the 1980s**
C. Fred Bergsten and William R. Cline/November 1982

4 **International Debt and the Stability of the World Economy**
William R. Cline/September 1983

5 **The Exchange Rate System, Second Edition**
John Williamson/September 1983, rev. June 1985

6 **Economic Sanctions in Support of Foreign Policy Goals**
Gary Clyde Hufbauer and Jeffrey J. Schott/October 1983

7 **A New SDR Allocation?**
John Williamson/March 1984

8 **An International Standard for Monetary Stabilization**
Ronald I. McKinnon/March 1984

9 **The Yen/Dollar Agreement: Liberalizing Japanese Capital Markets**
Jeffrey A. Frankel/December 1984

10 **Bank Lending to Developing Countries: The Policy Alternatives**
C. Fred Bergsten, William R. Cline, and John Williamson/April 1985

11 **Trading for Growth: The Next Round of Trade Negotiations**
Gary Clyde Hufbauer and Jeffrey J. Schott/September 1985

12 **Financial Intermediation Beyond the Debt Crisis**
Donald R. Lessard and John Williamson/September 1985

13 **The United States–Japan Economic Problem**
C. Fred Bergsten and William R. Cline/October 1985, rev. January 1987

14 **Deficits and the Dollar: The World Economy at Risk**
Stephen Marris/December 1985, rev. November 1987

15 **Trade Policy for Troubled Industries**
Gary Clyde Hufbauer and Howard F. Rosen/March 1986

16 **The United States and Canada: The Quest for Free Trade**
Paul Wonnacott, with an Appendix by *John Williamson*/March 1987

17 **Adjusting to Success: Balance of Payments Policy in the East Asian NICs**
Bela Balassa and John Williamson/June 1987

18 **Mobilizing Bank Lending to Debtor Countries**
William R. Cline/June 1987

19 **Auction Quotas and United States Trade Policy**
C. Fred Bergsten, Kimberly Ann Elliott, Jeffrey J. Schott, and Wendy E. Takacs/September 1987

20 **Agriculture and the GATT: Rewriting the Rules**
Dale E. Hathaway/September 1987

21 Anti-Protection: Changing Forces in United States Trade Politics
    I. M. Destler and John S. Odell/September 1987

22 Targets and Indicators: A Blueprint for the International
    Coordination of Economic Policy
    John Williamson and Marcus H. Miller/September 1987

23 Capital Flight: The Problem and Policy Responses
    Donald R. Lessard and John Williamson/December 1987

24 United States–Canada Free Trade: An Evaluation of the
    Agreement
    Jeffrey J. Schott/April 1988

25 Voluntary Approaches to Debt Relief
    John Williamson/September 1988, rev. May 1989

26 American Trade Adjustment: The Global Impact
    William R. Cline/March 1989

27 More Free Trade Areas?
    Jeffrey J. Schott/May 1989

BOOKS

IMF Conditionality
John Williamson, editor/1983

Trade Policy in the 1980s
William R. Cline, editor/1983

Subsidies in International Trade
Gary Clyde Hufbauer and Joanna Shelton Erb/1984

International Debt: Systemic Risk and Policy Response
William R. Cline/1984

Economic Sanctions Reconsidered: History and Current Policy
*Gary Clyde Hufbauer and Jeffrey J. Schott, assisted by
Kimberly Ann Elliott*/1985

Trade Protection in the United States: 31 Case Studies
Gary Clyde Hufbauer, Diane T. Berliner, and Kimberly Ann Elliott/1986

Toward Renewed Economic Growth in Latin America
*Bela Balassa, Gerardo M. Bueno, Pedro-Pablo Kuczynski, and
Mario Henrique Simonsen*/1986

American Trade Politics: System Under Stress
I. M. Destler/1986

The Future of World Trade in Textiles and Apparel
William R. Cline/1987

Capital Flight and Third World Debt
Donald R. Lessard and John Williamson, editors/1987

The Canada–United States Free Trade Agreement: The Global Impact
Jeffrey J. Schott and Murray G. Smith, editors/1988

Managing the Dollar: From the Plaza to the Louvre
Yoichi Funabashi/1988, rev. 1989

Reforming World Agricultural Trade
Twenty-nine Professionals from Seventeen Countries/1988

World Agricultural Trade: Building a Consensus
William M. Miner and Dale E. Hathaway, editors/1988

Japan in the World Economy
Bela Balassa and Marcus Noland/1988

America in the World Economy: A Strategy for the 1990s
C. Fred Bergsten/1988

United States External Adjustment and the World Economy
William R. Cline/1989

Free Trade Areas and U.S. Trade Policy
Jeffrey J. Schott, editor/1989

SPECIAL REPORTS

1 **Promoting World Recovery: A Statement on Global Economic Strategy**
by Twenty-six Economists from Fourteen Countries/December 1982

2 **Prospects for Adjustment in Argentina, Brazil, and Mexico: Responding to the Debt Crisis**
John Williamson, editor/June 1983

3 **Inflation and Indexation: Argentina, Brazil, and Israel**
John Williamson, editor/March 1985

4 **Global Economic Imbalances**
C. Fred Bergsten, editor/March 1986

5 **African Debt and Financing**
Carol Lancaster and John Williamson, editors/May 1986

6 **Resolving the Global Economic Crisis: After Wall Street**
Thirty-three Economists from Thirteen Countries/December 1987

7 **World Economic Problems**
Kimberly Ann Elliott and John Williamson, editors/April 1988

8 **Economic Relations Between the United States and Korea: Conflict or Cooperation?**
Thomas O. Bayard and Soo-Gil Young, editors/January 1989

FORTHCOMING

Foreign Direct Investment in the United States
Edward M. Graham and Paul R. Krugman

Equilibrium Exchange Rates: An Update
John Williamson

Oil Crisis Intervention: A Blueprint for International Cooperation
Philip K. Verleger, Jr.

Exchange Rate Policy Making in the United States
I. M. Destler and C. Randall Henning

The Debt of Low-Income Africa: Issues and Options for the United States
Carol Lancaster

International Aspects of United States Tax Policy: An Overview
Daniel J. Frisch

Europe, the Dollar, and 1992
Stephen Marris

The United States as a Debtor Country
C. Fred Bergsten and Shafiqul Islam

Pacific Area Trade: Threat or Opportunity for the United States?
Bela Balassa and Marcus Noland

Trade Liberalization and International Institutions
Jeffrey J. Schott

Reciprocity and Retaliation: An Evaluation of Aggressive Trade Policies
Thomas O. Bayard

Third World Debt: A Reappraisal
William R. Cline

The Politics of International Monetary Cooperation
C. Fred Bergsten, I. M. Destler, C. Randall Henning, and John Williamson

The Taxation of Income from International Financial Investment
Daniel J. Frisch

Energy Policy for the 1990s: A Global Perspective
Philip K. Verleger, Jr.

The Outlook for World Commodity Prices
Philip K. Verleger, Jr.

EC 1992: Implications for the World Economy
Bela Balassa and Jeffrey J. Schott, editors